More Praise for Cynthia F. Davidson's
THE IMPORTANCE OF PARIS

"Wow. Your book is fantastic! I've been reading the sample of your book on Kindle and enthralled. I'm learning so much about history through your eyes and enjoying Paris at the same time. Super good job with language and descriptions and history!"

— Linda Joy Myers, President of the National Association of Memoir Writers

"Above all I admire your frankness about the people you met, your parents, and your love life. Very brave to put so much of it down on paper for all to read, and it makes a riveting story."

— Fiona Dunlop

"I love the raw honesty in your writing, the perfect blend of history, political intrigue, and enough personal detail, albeit some very steamy details...I'm still in Paris with your 'phantom lover' and wishing I took more chances in life. You have a hit here and maybe a movie too."

— Naide Aymelek

"A book about love in all its forms: love of place, love of country, love of ideals, love of learning, erotic love — how fraught it all is, and how beautiful, necessary, and difficult. Transcendent."

— Alison Veres

"I think this book is incredibly important. Cynthia imparts knowledge on the intricacies of cross cultural connections and conflict by letting us into her home(s), her journal, even her bedroom. As a result, readers are forced to wrestle with themes that have been easily cast aside by Americans who find Middle Eastern history/conflict too abstract, convoluted, or even uncomfortable."

— Sheila Dobbyn

"Lovely and lyrical! I feel like I know you."

— Jana Rice

"...a real page turner."

— Barbara Ganim

"...a very timely book for me personally. Not only does it takes the reader so very skillfully behind the scenes, as a witness to their exquisite beauty and joy, along with their abject horror and shame, but it also reveals a shared past: roads I have taken and not taken, things said and not said, questions asked and not asked, answers given and not given, truth told and truth untold — all with significant effect. Through the book I'm able to explore all of these, returning to those many points of choice, of acting, of saying, of asking, of answering, and of revealing. My own story suddenly has taken on new dimensions, shape-shifting me in the process."

— **Karen Hutchendorf**

The Importance of Paris

Loves, Lies, and Resolutions

a memoir

Cynthia F. Davidson

To each reader who needs to tell their own story.

CONTENTS

TIMELINE
life & war

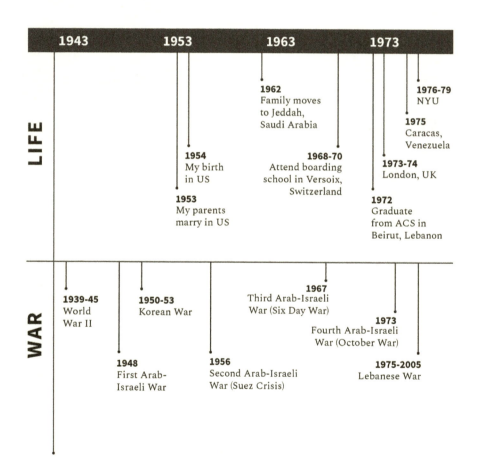

1943   1953   1963   1973

LIFE

1962
Family moves
to Jeddah,
Saudi Arabia

1976-79
NYU

1975
Caracas,
Venezuela

1954
My birth
in US

1968-70
Attend boarding
school in Versoix,
Switzerland

1973-74
London, UK

1953
My parents
marry in US

1972
Graduate
from ACS in
Beirut, Lebanon

WAR

1939-45
World
War II

1950-53
Korean War

1967
Third Arab-Israeli
War (Six Day War)

1973
Fourth Arab-Israeli
War (October War)

1948
First Arab-
Israeli War

1956
Second Arab-Israeli
War (Suez Crisis)

1975-2005
Lebanese War

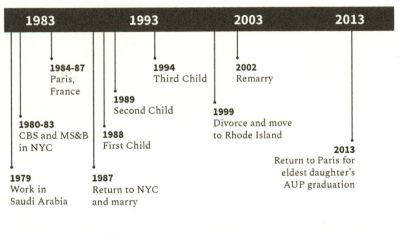

1983 **1993** **2003** **2013**

1984-87
Paris,
France

1994
Third Child

2002
Remarry

1989
Second Child

1980-83
CBS and MS&B
in NYC

1999
Divorce and move
to Rhode Island

1988
First Child

2013
Return to Paris for
eldest daughter's
AUP graduation

1979
Work in
Saudi Arabia

1987
Return to NYC
and marry

1983
US Embassy and
barracks bombed
in Beirut

2001
September 11
Attacks in US

2010
Arab Spring
begins

2011
Syrian Civil
War begins

1982
Israel invades
Lebanon

1991
Iraq invades Kuwait, US
and coalition forces engage
in Gulf War

2003
US invades Iraq
and Afghanistan

PROLOGUE

Paris has a soul and she'll test yours.
Will you sell out or stay true?

Seekers of transformation have been flocking to the City of Light for centuries: artists, mystics, writers, revolutionaries, royals, and refugees. And twenty-seven million tourists a year were making Paris the most visited place in the world when I went there for a ten day vacation in January 1984. A month later, I put my affairs in order and returned, to become one of the two million who call Paris home.

My home had once been in another Paris, the "Paris of the Middle East" Beirut, Lebanon. Having come of age in that former Levantine colony of France, I believed I belonged there. But shortly after I turned twenty-one, Lebanon devolved into a gaping, bleeding war zone. Those of us who witnessed its demise can hardly believe the Beirut we knew is gone. The promise of its heydays lives on in our memories.

During the two decades of my most formative years, my family made our home in the Middle East, although we had all been born in the US. My American expatriate parents might have stayed in their Beirut apartment if Lebanon had not become another casualty of man's inhumanity.

The Lebanese Civil War almost finished us: my sister was shot in Beirut, my father kidnapped, our apartment looted, and friends disappeared. Some were tortured and killed. Worse yet, some became torturers, killers, and black market profiteers. While others have the luxury of ignoring what went wrong in Lebanon, we who lost everything familiar there crave a decent explanation for its disappearance.

The nightmare of that faux Paris still had me in its thrall when I moved to France at age twenty-nine, determined to discover what had gone wrong in Lebanon. The ongoing fighting made it too dangerous to return to Beirut for answers. After the invasions of the Syrian and Israeli armies, my parents finally gave up and returned to America in the summer of 1982, after twenty-one years in the Arab world. Each member of my family struggled to readjust to life in the US after being abroad for so long. In addition to what was lost in the fighting, we had also lost our foothold in the world at large, and this wreaked havoc on my sense of belonging and identity.

Thoughts of Lebanon's ruination preoccupied me. As the war raged on during my twenties, I dreaded having turned my back on a place and a people when they needed their friends the most. I didn't know my grieving process had a label, and a form of treatment, until years afterward when the term "post-traumatic stress disorder" came into vogue. Desperate to draw conclusions and be done with the torment, I decided the best way to come to terms with the war was to find out what had caused it.

That meant finding someone with deep knowledge of the how and why. Only survivors had any credibility with me. Who else could be trusted to explain the reasons behind such devastating violence? Furthermore, it had to be a Lebanese national who had been there, not some foreign analyst, or a pundit with an agenda. Surely a local person was better qualified to tell the world what had gone wrong in Lebanon. If my country, the US, had fallen apart in a civil war, I would want a fellow citizen to explain the lived truths of our story.

Apart from nationality, I wanted to hear it from another woman. And I chose Georgina Rizk. Not because she had once been Miss Universe, but because the multiple tragedies she had endured since wearing that crown had left her fatefully suited to the task. Her involvement with people from opposing sides of the conflict had transformed her into a cipher, with insights from more than one perspective. So I put my faith in this search for the truth, via another person, without fully realizing the risks of such a plan. Nor did I comprehend the limits of logical, factual quests, which rarely repair our hearts or restore trust, in others or ourselves. My psyche steered me towards a female survivor, and a French city, each with their own experiences of wars and healings. Living in Paris put me through a process as peculiar as it was unexpected. And although my three-year cure in France came close to killing me, this memoir is a testament to how Paris managed my transformation. *Vive la différence.*

Chapter 1

CHERCHEZ LA FEMME /
LOOK FOR THE WOMAN

The most subversive thing a woman can do
is talk about her life as if it really matters.

— MONA ELTAHAWY

Autumn 1983

My doorway to Paris swung open inside a Manhattan art gallery because I needed a push from the universe and a complicated story demands a simple starting point. On that crisp autumn evening in 1983 the transformative ingredients were deftly stirred together although it would take me another five years to grasp their full significance. I had come out to celebrate the accomplishments of a dear friend on the opening night of her retrospective exhibition. Thirty-five years worth of Lilian MacKendrick's artwork covered the well-lit walls of Wally Findley's 57th Street gallery. Despite the many ups and downs, a Great Depression, and two World Wars, she had never stopped painting. Her gumption and creativity were galvanizing and one of her canvases was about to create an opening for me. Depicting a desire too disguised for me to recognize, it also revealed who I would become after Paris.

With the sun sinking between the priapic towers of New York City, I wove through the crowd, searching for my well-traveled friend. Nearing eighty and thronged by admirers, she was holding forth, oblivious to envy at least for tonight. After congratulating her, and kissing both her deserving, powdered cheeks, I slipped away to admire her canvases. Leaving the canapé nibblers and wine goblet wavers spouting about art in the front rooms, it was Lilian's *oeuvre* and her artistic development that impressed me. Seeing all those paintings reunited was like reading an autobiography, with each reassembled scene highlighting an enduring theme in the overall story.

3

In one still life, a pair of gold-rimmed spectacles rested upon a sumptuously embroidered tablecloth. What had their wearer seen? The finely rendered porcelain, the crust on the plate, even the unseen dessert enticed a viewer to pull up a chair and join the after-dinner conversation. Her more recent canvases were full of vivid gardens in riotous bloom. In the years since her husband's death, her color usage had intensified considerably.

We had met during my student days at New York University when Lilian was already in her seventies. Still at her easel every day, with the natural light streaming through the south facing windows of her Central Park South apartment, she worked with her radio tuned to the classical music station. I knew all this because she'd asked me to sit for her, suggesting I wear things from my Middle Eastern days. And that's how a portrait of me, in a floor length orange silk Moroccan caftan bedecked with golden jewelry from Arabia, had been painted. Unable to afford her work, I wonder where that picture of me before Paris has ended up.

Continuing my tour of Lilian's canvases, with their American, Asian, and European settings that evening in the gallery, I recalled her stories of famous friends in far off places. Some had hosted her at their estates expecting her brushstrokes to immortalize their decor and properties. At one of Lilian's previous Paris shows, the Duchess of Windsor, Mrs. Wallace Simpson, had purchased a painting but it took Lilian two years and ten written reminders to get paid for it.

At the rear of the Wally Findlay gallery, it was quiet and peaceful. And there I discovered a larger than life-sized portrait of a rosy skinned mother nursing her babe in arms. The softer, blurrier style indicated earlier work. An idealized scene it was, for I knew Lilian, the Brooklyn raised daughter of Russian émigrés had vowed, as I had, never to have children after what we had seen of the world. She had confided this several months after our initial meeting at an upstate retreat center. Our friendship had commenced after she complimented me on the long *jalabiya* (dress) I was wearing to dinner that evening in the country. At breakfast the following morning, I gave it to her, and that gift sealed our mutual adoption. Growing up in the Arab world, I had learned about the evil eye, which taught offering an admired object was preferable to causing envy and resentment, and the possible loss of a friendship. Our stories are also gifts. Perhaps we risk envy, resentment, and friendships when offering them.

Lilian became my chosen New York grand aunt. Since moving abroad at age eight, I had seldom seen my blood relations in America, and was grateful to become this widow's adopted niece. Being raised overseas, and relocating often, had taught me the importance of finding an anchor in each new place. Elder, wise women usually fulfilled this role and Lilian was the quintessential New York City guide. Firmly rooted in Manhattan, she was a fount of information on subjects of all sorts, and could dish the dirt on society families and the friends of those I considered dating. We dined regularly in her Central Park South apartment, where she whipped up walnut sauced noodle dishes in her compact kitchen and tossed salads, carefully cutting out the white stem sections of her romaine lettuce. Those meals were served upon her miscellaneous collection of Chinese crockery. Eventually I noticed some of these dishes were featured in her paintings, along with the bouquets I brought her.

That evening at the gallery a bearded man approached me.

"Do you like the painting?"

His accent was decidedly Eastern European. The face was kindly, the brown eyes crinkling at the corners, his dark hair straight and shaggy.

"Yes, it's my favorite of them all," I replied, looking again at the mother and child. The portrait was full of sunlight and fresh air. The colors were warm and inviting as if the breeze of a summer afternoon was wafting through.

"I like it the best too. Although it is not recent, I think it is her best effort. I'm also a painter," he said, stepping nearer as if my reply had granted him permission. From his back pocket he drew a folded brochure and handed it to me.

As I took it, an officious fellow strode over. He draped his arm around the artist's shoulders with great familiarity and declared, "So, I see you've met Zvonimir. We are very proud of him. We showed his work here last month and he broke a New York record. It was his first one-man show in America and we sold every one of his paintings in the first three days."

I regarded the bearded man's rumpled nondescript clothing. He grinned, revealing adult braces on his teeth. The gallery manager turned to greet someone else going by and left us standing alone together.

"May I congratulate you?" I said, offering my hand.

"Thank you," he replied modestly, clasping my fingers in his warm palm.

He explained he had been born in Split, a city on the Adriatic coast of Yugoslavia (now Croatia). That explained the accent. Although I had heard of a French island called Reunion, I'd never imagined a place called Split.

We chatted about Lilian's work and art in general. When another person approached to speak to him, it gave me a moment to peruse the brochure. His bearded photograph was on it, along with several paintings of seaside villages. A timeless world, far removed from the urban clamor of New York, with smooth, egg-shaped stones glistening beneath the clear seawater, lapping at the rocky shoreline. Each individual pebble had been rendered with several painstaking shades of paint. The labors of a patient love. On another canvas a cluster of handmade wooden boats rested upon the calm surface, each brightly colored, and unique yet belonging together, like the members of a family. A flaring red umbrella distinguished one.

Noticing me studying his work Zvonimir continued his story. "I starved in Paris for ten years, painting scenes for tourists to earn money while I studied, but I learned. This style is called hyper-realism."

The prices for his canvases were in the $60,000 range. It was fair to say he had made it as an artist. My struggling inner writer felt distinctly encouraged by his presence.

"Would you like to see my work?" He invited me to his borrowed studio in midtown Manhattan. The address was walking distance from my office.

"Why don't you come tomorrow? I'm going back to Europe next week."

* * * *

The following afternoon, I left my Lexington Avenue office for that rendezvous. Still wearing my corporate consultant disguise, with my long hair pinned up, I felt giddy. Things were shifting. I was being shown a glimpse of my future when I would escape it all. One day I would even inhabit a seaside landscape, much like the ones portrayed in his paintings, but I would move there of my own volition, not following some fellow's invitation.

After buzzing me into the building, Zvonimir came down the stairs to greet me.

I asked with a grin, "So, you've invited me 'up to see your etchings.' Do you use the same line with every woman?"

We laughed a great deal that evening. After my inquiry he explained his name, Zvonimir, meant, "Ring the Bell of Peace." That meaning resonated deeply, generating ripples of hope in my war-torn psyche, gestating some future potentiality.

Our affair began soon afterwards, in that turpentine scented studio with its convenient couch bed, where he slept when staying in New York. Large commissioned works kept him busy with his paint and brushes, hour after hour. A bright electric light bulb, pulled close to the canvas, illuminated each wet brush stroke. Perhaps being alone all day made him such a lusty lover. I was hardly the first to be an artist's muse but trying on that role called much into question. It stirred up what would only be learned when muses of my own materialized.

Zvonimir did not ask me to sit for him like Lilian had. He did not paint portraits. Instead he asked me to be his "witch" and inspire him. At the time I did not ask why he'd chosen me, nor consider why I had complied so readily. Another affair, with an Egyptian diplomat, had recently ended. Mahmoud and I had remained friends but I felt free to do as I pleased. I had yet to reckon with how hunters perceive their prey. For those lessons, I would have to preempt their tactics, and Paris would be my proving ground.

As the leaves fell away that autumn of 1983 I shed some more naiveté. The war news[1] from Lebanon was as bad as ever, intensifying my obligation to deal with it. Only a corollary blast of creativity could boost me out of a downward spiral. The combined poles of duality, of Lilian and Zvonimir, profoundly energized me. They touched off a self-sustaining reaction. Heartened by their examples, a belief in my own art burgeoned. Perhaps my pen could perform similar feats, of poetry and writing, if I made an equally complete commitment.

That winter in a dream, I saw myself cutting off my long braid, to make brushes for Zvonimir to paint masterpieces with. How often we project upon others the gifts, and the faults, we are not ready to accept. Three months later he invited me to meet him in Paris on vacation. There a similar pairing would occur, when the inspiration of a Lebanese refugee named Georgina Rizk, would combine with the influence of another man. But it would take me awhile to recognize the repetition of that duel gender pattern.

* * * *

How did I become the sort of person a woman paints and men invite to Paris to be their personal witch? My search for those answers took me back thirty years, to the moment when the die was cast, by another man seeking a woman.

The Korean War was on then, adding its harrowing chapter to the interminable history of men's refusals to be reconciled. A skinny sailor serving on an aircraft carrier was glad for the R&R of a shore leave. His Navy buddy invited him to York, Pennsylvania, where the Connecticut raised Andrew Norman Fetterolf crossed paths with Lucille Anne Trout. That very first night he vowed to marry her. Although she had laughed off the "tall, dark handsome stranger," within a year they were standing at the altar. Dad was nineteen and mom twenty. Their needs set the mold for me. I arrived seven months later, weighing over eight pounds, and definitely not a preemie. This made the tongues wag, since my mother wore white to her church wedding, which was still a big deal in WASP America during the 1950s.

The details of my conception remained a mystery to me until my twenty-first birthday in the spring of 1975. By then I was living on my own and working in London. My father flew the five hours over from his job in

---

[1] Two hundred and forty-one US Marines had died that October when their barracks and the French garrison were truck bombed outside Beirut. That was the worst loss of US military lives since the end of the Second World War.

Beirut to celebrate that milestone with me. None of us suspected then just how much our lives were about to change when the Lebanese war erupted the following month. At my birthday dinner the truth serum of too many beers loosened my father's tongue. He bragged, with pride in his voice, "You were conceived in a moment of passion, on your grandmother's front parlor sofa, on the night of the fourth of July."

I felt warm and justified in that moment. Another couch, and the friction of mutuality, which so often sets our lives in motion. His story explains the nature of my passionate existence. Some are born to put out fires and defend the status quo while others are born catalysts like me. Our job is to ignite change. Carrying the sun star heat, we burn off falsehoods and breach separations. Both a source of torment and the secret to preservation, this capacity for ecstasy determined what kind of woman I would become, more than anything else.

To describe these characteristics my father employed the language of astrology: "We're all fire signs." Figuring celestial navigation from his seat in the cockpit as a flight engineer predisposed him to this version of sense making. I inherited his fiery curiosity, if not his methods, about whatever engineers our human flights of fancy and practicality. He and mom are Sagittarians, my brother and I Arians, and my sister the Leo. Adapting to this excess of combustion, smoke, and sparks was an essential aspect of my upbringing. Each member of my nuclear family clamored for the available oxygen and attention. Within our family crucible my mother became the merchant poet, my sister the artist scapegoat, my brother the recording engineer musician, and my father the afflicted truth teller. This childhood familiarity with fire forged my tolerance for its annealing effects. But the scale of firepower that overwhelmed Lebanon severely tested all of us. It would also try me in Paris.

In addition to the details of my conception, dad recounted his reactions to the news of my birth on March 27, 1954. "I was so excited to meet you, I locked the keys in my car at the medical center of the Naval Air Station in Patuxent River, Maryland." Expecting his firstborn to be a son, dad treated me like one, complete with firearms training and track and field coaching. A born daddy's girl, I remained a tomboy for as long as I could. On my parents' second wedding anniversary, on August 22, 1955, their second child and second daughter Karen was born at two o'clock. Mom's coveted son, Craig, came four years later.

Though he never wrote them down, my father was full of fanciful stories, bawdy jokes, and salty sailor talk. When revving up the engine before shifting gears, he would tell us kids tiny Chinamen were running beneath our car. And, according to him, our mother had been a mermaid when they'd met. Too young to connect this to the fact her maiden name was Trout, I was aghast when he claimed to have married her "because when I cut off her tail, she grew legs."

Not content to remain a Navy wife, mom encouraged dad to quit his machinist job in the military, "Follow your dream of flying airplanes." They moved to Tulsa, Oklahoma so he could go to flight school. Mom helped to pay their way, working as a ticket agent for Braniff International Airways. When my sister arrived sixteen months after me, she slept in a bureau drawer since I already occupied the crib in our trailer home. A breech baby, Karen seemed reluctant to enter this world, and had to be coaxed to take her first breath. Perhaps she knew how fraught her existence would be.

A beautiful, blonde, artistic child, with hazel green eyes like our mother's, she grew up to model in Beirut and New York City. One of her nicknames was "petite Brigitte," after the famed but troubled French actress, Brigitte Bardot. By the time my blue-eyed brother Craig arrived in the spring of 1959, we were living in Long Island, New York and Dad had achieved his dream. He was flying Boeing jets for Trans World Airlines. Mom was busy caring for the three of us, and sometimes managed to host Emmonds costume jewelry shows in neighbors' homes. For the next fifty years she kept her hand in, always working on something, going along with everything dad did, and sometimes taking the lead.

She never mentioned her side of my conception story. How many women do? We call his stories history. What are her stories called? All of this transpired in the decade before dad took us off to Arabia to begin our expatriate adventures. While overseas for those next two decades, I would learn men the world over can't seem to get enough of women or warring.

CYNTHIA F. DAVIDSON

Chapter 2

RAISON D'ÊTRE /
REASON FOR BEING

They do not feel bound by customary rules of conduct and
have not yet found an inner law that would replace them.

— MIRRA ALFASSA

January 1984

Zvonimir was not the only man who had asked me to join him in Paris that
January of 1984. Nabil had also invited me, but he represented the past, and
everything I needed to put behind me. While speeding towards my job in
New York City on my morning commuter train, I took stock of what Nabil
and I had in common, before our rendezvous in Paris tomorrow evening.
With the sunlight glinting off the snow along the tracks, I reflected upon
our mutual experiences in mythical places. Our kinship was based upon our
endangered memories. We were both expatriates, educated in Beirut. After
nine years of disintegrating war (so far) Lebanon's former allure lay buried
beneath the rubble. Both of us had also lived and worked in Jeddah, Saudi
Arabia, another city being rendered unrecognizable, for other reasons
entirely. Oil money and modernization had turned the ancient Red Sea port
into a disorienting hodgepodge of crumbling coral block buildings and
spanking new skyscrapers.

The more recent monstrosities dwarfed the white washed walls
surrounding the prehistoric tomb of Eve, for my old hometown of Jeddah
had been named in her honor. *Jidda*, the Arabic word for grandmother, the
Mother of us all, marooned between the ruins of modernity. I had often
passed her gravesite, speculating about its secrets, but the gates were locked.
Legend said the Garden of Eden had been just south in present day Yemen.
The Muslims called those times *Jahaliyyah*, "The Age of Ignorance," before
the revelations of Prophet Muhammad and the founding of Islam, in 640
CE. Perhaps Eve's followers had not been so ignorant after all. Our

blighted times might benefit from some remedial balancing of matriarchal wisdom.

The train rattled on and my thoughts returned to Nabil, yet another man, in search of what could only be offered by a woman. More than once he had traveled to visit me in the US, and I understood what he was looking for, but did not feel it was my job to provide it. A dozen years older, recently divorced and beginning to bald, he was hoping our companionship might lead to more, but I felt no physical chemistry. Our serial displacements and psychic dislocations did make for an odd bond however and I found it easy to empathize with him. During a nostalgic moment he had shared his feelings about leaving his observant Muslim family in Damascus for college in free wheeling Beirut. "The day our American professor told the class God was a man-made concept, my world fell apart." The intimacy of this and other admissions had stayed with me, along with his assertion, "you are not like other Americans." He had meant this as a compliment, and I took it as such, having heard it often by then.

A far more pliable second grader when my father's commercial aviation job with TWA took our family to Arabia in 1962, I'd grown up to become a TCK (third culture kid), as psychologists later dubbed us. Imprinted by the culture where I was raised, I had adapted more to it than the culture my parents had come from. At the outset my folks had not expected to stay in the Arab world for over twenty years. So we had not prioritized things, as we might have done in hindsight, like properly learning the language. Although we spoke *matbaki* (kitchen) Arabic, well enough to get by, I later learned to read and write it at university.

To continue my education, I had to leave our Arabian Desert home at age fourteen, for boarding school in Switzerland and Lebanon. More cultural experiences were layered on in the French speaking part of Switzerland, at Collège du Léman during my freshman and sophomore years. But I missed the Middle East, and transferred in 1970 to the American Community (high) School in Beirut, Lebanon, to become a boarding student there, for my junior and senior years. Our home was still in Jeddah, where I returned regularly, until dad made his next move. After eleven years in Arabia, he took a job with MEA, Middle East Airlines, in Lebanon. Mom was glad to leave the desert for cosmopolitan Beirut. Having often vacationed in that "Paris of the Middle East" we knew it well, and our home was easily re-established there in the summer of 1972. This relocation coincided with my graduation from ACS, the high school whose lovely Mediterranean campus bordered the American University of Beirut, where Nabil had earned his accounting degree.

By the time Nabil and I met in 1979 he was based in London and Jeddah. He traveled extensively for his job, as a financial officer for the various holding companies of Mazen Pharaon,[2] the man who introduced us. A family friend since my girlhood days in Arabia, this Syrian-Saudi business tycoon was born in 1939. Mazen's family had also been expatriates, and had lived in Paris when his father served as the first Saudi ambassador[3] to France. Multilingual and well connected, Mazen had gone to European schools and earned his engineering degree in Germany. My early life in Arabia was greatly influenced by this network of relationships and they would also affect the outcome of my days in Paris.

Instinctively people like Mazen, Nabil, and I gravitated towards those whose initiations were similar to ours. Befriending fellow expatriates was easier than forming ties with people who had never left their countries of origin. The latter were rarely interested in issues that concerned us, so we politely attempted to fit in, rather than mention what further distanced us. Besides the wars we had seen, each of us had survived culture shock, that lengthy convoluted process of adjustment and adaptation. Our beliefs had been called into question often enough to increase our tolerance for doubts and differences, or so I presumed.

When Nabil had been told, "God is a man-made invention" it launched a continuing process of reconsideration, about how he was raised, and what had formed his character. The Qur'an had dominated Nabil's childhood in much the same manner as the Bible had guided my Christian upbringing, and the Torah circumscribed Jewish lives. According to Islam, we were all "People of the Book" who shared many of the same stories, since our patriarchs-in-common had decided God was singular and male. How

---

[2] The fortunes of the Pharaon family had risen and fallen in an unlikely series of events. Mazen's father, Dr. Rashad Pharaon, had been a refugee, forced to flee from Syria in the 1930s for participating in the Syrian resistance movement against the French. France occupied the Levant (territories of present day Syria and Lebanon) between the first and second world wars. Dr. Rashad Pharaon was a wanted man, hiding out in the Arabian desert south of Syria, when he met Abd al-Aziz Al Saud. The new king of modern Saudi Arabia, Abd al-Aziz had consolidated the tribes and territories of the Arabian Peninsula in 1932 when he declared Saudi Arabia an independent country. Five years later, in 1938, oil was discovered in Arabia's eastern province. American geologists searching for water had found vast petroleum deposits. The discovery of that black gold, and the rising global demand for it, altered the destiny of the Bedouin tribes. It also spawned the founding of the world's richest corporation, Saudi ARAMCO, with revenues of 465.5 billion USD in 2017.

[3] Dr. Rashad Pharaon, a multi-lingual physician, became a close advisor to the new King Abdul Aziz Al Saud, who needed help from those with experience beyond his Arabian territory. Rumor has it that Dr. Pharaon earned the trust of the royal family by curing them of syphilis. Going on to advise several more Saudi kings, Dr. Rashad Pharaon was assigned to many diplomatic posts in Europe, where some of his children, three sons and a daughter, were born.

intensely reassuring to believe a single good book contained all necessary instructions for being a good person. Yet if such certainties remained unexamined, they could ignite conflicts when one lived and worked with those from other countries.

I also questioned my upbringing, and things like the authority of those who had failed so miserably to keep us safe. What others believed in often surprised me, like the time I heard the well-traveled Mazen confide his fatalistic assessment of Arabia's good fortune. "Allah gave the oil to Muslims as a test. If we don't remain faithful to Islam, a great calamity like an earthquake will come. Then the oil will go too deep into the Earth to be recovered. And we'll go back to living in our tents."

Which truths did I believe? And by what process could the false be distinguished from the true? By now I was familiar with these mental gymnastics. And I had learned enough psychology to understand my personal need for definitive answers was a universal trait. But my preoccupation with the war in Lebanon, and its torturous refusal to end, had become a serious roadblock. Lacking the answers to the most basic questions, like what had caused the war and why it wouldn't stop, had made me lose confidence in normal life. It seemed criminally irresponsible to marry or start a family only to subject newborn innocents to what my family and friends had been through. To resolve these festering preoccupations I needed to find "the truth that would set me free." But who possessed it?

At least Nabil and I shared these concerns and enjoyed each other's company. So I had agreed to meet him in the City of Light on my upcoming vacation. He had offered to pay my airfare and hotel expenses. I had thanked him for his generosity, but demurred. I explained my preference for paying my own way and said I would "stay at a friend's place." Zvonimir had already arranged things with Zemira, his Croatian compatriot, who lived in Paris. The importance of independence to seekers of the truth is more obvious to me in retrospect. Without the first, the quest for the second gets tainted.

* * * *

When my train arrived at Grand Central, I hurried from the station, heading down Lexington Avenue to my midtown Manhattan office four blocks away. I walked briskly, because it was cold and this was the only exercise I was likely to get, before spending the next eight hours at my desk. My rolling wheeled suitcase was also in tow, as this was to be my final day of work, before my ten-day vacation in Paris. The anticipation of flying there tonight added some spring to my step. Relieved to be out of the icy wind a few minutes later, I ducked into my building and greeted our receptionist and colleagues passing in the hallway. After stashing my bag and hanging my coat on the back of my office door, I drew my chair up to my desk and marveled for a moment at how closely woven my current career was with my expatriate past.

In retrospect, this management consulting job with MS&B, Inc. international relocation experts, seemed a perfectly straightforward choice. I screened, selected, and trained expatriating executives and their families, preparing them to live and work abroad as I had done. But job counselors in the early 1980s were not recommending cross-cultural training work because the field was too new to appear on the outplacement radar. What had conveyed me here had not been logic but my stubborn love. Although the Lebanese war had forced my family to return to America, I had not relinquished the thread of longing and belonging that kept me tethered to our former friends and fellow expatriates, like Nabil. This deeply felt connection, to my tribe of modern global nomads of all nationalities, had drawn me into this specialized branch of management development. I was proud to work with our firm too as we were considered the best in this brand new business.

Being well compensated now for sharing my hard-won wisdom increased my appreciation for the value of our particular skill sets, and our personality traits, in the globalizing business community. The right attitudes are crucial to success overseas. Years of experience had honed my awareness of the qualifications for membership. While anyone could memorize foreign assignment facts, the psychological orientation was the deciding factor. Genuine interest and innocent ignorance were more forgivable than superiority complexes or outright refusals to learn. Delivering cross-cultural training programs kept me focused upon the personal growth and development needs of those determined to overcome the stereotypes of their passport nationalities. And I was relieved to find my peripatetic existence had actually prepared me for an occupation, which suited my clients' needs as much as my own.

Before tucking into the day's to-do list, I took my mug to the kitchen alcove down the hallway, to make a cup of tea. Waiting for the kettle to boil, I reminisced about our checkered experiences as an expat family. Despite the rupturing war, and all that remained unresolved, I was still glad we had gone overseas. We were programed to. Our very DNA was encoded with wanderlust. Our immigrant forbearers — English, French, Scotch-Irish, and German — had also left their lands in search of better lives. And when economic necessity challenged my parent's generation, they simply reversed direction, heading East instead of West. Through it all, or perhaps because of my inherited cellular memories, I harbored a persistent belief: people ought to be free, to travel and live anywhere, to work everywhere, to use anybody's ideas or money, and marry whomever they want. What else was freedom for? In my bones I felt the American immigrant experience was a continuous experiment in the limitless mixing and matching of individuals and opportunities. By taking people in from the world over, hadn't we been primed to learn the multicultural, multiethnic lessons necessary for peaceful co-existence?

Yet even in America I knew this was wishful thinking. My assumptions were the result of my expatriate experiences and we were a tiny minority without political representation. Despite numbering several million, we expats had no elected representatives to protect our interests, although we paid taxes like every other American citizen. Expatriate Americans faced other handicaps too. We were the only citizens required to pay income taxes to our home country while working abroad. These were in addition to those paid to the governments of the countries where we earned our living offshore. This penalty was a great disadvantage as it made American managers three times more expensive to hire than other nationals. Additional prejudices hampered our individual chances in this globalizing era and my family had encountered most of them.

I didn't like to dwell upon the violence we had seen in Beirut but looking at life from the wrong end of a gun reveals the sadder truths. People who were supposed to protect us had often failed to recognize the dangers. And even supposed safety nets, like insurance policies, were cleverly worded so as "not to be liable for coverage during war or civil war, whether the conflict was officially declared or undeclared." We knew we were on our own when the war started in Beirut three years after my parents relocated there. Our apartment had been looted, my sister shot, and my father kidnapped. Thankfully, they had survived, but the continuing fighting had ended our lives as an expatriate family in 1982.

I understood the primal urge to lash out and hurt others after being wounded but after what we had suffered, I knew exactly where those cycles of retribution led. I wanted them to stop. Why did human beings waste their time and money perfecting more lethal ways to kill each other instead of discovering how to end wars? What captured my imagination were innovations in conflict resolution and reconciliation, and more efficient means for preserving peace, by honoring legitimate needs. So I had found my sense of purpose in work, which enhanced multiculturalism and prevented further violence. In my job, I was laying the foundations for good global citizenship one client at a time. Yes, it was a drop in the global ocean, yet I believed expatriates of goodwill and positive intent could push the human dial towards progress. If not, we might be doomed to the same fate I had seen unfold in Lebanon.

The kettle boiled. I turned off the burner and poured hot water over the Earl Grey tea bag in my cup. Warm mug in hand, I headed back to my office, contemplating the recent history my family had been a part of. In the short span of our lifetimes, we had seen Americans go from being openly admired to heartily despised in the Middle East. This was hardly my family's fault. Yet it was also true that American foreign policies of the past forty years were partially responsible for the violence, which had driven us, and many others, from our homes in the Arab world. And because things had gone so badly, I was determined to figure out why. Back at my desk now I thought about our personal goals and how every person's played out against the larger backdrop of socio-economic cycles. To link the larger causes with their small effects, just in the lives of my family, I had to parse out the reasoning behind our decisions. The major turning points revolved around three eternal themes: love, work, and war.

Dad had gone overseas for the first time because of the Korean War and his work on an aircraft carrier had solidified his love of airplanes. If he hadn't lost his job in one of commercial aviation's infamous boom-bust cycles, I might've grown up in Huntington, Long Island, New York. We had lived there in my early years so dad could commute to Idlewild airport to fly Boeing 707 jets for Trans World Airlines. Another act of violence had been the reason for renaming that airport JFK, after the 1963 assassination of American president, John F. Kennedy.

When my father was laid off in 1960, the mortgage on our split-level ranch house quickly became unmanageable, and our relatives had no money to spare. Although only a kindergartener, I understood things were serious when my parents requisitioned the contents of my piggy bank to pay for a quart of milk.

Dad found temporary work with Lufthansa, the German airline. He rotated out a couple weeks each month, to fly the newly purchased American Boeings, until enough German crewmembers could be trained to fly their imported jets. Our German surname Fetterolf must have been an advantage in the hiring process. Dad relished reconnecting with his father's culture of origin. *Deutschland uber alles*. Born in 1933, he'd been bullied at school for being a "Kraut" during the Second World War.

In his den I discovered his German history books and William Shirer's *Rise and Fall of the Third Reich*. Seeing pictures of Holocaust victims as a child, I never forgot their skeletal frames, gaunt faces, and sunken eyes. They were my first warning: the horrors in our world were real. Those concentration camp survivors staring out from black and white photographs turned me into a witness. People do terrible things to each other. And if we do nothing to prevent this, we risk becoming the next round of victims and victimizers. The forces of evil were still with us, as revealed in casual remarks and racist, sexist jokes. My father repeated them, like the one he overheard from a Lufthansa pilot. After reporting to the control tower that one of their passengers was missing, another pilot had radioed in reply, "Lufthansa, the German airline, have you checked your ovens?"

A letter from TWA arrived at our Long Island home while dad was away in Germany. It explained the company had signed a contract to help manage Saudi Arabia's fledgling airline. Like the Germans, the Saudis had bought some Boeing jets, eager to build their own commercial aviation company. Laid off TWA employees were offered first dibs on these new jobs in Jeddah, Saudi Arabia. My mother responded to that letter, thinking a year or two overseas would be a good way to save up a nest egg. She never imagined remaining in the region for the next two decades but by the summer of 1961, my father was living in Jeddah, flying Boeing jets for Saudi Arabian Airlines. We joined him the following summer. Over the years he trained Saudis to fly their own planes as the process of Saudization got underway. Much to the chagrin of TWA, whose Kansas City-based management team had milked this "cash cow" for as long as they could, foreign crewmembers were eventually phased out.

No real cows had grazed in the Arabian Peninsula, where not a single river flowed. As I removed the tea bag from my mug, and tossed it into the garbage bin beneath my desk, I recalled the countless tiny cups of scalding tea we'd drunk during our decade in that hardship post. Mint was often added in Jeddah but never milk. Arabia was a proud but poverty stricken place in the 1960s. We arrived a decade before the rising demand for petroleum made the Saudis rich. Thanks to the foreigners, including those who discovered the black gold beneath its burning sands, the money poured in. Too much money is almost as bad as not enough. The oil wealth also induced an ongoing case of cultural schizophrenia, exacerbated by the presence of expatriates like us, who had adaptation challenges of our own.

Expat hires had to prove they could adjust to their jobs' unusual demands before their families were allowed to join them. Spending the first year on bachelor status in the Wahhabi[4] Muslim culture of Saudi Arabia meant no bars, few restaurants, no (legal) alcohol, no movie theatres, no television, few phones, and no girls to "take the edge off." The lack of all amusements added to the stress and strain of relocating far from friends and extended family. More than half the expat employees failed to adjust. They were shipped back home to the "Land of the Round Door Knobs,"

---

[4] The Saudis practice a strictly observant Wahhabi version of Islam. Arabia is considered the Muslim Holy Land because the Prophet Muhammad was born there and proclaimed the religion in 642 AD. One billion of the world's Muslims face the Holy City of Mecca in Saudi Arabia each time they pray — five times a day for the devout. It was explained to me that alcohol and other intoxicants are forbidden to Muslims because no one can get drunk and sober up between two prayer times. Approaching the Creator, Allah, in an inebriated state would be the height of disrespect. My Muslim friends also told me they believed Islam was "the updated word of God" because the Qur'an came after the Torah and the Bible.

one of our expat nicknames for the US. Most doors in other countries have levered handles.

This fifty percent failure rate necessitated a more thorough screening process and some proper preparation methods, of the kind my consulting firm provided. Our overseas moves, and my subsequent schooling and work in other countries, had qualified me for my current career. Companies could not afford to keep sending people who had to come home early from their overseas assignments. For the cost of a single expat failure, we could train an entire department. My three-day pre-departure programs mixed general and culture-specific information expatriating employees (and sometimes their families) needed to know before they left. I administered Cross-Cultural Inventory tests, explained culture shock and coping strategies, and the specific stages of adaptation, using videos and other materials. Participants learned to identify cultural values, and the causes of critical incidents, which flared because of our differences in cultural conditioning.

Sometimes I shared critical incident stories from my own experience, like the time I'd been at lunch in Mazen's Jeddah home and heard his conversation with a former US diplomat. The American was representing a major US defense contractor and he was trying to convince Mazen to become their Saudi joint venture partner. The small talk began with *de rigueur* questions about the family.

"How is your father?" Mazen inquired politely. I knew he was also using these inquiries to assess the character of this guest.

"Oh, my dad's fine. He's old and he's getting a little deaf. We took him out of the nursing home for Thanksgiving."

The atmosphere in the room chilled perceptibly. Mazen had already made up his mind. I realized he would never agree to go into business with this man. Saudi Arabia is the only country in the world named after a family, the Al Sauds. Anyone who left his own father to live with strangers in a nursing home could not be trusted to care for a foreign business partner. I doubt the retired diplomat understood what he'd done wrong and who would tell him. In the absence of any cross-cultural training, or local friends — who can correct our mistakes — most expatriate foreigners tend to blame their failures on other nationals. Requesting honest feedback requires rare fortitude but it makes a lasting difference and definitely sets you apart. So does learning the language.

I could train people to go anywhere because our programs included returned expats, area experts, and carefully chosen nationals who helped me facilitate the culture specific segments, the history, politics, and customs of whatever country my clients were moving to. Staffing these programs required a wide network of these resource people. I constantly collected contact information on male and female nationals, as well as recently returned expats from many countries, to keep up with demand. Ideally these people had resided in the same city our clients were relocating to. Fellow expatriates gave the best advice on daily life details, such as which neighborhoods were best for expats to live in, and where to shop for American consumer goods and comfort foods.

Resource people had to be articulate about the cross-cultural challenges and I encouraged truthfulness about the hardships. Painting too rosy a picture would not prepare newbie expats for the inevitable isolation, alienation, and loneliness. They would be far from friends and extended family just when they most needed their support. Living abroad, and getting a job done, is nothing like being on vacation. And coping in another language can feel as exhausting as a 24/7 exam. These situations can build character and strengthen family relationships but I had also seen them trigger divorces, domestic violence, and nervous breakdowns.

Most Americans went overseas with no orientation or cross-cultural training but even without leaving the US, diversity issues can destroy business deals as some spectacular failures have demonstrated. Ignorance and arrogance are a costly combination. One of our corporate clients had just lost a huge joint venture opportunity with the Chinese because they did not understand what "saving or losing face" means in Asian cultures. After inviting their potential partner to visit their US manufacturing sites, the American CEO sent his chauffeur to meet the arriving Chinese CEO. But the man never arrived at their headquarters. When he did not see his American counterpart at the airport, he promptly returned to Shanghai. When someone has flown halfway across the world to negotiate a very big deal, the least you can do is show up at the airport.

I'd written up many of these case studies to explain the expensive pitfalls of unexamined beliefs, language barriers, and assumptions. Savvy expatriates could learn how to avoid such gaffs. Our type of training had originated in the US Navy after Admiral Zumwalt decided to outport American ships in the 1970s. The unruly behavior of American sailors during shore leaves had caused serious incidents in multiple countries. A team of organizational psychologists had been brought in to study these cross-cultural challenges and suggest solutions. We had since refined their coursework for corporate use, but we still had to prove its worth to skeptics in the management-consulting marketplace, as few companies had addressed the human challenges inherent in their globalizing business strategies.

When selling our programs to human resource executives, I explained it was like buying insurance, to offset the risks of sending American staff overseas, or bringing non-Americans to the US. By then we had the research to prove that living and working abroad tops the psychological impact scale. Foreign assignments can cause as much severe stress, anxiety, and depression as death, divorce, or going to jail. More than thirty percent of US employees are unable to adapt to daily life in other countries and return early from their assignments. Some of the reasons for these failures are predictable: poor screening and selection, unexamined attitudes, or unrealistic expectations. Those who show no interest in learning the language or enough customs to fit in tend to be rejected by local people. The same is true when other nationals come to the US, France, or elsewhere. But how much adaptation is enough to become fully accepted?

Repatriating families and their household shipments early was expensive and embarrassing for everyone involved. It made the recruitment of replacement expat managers doubly difficult. Measuring these dollar costs was easier than calculating the damage done to corporate reputations by unprepared employees. Some expats had caused international problems, when doing things like making and selling "bathtub gin" in Saudi Arabia, where the practice was lucrative but illegal. It earned you forty lashes in a public square and prison time if your company lacked the clout to get you deported after contravening local laws.

For several hours, I tucked into my to-do items and managed to check off most of them. When my stomach started growling, I rode the elevator downstairs to grab a quick takeout lunch from the nearby Korean grocery store. The January wind blew my coat open as I rushed across the avenue to the brightly lit store with its steamy windows and mounds of fresh mangos and bok choy. Once inside, I filled a clear plastic container with salad bar items, like sushi and extra slices of pickled pink ginger. Hot soups also beckoned. While ladling New England clam chowder into a paper cup, and securing its round white lid, I was struck by how remarkable this was — to have such a smorgasbord of traditional and fusion foods to choose from.

"Life ought to be like this," I thought, waiting in line to pay at the register. But the freedom of so many choices could be frustrating and confusing, unless one welcomed novelty, and had ways to discern and decide.

Back upstairs I ate alone at my desk, hoping to call my old beau Mahmoud, before things got too busy again. Despite no longer being a couple, I wanted to arrange something for his upcoming birthday. After locating his card in my Rolodex, Deputy Permanent Representative to the United Nations for the Arab Republic of Egypt, I dialed his number.

Mahmoud was also my best Middle Eastern resource person. The epitome of a tall, suave diplomat, he had lived in New York for several years and understood Americans. He deftly explained the nuances of Arab culture. His humor, charm, and excellent English instilled a sense of confidence in program participants preparing to live in Egypt. While working at the United Nations, he was completing his PhD in political science.

Last month we had gone to see the film *Moscow on the Hudson* about a Russian defector to the US. Mahmoud had known Russians during his service in the Egyptian Air Force. The USSR had been Egypt's ally and he had learned enough of the language to get by. Before we got into his car that evening for the drive to the theater, Mahmoud used a small mirror on an extendable metal wand, to check beneath the vehicle for explosives. After the movie he checked again. His vigilance was understandable. Ever since his President Anwar Sadat signed the Camp David Peace Accords, sponsored by US president Jimmy Carter, Egyptians everywhere had been targeted, spit upon, and worse.

I still had some hope when seeing that agreement signed four years ago. The Israeli and Egyptian adversaries had shared the 1978 Nobel Peace Prize, the first time any Arab leader had received it. But the situation in the "Muddle East" (as we called it in frustration) had spiraled downwards since that historic three-way handshake between President Sadat, Israeli Prime Minister, Menachem Begin, and US President Jimmy Carter. That "bought peace" had cost Sadat his life. Three years later his fellow army officers assassinated him during a parade to commemorate Egypt's "Ramadan War" victory against the Israelis in 1973. Referred to as the "Yom Kippur War" by the Israelis, outsiders called it the "October War." The Camp David Accords greatly emboldened the Israelis who would not have dared to invade Lebanon in 1982 if the Egyptians had been ready to fight. That treaty had directly affected the fate of my family too.

And, whether they knew it or not, my fellow American taxpayers were on the hook for the endless bills created by those Camp David Accords. The US government had pledged several billion dollars worth of annual subsidies to the Egyptians and Israelis. Much of it was in the form of military aid: tanks, gunships, and fighter jets. Some of the American defense contractors involved in these exchanges, like the F-16 fighter jet manufacturer General Dynamics, were clients of mine. I knew they could not afford peace in the Middle East. Their sales revenues were directly dependent upon continuing instability and protracted conflicts. Most Americans were quick to blame the Arabs and Israelis for not being able to get along while failing to notice the culpability of American foreign policies. Our economy had shifted during the Second World War and now relied too heavily upon the military industrial complex President Eisenhower had warned us about in his 1961 speech.[5]

---

[5] "[...] we must guard against...the military industrial complex. The potential for

The Palestinians had fared the worst. They were furious when Sadat and Carter sold them out with nary a consultation. The agreement withdrew Israeli troops from captured Egyptian Sinai territory but not from any portion of occupied Palestine. From their wretched refugee camps, the Palestinians made life dangerous, especially for Egyptian government representatives like Mahmoud. Agitating and demonstrating for the return of their homeland, the Palestinians employed every strategy they had seen work for the Jewish people, who had managed to retrieve *"Eretz Yisrael"* after 2,000 years of Diaspora. Some Palestinians still possessed the keys to the homes they were forced out of in the first war of 1948 when a UN mandate created modern Israel.

The phone rang and rang. Mahmoud was not in his office. His receptionist picked up. I left a message suggesting we arrange lunch before the end of the month. I was still fond of "Moudi" as I called him in private. Mutual friends introduced us, explaining the divorced Mahmoud was quite a catch. Our affair had been intense, and it inspired some lovely poetry, but I saw no future in being anybody's wife or mother. After what I'd seen of events in the Middle East, and my family's experiences during the Lebanese war, I had vowed "never to bring children into this rotten world."

* * * *

The rest of Friday went by in a blur. The sun had already set when I left the office with my suitcase and hailed a Yellow cab for my ride to JFK airport. For my job, I did a lot of traveling, but this trip was strictly for fun. For the next ten days in France I was free to do whatever I wanted. Feeling elated, not even the rush hour traffic bothered me. I left those worries to the driver and relaxed in the back seat. Tomorrow morning in Paris, I would meet Zvonimir's friends Zemira and Hugette, and see Nabil for dinner in the evening. The women's addresses and telephone numbers were in my handbag. I was curious about them and knew they probably wondered about me. What to ask or tell? This was not an occasion for the canned speech I recited for my work life introductions. What did they need to know? How much easier it would be if we could peek inside each other's heads. As a child I had peered into a hollow, spun sugar Easter egg and seen the 3D imagery secreted inside. My head was like that egg. Anyone looking through my ear would discover the desert dunes of my childhood environment.

---

the disastrous rise of misplaced power exists…only an alert and knowledgeable citizenry can compel the proper meshing of the huge industrial and military machinery of defense with our peaceful methods and goals, so that security and liberty may prosper together."

As the taxi wove through the streets on the way to JFK airport, I sank into that semi trance-like image-receiving state, so relished when traveling. My best insights came during these journeys in cars, trains, and planes though I had yet to understand the science behind this. Moving through landscapes can synchronize the right and left hemispheres of our brains and alter our consciousness. Tonight a celluloid filmstrip spooled through, starting with the sepia-toned photographs my father had taken in 1961, to show us where we were moving to. Although I was on my way to France this evening, I did not think it odd that my psyche was serving up twenty year old images of Jeddah's dusty, unpaved roads and scrawny donkeys pulling water carts, fashioned from repurposed oil drums. Like anyone else's remembered streets and scenes from childhood, my impressions of our previous homes in Arabia were replaying, reassuringly. Like safely secreted talismans, these reminders of my first experiences with relocation were preparing me to walk back out into the world again.

Dad had mailed those initial photos from India, Pakistan, Turkey, and Nigeria — wherever his work flights took him. Saudi postal services were notoriously unreliable and pictures were often confiscated. His onionskin airmail envelopes arrived at our Long Island house, their upper right-hand corners covered with multicolored stamps, and heavily franked in Arabic calligraphy and other alphabets we had never seen.

On the back of one snapshot, dad had noted he was running out of developing fluids in his makeshift darkroom. Cameras and photography supplies were scarce in Arabia where the "reproduction of human or animal form" was considered *haram* (forbidden) by Islam. While staring out the cab window at the New York City pedestrians, bundled against the cold, I recalled the controversial decision to photograph Saudi women unveiled, for their official passport pictures in 1975. This step had been necessary to prevent identity fraud, since anyone could travel beneath those black coverings, if their features remained indistinguishable.

The sight of unveiled women in Wahhabi Arabia was a big deal. Uncovered female faces on television screens had provoked riots a decade earlier when broadcasts first began in 1964. While defending the TV stations, the police had fired upon the protestors, and one death brought dire consequences. The brother of the dead man assassinated the modernizing King Faisal in revenge. All three were related members of the Saudi royal family. The killer was the king's nephew and even shared the name Faisal. In the spring of 1975, King Faisal had bent to receive his nephew's customary kiss of respect during a majlis meeting in Riyadh, but instead he'd received two bullets in the head. Since majlis meetings were public and televised, the cameras were rolling, and the crime was captured on film. That June, the culprit was publicly beheaded with a sword after Friday prayers, as is the Saudi custom. But conspiracies continued to circulate about that killing. The assassin had gone to college in the US and some were sure the CIA had put him up to it, after King Faisal's 1973 oil embargo had quadrupled the price of gasoline following the October 73 War.

Change in the Arab world came at a much higher cost than most Westerners could appreciate. I had grown up under the reign of King Faisal and his death affected me more than the assassination of far away JFK in the previous decade. The king was killed two days before my twenty-first birthday. His violent passing marked the definitive end of my childhood, and then war broke out in Beirut the following month, of that watershed year 1975.

The cab pulled up to the curb at JFK airport. I paid my fare and went inside to check my bag and get my boarding pass. Those chores completed, I headed for the departure gate, relieved to be early for my Paris flight. Glancing around at my fellow passengers while waiting to board, I wondered if any of them were first-time flyers. My first flight had been taken from this airport. At age eight in 1962 I had not known enough to be afraid. A twelve-hour transatlantic crossing on a Constellation had been my memorable initiation to a lifetime of travel. Now twenty-nine, and a veteran of countless trips, I still loved flying. Awaiting our boarding call tonight, while sitting in my molded plastic seat at the departure lounge, I invited the sensations of my initial voyage to return, The sounds were first, the distinctive droning hum of those four propeller engines, vibrating through the "Connie's" metal skin. They had lulled me safely to sleep. My thirty-year-old mother, six-year-old sister, and three-year-old brother were with me on that flight, as we were off to join dad in Jeddah. Having a father who flew airplanes for a living had definitely increased my aviation comfort level. Flying had become as routine for me as hopping on a bus with wings. And dad's habit of packing a suitcase to go to work had set some of my expectations for I happily did the same in my job.

In hindsight, knowing what I did now after all those years overseas, what might I have done differently? Knowing how difficult my re-entry to America had been decades later, I think I would have taken some precaution, to stay connected to my homeland. Perhaps in retrospect, I should have scooped some soil from our Long Island yard and kept it in a jar, to swallow some granules regularly, to preserve the connection. But no one had suggested such a medicine. Instead I had ingested the dust of the dunes and fallen unforgivably in love with Arabia.

There we often heard the saying, "You can take the Saudi out of the desert, but you can't take the desert out of the Saudi." That expression also described us expat brats, who grew up in that desert, yet had to depart from it. Despite how inconvenient and impolitic our attachments were, our formative years remained as deeply embedded in us as the ground beneath anyone's childhood place. As one homeland turns another towards terrorism and endless war, we embody all their conflicts.

The boarding announcement interrupted my reverie. Standing to take my place in line I couldn't shake the memories. They came unbidden now, like the heat and humidity that had hit us like a wall when the aircraft door first opened in Jeddah. Tonight at JFK we have the convenience of a jet way, but twenty years ago in Arabia, a set of mobile metal stairs had been rolled up to our plane. Descending them, the night wind coming across the desert had imprinted me, filling my nostrils with its distinctive scent, and entering my body. It was accompanied by the sound of echoing syllables, *As-salamu alaykum*, the Arabic greeting, "Peace Be Upon You."

Ironically, we would come to know war personally in this Arabic-speaking region of the world, where the greeting was about peace, *salam*. I could tolerate these contradictions, but what I found psychologically debilitating now, was the irreconcilability of competing realities. That original Jeddah airport, with its nearby stucco walled compound, containing the Saudi Arabian Airlines offices and my Parents Cooperative grade school, were all gone. Demolished in the rush to modernize. Not knowing what had replaced them made me cling even harder to what I knew no longer existed. This was an odd headspace to inhabit. My only other choice was to accept the unknown. Harboring that black hole of doubt meant I didn't know what was real anymore.

Why these particular memories this evening I wondered while settling into my assigned seat on board the plane. I was on my way to Paris not the Middle East. As the cabin crew readied us for takeoff, the remembrances continued, and it took too much energy to resist them. Perhaps this internal trail was leading to something requiring my attention. I went along, recalling the rest of our welcome to Jeddah in the summer of 1962. Once inside the rudimentary concrete block terminal of the former downtown airport, we retrieved our suitcases. Setting them upon the long low counters, we opened them for inspection. The custom agents had riffled through our belongings in search of contraband: girlie magazines, alcohol, or pork products.

When finished, they marked each bag with their powdery sticks of chalk, as white as their long-sleeved, floor-length cotton *jalabiya* robes. Their clothing was perfect for their climate. Never colonized by the West, the Saudis had not been forced to adopt the dress code of any overseers. Instead it was the expats who sweated mercilessly in the inappropriate attire of suit jackets, trousers, knotted ties, buttoned shirts, socks, and closed toed shoes.

Dad met us at the airport and drove us to our new home in the Alireza building downtown. He explained Jeddah had two paved roads: one led to

Mecca, the other to Medina to ease the journeys of the Hadji[6] pilgrims. Our comparatively modern third floor apartment had balconies, high ceilings, a wide stairway, and whitewashed cement walls but no elevator. Burgundy colored shutters could be pulled shut over the windows for shade from the relentless sun. The older houses in our neighborhood were constructed of coral blocks, cut from the nearby Red Sea reefs, plastered and painted over. These also had balconies, with distinctive latticework screens of imported wood. This luxury allowed the womenfolk to peer out and enjoy the fresh air, without donning their oppressively hot veils. The higher status females seldom left their rooms. Their men took care of them; the husbands, sons, or servants ran the errands and shopped in the *souk* (bazaar).

Tonight I looked around the aircraft at my fellow female travelers. Not a single one was veiled or wore a scarf over her hair. What adventures or affairs might they be off to? Ruefully I recalled my father's many dalliances. As a flight crewmember who spent more nights away in hotel rooms than at home in the marriage bed, he had taken advantage of his opportunities to be with many women. Why? My mother was more attractive than most of them. She could have used his absences to conduct her own affairs yet she seemed to prefer wielding some moral upper hand. One time when she discovered another liaison, mom had packed up my father's clothing and thrown his things out on the porch. But living in Arabia, where women were not allowed to drive much less make their own living, she could hardly fend for herself. Depressed for days, she remained in their darkened bedroom, making up her mind. She took him back but she seethed with resentments I could sense. Her decision appeared to be based upon the belief all men were like that. "Better the devil you know." Observing my parents power struggles as a child had been instructive. I viewed martyrdom as another choice to be avoided.

My father's behavior had certainly colored my expectations about men. As our plane taxied onto the runway for takeoff, I thought wryly about why the front end of the plane was called a cockpit. Growing up I had heard my dad's litany of sexist expressions. A holdover from his Navy days, those phrases had stayed with me.

---

[6] All Muslims are expected to visit Mecca and Medina at least once in their lifetimes. As a kid, I watched the faithful come by the growing millions in ships and planes each year, to make this *Hajj* pilgrimage and fulfill their religious obligations. In Saudi Arabia there is no separation between government and religion. The Qur'an (Koran) is considered the constitution and the Saudi kings call themselves the Guardians of Islam. Tens of millions of petrodollars have circulated from the hands of Americans, paying to fill their gas tanks, to the Saudis who've used them to support Muslim charities and the construction of mosques around the world. Oil helped to make Islam the world's fastest growing religion and some of this money has supported its extremist groups.

"Women are like buses, there's another one every five minutes."

And "Find 'em, fuck 'em, forget about 'em."

"Show me a man who won't go down on his wife, and I'll show you a woman I can steal."

Had my mother ever asked him not to talk like this around us kids? I remembered distinctly the day my dad washed my mouth out with soap, at age twelve, for repeating the risqué jokes I heard him tell. Had he realized the irony?

Another one of his expressions was, "A woman should be a lady in the living room, a chef in the kitchen and a whore in the bedroom."

Forever searching for women, he denigrated what he couldn't bear to live without. It was a confusing legacy. Although he constantly broke his marriage vows, he expected my mother to keep hers. As far as I know, she did.

"Put up and shut up," was one of her expressions. "You made your bed, now lie in it."

My father had never said anything about what men should be like. I was still trying to figure that out.

Technically I'd "become a woman" in Arabia, with the arrival of my menses at age twelve. My mother had trussed me up with menstrual gear and informed my father.

He congratulated me, clapping me on the back, "You're a woman now."

"I don't want to be a woman!" The echo of that yell had stayed with me.

Besides my father's comments about females, I also knew what happened to the Saudi girls around me at puberty. They put on their veils and wore them for the rest of their lives. Dependent upon their parents, even to find them husbands, they perpetuated these restrictive cycles. This ensured their lives remained as circumscribed as their mothers. Under Sharia law they might have to share their husband with three other legal wives. Some insisted this was familial love and protection, but to me it seemed designed to thwart possibilities for change. The rules preserved the power of those who already possessed it. Progress is threatening to those who already enjoy the freedoms of choice.

Our jet revved its engines, and we raced through the darkness down the runway. I welcomed the familiar thrill of takeoff. Seeing Paris again would be wonderful, and being with Zvonimir and Nabil, but I had an ulterior motive for making this trip. It was time to face it. My secret, unspoken hope was to find Georgina Rizk. I needed to hear from her what had gone wrong in Lebanon. Georgina had literally represented her country, first as Miss Lebanon, and then as Miss Universe in 1971, only four years before the war started. But the beauty pageant part of her life interested me far less than her story of what had happened after she became the first, and only Arab woman to wear the Miss Universe crown. Now thirty, only a year older than me, she was already a widow and a refugee. All the glamour had done nothing to preserve her from the violence in Lebanon. A car bomb had killed her husband Ali Hassan Salameh five years ago in 1979 before their son was even born.

By then my worries about that war, and the safety of my family and friends, were consuming me. I had latched onto the idea of writing a book as a way to deal with it. To keep from drowning in a sea of violence and chaos, I would cobble together a raft of paper and ink. Though writing was the flimsiest of things, at least I had practice doing it. And Georgina's tragedies had touched me deeply, in part because we had friends in common, and because her range of relationships mirrored mine. Born Christian, she had converted to Islam and married a Palestinian refugee. Her life story illuminated so many facets of the war. When the war scattered us, I had lost track of her and many others, but had heard through the grapevine she was now living in France. Although we had gone to some of the same parties during our Beirut heydays, Georgina had no reason to remember me. I couldn't just roll up and request her collaboration, even if I managed to get her contact information in Paris. What I needed was the right introduction, to be recommended by a friend she trusted. That would smooth the way. Even before the war, having the right connections in the Middle East was important. The factional fighting had made this requirement more crucial than ever. Could my network of Beiruti friends be revived or replaced?

Too tired to think anymore I dozed off, trusting the silver jet to carry us across the darkness of the Atlantic Ocean, whose waves rose and fell, more than thirty thousand feet below us.

When the stewardess woke me later to ask if I wanted a meal, I had been dreaming of Mazen, the mutual friend Georgina and I had in common. The details evaporated upon waking so I dredged my memory for my earliest recollection of him. What surfaced was the time he had taken our family to see the horse he had recently purchased. He knew I loved horses and longed for a real one. All I had to play with were my wooden, plastic, and glass horse statues. My favorite was a black one from the TV series *Fury*.

"His name is Fury," he told us. "You can ride him whenever you want."

Mazen had entered our lives in my preteen years though I could no longer remember exactly how. It had probably been via a party. My young, socially active parents had attended many soirees in Jeddah. There was nowhere else to go at night, except each other's houses and the embassies, where the illicit alcohol flowed. Making any Saudi friends was unusual as most expatriates lived on company compounds that were off limits to locals. All foreign workers occupied housing rented by the companies who sponsored their visas and work permits as non-Saudis were forbidden to own property in Arabia.

Inside those segregated housing areas were western style bungalows and pools where women could even wear shorts and bikinis because Saudis were not allowed to enter these compounds. ARAMCO, the Arabian American Oil Company, had set this precedent in the 1930s. Both sides had their reasons for limiting fraternization. The policy tended to reinforce stereotypes because genuine relationships could not form naturally. Even the simplest social courtesies were impossible. For example, you could not accept a dinner invitation to a Saudi home because you could not reciprocate since they were forbidden to visit your house if you lived inside a compound.

Tall concrete walls surrounded most private properties in Arabia. Many Saudis built extended family compounds, with enough land to build individual homes for their sons' wives and offspring. As kids, we often walked along the tops of those high, connecting walls when exploring. Such an appropriate metaphor, for we were also traversing cultural walls and boundaries best appreciated when viewed from above rather than down in the trenches of warring worldviews. I felt fortunate never to have lived on one of the compounds in Jeddah, although our friendships with Saudis did bring unforeseen consequences.

I dozed off again, no closer to discovering any reason for all these Jeddah flashbacks tonight. But my Arabian days, and my years in Beirut, were about to form the common ground for several enduring friendships upon my arrival in Paris.

Chapter 3

JOIE DE VIVRE /
GLAD TO BE ALIVE

If you love life you also love the past because
it is the present as it has survived in memory.

— MARGUERITE YOURCENAR

January 1984

The weather was bright and glorious when I stepped from the smooth metal tube of the plane upon landing at the Paris Charles de Gaulle airport next morning. Not sleeping well on the trans-Atlantic flight, I was in a strange mood as the sights and sounds washed over me inside the circular, donut shaped terminal. Riding the rubberized escalator that conveyed all passengers through an open, center space, I felt we were being invited to regard our journeys from all 360 degrees. The airport was named after the former French president, and Second World War general Charles de Gaulle, who had already passed into history.[7]

While waiting my turn at immigration control, I noted the French official inside the glass booth wore the same type of flat-topped hat de Gaulle had. I passed him my American passport.

"Is your trip for business or for pleasure?" he asked.

"Pleasure," I replied with a smile.

He stamped my passport with a six-month visitor visa. Heading for the baggage claim area to retrieve my suitcase, I thought about de Gaulle's wife,

---

[7] In the decade before my birth, American troops had helped to liberate France from Nazi German occupation. De Gaulle had led the French resistance, and the provisional government, from outside the country during the Second World War. He later opposed the American war in Vietnam, a former French colony, and he dared to take France out of NATO, the North American Treaty Organization.

whose picture I had never seen. I knew the current French president, François Mitterrand, lived with his mistress and had an illegitimate child. Word was Mitterrand had to pay his wife to appear with him at state functions. Men, they made all the rules to suit themselves, and forced us women to break them.

I queued for a cab and was soon climbing into the back of a small white Mercedes. The driver had the radio on. As the wintry scenery went by — the bare trees, emptied fields, and shuttered grey buildings — I sank into the leather seat and took it all in. The song lyrics of the popular station re-immersed me into the French language and made me feel as though the use of an atrophied limb was being regained. As we pulled onto the Périphérique encircling Paris, I recognized the opening notes of a tune not heard since my Beirut days, *"Paroles, Paroles"* ("Words, Words.") That music evoked the places where I had heard it: coming from the dashboard radio of the red Volvo driven by my Lebanese fiancé Ayman Choucaire, and the speakers in the Caves du Roy nightclub, where I had danced with friends. Georgina Rizk had also recorded this song before Beirut fell apart. The reminder seemed significant.

Today is was Dalida's voice warning about "easy words, fragile words…fake words you sow in the wind, listen to…my only truth."

A lump thickened in my throat. Simultaneously sad and glad to hear this song, I rolled the window down, needing the air of the here and now, to bring me back to the present. Dalida's lyrics would prove prophetic. (Three years later the lovelorn entertainer from Egypt would take her own life in Paris.)

I had given the taxi driver the address of Hugette Connier, one of Zvonimir's friends, unsure if Zemira would be awake or at home when my flight arrived so early on a Saturday morning. The cab's tires were soon rolling over the cobblestoned streets of the seventeenth arrondissement where Hugette lived. The cafe and shop windows shone in the bright morning light, as the Paroles music ended. I promised not to forget this poignant welcome back to Beirut, which had doubled as my welcome to Paris.

A few moments later, Hugette ushered me into her apartment, one of those turn of the century, five-story buildings with their floor-to-ceiling windows. Her greeting was warm and her English excellent. Delightful, blond, and middle-aged, Hugette had married an American expatriate executive, who was posted to Paris shortly after the end of the Second World War. Unfortunately he died of a heart attack in his early forties. They had no children.

Hugette explained she had known Zvonimir for many years and relayed his latest news.

"He hit his foot with an axe while chopping firewood. The Yugoslavian government has taken all the heating oil to Sarajevo, to keep the tourists warm at the Winter Olympics. The people have to make do with their woodstoves if they have them. He will arrive a day or two later than planned."

Knowing how expensive it could be to rebook airline tickets, Zvonimir had insisted I come anyway as he knew I would also be seeing Nabil. This accident was one of several strangely fortuitous events which conspired to keep me in Paris. Hugette and I would remain friends after this initial meeting. That week we ate the first of our many lunches together at the Champs-Élysées office of Air France where she worked. Every Thursday, their cafeteria served a stellar version of the North African couscous dish.

Later on the day of my arrival, I met Zemira, Zvonimir's other gal pal. Equally friendly, she spoke no English, but her Croatian accented French was easy to understand and she had no difficulty with my Lebanese accented French. Her apartment was tiny, but conveniently located. Right away she gave me her spare key, explaining her late working hours at a nearby restaurant.

"You must be free to come and go," she insisted.

Brunette and divorced, she was in her late thirties, with a teenage son and her mother to support, back home in the Croatian part of Yugoslavia. For the last fifteen years she had lived in Paris, saving money. She hoped "to build a little stone house" of her own one day, like those I had seen in Zvonimir's paintings of villages along the Adriatic coast.

The delay in Zvonimir's arrival gave me some free time, but the first thing I needed was a nap to cure my jet lag. When Zemira unrolled the extra mattress on the floor, I gratefully curled up on it. If Zvonimir had been there as planned, I may not have met so many other people that first week in Paris. In hindsight it all seemed *maktoub* (destined).

* * * *

Refreshed from my nap, showered, and changed, I met Nabil for drinks at the Hotel George V that evening, as previously arranged. Just off the well-known Avenue Champs-Élysées, this luxury establishment with its plush carpeting, heavy satin curtains, gilt paint, and rich Arab clientele was already familiar to me from previous trips to Paris. Mazen had brought me here, during my university days, and introduced me to movers and shakers in Saudi government and business circles.

The Hotel George V would remain a fixture in the coming three years. When meeting Nabil there for our tête-à-tête, I noted the differences between these ritzy surroundings and Zemira's modest lodgings. In her miniscule home my knees almost touched the porcelain sink when sitting on the toilet. Paris would be full of such contrasts and they would instruct me in ways I had yet to imagine.

Nabil's greeting was sincere but we were soon arguing. It started when the waiter asked for my drink preference and I replied directly. Nabil considered this a breach of etiquette. To his way of thinking, the man dealt with other men, and protected his woman from such interactions. A well-traveled executive, I was accustomed to ordering for myself, though I understood why Nabil thought the way he did. His behavior was valid in the Arab world where women needed men to care for their needs. Nevertheless, we had gotten off on the wrong foot, and things continued to sour.

In the following discussions that evening we also had a bit of a *contretemps* about love. I had recently decided, thanks to the influence of Lilian and Zvonimir, I was going to live for it as poets, artists, and creative people do. This was in keeping with my growing desire for truth and closure. Nabil found my idea foolish in the extreme and naïve for a woman of my age. By now, he assumed, I should have outgrown such idealism. I was almost thirty. In his eyes, it was high time to be sensible, and make a good match, settle down, and raise a family. But I couldn't. Not with him nor anyone else. I didn't believe in security. The war had proven it was nothing but a pack of lies.

Nabil had forgotten to pack his toothpaste, so we went to buy his particular brand from a pharmacy across the street. This was another lucky mistake, because just as we reached the sidewalk, an old friend of his walked by. They greeted each other warmly. Both AUB alumni, Nabil introduced me to Waddah, his barrel chested, mustachioed pal, who generously invited us to dinner that evening at his place.

Waddah returned to collect us from the hotel in his Range Rover. Being driven through the City of Light on my first night there was thoroughly charming, and I felt as light as air. Waddah's quiet apartment was in the fourth arrondissement, the old Marais district, and faced a serene inner courtyard. His home was an eclectic mixture of Western efficiencies and Middle Eastern comforts. The soft, stuffed pillow furniture was covered in a striped fabric that could have come from a souk in Baghdad, Beirut, or Damascus. On my visit to the bathroom I peeked at the modern kitchen, with Italian stone counters, custom-built cabinets, and brand new appliances. Each room was full of paintings, tastefully arranged, and they covered most of the walls. My eye was drawn to a brightly colored bird and a woman, by Corneille, and the desert-toned works on parchment paper by Henein. What I liked best was the smooth sculpture of a black bird, with folded wings, lying upon the coffee table in the living room. For quite a while that evening, I held it in my hands, feeling the stone grow warm.

A Moroccan woman came to cook for the party that night. The food she prepared was superb, but eating it left me feeling conflicted. These flavors recalled past savories but now they were mixed with the present ashes of Beirut. Was it wrong to enjoy this meal when so many went hungry and homeless in war-torn Lebanon? I decided to eat the food gratefully, having also seen how useless sentimentality was. It saved no one.

Our group included Henein, the Egyptian artist, whose work hung on the walls, his wife, and an English woman named Fiona, who managed Waddah's Paris art gallery. Her humorous French artist paramour was also there. The rest of the guests sounded Lebanese. The ambiance crackled with jokes and double-entendres in three languages. I enjoyed myself, more than I had in a long time. Nabil seemed miffed however, not being the center of my attention.

Unlike the Syrian born Nabil, Waddah's family hailed from Iraq. They both had Lebanon and AUB in common and the fact that neither man could return to their respective homelands. Both Syria and Iraq were in the grip of absolute dictators, Hafez al Assad and Saddam Hussein. My guess was they had left, rather than do their compulsory military service. This would make it difficult to go back even if they wanted to. A dozen years older than me, both Nabil and Waddah were childless in their early forties — very uncommon in the Arab world, where fatherhood and family are prized above all else.

Waddah had been an artist and photographer, although he had given these up by 1971, to go into the business side of art. His gallery was named "Contact" but the war had crushed it, literally and figuratively. Like so many others, who lost everything in Lebanon, Waddah had to start over. With the help of investors, he managed to open another gallery, in Paris in 1979. Although I had never seen his Contact gallery in Beirut, I knew its neighborhood well, having frequented that section of the city. It was walking distance from our ACS dormitory near the seaside Corniche, skirting the rocky western edge of Beirut. To reach the uptown Rue Hamra area with its boutiques, bookstores, and chic cafes, you climbed a long stone staircase bordering the AUB campus. Due to the pungent odors, left by those who relieved themselves there, we students nicknamed them the "Stinky Steps." Piss and shit seem apt metaphors for what we fail to plan for and try to ignore. Whether it was hunger, or eliminating what came after eating, even these legitimate needs troubled our world.

Before we left his place that night, Waddah invited Nabil and I to join him again for dinner the following evening. This time the venue was Tse Yang, a gourmet Chinese restaurant, walking distance from the Hotel George V. Ever the master of ceremonies, Waddah introduced everyone as we took our seats, and he ordered the food for our group. In addition to the gastronomic delights of the dishes, he chose wines for each course, starting with the white Vouvray for the hors d'oeuvres, and a well-aged bottle of rich red Bordeaux for the main meal. Poured ceremoniously from its bottle, over a candle flame into a crystal decanter, this precaution prevented any dregs from reaching our goblets while the heat enhanced the flavors of the mature Bordeaux. The mingling tastes were magical and so was the dessert. A pan of piping hot apple slices in a melted caramel sauce was poured into a bowl of ice water, crackling to hardness right beside our table. All this was polished off with a bottle of rosé champagne. Not a drinker, I couldn't finish a single glass, and was already tipsy.

Another AUB alum was at the table that night, Maurice. Like Waddah, he had family ties in Iraq, although he was Christian. High spirited and cheerful, Maurice cast the others in greater contrast: Nabil acting like a fussy, old maid and Waddah with an artist's tinge of mercurial moodiness.

After the introductory niceties at the Tse Yang restaurant that evening, Maurice pointedly asked me, "Why have you come to Paris?"

"I'm hoping to find Georgina Rizk," I explained, a tad too earnestly. "We used to go to some of the same parties in Beirut. I believe her story could explain what went wrong in Lebanon to those who've never been there. I would like to write a book about her life."

He nodded, and relief flooded me. I did not need to explain any more.

"She lives here in Paris. I'd be happy to help you contact her," he offered.

My spirits soared. After years of privately incubating this intention, here was the chance I had sought. Perhaps my plan was not so crazy and could even happen. Anticipating that prospect made me giddier than the combination of wines. As the evening ended, Maurice invited Nabil and I to join him for dinner the following night, having assumed we were together.

I immediately answered, "Yes, I'd love to."

Nabil bristled, feeling it was up to him, to accept or decline this offer. Maurice might be muscling in on his date, but it would have been gauche for him to say no, after I had just said yes, so he acquiesced.

Tonight, I gave Waddah a few of my poems, by way of thanks. And I resolved to make more copies to share with Maurice tomorrow evening. Having told them I was a writer and a poet, I felt it was important to prove I was serious, not just some dilettante playing at it.

"Fait Accompli"

In a world too full
of alien blue
eyes, I turn to you,

appearing like a ghost
from the past, wearing
the mask of my memories.

I can hear your eyes
ringing, like dark bells,
calling me back to Beirut.

Back to the ravaged country,
where the losses are,
too great to count.

Where we left our lives,
and abandoned our histories.
to the war that brought us

here, to face the choice
of futures wrought from
the ruins of our past.

I ask your eyes
what to do, and they say,
"What is true."

[Excerpt from *Measuring Distances* poetry collection]

Waddah suggested we meet to discuss the poems and passed me his business card. On a strip of paper torn from my agenda book, I wrote down Zemira's number, and said I looked forward to talking with him before my return to the US.

* * * *

Before falling asleep on Zemira's floor mattress, I reviewed the evening's events. What I treasured most about tonight, besides Maurice's offer to help me contact Georgina, was how much the ambiance resembled the Beirut I remembered. This circle of AUB alumni in France was the closest I had come to recreating what had been lost. I wanted more, despite the ache of longing, for everything unresolved about my past. So much potential had been squandered in Lebanon.

I remembered how I'd felt like a country bumpkin coming up from the desert to visit Beirut on vacation. In Arabia we had no telephones, television, movie theatres, or restaurants, except the lone "Kilo Ten" on Medina Road. My experiences had left me profoundly confused. The women around me wore veils in public, were forbidden to drive, and could not go out alone. Yet a mere three hours flying time north of Jeddah, women like Georgina Rizk were cavorting in bikinis, wearing hot pants and miniskirts on the covers of Beirut's glossy magazines. Which world did I fit into? The need to decide where I belonged and what sort of woman I wanted to be was also resurfacing here Paris. The fancy hotels, flashy boutiques, and nightclub shows at the glitzy Casino du Liban had turned my head in Beirut during the years when it had epitomized the jet set lifestyle, for those who could afford it. In the 1960s and early 1970s the manicured, well-coiffed types wore the latest French and Italian fashions, wined, dined, and danced until dawn at posh nightclubs like Les Caves Du Roy. That was Georgina's milieu. And by winning the Miss Universe pageant in 1971, she had helped put Lebanon on the map. Yet when the war broke out a scant four years later that veneer of glamour degenerated overnight. Once again clashing realities had forced me to decide, which was true: Beirut's prior sophistication or its current savagery?

Ruefully I recalled how AUB had turned down my application in 1972 when I graduated from the high school next door. Their small quota of American students had been exceeded for that year. Preference went to Arab students because AUB's mission was to educate the region's future leaders. Despite the fact AUB had turned me away, it was one of the few institutions my tax dollars supported in the Middle East that I agreed with. Obviously the US government expected to leverage its cultural and political advantages by funding the institution but I believed in education for its own sake. The British and French had also set up their own schools after invading the Levant at the end of the First World War. But the ravages of the Second World War had ended their colonial ambitions and forced their armies to depart. Thirty golden years of relative independence had followed in Lebanon.

When the war began in 1975, it interrupted any possibility of finishing a degree if I had gone there. Instead I spent my next four years after high school working: first in Beirut, then London, and Caracas. My higher education was not resumed until most of my fellow classmates were finished with college. By then I had returned to New York, where I got my bachelors degree in journalism and Middle Eastern studies at New York University. In a hurry, I had finished my studies in two and a half years instead of four, intending to return to the Middle East as soon as possible as a reporter.

I understood AUB had not been created for the benefit of lonesome expatriates like me, but meeting these refugee alumni increased my appreciation for its incalculable importance. When AUB first opened its doors in 1862, the US was suffering its darkest period. A civil war was raging over issues of slavery and succession. Now another civil war raged in

Lebanon. The intervening one hundred years of education had not prevented the slaughter from reoccurring.[8] Did studying the liberal arts encourage the growth of democratic ideals, beliefs, and values? That idealism had not panned out. The local situation was a lot worse now. Why? Because people lacked the peaceful means for sharing their resources and resolving their conflicts, or because the machinery of war was too readily available and too profitable?

The first college of its kind in the old Ottoman Empire territories, AUB had continued to innovate, managing to shed its overtly Christian missionary beginnings. By refocusing upon what the locals needed and wanted, the university provided practical training to the growing middle class of professionals, entrepreneurs, economists, and doctors. Its teaching hospital had remained the best in the region. In 1975, my own sister had gone to their emergency room for doctoring after being shot. AUB's secular curriculum had maintained its relevance to the increasingly diverse student body, which included my former fiancé, Ayman, a member of the Druze Muslim minority.[9] What had happened to him during the war? It had been years since I'd heard any news beyond the fact he managed to survive the fighting, was married to a French woman, and working for a French bank.

Rolling over on my mattress in Paris, I thought of how grim the future looked for Lebanon, even those lucky enough to attend AUB. Classes had been suspended. The ongoing war made it too dangerous to risk the lives of students and faculty. Thirty AUB staff members were already missing, kidnapped, or presumed killed. I fell asleep doubting any of us would ever see the city or the university again.

* * * *

In the daylight, things seemed more hopeful. The following afternoon I went for a walk, determined to cover the five kilometers between Zemira's apartment and the Hotel George V. The January cold was bracing but I needed the exercise and wanted to enjoy Paris on foot. Only my third day here, and already my new contacts had rekindled my plan to write about Lebanon via Georgina's life — if I could convince her to do it when we

---

[8] Dr. Daniel Bliss, a Protestant American missionary had established AUB, first calling it the Syrian Protestant College, and then changing the name four years later. American missionaries realized by then how unrealistic their attempts were to Christianize the Arab Muslim world. It was decided to maintain a foothold, and wield some influence in the Arab world, via higher education.

[9] A somewhat secretive, thousand-year-old sect, with a mystical, unitive version of Islam, the Druze forbid polygamy, slavery, and circumcision. They do not proselytize nor allow conversion to their faith. Unusual for the Middle East, they also believe in equality for women and the separation of church and state.

met. While packing for this trip, I had dug through my files to locate the early draft of my book proposal. After jotting down a rough outline in 1979, I refined my ideas over the intervening years, deciding to write an Arab version of *Gone With The Wind*. Although Margaret Mitchell's 1936 novel was fiction, its well-received format proved audiences could learn the history of a civil war via the experiences of a woman and her family.

While negotiating the Parisian streets at rush hour, I wondered about Georgina's life here. After all she had been through, was she happy in Paris, or did she yearn for peace so she could return to Lebanon? Born to Christian parents in Beirut in 1953, Georgina had lived a remarkable life for an Arab woman. I reviewed her high and low points while striding along. After high school, she worked as a model instead of going to university. Becoming a professional beauty queen, she had won the Miss Lebanon title in 1970. Mazen had bragged to me about paying all Georgina's expenses for the trip to Miami, Florida so she could compete in the 1971 Miss Universe contest, which she won.

What had Mazen expected in return?

After winning the Miss Universe title, the stunning, hazel-eyed, auburn-haired Georgina could have had her pick of men. Why did she fall in love with Ali Hassan Salameh of all people? Her choice had shocked her family, friends, and fans. They could hardly imagine her with such a controversial character, despised by her social set. Salameh had multiple counts against him: he was a Muslim, a Palestinian, and a refugee, a dozen years older. Their affair occurred during the time of the war, when Georgina's fellow Christian Lebanese were vowing to "eradicate the Palestinian problem" by killing any refugees who did not leave. But where were the Palestinians supposed to go? There were few options. On the run since the immigrating Zionist Jews began forcing them out before the First Arab-Israeli war in 1948, they had lost more territory since, in the ongoing series of wars: in 1956, 1967, 1973, 1982...

Palestinian militants like Ali Hassan Salameh and his boss Yassir Arafat knew they were not just fighting the Israelis, but their backers, the deep-pocketed American empire. Not even the Soviet Union had sufficient resources to defeat the US. With their backs to the proverbial wall, the Palestinians had tried to take over their neighbor nation of Jordan, in what became known as the Black September of 1970. Having lost that bloody attempt, they fled over the border into Lebanon. Their well armed, battle hardened presence soon tipped the precarious Lebanese political balance. By the spring of 1975, the unstoppable war was in full swing.

To become Ali Hassan Salameh's second wife in 1978, Georgina had converted to Islam. His existing Palestinian wife, Nashrawan, had borne him two sons and he did not have to divorce her. As long as the husband can provide for each one equally, Sharia law allows four simultaneous wives. Depending on which side told his story, Ali Hassan Salameh was a famous "freedom fighter," or a reviled "terrorist." After his involvement in planning the Munich Olympics hostage taking of 1972, the Israelis and many others put him in the latter category. In the botched rescue mission by the German police, eleven Israeli coaches and Olympic athletes perished, as well as five Palestinian commandos. This earned Salameh the top spot on the Israeli intelligence organization's hit list. Seven years later, those Mossad security agents finally assassinated Salameh with a Beirut car bomb, when Georgina was four months pregnant.

I never found out where Georgina had ended up after that and I shelved my budding biography project. Too consumed with earning my own living, I had little time to spend on such a long shot. But knowing we would both be in Paris this month, I had buffed up my proposal and run off a couple copies to bring along, just in case. They were stashed in my roomy purse now, ready to show to Maurice, or anyone else who might help me revive this project.

As the purpling twilight tones streaked the sky, my booted steps neared the cobblestoned Place de l'Étoile, the star shaped roundabout at the heart of modern Paris. While waiting at a red light, I regarded the massive Arc de Triomphe standing in its center. Commissioned by Emperor Napoleon in 1806, that monument symbolized the glory days, when France was Europe's largest nation. Perhaps the French had expected only greater triumphs, yet their empire had dissolved, like all the others.[10]

With the cars roaring past, I recalled the smaller replica of this arch, at the bottom of Fifth Avenue in New York's Washington Square Park. Standing in the center of the NYU campus, I had often passed it during my university days. Named in honor of the first US president, it was another reminder of our debts to the French. Without the strategic help of nobles like Lafayette, and the financial assistance of King Louis XVI, our seven-year rebellion against the British Empire, our American Revolution may have failed.[11]

---

[10] The Americans replaced the French in Vietnam, where war taught us about the limits of empires. Saigon was once called the "Paris of the Orient." Now Ho Chi Minh City, it was named after the Vietnamese revolutionary who once called Paris home. While the French occupied his country, he had lived in France trying to get his land back, and later turned to the Soviets and the Chinese Communists for help.

[11] The first American Ambassador, Benjamin Franklin, lived in Paris for nearly a decade. He convinced French King Louis XVI to loan money to the fledgling United States to overthrow the colonizing English King George III. The French monarch also sent arms and fighters, including the Marquis de Lafayette, who became an unlikely hero in the American Revolution. My mother's LaMotte side of the family were cousins to that French aristocrat. Lafayette helped to draft the revolutionary Rights of Man and the Citizen Declaration, which remains part of the

The light changed and I crossed the edge of the Place de l'Étoile to take one of its best-known spokes, the Champs-Élysées. The last rays of the sun cast a pearly iridescence across the pale grey stone buildings as Paris turned into the City of Light. This sobriquet dated back to 1900, when electricity began to illuminate the French capital. But it also referred to the earlier Enlightenment era, which had put an end to royal rule. When revolution rolled through France, the same King Louis XVI was forced to bare his neck to the guillotine, along with his wife Marie Antoinette, and his mistress, Madame de Pompadour. Their executions were carried out at the bottom of this avenue, now called the Place de la Concorde, where the three thousand year old Egyptian Obelisk of Luxor had more recently replaced the grisly Madame Guillotine.

At night Paris felt different, glittering, and haughty. This evening it was also quite cold. Tucking my chin into my neck scarf, I picked up my pace to the George V. The hotel was named after the English king whose granddaughter Queen Elizabeth II was now the Queen of England. Her uncle, Edward VII, had abdicated to marry "the woman I love," the Pennsylvania born American divorcee, Wallis Simpson. Had it been love? Or something else?

I was on the Champs-Élysées now, named after the mythical Greek Elysian Fields. That sacred burial ground was a far cry from the reality of this broad commercial avenue. Rather than a resting place for virtuous and heroic souls, vanity ruled here. Immense plate glass windows fronted the expensive designer boutiques, reflecting the images of each passerby. I tried to roll back time, if not to the Greek Elysian Fields, then at least to the pre-revolutionary days when horse drawn carriages had clattered down this road, currently clogged with cars. Those carriages had carried the trendsetters of bygone centuries, who were often the mistresses of the French kings. Royal marriages were political alliances not romantic pairings. Some of those women had done a lot more than play dress up, though their portraits could only depict their powdered wigs and hairpieces, festooned with ribbons and plumes. The educated hostesses had artfully mixed the social classes in their influential salons. Introducing royals to gentry, and writers to artists and philosophers in their candle-lit rooms, these women had been the first to facilitate the free exchange of ideas during the eighteenth century Age of Enlightenment. Ironically, the spread of science and rational thought had broken the stranglehold of the church, and hastened the demise of European monarchies and aristocracies. But these changes had also brought lasting progress to France and the rest of the world. Surely some of those paneled rooms, where those society doyennes

---

French constitution, as does the American version, in the US Bill of Rights. Those ideals fueled revolutions elsewhere and ended royal rule in dozens of countries.

had convened their soirees, still existed behind the facades of these ancient regime buildings.

After the edgy, masculine severity of Manhattan, with its angled surfaces and the "get to the point" sharpness engendered in New Yorkers, Paris felt as curved and undulating as the female body. This was generating a greater awareness of my own femininity. The rounded balustrades, ornamental ironwork and decorative cornices were practically flirtatious, as their pretty details beckoned you to take another look. My initial introductions to Parisian fashionability had been in the homes of wealthy Saudis and Lebanese, who preferred European clothing, and furnished their formal sitting rooms in the gilded Louis XVI style. I recalled those petit point chairs and couch cushions, marbled clocks and French fabric flourishes, with their scenes of bosom heaving ladies in long satin gowns and elaborate hairdos, cavorting in faux European woodlands. Meanwhile the desert lay incongruously beyond the walls of those villas and palaces. Another instance of the bipolar reality I had grown up in. How odd to mimic the style preferences of a doomed king. Louis XVI had an era named after him, but he and most members of his court died in the Reign of Terror following the 1789 French Revolution. For me the lasting lessons were in the reasons for their violent endings.

Continuing my Champs-Élysées stroll, I thought of the salons hosted by influential Arab women, who fulfilled equally important roles during times of great upheaval in the Middle East. Our Beirut street was named after one of them, Rue May Ziade (1886-1941). The poet, author, and hostess had been born in Nazareth, when the city was still under the six hundred years of Ottoman Empire rule, which did not end until after the First World War. Her father was a Lebanese Maronite and her mother a Palestinian Christian. Between the World Wars, May Ziade's Wednesday salons had mixed the social movers and shakers of her day. Seeking to wrest their independence from the colonizing Europeans whose rule had replaced the former Ottomans, they debated the burning issues in her living room.

Education made the difference for May Ziade. She had gone to a French run convent school in the mountains above Beirut where her wide reading opened her mind. Thanks to inspiring books from abroad, she also became a multilingual translator of French literature, in addition to penning her own books, articles, and editorials. Her work often appeared in her father's influential newspaper where she told her readers about ideas gleaned from overseas thinkers and philosophers as well as the concepts being debated and adopted by the local politicians, novelists, and artists attending her salons. Although May Ziade never married, she did conduct a long distance love affair with the famous Lebanese poet and illustrator, Kahlil Gibran for nineteen years, as their letters later revealed.[12]

My walk had not taken as long as expected. With the Hotel George V in view, I took a seat at a cafe across the street until it was time to meet Maurice and Nabil for dinner. My midtown Manhattan walks rarely invited me to linger or savor such a cascade of memories. No sidewalk cafes there (yet). New York was brusque and transactional whereas the seven thousand years of Parisian history evoked almost too much. To tune into these enchantments, I would have to slow down, and sync up with a completely different rhythm. Otherwise Paris would be too disorienting. How to stay grounded while exploring this mesmerizing multiplicity of past and present realms?

The permeating warmth of the café crème helped to center me in my body. This sensation of inner comfort encouraged outward experimentation, and I invited the memories to come, to transport me, near or far. I focused upon the anchoring solidity of the Hotel George V. Remaining attached to a reference point, a significant person, airport, or hotel kept my psychic roamings better organized and easier to return from. With the George V firmly in sight, I widened the opening of my mind. The image of The Phoenicia quickly superimposed itself. The first great hotel I had known, Beirut's Intercontinental, with its centering courtyard, tiled oval pool, and 450 rooms. This had been my vacation playground during childhood and adolescence.

Today, after all the fighting, it was a gutted, blackened hulk, frequented by snipers. Could both truths co-exist? Holding such divergent realities inside me was exhausting. Should I choose one and banish the other? I blinked and brought myself back to Paris. I took another sip of my coffee, unable to resolve my prior experiences with the despairing realities of the present.

I released my mind again and it took me to another hotel, one that remained unchanged: the Waldorf Towers, in New York City. No conflict to overcome here. Through its grand lobby I had seen Saudi royalty, Frank Sinatra, and Gina Lollabrigida and enjoyed elevator rides with the band members of the Bee Gees, and Imelda Marcos, first lady of the Philippines.

---

[12] Despite his success in America, with his bestselling books like *The Prophet*, Gibran was lonely. His patron, Mary Elizabeth Haskell, was a prominent Protestant school matron in Boston. Fearing the cultural backlash of her peers, she rebuffed his marriage proposal. She bankrolled his stay in Paris but Gibran died of alcoholism in New York at age forty-eight. He and May Ziade never met. When her parents passed, May's family tried to steal her inheritance. They connived to get the childless spinster committed to an asylum in the Lebanese mountains. Eventually released, May left for Egypt where she died alone at 55, another tragic ending.

Like Georgina Rizk, Imelda had begun as a beauty queen, singer and aspiring actress. She had also married a politician who later became president. Had Georgina expected to become the first lady of a restored Palestine when she married Salameh? What if he had lived? So many what-ifs. And which decisions had prevented better outcomes? During their decades in power, the Marcos family had grown increasingly corrupt, stashing millions in overseas bank accounts. Last year in 1983, the assassination of an opposition leader had finally forced them into exile. Would something similar have happened to Georgina and Salameh?

Releasing this train of thought, I refocused upon the George V. What are luxury hotels good for? When stepping inside these deluxe establishments, you entered an altered dimension. Unlike personal homes or office buildings, hotels were neutral zones. Like tiny Switzerlands, they were safe havens, where people could rub shoulders with those outside their cultural and social orbits. Whether mixing by accident or on purpose, the world needed such spaces. They were a bit like the old salons, minus their clever hostesses.

But posh hotels are also places of privilege, where the heady allure of money and luxury mingled with indulgence, flattery, and risk. The constant tension of arrivals and departures heightened the sense of chance. Moments mattered because they were limited. Whether staying overnight as a guest, or coming only for drinks or a meal, those experiences forced you to make up your mind. My inner sybarite wanted more but it bothered me to know how some of the money was made by those who could pay such exorbitant prices. I checked my watch and ended this reverie. Time to go. I signaled for the check.

Nabil and Maurice were waiting in the George V lobby. We walked a few blocks to a bistro. Settling into our seats, the men began discussing a construction project in Canada. I studied the room, drinking in the surrounding details, determined to have this city instruct me. What distinguished this institution of French gastronomy? Bistros were more than their menus and settings of upholstered banquettes and polished brass work. The waiters all wore white shirts with cuffs, collars, and bow ties. Their black trousers were sharply creased. Long white aprons extended to their knees, the tops folded down, just so, around their slim waists. No housewife wore such an apron. These men moved with a practiced precision and flair rarely seen, even in expensive American restaurants, unless the staff had European accents.

In the US, teenagers and college kids waited on tables. The job was seen as a stepping-stone for those working through school or some income for actors between gigs.

"Hello, my name is Joe, and I'll be taking care of you tonight."

Such instant first name familiarity was not how things were done in class-conscious France. Service, as practiced by Europeans, Asians, and Middle Easterners was the product of a far more rigid system imposed for centuries. Those accustomed to servants wanted to keep them. In "I-can-do-it-myself" America, few wanted to wait upon anybody else. And being waited upon made most (middle class) Americans feel uncomfortable.

But these waiters had a hoary pride American tourists were not prepared for. In the finer establishments of Paris, waiting upon the clientele was an end in itself, an actual profession. Both sides were expected to observe proper protocol. When done well, this *pas a deux* (duet) was beautiful to behold and partake in, despite the implied status differences. This prescribed routine between diners and wait staff was obvious tonight in the polite gestures: a raised eyebrow, a slight head nod, a finger barely tapping the base of a wine goblet. Every movement was understated and formal, nothing so gauche as a raised arm or a raised voice. In this smooth ballet, one noticed only the occasional flourish, as when a hot dish was set down with a flick of the wrist, or the corner of a spotless napkin wiped a droplet of sauce from the edge of a wide porcelain plate.

Newcomers did not know the signals. They were already anxious about reading the menu and pronouncing their order in French. No one enjoys being intimidated. Visitors felt inadequate when faced with the starchy *de rigueur* of these waiters. Paying a lot for such cool treatment could add to the outrage. The French were equally liable to impatience. My uncle had once been escorted out of a provincial French restaurant by the chef himself, in a snit, after Wayne asked for a Coke with his three star meal.

Tonight when it came time to order, I chose escargot and turbot, foods never eaten in the US, but reminiscent of Beirut. Maurice said he "had a little gift" for me. Nabil frowned as his friend passed me a piece of Hotel George V stationary. Upon it, he had written Georgina's address and phone number in pencil. Tears of gratitude welled in my eyes. For years I had sought this information, hardly daring to hope I would ever have it. Maurice proceeded to regale Nabil and I with stories about Georgina's loud and frequent parties. According to his friends the Burkes, an American expatriate family who lived in the apartment directly beneath hers, those soirées continued until dawn sometimes.

Chatting with the gregarious Maurice was easy. By some shared timing instinct, we occasionally attempted to draw Nabil back into the conversation. But he grew more sullen as our exchanges grew more animated with the food and wine. At the end of the meal, Maurice invited us back to the apartment he shared with his brother on Avenue President Wilson. "It's near enough to walk to."

As we left the bistro, I turned up my coat collar. The night air was frosty. To my left, the Eiffel Tower blazed, like some oversized Cupid's arrow of black metal lace pointing dramatically skyward.

His third floor apartment was in one of the older buildings, with an ancient caged elevator nestled between the curving stone staircase. Once inside, we crossed the creaking parquet floors, and pulled off our coats, to sit upon the pale blue sofas and chairs.

Maurice declared, "I want to fix you a special treat. White coffee." Then he disappeared down a long hallway toward the kitchen. I admired the artwork on the walls: paintings, watercolors, and sketches in all sizes. The hodge-podge was decidedly Middle Eastern in theme but lacked the selectivity of Waddah's critical eye.

Returning with the hot, clear liquid, Maurice poured it into the tiny, traditional, handleless white china cups. The taste was of roses. Despite my pleas, he refused to divulge the ingredients, saying only, "It's a secret, but it has no caffeine, so don't worry. Here, have another cup," he insisted. This time I sipped slowly straining to decipher the concoction.

"What would you like to hear?" Maurice asked us, indicating the sound system and the collection of cassettes filling the lower shelf of the built in bookcase.

"Oh Fayrouz, please, if you have any of her music," I replied, forgetting to defer to Nabil.

He had retreated into his shell since taking a seat on the couch. Maurice found a cassette tape and soon the bell tones of her soprano voice filled the room. "*Biladi, Biladi*" (my country, my country) Fayrouz sang. My tears brimmed again.

Maurice noticed the change, regarding me with some concern from across the room.

"It's alright," I reassured him. "Hearing her also makes me happy." I wanted the music to continue. Though it reminded me of all that was lost, it made me feel less lonely. In this moment I felt closer to "it" than I had ever had in New York.

Later, as Nabil repeated for the third time that we really had to go, I handed Maurice the copy of my Georgina proposal, along with a couple of my poems. I thanked him for a wonderful evening.

"I'm returning to New York on Monday morning, but I'll be back. I'd really like to talk with Georgina."

"If you come back, call me. I'll see what else I can do to help you." He gave me his card, taking up a pen to write his private number on it. Handing it to me, Maurice asked, "Do you know the meaning of Rizk, Georgina's family name?"

My cheeks reddened. Had I forgotten? Or had I never thought about it? I shook my head.

He replied softly, "Rizk means a gift from God, an effortless abundance."

* * * *

The following day Nabil and I ate lunch at the hotel before his flight to London. Things had grown awkward between us. The trip had not turned out as he'd hoped. I was getting along better with his friends than with him. Nevertheless I thanked him sincerely for the introductions, and chided him to keep in touch as we waited for the taxi that would take him to Charles de Gaulle airport. After our goodbyes I walked the cold but sunny streets back to Zemira's little apartment, relishing my freedom, and the fact Zvonimir was due to arrive in a few hours.

* * * *

Later in Zemira's modest room, we embraced for a long time. Zvoni's large bandaged foot altered his familiar form. His doctor had insisted he wait to travel until the wound fully closed, but he had disobeyed, and the wound throbbed. We laid down so he could elevate his foot. At his insistence I supplied my news, regaling him with tales of the coincidences and the people I'd met, who might help me with my Georgina project. He teased me about my rich Arab friends before pushing me gently into the pillows where kisses ended our conversation. That evening we left the apartment only long enough to share a simple meal at a quiet restaurant a few doors away.

In the morning, despite Zvoni's limp, we went shopping. He had a long list of items to bring back, which were unavailable in Yugoslavia. Touring the Galerie LaFayette department store left me dizzy. Zvonimir bought me a bottle of First perfume by Van Cleef & Arpels and a pair of decorative hair combs. Exhausted we returned to Zemira's place that afternoon for a lovely nap and some lovemaking in the fading winter light. He pretended to be a small boy, and me, the enchantress, initiating him.

"You do make love like a beautiful witch," he whispered holding me close.

That night I wondered about real intimacy. If I behaved as he preferred, rather than being myself, what would change? The idea of sex being reduced to a performance, instead of being inspired, would turn pleasure making into a chore and kill the magic. Being true was more important. If I lied about the basics, I hardly deserved the truth from anyone else.

The next night we ate out with a merry group of Zvonimir's friends who knew each other well. One was a charming hairdresser named Freddie (Frederique) who had her own salon. After dinner, she took us all for a spin in her Alfa Romeo to see Paris by night, and admire the jewels of Her lights. Once again, I felt wonderfully blessed and totally spoiled.

The following morning, Zemira surprised us with a gift of fresh croissants. Dipping them into the bowls of milky reheated coffee, we discussed the day's plans. Zvoni still had shopping to complete before his departure the next day. He phoned his wife. It was impossible not to overhear their conversation in the little apartment. Though others believed there was nothing wrong about affairs, I would never feel right about dating a married man. Now that I knew about his wife, I resolved this relationship would have to end before too long.

When Zemira went to work, and Zvoni left to do his shopping, I set off on foot for Place Victor Hugo and the Rue Georges Ville. In my hand was the scrap of paper Maurice had given me with Georgina's address and phone number. I had checked the map in the *Paris Par Arrondissement* guide beside the telephone. Possessed by an urgency to get there right away, I hadn't thought much about what to do once I reached her building, and decided to figure that out on the long walk there. Going out the door, I felt an invisible hand on my back, propelling me across town, with another copy of my Georgina book proposal in my handbag.

The frigid weather made my ears ache, and I double wrapped my scarf, glad the sky was blue at least. Striding down the beautiful wide boulevards, bequeathed by Baron Haussman's controversial nineteenth century city planning, I felt the beauty of Paris seducing me to stay longer. What a wonderful city even for pedestrians. Soon I was standing at the right address. The pre-war, five story gray granite building had fanciful carvings around the windows. Pushing on the silver button that released the outer door latch, I was suddenly inside the foyer. On the wall to the right was an intercom panel, with the residents' names labeling the buttons. The second, inner set of locked glass doors would not open unless someone buzzed you in. Seeing the name Rizk on the intercom panel made me feel faint. To be this close was almost too much to take in.

I realized anew just how far this self-assigned task would take me from my present life course. Even if Georgina said yes to the idea of telling me her story, everything would have to change for a book about her life to become a reality. Nothing is easy, especially when working with people from the Middle East who have legitimate reasons to distrust Europeans, Americans, and each other. Georgina's reasons were more dire than most since the assassination of her polarizing husband and her conversion to Islam. For a long moment I considered giving up the whole idea.

Turning away now, before initiating anything with Georgina, meant my fantasy would never be marred by reality. Inside imagination's cave, my intention could safely hide, like my other unexamined memories of Beirut before the war. Contemplating this project, without daring to attempt it, had helped me survive. But if I staked everything on it and failed to accomplish it, where would that leave me? And what about the risks to Georgina Rizk?

How long might that take to gain her trust, and by what process exactly? I knew "they" would have to check me out and delve into my background. Her husband Ali Hassan Salameh had been high up inside the Palestinian Liberation Organization (PLO), and the chief of their elite intelligence unit, Force 17, the Palestinian equivalent of the Israeli Mossad. He had been the heir apparent of current PLO leader Yassir Arafat. Rumor had it Georgina was still on Arafat's payroll. So even if she wanted to collaborate with me, how much of the truth would they allow her to tell?

How much did she know, and could she share the real reasons behind the destruction of Lebanon? More of my doubts reared up. Few cared about the fate of such a small country. A book might never appeal to enough readers to cover the costs of writing it, much less make a difference. From personal experience I knew how few were interested in the region or its history, after watching their eyes glaze over when I mentioned my own years there.

If I made this commitment, it had to be total. Half-heartedness would never work and it might be the hardest thing I had ever attempted.

Georgina would probably say no, but what if she said yes?

I remembered the Arabic proverb, "How far the eye can see, how short the arm can reach."

Just below the Rizk bell was a button labeled Burke. A perfect option. Maurice had told me about this American expatriate family who often endured Georgina's all night parties. Knowing they had lived in Saudi Arabia would provide an instant kinship. I pushed the button and heard the bell ring nearby.

A woman answered, "Who is it?"

"Hello, are you Mrs. Burke? You don't know me, I'm Cynthia Fetterolf, a friend of Maurice's. I happened to be in the neighborhood, and would like to meet you, if you have a moment."

"Just a minute," she replied. The glass door lock buzzed opened and a pert blonde woman came out of her ground floor apartment, extending her hand.

"I'm Janet Burke," she said. "Come in, come in. Pardon my appearance. I was washing the windows. We only recently moved in here."

I liked her immediately. "I could come back another time," I offered, explaining I was visiting Paris, but had to return to New York next week.

"It's alright. If you don't mind the housecleaning mess, at least have a coffee with me."

Greatly relieved, I followed her inside. For the next three hours we chatted like old friends, trading stories about our Jeddah years. Janet had been there the last five years and brimmed with news about changes in the country. I had not been back since 1979 when I spent a year working there after completing my university degree. Briefly I explained my Georgina project and showed her the book proposal. "I have to slip this copy beneath Georgina's door but I will gladly bring you another one."

Janet had never heard of Georgina until moving here. Now she was too close to the woman's noisy parties. "My husband Tom probably knows more. He's due back any minute."

After another half an hour, I knew Zvoni would be expecting me, and Janet still had her windows to finish. I apologized for bursting in on her. "Would you like to join me for lunch tomorrow? I'm meeting Hugette, a French woman who works at Air France. I think you would like each other."

Janet needed to make friends in this city, especially with those who spoke English. Hugette and I had already planned to meet and I was happy to share this friend of Zvonimir's, met on my first day back in Paris. Janet had never studied French. This put her at a distinct disadvantage here where speaking the language made such a difference. Even when you did know the language, making friends in another country was never easy. After exchanging phone numbers, we agreed to meet at the main Air France office on the Champs-Élysées where Hugette worked, at twelve thirty the following day. In the meantime, I would call Hugette and make sure it was all right to include Janet. After saying goodbye to Janet Burke, I climbed the stairs to ring the bell at Georgina's apartment door. When no one answered, I slid the envelope with my proposal, a few poems and a handwritten note under the door.

* * * *

Three days later in Zemira's apartment, I was happily reviewing everything that had happened since my arrival in Paris. Although Georgina had yet to respond to me, as far as I could tell, I still had hope. I had left Zemira's Paris number, and her call may have gone unanswered, since we were out a lot. Zvonimir had made it safely back to Yugoslavia and I had followed up Waddah's invitation to visit his gallery. He introduced me to his manager Fiona, the Englishwoman I had met briefly at one of his dinners. Waddah was often away, traveling to buy art and sell it, especially in Saudi Arabia.

I thought him curiously unexcited about what was being displayed on his own gallery walls. Most of the paintings were abstract and not exactly standouts. When I asked about the canvases, he scathingly referred to the Saudis who bought them, as "visual illiterates."

His candor was both surprising and refreshing. Because the strictly interpreted version of Wahhabi Islam prohibited the reproduction of human or animal forms, Waddah had to scour the market for the bland art Saudis found acceptable for public display. Most of the work he sold in the Kingdom was destined to decorate the brand-new ministries and office buildings. Staring at the geometric designs, stylized Arabic calligraphy, and smudgy landscapes made me recall the more attractive artwork that had hung upon the walls of our family home in Jeddah.

My mother collected paintings and her taste extended well beyond what the Saudis deemed acceptable. She had purchased several fine portraits, including one of a bespeckled Muslim cleric with a Qur'an open before him. The artist was an Indonesian Muslim[13] named Bawazir. He had come to Arabia to fulfill his religious duty by making the hajj pilgrimage to Mecca and Medina, and remained afterwards. The expat community in Arabia recognized the value of Bawazir's work but I doubt the locals bought it. The artist was probably worried about the *Mutawa*, the Saudi religious police. If they find out about his art they would punish him for reproducing human forms. Under their strict interpretation of Sharia law, he could be lashed or worse for this transgression, and his paintings would probably be seized and destroyed.

The full name of the Mutawa translated to The Committee for the Promotion of Virtue and the Prevention of Vice, akin to the repressive punishments meted out by the Puritan fundamentalists who founded their colonies in New England. The Mutawa patrolled the streets, making sure all shops closed at prayer times, five times every twenty-four hours. They enforced other religious laws, keeping the sexes segregated and making sure women were properly chaperoned and veiled and not driving automobiles. Dressed in their white *jalabiyas*, with *ghutras* (*keffiyeh*/scarves) on their heads, and cloaks over their shoulders, they often carried bamboo rods. Zealous Mutawa had even spray-painted the bare legs of Western men who offended Islam by wearing shorts in public.

While we were touring his gallery, Waddah invited me to dinner that evening with his business partner visiting from London. The restaurant, Casa Olympe, was another superb choice. Run by the female chef, Olympe Versini, it featured minimalist nouvelle cuisine. Eight of us enjoyed an exquisite meal, and Olympe came out of her kitchen afterwards to speak with Waddah, who obviously patronized the place.

I was impressed that he knew the finer dining establishments, not just the tourist traps of Paris, which were also plentiful. At the end of the evening he drove me back to Zemira's place.

"Won't you join me tomorrow?" he asked as I got out of the car.

It would be the final day of my vacation.

"Yes," I agreed, pleased and curious. Where might this lead?

* * * *

---

[13] Indonesia, a non-Arab country, is home to the world's largest Muslim population.

On the last full day of that January vacation, before my flight back to New York, Waddah picked me up from Zemira's apartment as promised. In good spirits he declared enthusiastically, "I'm going to show you my favorite part of Paris."

We drove to the fourth arrondissement and he parked alongside an apartment building that faced an ancient central square. I noted the name, Place des Vosges, while getting out of the car. Throughout Paris, the street names can be seen written in white on blue metal signs, bordered with green, and displayed high on each corner.

As we toured the area Waddah supplied the details.

"King Henry IV [aka Henri Quatre, the first of the Bourbon Kings] gave this land, free to members of his entourage, but there was a condition. Everyone had to build to the specifications of his architect's uniform design. The king's apartments face the queen's," he added, with a sweep of his arm. "When they lived here it was called the Place Royale."

Located not far from the River Seine, this land had once been a boggy marsh where tournaments and duels were held. During a celebratory jousting contest here in 1559, King Henry II died after being wounded accidently. That incident had far-reaching consequences, which affected my very own family. The dead king's very Catholic widow, the Italian born Catherine de' Medici, was determined to eliminate any alternatives to her authority. She encouraged their son, King Charles IX, to order the massacre of the Protestant Huguenots. That infamous slaughter began on Saint Bartholomew's Day in August 1572 and the River Seine ran red with the blood of my French Huguenot LaMotte ancestors. Though I refrained from mentioning this to Waddah, I felt some empathy for him, a minority Shi'a in the largely Sunni Muslim world, where massacres continued to occur.

The calm beauty of the place, ringed by sloping mansard roofs, belied its turbulent history. By 1612, the area had become a perfectly pleasant square, 140 meters by 140 meters. It also became the European prototype for royal city planning. Many famous Parisians had lived here, including Madame de Sevigne (1626-1696), the French aristocrat and literary icon, whose salons were equally celebrated. She had been born on the south side of this square. After the French Revolution swept the royals away, the Place Royale square was renamed Place des Vosges, for the mountainous Vosges region, the first to pay taxes to the new revolutionary government in 1799.

That Sunday afternoon, Waddah escorted me to address #6 saying, "This was Victor Hugo's [1802-1885] home."

We entered what was now a museum dedicated to the well-known Frenchman. The author of *Les Misérables* and the *Hunchback of Notre Dame* had been exiled for sympathizing with the poor. Like us, he'd become an expatriate, spending almost two decades away from France in the British

Channel Islands. After climbing the wide, worn stone steps, we visited the high-ceilinged rooms. The dark, heavy furniture dated from the days before electricity and running water. I imagined servants collecting the smelly chamber pots from beneath these curtained beds. On the wall of an upstairs room, I stopped to admire the portrait of a young woman, swathed and hatted in luxuriant furs.

"That is my favorite," said Waddah.

The person in the painting was Juliette Drouet (1806-1883), Victor Hugo's mistress. She had given up her acting career to become the author's secretary and travelling companion. Later in the downstairs gift shop, I discovered the artist was C.E. Champmartin when I read the back of the postcard featuring the portrait. I purchased two, and mailed the first as a thank you to Waddah, and taped the other into my journal as a reminder of another road taken by a woman in Paris.

After the Victor Hugo museum, Waddah guided me through the cobbled lanes of the Village Saint Paul neighborhood. Eventually we arrived at Pont Marie, where we paused to look upstream and down. The unsettling power of the River Seine swirled beneath us with the unquenchable force of life itself. Waddah pointed at Île de la Cité, the larger of these two islands in the river at the ancient heart of Paris. Dominated by its flying buttresses, Notre Dame cathedral, Our Lady is easy to spot. Completed in 1345, its Dark Age gargoyles and chimeras were designed to frighten the superstitious and uneducated into regular church attendance and almsgiving to support the clergy.

"Now I shall take you to the most famous ice cream maker in all of Europe here on the smaller Île Saint-Louis. Surely you need a nice hot cocoa too, after all this walking in the winter cold?"

With an enthusiastic, "Yes!" I took his arm for the first time.

We crossed the remainder of the stone bridge to the smaller, quieter island, named after the pious King Louis IX, who died in 1270, the only French king ever canonized as a saint. The island's peacefulness was palpable. Like Place des Vosges, it was another haven in the midst of bustling Paris. Little did I realize on my first visit that Île Saint-Louis was about to become my next home.

At Berthillon, we were relieved to find a table. Our numbed fingers soon warmed around steaming cups of milk chocolate. We savored the icy *nougat au miel* and *marron* (chestnut) *glacé* served in clear glass dishes. After we'd finished the ice cream, Waddah took my hands in his. Our knees were touching beneath the round marble topped table.

He looked long into my eyes and repeated the word I had said on the bridge, "Yes."

My insides were somersaulting.

We continued to chat about art and poetry. He commented on my "Fait

Accompli" poem, saying, "It got a bit biological in some places."

I was pleased he had given some thought to the lines instead of just saying he "liked" it.

He spoke about his Iraqi homeland and how his family had fled in the wake of the 1958 revolution. It had been the bloodiest uprising in the Arab world. The entire royal family had been murdered and their bodies dragged through the streets to ensure no more monarchies[14] could be re-established in Iraq. Afterwards, a series of coups d'états eventually brought Saddam Hussein to power. Even before he seized the presidency in 1979, Saddam, a Sunni Muslim army officer, had harassed the Christians, Kurds, and the Shia Muslim minority.

Waddah didn't need to tell me about Saddam Hussein's ruthless consolidation of power over Iraq during his twenty-four year dictatorship.[15] I didn't want to interrupt the flow of his words to ask clarifying questions. Having never been to Iraq, I was experiencing what others probably felt when listening to me go on, about places they had never seen.

With conviction he said, "I wish I could take you to see the Imam Hussein shrine at Karbala. People take their dead there because it is such a calm place. They carry the corpses around the tomb to settle their spirits. Nearby is another holy shrine, but that one, Al-Abbas is more turbulent. The martyrs are buried inside its walls."

He explained the tomb's power. "They take disputing friends or lovers there to swear their lives, their truces, or their truths on the temple. Inside is a silver cage (holding the saints' remains). The penitents hold on to the bars as they chant, pray or beg Allah, throwing their tokens, money, or gifts of jewelry through the bars, sometimes tying green strips of cloth to the metal

---

[14] After their invasion of Egypt in 1882, the British added Palestinian, Jordanian, and Iraqi territory to their empire. They installed their Hashemite friends as puppet kings in the lands they seized, placing Abdullah in Jordan and Faisal II in Iraq, without bothering to consult the local populations. The Hashemite dynasty had originated with the Prophet Muhammad's great grandfather. From the tenth century up through the end of Ottoman rule, this family had governed Islam's Holy Cities Mecca and Medina. In 1932 the first modern Saudi King, Abd el Aziz al Saud removed them, and took over the Holy Cities.

[15] Saddam Hussein's prisons filled, his executions were brisk, and he declared war on his neighbors, Iran and Kuwait. This sociopathic behavior is a personality trait shared with other despots. Saddam kept his generals too busy to mount a coup against him knowing that was how he'd taken over. By 1991 he had the largest standing army in the Middle East. After a disastrous eight-year war with Iran, he marched his men into Kuwait. This triggered the first American war in the Middle East when President Bush Sr. ordered US troops to protect our oil-producing allies. "Saudi Arabia declared war on Iraq, but they gave the contract to the Americans, "was the joke Arabs told each other.

lattice work when making vows."

As Waddah spoke of these ancient places and people, Paris fell away. I felt transported back to the desert of my childhood and had a premonition, of some vow he and I might make. The familiarity of his accent activated the perpetual rippling of those inner dunes. Both of us loved those much-maligned lands. They formed the common ground of our rapport. Not having to explain any of this, bound us together here in France, so far from where we'd been. Immense relief flooded me for the shared sorrow we felt was as real to us as it seemed unreal to others. Speaking of those tombs breathed life back into their memory, and kept them and those who loved and remembered them, alive. My poems were my attempts to preserve what threatened to die in the distance. If we combined our memories, in this third place, would it improve our chances to survive or thrive?

Growing up in Arabia, I knew about the strife between Waddah's Shia minority and the Sunni majority. Many times in my training programs, I had explained these Muslim differences by comparing them to the rifts in Christianity. Theologically, the Shia were similar to Catholics. Their ayatollahs were a bit like popes. Protestants, the Puritan founders of the US, were more like Sunnis since they refused any intermediaries between themselves and God.

Of the world's one billion Muslims, only ten percent were Shia. Their line followed the Prophet Muhammad's son-in-law Ali who was murdered when his father-in-law died. The battles over succession had been bloody. Both Ali's sons had died violently: Hassan by poison and Hussein on the battlefield. Without a peaceful process for sharing power, violence prevailed. For centuries the Catholics and Protestants had savaged each other, when not focused upon a third enemy, like crusading against Muslims in the Holy Land. Some continued to wage these conflicts today.

Outside it grew dark. The Burkes were expecting me for drinks and dinner tonight. "Are you free this evening?" I asked Waddah. "Would you like to come along to my friend's house for dinner?" It would be one way to repay him for all his invitations.

"I have nothing else planned," he replied.

I went to the back of the Berthillon ice cream shop and used the pay phone to call Janet. Could she accommodate an additional dinner guest on such short notice?

"Sure! I'd be happy to make another friend in Paris," she responded, reminding me of how much she'd enjoyed meeting Hugette, at our Air France luncheon earlier this week.

Waddah and I walked back to the Range Rover arm in arm. Cruising slowly through the Paris Sunday streets at dusk, he put an old Barbra

Streisand cassette in the tape deck. I sang along to the songs I knew. "Oh my man I love him so…"

We arrived at the Rue Georges Ville building and found a parking space right outside the door. We smiled at each other. The Goddess of Fortune was nodding at us. After he switched off the ignition, I leant over to give Waddah a good luck kiss. A dam was breaking. My head and stomach were tumbling. Was I was falling in love?

Dinner at the Burkes was delightful. The simple home-cooked meal was a welcomed respite from our recent gourmand extravaganzas. Waddah was at ease. His dark eyes shone across the table and mine sparkled in return. By ten thirty we took our leave, knowing Tom had to work in the morning, and I had a flight to catch back to New York. Tom and Janet insisted that I consider their home as my Paris base if I returned to work on the Georgina book.

"After all, she lives just upstairs."

Nowhere else could be more convenient. Over dinner we discussed the project. Tom thought it would be a hit. Waddah did not say much. After bidding everyone adieu, we stepped outside into the cold darkness.

As he held the car door open he whispered in my ear, "Come. Spend the night with me."

We embraced on the sidewalk, our bodies pressed together for the first time. He smoothed my brows, cheeks, and forehead with his fingertips as he kissed me. Our shared heat melted any resistance. And I repeated what had become our word: "Yes."

Later in his room, he carefully closed the long shutters over the windows before turning to undress me slowly and deliberately. Then he removed his own clothing. Left around my neck was the red ribbon from the bow of my blouse as he gently lowered me to the silken coverlet of his bed. His body was thick and brown, his tongue tart with the taste of tobacco, as he sank into my flesh.

Swooning beneath him I cried in French, "*J'étais fait pour toi.*" (I was made for you.)

From above he repeated my words, grasping me harder, "Yes, you were made for me."

Afterwards, while we rested, I took hold of my long hair and drew it across his naked back. He sighed.

"It feels like a summer breeze."

Soon we were taking each other again, fitting and moving together as if we'd been lovers all our lives. The intense pleasure and deepening joy made me want to weep.

In the morning, as I finished dressing, I removed the red ribbon from around my neck. Carefully I tied it to a small hook on the wall above his bed. Perhaps a painting had hung there. I was thinking of Eve's tomb and the shrines he had told me about in Karbala and the strips of cloth pilgrims fastened to the tombs. Wasn't I a pilgrim too? Seeking some blessing, some mercy, some love?

Waddah looked at the ribbon and declared, "By February, roses will be growing from it."

"And laughter and tears too perhaps," I added.

* * * *

We held hands during the drive to the airport the following morning. Parking beside the terminal entrance, Waddah repeated for a third time, "I will miss you. It will be a long February. Come back and stay longer next time. Stay with me."

"I will," I assured him before getting out of the car.

"And write."

"I will."

Walking through the round cavern of Charles de Gaulle airport, towards the smooth metal tube that would whisk me away from everything I wanted, he could not see my hot, silent tears already flowing.

Chapter 4

LE POURQUOI /
THE WHY

A tout pourquoi il y a (un) parce que.

Every why has a wherefore.

— FRENCH PROVERB

Three days after my Paris vacation, I was back on my morning train, riding from Greenwich, CT to my job in Manhattan. A fellow commuter shook open his fresh copy of the New York Times and the headline blared, "University Head Killed In Beirut; Gunmen Escape." The death of Malcolm Kerr, AUB president, dominated the front page.

Stunned, I asked to borrow the front section of the paper with a tremor in my voice, and quickly scanned the newsprint columns. Kerr had been shot twice in the head, right outside his office door, in broad daylight. No group had claimed responsibility. No one knew why he had died or which group had hired this pair of assassins.

Reading the story catapulted me right back to Beirut and the place where he'd died. I had often walked through that area of the campus during my boarding school days. If anyone had seen his killers, fears of reprisal would discourage them from coming forward. Without witnesses or suspects, Kerr's name would join the ever-expanding list of revenge killings and kidnap victims. The survivors included my sister Karen, my father, and Georgina. The deceased included Georgina's husband Salameh and Lebanese president elect, Bashir Gemayel along with hundreds of others.

Unsolved shootings are as common as dust in Beirut. No one had ever been held accountable for the crimes committed against my family either. Kerr's shooting jolted me, reopening the jagged events of nine years ago. Staring out the window I recalled the opening week of the war, in April 1975, when two Palestinians had fired their AK 47 automatics at a passing

Peugeot with Lebanese license plates. Twenty-seven of their comrades had just been massacred by Lebanese Christian militiamen in a bus across town in Ain el-Remmaneh.[16] Craving revenge, the pair had sprayed the hot lead from their curved ammo clips, at whatever target they could find. *Rattatatat.* They were past all caring about who might be inside the vehicle.

One of the sixty some bullets flying at the Peugeot pierced the front door on the passenger side and penetrated the flesh of my sister's hip. Another bullet exploded the windshield, grazing the forehead of her boyfriend at the steering wheel. Half a centimeter closer and the two of them never would have made it to the AUB hospital emergency room that night. Digging the bullet and door fragments from my sister's body proved far easier than healing her torn psyche. My sister would be in and out of NYC hospital psychiatric wards throughout the following decade. On the darker days she picked scabs from her forehead, convinced they were pieces of glass from the shattered windshield, working their way to the surface.

The identities of the pair who shot my sister would never be known. There were no officers to report the shooting to since the police force had scattered once the war started. I doubt the men who shot her have fared much better and neither has the country. Lebanon barely functions as a modern state, going two years at a stretch sometimes without a president, after the assassinations of so many politicians. Lebanon harbors more refugees than citizens now. On my worst days, I too have seethed with the same volatile mixture of helplessness and rage about all of this, and can understand how it inspires some to strap on those vests of finality.

Needing to reel myself back in, to the here and now, I concentrated upon the grounding reality of the rocking train. To refocus my thoughts, I started listing those who might have reason to kill Kerr. The most obvious were the Palestinians or the Syrians who vied daily for power and territory. Or it might have been Iran's ayatollahs who ordered the hit. Their Shi'a Hezbollah "Party of God" ran the meanest streets in Lebanon's poorest neighborhoods and Kerr was a convenient symbol of the "Great Satan Uncle Sam" their most convenient target. I wondered what Waddah might say about this.

Even the Israelis might want Kerr out of the way. Considering so many possibilities made my head throb. As the wintry scenery rushed past my commuter train window, I considered why the Israelis might have targeted him. The Israelis barely tolerated American Arabists like Kerr, who knew too much, and often made recommendations that contravened Israeli plans. Arabists understood the context, the players, and the finer points in Mid

---

[16] The Ain el-Rammaneh incident involved the Phalangist Party's Kataeb Regulatory Forces (KRF) militia and the Palestinians who refused to be diverted from their route, fearing an ambush.

East politics. Their firsthand connections far exceeded those of deskbound Pentagon employees, military advisors, and US intelligence analysts back in Washington, who rarely spoke Arabic. Walking the thin line of neutrality between such ferocious foes was exceedingly difficult. Each side cast you as the other's patsy.

Living in the region, the Israelis were a lot closer to the key decision makers on the ground. They instigated much of the covert action, often casting the blame for their assassinations upon other groups. Of course they preferred to control what Americans knew about the Arab world as the Israelis had more to gain or lose. Israel's very existence depended upon the American empire's ambitions, money, and military might, "in a sea of Arab Muslims," but it took too long to school each new US administration. Arabists like Kerr were a threat precisely because they knew the long game the Israelis were playing and how the tail wagged the dog.

Arabists. I was labeled one upon my return to the US. The assumption was we had "gone native." Because we knew the language and had friends there, we so-called Arabists were judged as too sympathetic to Arab causes. Did sentiment cloud our judgment? Surely ignorance and projection clouded Israeli and American Jewish attitudes about Israel and Zionism, yet these were rarely interrogated as vigorously. The prejudiced and the privileged have a universal tendency to dismiss any talk of justice. As I saw it, the Palestinians were a lot like the Native Americans. They had done nothing to deserve the ire of the Europeans, who routinely fled their own continent because they could not get along with each other. The Palestinians were not responsible for the latest European Holocaust yet they were paying for it with their current homelessness. If the homeland argument was valid for one, it was valid for all. Palestinian territory had been under Ottoman rule until the collapse of that empire after the First World War. The British and French replaced the Ottomans, divvying up huge swaths of land in their secret Sykes-Picot agreement.[17]

By the end of the Second World War, the depleted British army was locked in combat with two adversaries: the local Palestinians, attempting to gain their territorial freedom, and the newly immigrated European Zionists, determined to create their own country in the same land. The UN partition of 1947 created the modern state of Israel, assuaging some of the European Christian guilt after the horrors they had permitted and/or perpetrated during the Second World War. Although the UN gave displaced Jews a place of their own to go after the Holocaust, this did not solve anything for

---

[17] The Sykes-Picot agreement was named after the two European diplomats who struck the deal to divide control and influence between their governments. The British retained what is today southern Iraq, Palestine, Jordan and Israel while the French got what became southeastern Turkey, Syria, Lebanon and northern Iraq.

the Palestinians, who have endured a mounting toll of injustices ever since.

How many Americans understand recent Middle Eastern history? Yet we bear the ballooning costs of the wars in the region as US taxpayers. Some of this ignorance is deliberately engineered. My corporate work, and personal life, had shown me how few took any interest in the area. Some resisted any additional information, from me, unless it confirmed what they already believed. This taught me a valuable lesson about assumptions. Most people prefer to reassert them rather than reconsider them. Even though they had never been to the region, they clung to their opinions, and argued with the facts I'd gathered firsthand. Labeling me an Arabist was easier than keeping an open mind and hearing me out. More than once I had lost my temper and retorted, "I never met an Arab or an Israeli who was called an Americanist."

In my view, the Kerr family exemplified the term Arabist, if anyone did. Protestant American do-gooders, the Kerrs had spent generations in the Middle East, trying to do the right thing, whatever that was in retrospect. In the eyes of the locals however, even if our intentions were purely positive, American expatriates were always representing the power of an empire, whether we agreed with that assumption or not. Americans were not the same as the old school colonists, European and Ottoman, whose occupying armies enforced their empire's political will, but the local people, so long repressed, had a deep psychological need for independence. After the harm and abuse by former invaders and overlords, they wanted to determine their own destinies. Recovering their autonomy and exploring their options was important. And yet this yearning for freedom was muddled by a paradoxical habit of seeking "help" from useful outsiders. All sides took advantage of this. During the Cold War, the USSR and the US had fought their proxy wars in the region, using high ideals or outright bribery as the means of persuasion. To their credit, the Lebanese had honed their masterful middleman skills after enduring centuries of occupation. They played the big guys off against each other, including the rulers of the Arab Gulf States, the Egyptians, and anyone else whose interests they could leverage against another's. This was how they had survived as such a small country. Less sophisticated Americans were often flummoxed by their charming politeness and extravagant hospitality as well as their cunning.

My family was also middle class Protestant American expatriates but we had not come to the region for reasons of religion, oil, or politics. Commercial aviation was cut and dried by comparison. Malcolm Kerr's parents had come as humanitarians, to rescue their fellow Christian Armenians, after the Ottoman Turks slaughtered a million and a half of them during and after the First World War.[18]

Thousands of Armenians had ended up in Lebanon, just like the Palestinian refugees, who learned from observing each other's plight. The nurse at our Beirut high school was the first Armenian survivor I had known. Listening to her soulful stories opened my eyes to how many human victims of war there were in the modern world. The Haigazian (Armenian) College was close to our Beirut apartment and my parents had heard it being shelled, looted, and set on fire during the fighting in our neighborhood. Educational institutions and information systems were the first to be destroyed by warlords, closely followed by the destruction of alternative sources of electricity, water, and food distribution networks. This gave each militia's black marketeers mastery over the misery of citizens caught between contestants, who then siphoned off their money. Setting up checkpoints, they demanded exorbitant fees for necessities, passage, and false protection, which provided the cash for purchasing more weapons and ammunition. This deadly cycle was common knowledge to all survivors.

Malcolm Kerr had not intended to be in Beirut during the fighting. He had only returned to act as the temporary replacement for David Dodge, the former AUB president, who was kidnapped in 1982.[19] Dodge spent most of 1983 in Tehran, flown there by his pro-Iranian Shi'a Muslim captors. Why had Kerr been killed now, in January of 1984, instead of being held captive like his predecessor? Surely Kerr was worth more alive. Hostages were often taken as bargaining chips, to be exchanged for cash or other imprisoned militants. Official US policy was never to negotiate or pay ransom, so there had been nothing in the news about any deal. But if the release of Dodge had been part of some promise that had not been kept, Kerr might have been killed as retribution. Would we ever know the truth? I thought of the agony his wife, daughter, and sons must be going through. Most of the public would see the news of Kerr's death today with scant appreciation for his sacrifice or what the rest of us had lost. The man had done his level best to educate us about what he had learned from living in

---

[18] Armenia was the world's first Christian nation. The Soviets invaded it after the Ottomans and the country did not regain independence until 1991. After the Armenian crisis the Kerrs stayed on in the Levant. Malcolm's father eventually became an AUB president and his mother, the university's dean of women students. The youngest of her four children, Malcolm had spent most of his life in the Arab world, becoming a rare Arabic speaking American scholar

[19] David Dodge's great grandfather, Daniel Bliss, founded AUB. A popular Ras Beirut street was named after him. We frequented Rue Bliss during my student days, along with the Uncle Sam's restaurant, the first to feature genuinely American foods like hamburgers, hot dogs, and French fries. The figurative Uncle Sam was no longer welcome in Lebanon and Rue Bliss now ran through the hell that Beirut had become.

the region and speaking the language. His deep understanding far surpassed what casual visitors could guess at.

I felt overwhelmed with sadness as the commuter express hurtled through the frozen New England landscape towards New York City. Another life lost. More wasted efforts. Tilting my head back, I closed my eyes, summoning happier days in Beirut to regain my equilibrium. Some things didn't change, like the varicolored Mediterranean, its waters shimmering in the sunlight. I listened for the screeching gulls in my memories, and the waves dashing upon the rocks, their spray flung upwards towards the Corniche where I had so often strolled. Recollecting the sea scent sent me deeper. And the remembered sensation of the salted breeze caressing my face closed the separation of a decade. I was back on that wide tiled boulevard bordering the shore below our high school dorm, a freshly baked *ka'ak* still warm in my hand. Those tasty pockets of dough, dusted with sesame seeds, were a common treat. "*Ka'ak ka'ak,*" called the vendors hawking their wares, toting them on boards set atop their heads. To my right, the AUB campus stood, as I faced the celebrated view of snow peaked mountains to the northeast. Such a beautiful spot, the country epitomized what the tourist brochures proclaimed.

"Lebanon, where you can ski in the mornings and swim in the afternoons..."

Certainly a place of contrasts, but today Lebanon was harboring as much horror as beauty. Barely one hundred and fifty miles long and fifty miles wide, how could so much mayhem fit into such a small space?

Still encased in memories I moved on to the well-tended grounds of AUB. Our high school sports teams had practiced on its courts and competed on its track fields. As high schoolers, we often cut through the campus, going to and from the uptown Ras Beirut neighborhood. (Ras meant "head" in Arabic, the rocky head of the harbor shoreline in this case.) Besides the natural beauty of AUB, I loved the ambiance created by its buildings, especially the Arabesque ones with curved archways and inner courtyards. Reminiscent of the Moorish architecture that characterized the Golden Age[20] between 711 and 1492 when Muslims, Jews, and Christians had coexisted peacefully in the Muslim Empire of Andalusia, in present day

---

[20] Another cycle of war and destruction had ended all that. After routing the Muslim Moors from Granada, the Christian King Ferdinand and his Queen Isabella had launched their Spanish Inquisition. To finance the expenses of their military conquests, they had demonized the Jewish minority, employing prejudice and propaganda to justify their theft of Jewish monies and properties. Some of that plunder had paid to outfit the three ships Christopher Columbus had sailed off in to trigger the devastation of the "New World." Hitler used the same logic, to rob and enslave Jews, gypsies, gays and anyone else he could crush to pay the costs of his Nazi megalomania.

Spain. That era fascinated me. Their collaboration had enabled art, medicine, and learning to flourish while the rest of Europe was sunk in the illiteracy of the Dark Ages.

My wandering mind's eye went back to the College Hall building and the AUB office where Kerr had worked. Though he knew the current dangers as well as anybody, I doubt he had stepped out that doorway yesterday expecting to die. Pausing internally, to pay my respects to the spirit of this peaceful warrior, I also felt the rising heat of my anger — another casualty in the fight against ignorance and historical amnesia. So easy to rally the troops to squeeze their triggers, while raising and educating a child, securing a family, and keeping a nation at peace was infinitely harder.

In my continued envisioning, I departed the AUB campus and turned to visit the unusual Ras Beirut neighborhood nearby. Thanks to the presence of so many educational institutions — AUB, ACS, the International School, and Beirut University College — this portion of Beirut was a model, multicultural enclave for several decades. Home to professors, students, merchants, booksellers, and cafe owners from the world over, we had enjoyed it without realizing how short its days were destined to be. Rubbing shoulders and relating to each other in those classrooms and cafes, we had indulged our curiosities, about the coexistence of faiths, philosophies, and political options. Tolerance had also proven to us just how profitable diversity could be, not just financially but intellectually and emotionally, for those who could embrace it wholeheartedly.

A lump thickened in my throat. Had I been lucky to grow up during that precious reign of peace or had it deluded me? My early Beirut experiences had made me believe in golden ages and multiculturalism. But when Lebanon descended into the nightmare of war, I'd been forced to witness its violent opposite: when the belief in peaceful coexistence faltered and ethnic and religious separatism surged back. Would another golden age bloom in my lifetime? Or would the cyclical pendulum continue to swing in the opposite direction?

I suddenly remembered Corniche Mary of all people. As a teenager, I'd seen her walking the seaside boulevard, below AUB, stopping to reapply her powder and lipstick. Rumor had it she plied her trade as a streetwalker there. The judgmental arrogance of my youth had softened into sympathy for her now. Had she survived this war? For the first time I connected the real Corniche Mary with my portent of impending doom about the future of Lebanon. While still living there, I had experienced an intuitive, recurring image, akin to a nightmare, in which I had "seen" the body of a lifeless woman. Hanging in an empty apartment, she had a black electrical cord wound tightly around her neck. The sea air and desert dust blew in through an open window, with no one there to care.

The tableau of that used up whore had lodged within my psyche before

I left Lebanon to live and work in London. A deep dread had accompanied this warning. Had the woman died by her own hand or had someone killed her? If she personified the fate of the nation, was it suicide or homicide? Were the Lebanese themselves at fault or were others to blame? Perhaps this message was personal, presaging my fate, if I had remained in Beirut. Unschooled in dream imagery, all I knew was that the woman had symbolized a warning about Lebanon for me.

The train slowed as we entered the tunnels beneath Grand Central Station. The daylight was snuffed out in the subterranean darkness. Women's lives and women's deaths. Men's lives and men's deaths, and everything we did, with and to each other, in between.

* * * *

Stepping out at the 42ⁿᵈ street exit, the cold wind rudely returned me to Manhattan's reality. On my way down Lexington Avenue towards my office, my teeming brain began to hatch a plan. For years I had wanted to put my Beirut demons to rest, by writing about the place and Georgina, and this Paris vacation had provided her contact information. What more was I waiting for? Kerr's assassination suddenly made it imperative. My mind was made up. I would move to Paris as soon as possible. I had work to do and the energy of a new love affair to push me through. As my steps quickened I began to plot the practical parts. How to make this happen and pay for it?

Later that morning, my boss provided the perfect opportunity to broach the subject. As our meeting about upcoming program scheduling concluded, he asked a perfectly innocent question.

"So, how was your vacation?"

"I had a great time. Paris is…quite the place."

Gathering the papers on the desktop between us, I almost wimped out. He would not want to hear what I had to say next.

"Actually, I want to go back there."

Realizing what we want in life is one thing but asking for it required more practice than I had in my late twenties.

His blond head jerked up from the calendar we had spent the last hour working on, "But you just got home!"

Home. Such an easy word for him, he spoke it without doubt or hesitation. Where was my "home?" It certainly wasn't here in New York City where we sat in the midtown office of our employer. Nor was Greenwich, Connecticut my "home" despite being my current address. The place I longed for was even further away in time and space than Paris, France.

His exasperated tone triggered my conciliatory response. "Look," I replied, weighing each word. "You know my history. I've lived overseas for most of my life. It's what I've known since I was eight years old. I'm an expat at heart and I miss being out in the world."

As soon as the words left my lips they sounded wrong, as though I didn't love my own country. Can stay-at-home citizens understand how expatriates feel more at "home" when abroad?

Not expecting any push back, my boss stammered, "You can't go off to Paris Cynthia! You're supposed to become our first female vice president!" Rising from the chair behind his desk, he stopped just short of saying, "How dare you!"

It was my turn to be surprised. From my seat on the other side of his desk the redness rose in my cheeks. Competing realizations ricocheted inside my brain. The part of me that loves being first felt flattered, yet such a promotion was the last thing I wanted. Though good at my job, climbing the corporate ladder sounded hopelessly naïve to me, some carrot and stick fairytale. After the hell of the ongoing war in Beirut, I could not believe in security. It sounded like a lie to me.

My Paris trip, and meeting so many survivors, had revived the reality of the war. And so had the news of Kerr's killing this morning. I had snapped right back into those conditioned responses, looking at the window — near our heads now — knowing at any moment an RPG (rocket propelled grenade) could come through it, if we'd been in Beirut instead of Manhattan. No matter what you planned, or how good you tried to be, a car bomb or an assassin could take you out, along with the rest of your family in an instant. And what could you do about it?

None of this concerned my boss. Knowing nothing about the region's history or recent events, how could he imagine such a bifurcated existence? Without the visceral shared experience, most would avoid dealing with these tragedies. Even when someone was interested, it was not easy to explain the confounding Middle East. I had often wondered where to begin with people who had never been there. Start with the dates of the wars and invasions by British, French, Syrian, and Israeli armies? Or list the massacres and assassinations of politicians, presidents, journalists, and CIA operatives? Even I had trouble keeping track anymore. So much had happened. Only three months ago, 241 US Marines had died, when their barracks were truck bombed outside Beirut. That was the single worst loss of US military lives since the end of the Second World War. My boss had no experience with this magnitude of catastrophe. And if I mentioned what really bothered me, he might assume I needed treatment and prescription meds. He would be unable to imagine how we handled such things. So I kept quiet like most survivors do.

Only my fellow sufferers understood how each terrible event rekindles our perverted hope. "This is rock bottom. Things are as bad as they can get. It has to get better now."

Yet each savage excess in Beirut had been eclipsed by the next horror and none had been the means to any end. They were merely plateaus in the continuing escalation of violence consuming the region. Like the concussive force of an exploding device, the news of Kerr's assassination had sucked the air out of me this morning on the train. His death held a message. Our time is limited. Don't waste it. Do what you must before it's too late. Facing the truth of Beirut had become my urgent priority.

My boss sank back into his seat with a grimace. None of this was his fault. He was lucky. He could watch the evening news without tearing up like I did when scenes of the latest carnage flickered across the screen. Having never walked those streets, sat in those cafes, or loved those people, his days were not cratered like mine. The traveled and traumatized relate to other worlds.

Neither of us had expected this impasse. While grasping for a segue, my fingers smoothed the dark blue wool of my skirt, touching upon another irony. Wearing this costume implied my collusion with the corporate culture and the management masquerade, which made his assumptions about me understandable. I decided then to cast my request, to go back overseas, as an example of practicing what our company preached. We specialized in the preparation of global executives and their families and I could live anywhere and travel to deliver our training programs for newly assigned expatriates. This lent my Paris plan another selling point.

While making these calculations my gaze rested upon my hands, now clasped in my lap. I noticed the familiar callus on the knuckle of my right index finger. A powerful reminder of what else mattered to me — writing. My pen wielding stubbornness had toughened that patch of skin and this practice had kept my scattered life from flying even further apart. My mother had encouraged my earliest attempts. By age ten I was rhyming iambic pentameter poetry. The passing years had proven my drug of choice was the lulling medicine of words.

I suddenly remembered other calluses on the foreheads of faithful Muslims where I had grown up. Just as I pressed my pen to page in daily devotion, they knelt and pressed their heads to their prayer mats, each of us attempting to relate to the same Great Mystery.

With that epiphany came a surge of courage. I told my boss, "I don't want to be a vice president. What I need is…time…to write."

My career-ending speech delivered in two short sentences. It was do or die time. I would be thirty-years-old this spring.

He shook his head and stared out the office window. By his way of reckoning, my truth did not compute, but he needed the revenue my work generated. Few in the executive education business could match my overseas experience and language proficiency. Traveling the world for our firm these past two years, I'd fulfilled our contracts with several Fortune

500 corporations, and my program evaluations proved my abilities to keep our clients happy. If we could come to some arrangement, I could do the same from Paris, though we had no office there yet.

Several stories below, the traffic bustled down Lexington Avenue and something moved on inside me too. An eerie weightlessness rose from my abdomen. Then I knew nothing could dissuade me anymore. The road had forked. Declaring out loud what I wanted had freed me. If I didn't quit now, it would cost me my quest, to know the truth about what had destroyed Lebanon. When Maurice had handed me Georgina Rizk's address, the universe had given me a green light. True, she had yet to answer me, but so far she had not said no.

My boss did not ask "why Paris," or what I planned to write about, so I couched things for him in business terms.

"I want to write a book," I ventured, "about my years in Beirut, Lebanon, the old 'Paris of the Middle East.' I need to get that place out of my system."

His eyebrows bunched quizzically. "But you said you wanted to go back to Paris! Didn't you mean Paris, France? Which Paris are you talking about?"

"Paris, France. I can't return to Beirut. It's too dangerous." The US state department had forbidden all travel to Lebanon for Americans after the 1983 bombings of the US embassy and the Marine barracks. "Some of my Lebanese friends are in France, waiting for the war to end. I can work on the book there."

On a roll I added before he could interrupt, "I could deliver our overseas programs on a freelance basis to help you out." That would also finance my start as a writer in Paris.

His phone rang.

"We'll talk about it," he replied wearily.

As he lifted the receiver I slipped out the door.

* * * *

Leaving his office, I felt as giddy as a skydiver strapping on a parachute. Two years earlier I had made a similar decision when nudged by an inner conviction. I had quit my job at CBS News. Despite the recession, when 2,000 white-collar workers a day were losing their jobs after President Reagan moved into the White House, I had followed my conscience. Isn't that what it means to be self-directed? Everything had worked out. My new career began when I responded to an ad in the Arab American Chamber of Commerce newsletter "Seeking Resource People Who Have Lived in the Middle East." As part of their preparation for a three-year assignment to Amman, Jordan I was paid to brief a Chase Manhattan Bank couple, about

Islam and expat life in the Arab world. Those two very pleasant hours, chatting with them in a mid-town office, were a revelation. The following week the company running those programs hired me full-time for a job in a business I had never even heard of until then. Perhaps something similar would happen in Paris.

On my way down the corridor back to my office, I considered what to tell my parents about my plan to move to France. Wasn't I continuing in their expat footsteps? They had been upset when I left CBS News.

"You're the only kid in your graduating class who got a job at a network and you're quitting?"

But they had also laughed when I told them about my decision to study journalism. Their laughter had inspired my "I'll show you" attitude. Already accustomed to their lack of financial support, I no longer depended upon their advice either. A decade ago, while still dressed in my cap and gown at my high school graduation, my dad had draped his arm around my shoulders to say, "Kiddo, the gravy train is over. Get out there and find a job."

My parents never gave me another penny. I doubted they had much help either. If we had lived in the US getting a job after high school might've been easy, but working overseas as an expatriate made it far more complicated for me. A valid residence visa and a work permit were necessary. The Yazbeck agency, my first employer in Beirut, had failed to pay my salary. With no legal recourse, all I could do was walk away. I had learned a lot since then.

Now, I enjoyed coming to work because I loved what I did for a living. It provided more than a paycheck. Cross-cultural management consulting offered me a sense of purpose, freedom, and dignity. And if that's what it meant to be working class, so be it. I rarely reminisced about my old job across town on West 57th Street in the converted dairy barn where the CBS Evening News was taped and broadcast from. In those days I had been a "junior miss" on the foreign correspondent totem pole. Supporting others in the field, I had waited for my turn to rotate out on an overseas assignment, and expected to cover the Middle East region where I had grown up. But my time in the newsroom had taught me what was missing from my classes at New York University's School of Journalism. To return to the Middle East and risk being kidnapped, raped, and/or shot for the sake of stories that were scrapped when the football games ran overtime, had cooled my ardor. Calling me disillusioned was an understatement.

My prior boss, Brian Ellis, the British-born foreign editor at CBS, had helped me see past the glamour of the network news business, and we shared a deeper understanding of the damage wars do. He had been the Saigon Bureau Chief during the Vietnam War, and the same week he had ridden one of the last helicopters off the US Embassy roof in April of 1975, my sister had been shot in Beirut.

I could still hear his voice, "Remember, seventeen million Americans are going to the fridge to get another beer, especially when it's a foreign news story."

Those foreign news stories averaged one minute and sixteen seconds. Hardly enough time to explain the complexities. Ergo, most Americans had little grasp of world events. In between the advertisements, which paid our salaries, the evening "news hole" was only twenty-three minutes. So we used shorthand terms like "Rightist Christians and Leftist Muslims" to sum up stories from Lebanon. This gave viewers a false sense of comprehension. Without mentioning others players, like the Mourabitoun or the Amal, the audience had no comprehension of what splintered these groups or the underlying motives fueling the fighting. Nor did they realize the extent of US involvement. Overly simplistic labeling was just one example of how coverage, or the lack of it, contributed to the continuation of the conflicts. The failure to connect the dots protected those who profited from endless war.

Our Managing Editor, Walter Cronkite, had put it another way. "We're a headline service designed to sell commercial time."

He expected audiences to read the newspapers for in-depth coverage but how many actually did?

Most viewers didn't care. More than one of my friends had candidly admitted, "It's been a mess over there for centuries. If they want to kill each other, let 'em."

I had bitten my tongue, recalling our awful history, the genocide of indigenous people, our Revolutionary and Civil Wars. The centuries of ethnic bloodletting in Europe had caused our own ancestors to immigrate. The poverty, violence, and religious persecution between Catholics, Protestants, and Jews resembled the atrocities between Shia and Sunnis today. Desperation triggered migration.

There had been other reasons for leaving CBS. I had discovered how little the network did for their employees overseas, when one of our female correspondents was captured by rebels in Angola, while covering that war. An Africa expert, she was a few years my senior. I admired her and hoped to become the designated Middle East equivalent. When she was seized, I paid attention, to see what would be done to secure her release. From their comfy midtown offices, the network executives made a few phone calls to State Department contacts and not much more. By chance some French paratroopers stumbled upon the abandoned camp where she had been left to die after the gang rapes. They got her to a hospital barely alive. Within six months the company had dumped her. Damaged goods she was, drinking heavily to cope with what had happened. The same or worse could happen to me. Kidnap victims in the Middle East were often held for years.

Most were never heard of again.

When Cronkite retired, and Dan Rather took his place, I cleaned out my desk. My heart was no longer in it. Why risk life and limb for so little? There had to be another way. My grandiose ideas, about helping Americans understand the world, expatriates, the forces of globalization, or how all this connected with the war in Lebanon, would never be accomplished in the corporate news business. What alternatives were there? Rather than reporting I could write a book. But who wanted another academic tome? Unless assigned in college courses, most of them remained unread.

That's when I decided to zero in upon a single life.

By telling one person's story well, readers might comprehend the source of these wars and conflicts. That option felt manageable. And since the majority of writing about wars was done by, for, and about men, I wanted to even the balance by telling a woman's story. Female survivors seldom told what they knew because no one asked. Our stories of suffering and loss embarrassed the men.

Leveraging the misery of others to get myself more airtime was not my motive for becoming a journalist. I wanted to find out the facts and share them, not see my face on the screen more often. The unhealthy egocentricity of celebrity and the ratings game made me recoil. My beliefs were out of sync with the culture of this business and I balked at the adaptation demands. I did not wish to become like the people around me. Seeing how decisions were made at headquarters, about which stories to cover or not, had opened my eyes. "If it bleeds, it leads." "Get us more bang bang." Chasing stories of unrest, coups, and wars was a rough way to make a living. And doing that while constantly bucking the system, as a female foreign correspondent, was even less appealing. The system was more likely to wring me out and leave me unemployed, or in drug or alcohol treatment by age forty.

I had not been prepared for the soul-searching phase when I left the news business. How to explain to others what I had yet to grasp myself? But starting over felt braver than staying and pretending. Getting what I thought wanted merely teed up the next challenge. Goals must be allowed to morph. Once I realized "this" was no longer "it" how to discern what to do next was vitally important.

* * * *

During my lunch break that day at work, I closed my office door and took the phone off the hook to further digest the day's news. Searching my office shelves I found one of Kerr's books, "The Elusive Peace in the

Middle East." Published in 1975, the year the awful events in Lebanon began, I reread the introduction in silent homage to the man and his quest for knowledge.

> *The best way to begin a book about peace in the Middle East is to acknowledge that this is not a promising subject. Everything in the historical record must encourage the most pervasive pessimism. While it is good to favor peace, comforting to suppose that peace is what the mass of ordinary people in the world desire, and tempting to ascribe the persistence of conflict to needless fears and misunderstandings, in the Middle East it is far too late for such simple-mindedness.*
>
> *Clearly we are contending with more fundamental difficulties, such that peace has been at best an intermediate objective for some and indeed a negative value for others. At key moments prolongation of the conflict has always been a tolerable price to pay, if it was a price at all, for the pursuit of other interests. This holds true not only for Israelis and Arabs but for the leading members of the United Nations as well, notably the United States.*

From beyond his grave Kerr warned us. The US, our own country, contributed to and benefited from the chaos. Ironically, if my family had not lived abroad, I may have never known about US shenanigans overseas. Nor been cured of the patriotic naiveté, which casts fellow Americans as "the good guys" and prefers to project the "bad guy" image onto anyone who refuses to play our political games. And those "games" could vary widely from one US administration to the next.

Still sitting at my desk, I asked myself, aren't we obligated to do something, when we know our government is complicit in causing so much suffering and using our tax dollars to do it? And don't we have a debt to those we have used? The Middle East provided my family everything: from our livelihoods to our friends and our home. Had Kerr believed, as I did, that our friends need us most during times of greatest hardship? Maybe that's why he had taken on such a dangerous job and died doing it. But what can a single individual accomplish in one lifetime? My longing and despair seemed useless unless it could be channeled usefully. I had to do something. Yet I also remembered counseling recently returned expats, "cut loose your past or it will drag you under." Shouldn't I practice what I preached?

Yet I had to give it one more try, to resolve things rather than repress them. My inspiration was hanging by a thread, of another wounded woman's life, Georgina's. What a tenuous method! Malcolm Kerr's approach had been institutional, the way men typically dealt with facts, making the objectives their business. But his learning had also been more intimate, and subjective, like mine. The sensory osmosis of growing up in Lebanon trumped mere book knowledge. Likewise our needs for closure were more than merely logical. Making up my mind about all this might be easier than patching up my foolish heart, for I'd fallen for a place and a people who could be as vicious to each other, as the worst domestic abusers. Beirut had been shaping me since childhood. And I had crossed boundaries most adult expats maintained, vis-à-vis the locals. That access was charged with negatives and positives.

Often criticized for having too many local friends, I would have known even less about what really went on in Lebanon without them. Ayman Choucaire, my "leftist Commie boyfriend" came to mind. My father had called him this when not referring to my former fiancé as "that creep." Dad didn't know the half of it, but thanks to that relationship, my entrée into Lebanese life went further than most foreigners. Through Ayman, I had met other AUB students, leftists, radicals, Palestinians, and their sympathizers. As far as I could remember, Ayman had never mentioned Malcolm Kerr by name, but we had both benefited from his bridging work. In the privacy of my office it was hard to stop the skein of unraveling memories so I leant back in my chair and let them come.

The Arabian Horse Club materialized. I had met Ayman there in the autumn of 1970. The riding stables sat on the southern side of Beirut, near the airport, at the edge of two of the dozen plus Palestinian refugee camps in Lebanon. Most of the grooms and employees came from those slums. The Farajallahs, Kamal and Leonie, owned and operated the Arabian Horse Club. Quite a couple they were. She was a Swedish former journalist. He was Palestinian. His alleged job was leading hunting parties, but this was a euphemism for his actual work, which was running guns, and smuggling people and contraband across the mountains and into the country.

These recollections brought back the scent of the evergreens carpeting the pine forest of the surrounding hills. We often rode through this area that fringed the stables, daring each other to approach the runway, as the jets were landing or taking off. Our nervous horses would rear in fear, straining to bolt as the engines roared overhead. My friend Liz Brown sometimes shared a cab with me to the stables after school or on the weekends. Both of us were happy to change into our khaki jodhpurs and black leather riding boots to escape the confines of our dormitory. Our friendship went back to the Parents' Cooperative grade School, where we'd met in third grade, because her father's geology job had brought her to Jeddah. Brainy girls, we shared an abiding love of horses, especially the beautiful Arabians.

One morning Ayman was riding his bay mare in the red sandy *manège* (ring) of the Arabian Horse Club when I cantered by. He was twenty-one and I was seventeen.

"Love at first sight," he later confessed. "It was your smile."

He took it as permission to court me with a single-minded gusto. I remembered his dark mustache; a much favored attribute among the Druze Lebanese: "A kiss without a mustache is like an egg without salt."

We shared the same March 27th birthday. His name Ayman meant "one who is right, blessed, and lucky" in Arabic. Born in the caul, his mother had saved and dried it, sewing it into a leather pouch Ayman wore around his neck for protection.

Soon I was coming and going from the stables in Ayman's red Volvo. By the time I completely succumbed to him, I was eighteen. Liz and I were probably the last virgins left in our senior class. Near the ages my parents had been when they tied the knot, Ayman and I made plans to marry and raise a family. The first time we went "all the way" Ayman so thoroughly pleasured me I thought people could see the light coming out of my body. Sharing ecstasy was a great gift. No one would take that away from me. It seemed a fair trade for my virginity.

There had been no blood. Not bleeding was controversial in the Middle East where female virginity was no laughing matter. Rich Lebanese girls in my beginners' classes at the Arabian Horse Club had voiced their hesitancy about swinging their legs over the horse's back for fear of losing their precious virginity. While suppressing my desire to laugh, I explained their hymens would not break by mounting a horse. I presumed regular exercise kept women's bodies more supple and flexible and this was why nothing had torn with me.

I gained a more thorough understanding of the value of virginity in that part of the world via another job. After high school I became a receptionist at the Beirut office of a gynecologist-obstetrician, Dr. Amin Mousalli. This half Lebanese and half Turkish physician earned a lucrative living, performing reflowering operations on Arab brides-to-be, since the appearance of blood on the sheets, after the wedding night, was a matter of life and death for many. His clientele included Saudi princesses, who may have enjoyed adventures while off at college in other countries, but needed the doctor's help, to be certain they still bled when wed.

Then I remembered the first time I had heard the name Waddah. In Arabic it meant, "bright or brilliant," a bit like my nickname Saniya. Leonie Farajallah had beckoned me over one morning at the stables, and I guessed she was about to assign me to teach a class of beginning riders.

Instead she said, "Come see this new horse. He just arrived from Syria. His name is Waddah. I'm not sure if I'll buy him or just help his owner sell him. He's an Anglo-Arab, the right size for you. Ride him and tell me how he goes."

The handsome roan, with matching reddish mane and tail, was already saddled up. As I put my foot into the stirrup and swung up onto his back, I felt the eyes of the people watching me. Proud to be chosen, I put him through his paces. Trotting and cantering around the red sand-filled manège and over the cavaletti, it felt like a crowning moment. A dozen years later in my New York office, this was the last ride I could remember at the Arabian Horse Club.

That week in Beirut I had dreamt of the exact same scene, however everything shifted ominously in it. Beneath me the red sandy ring hardened and the ground grew steeper and rockier. The sky darkened with an oncoming storm. The red horse I had been so proud to ride and be seen upon was transformed into a thickly tufted Ram, my astrological sign. Even in a dream, I was embarrassed to be seen on the back of this wooly animal, with his curling horns, red eyes, and cleft hooves. Soon the ground was nearly vertical. We were on a mountainside barely making headway against the stiffening wind and pelleting rain. The weather became so fierce, I feared for my life and the animal's. Spying a low stone hut, the kind shepherds use when guarding their flocks, I reached it just in time. Once the ram was safe inside I bolted the door shut and woke up.

The details and accompanying emotions of that decade-old dream remained as vivid inside me as the New York skyline outside my office window this afternoon. Ayman's red haired uncle, a Syrian psychic, had interpreted the dream for me, warning that a storm of trials and tribulations were coming. He had endured such calamities, surviving imprisonment and torture by the goons of Syrian dictator Hafez el Assad. His fingernails had been pulled out and his feet scarred by beatings. His interpretation of my dream had proven true, personally and politically. The war broke out in Lebanon not long after. He also predicted correctly, "For many years you will put your power away…and you will not marry Ayman."

My visit to alternate reality was interrupted by a knock on my office door. Returning from my past to the here and now was wrenching. I called out with exasperation, "Come in."

The office manager poked her head inside my door, smiling mischievously, "A bouquet has just been delivered at the main desk. It's for you."

In a daze I stumbled through the hallway to the entrance area. On the polished stone countertop sat a tall vase overflowing with red roses. Attached to the cellophane wrapping paper was a small envelope. I pulled out the note card, thinking I should read it in private, but the suspense was too great.

"And I love you infinitely." — Waddah.

Chapter 5

L'ÉDUCATION SENTIMENTALE / THE SENTIMENTAL EDUCATION

It is not what France gave you, but what it
did not take from you that was important.

— GERTRUDE STEIN

Anxiety started to seep in that evening after work, as I wove through the rush hour crowds on my way to Grand Central Station to catch my train back to Greenwich, Connecticut. Could I support myself in France and still have time to write? Would there be enough freelance work to pay my bills? If I didn't try, I would never know. Staying in the US would never cure what plagued me. I knew others who had never gotten over a person, a place, or a severe disappointment. For me, the Middle East was all three of those rolled into one, and I had to do something to face those demons.

I had noticed this emotional limbo in Mahmoud's life before recognizing it in my own. After the trauma of wars, divorce, and the 1981 assassination of his President Sadat, Mahmoud's future was on an indefinite hold. Without closure, the energy for making emotional commitments to others was unavailable. Stuck in non-evolving orbits, our dreams and expectations shrank, while cynicism hardened to a crust that kept us separate. Having watched others drown their sorrows in drink, drugs, or fanaticism, I was still hoping to make my personal peace with what had happened to me, my family, and the Arab world. If the region could never find peace, would my own life fail to return to normal? Swearing to never bring children into this rotten world was proof of how badly I needed closure. Would Paris provide it?

"All aboard," called the ticket collector as I ducked onto the Metro North train just before the doors squeezed shut. Relaxing into a window seat, my mind wandered while other commuters stashed their hard-shelled briefcases in the overhead racks and settled with their rustling papers and magazines. Once the train had rolled beyond the underground tunnels, I reached into my oversized purse to extract a battered black and white Mead notebook. Volume #40. Eight years of journaling had proven I could keep a promise to myself at least, even if the world was going to hell. Since returning to the US for college, I had maintained this daily writing practice. Like a needle my pen was, suturing the rips and tears between then and there, and the here and now.

My poet friend Bonnie had recently asked why I kept a journal. I had joked, "It beats paying a shrink $100 an hour to listen to me."

No one in my family had ever gone to therapy. We didn't believe talking to strangers would solve our problems. "Pull yourself up by your bootstraps" was the advice my parents had given. No mention was made about what to do when this method failed.

Tonight I turned to a fresh page and sketched a rough timeline of my travels and our family homes, setting the context for this next move to Paris.

1950s in US
1960s in Arabia (boarding high school in Switzerland 1968-1970)
1970s in Lebanon (boarding high school in Beirut 1970-1972)
1973-1974 in England
1975 in Venezuela
1976-till January 1979 in US at NYU
1979 in Arabia again
1980s in US
1984 Paris, France?

All these transitions. What had kept me on the move? Love, wars, and work, the necessity of earning a living. Since my junior and senior years at boarding school in Beirut I had worked. Besides my previous babysitting jobs in Jeddah, I had taught beginning riders to help pay for my own lessons at the Arabian Horse Club. Spending the bulk of my free time as a teenager at Leonie's stables on the outskirts of the Lebanese capital had insulated me from the student drinking and hashish smoking common during my boarding school days. And it had steered me towards a potential career in the equestrian world. When I applied to a riding school in England, to go earn my instructor's degree with the British Horse Society, Leonie wrote my letter of recommendation. Once in the UK I discovered the power of the media, and it relegated my interests in the equine realm to the status of a hobby, rather than a vocation. In Arabia I had not been exposed to television news or newspapers growing up but in 1973 I avidly followed the reporting on the Arab oil embargo and the October War. The amount of misinformation had shocked me. But it served to plant a seed. My desire to know the truth and tell it blossomed into a consuming need. By then, I also understood my poetry would not pay my bills, so I began to redirect my writing goals towards the practicalities of the news business.

When my savings ran out, I left the stables in Aldenham and took the train to London, to look for a job. I was down to my last forty pence, and had a hotel bill I couldn't pay, when I found a position in the travel and visa department of the United Arab Emirates Embassy. Eventually, I was working directly for the U.A.E. Ambassador, Mahdi Al Tajir. In my time there he became the world's richest man, with his picture on the cover of Time magazine. A few decades later he would turn his sleepy Dubai hometown into a world-class city.

Having established my independence, I shared my decision to become a journalist with my parents. Their derisive laughter was painful but I had known my father could imagine nothing higher for a girl like me than "marrying a Marine and having a passel of kids." He had wanted to become a Marine right after high school but the Corps rejected him and he had settled for the US Navy. They say the unlived dreams of parents are powerful motivators for their children.

Despite my determination to become a journalist, it proved impossible to get a work permit for that job as a foreigner in the UK, with its surplus of wordsmiths. After recounting this depressing news, to my best friend in London, Rosario invited me to come to Caracas with her.

"You can stay with me and my family until you find a place." Having just completed her comparative jurisprudence degree, Rosario was heading home to work in the Venezuelan diplomatic corps like her father, a former ambassador to Lebanon.

I accepted her offer immediately. After counting twenty-seven straight days without seeing the sun in London it was time for a change. South America turned out to be nothing like the Middle East, although the Venezuelan economy was also beholden to petroleum, and rife with corruption. Enrolling in Spanish classes, and volunteering/working at the English language Daily Journal newspaper, I quickly realized I could never support myself in the news business without a college degree. Getting one meant finding a way to pay for it.

After spending less than a year in Caracas, I returned to live in the US for the first time since second grade. This was by far my most difficult relocation; I had not expected to feel like a foreigner in my own country at age twenty-two. This was another reason why Paris beckoned so strongly now. I knew how to be an expat. Although I looked and sounded American enough, I had missed too much: the Vietnam War protests, the civil rights movement, women's liberation, and the hippies. My memories were catalogued by wars and events in the Arab world, like the Six Day War in 1967. I had helped dad paint the top half of our car's headlights black then, to prevent Israeli jets from strafing us, if we had to flee across the desert at night. American expats also had to worry about being targeted by angry Saudis due to US government support for Israel.

My severe case of re-entry culture shock made me eager to get back overseas. Just as soon as my college courses were completed in January 1979, I returned to Arabia to work for that year. Not even waiting for my commencement ceremony, my NYU diploma came by mail. Not knowing how common re-entry culture shock was among returning expats, I had only learned of this diagnosis during my cross-cultural course work a few years later, while being certified to train others to cope with it. Attending university in the US revealed just how deeply my Middle Eastern decades had affected me. What smelled good, which foods I craved, which jokes were funny, and my romantic preferences were out of sync with my fellow Americans. What they thought exotic seemed familiar to me and vice versa.

While in Arabia my mother had tried to maintain some cultural continuity for us. She had even packed cans of cranberry sauce for future Thanksgiving dinners, and decorations for an artificial Christmas tree. Bibles were forbidden, yet she hid hers among the modern conveniences in our household shipment, determined to teach Sunday school. For a while she managed to do it. In the Muslim Holy Land, we lived a lot closer to where the renegade rabbi Jesus had walked, but churches and Christian holiday celebrations were not tolerated, though we managed to quietly observe them. The inability to convert Muslims to Christianity echoes the West's failure to convert them to democracy.

Coming of age, as a minority in a foreign country, I felt the clash of values competing for my loyalty. This awareness served as an odd inoculation against that feverish infirmity, when one is held captive by a set of beliefs, without realizing it. In cross-cultural training we spoke of how the fish can't tell you about the water until it's taken out of it. If we have the courage to stand apart from our cultures of origin long enough to re-examine what we think, and why we feel the way they do, we can make other choices. Individuals can deprogram themselves. Otherwise human beings would never have progressed beyond caveman thinking, the divine right of kings, or believing the earth was flat and the sun revolved around us. Knowing how quick all sides are, to judge others harshly for not being cast in their images, is evidence of the blindness of their prejudice, at least for me.

* * * *

As the metal train wheels scraped the steel tracks tonight, the sound reminded me of dad's guns. Mom also hid those inside the moving cartons shipped to Arabia. Their disassembled parts were secreted between innocuous items: the bullets went inside the vacuum cleaner body, and the rifle barrels and wooden stocks were wrapped separately, between our bedding and clothing. A lifelong member of the National Rifle Association, dad gave me a Remington .22 rifle for my twelfth birthday in Jeddah. By then I was a good shot. I also helped him cast bullets and clean the gun collection, which included a Luger pistol and Mannlicher rifle. What had registered in my young mind was Man Licker, a murderer of men, before I'd seen the name written down. I discovered that gun had quite a kick after examining the bruises on my shoulder after firing it.

Ammunition was not readily available, and purchasing it would have been illegal, so we made our own. Melting down scrap metal from the airline machine shop, we poured the molten mixture into molds. I learned how to resize and refill empty casings, and replace used primers with new ones, carefully measuring out the gunpowder. In the desert we often practiced shooting, using paper targets, or cans and bottles tossed in the air. Some nights the expat guys would drive out of town to shoot foxes in the canyons. They would shine their car headlights into the sandstone crevices and aim for the twin glow of the foxes' eyes.

A decade later, after my sister Karen was shot in Beirut, my struggle intensified with the legacy of guns as the solution to human problems. Yet I also understood firsthand the momentary, seductive power you felt when pulling a trigger. With the proliferation of firearms, across the Middle East and elsewhere, the propensity for violence has increased, not the practices of peace. Once enamored of their weapons, people became even less inclined to seek alternatives to them.

I shifted in my train seat. How far from Paris all this was. Staring at the blackness beyond the Metro North train window I realized for the first time my dad had been the same age I was now, twenty-nine, when he went off to Arabia. By then he had a wife and three little kids. All I have is a mass of unresolved issues, topped off by this harebrained scheme to move to France, in an absurd effort to convince Georgina Rizk to tell me the story of her sad life. She has more reasons to refuse my request than grant it.

At least my father had a contract when he left for Jeddah in 1961. Trading in his Lufthansa uniform, with its insignia of a dark bird inside a yellow circle, he put on the Saudi Arabian Airlines one, with its embossed green and gold logo of two swords crossed over a palm tree. He wore it for over a decade before moving on to work for the Lebanese airline in 1972. The emblem of the palm tree with its pair of crossed swords also represents the royal Al Saud family of Saudi Arabia.

Our family certainly has no nation named after it. Like most nonindigenous North and South Americans, our ancestry is a scrappy mix of German, Scotch-Irish, English, and French desperados. To make it in the "New World" my ancestors ditched their old world ways and languages, never expecting to see the old countries again. If I had been born before the jet age, perhaps I never would have seen the US again, like my forebears who never returned to live in Europe.

I did return to Jeddah though, to work in 1979, and even revisited our first home there. The Alireza building[21] had been eclipsed by higher apartment towers. Looking up at the balcony of our apartment again, I remembered how mom managed to turn our third floor apartment into an appealing home. Raw sewage flowed into the basement however, whenever the toilets were flushed. As no one seemed able to fix this problem, we moved to the Medina Road side of the growing town, to spend our remaining Jeddah years in a Sharbatly villa, which had once housed the Egyptian embassy and residence.

Looking to the right side of the train tracks as we hurtled north towards Greenwich, Connecticut I thought of our former US home sitting just across these waters of Long Island Sound. After my parents sold that turquoise and white house, we had nothing specific to root us in America. The first five years abroad had inexorably turned into ten, then fifteen, and twenty. The few times we had visited the US we stayed in York, Pennsylvania at the semi-detached house of my maternal grandparents. (After my parents gave up on Lebanon in 1982, they decided to resettle there, where mom had grown up.) On one of those rare occasions when we were all together in the US we made a pilgrimage to the old Huntington, Long Island place. Driving past that split-level ranch house, I had been surprised to see it was still there, frozen in time. Too small to contain us after all our travels and trials, I was glad we had traded those neat suburban tracts for the wilderness of the Arabian Desert.

As we slowed into the Greenwich train station, I spotted some cedars among the evergreens along the tracks, reminders of the green Biblical cedar in the center of Lebanon's white flag. Its bands of red looked as

---

[21] The Alireza building was named after the successful Saudi merchant family who had built it. Their son Ali Alireza was one of the first in Jeddah to attend college in the US. In 1945 he came back from California with a degree and an American wife, Marianne. She wrote a book about their twelve years together *At The Drop of the Veil.* I encouraged my clients to read it especially if they were moving to Arabia. Marianne and Ali divorced before he became the Saudi Ambassador to the U.S from 1975-1979. During my journalism days I got to know him. Ambassador Alireza died unexpectedly, of food poisoning caught from salmonella-tainted aspic on the hors d'oeuvres, during a trans-Atlantic Concorde flight.

though the edges of the flag had been dipped in blood. Since first raised in 1943, so many had sought shelter under it. Imperiled people of all kinds had fled to Lebanon, not just Armenian and Palestinian refugees. Those from the surrounding countries were escaping poverty, censorship and compulsory military service in the wars waged by corrupted kings and dictators, in Iraq, Syria, Egypt, and elsewhere. Hoping for any kind of alternative — communism, fascism, socialism, or democracy — they'd projected their fantasies of freedom upon the Lebanese canvas. But the Levant wasn't empty. It was run by families whose sense of entitlement predated the founding of the American colonies. The modern imported dreams collided with an existing tribal system, of well-established warlords, both Christian and Muslim.

Getting off the train in Greenwich I realized this upscale enclave was as far as one could get from Beirut's teeming slums and refugee camps. There the burgeoning population of stateless people competed for the meager job prospects, toiling as drivers, cooks, maids and guards in Beirut's swanky hotels and villas. Some had helped to build the high-rise luxury apartments overlooking the Mediterranean, while fashioning their homes from construction site leftovers. They knew the system was rigged against them, yet they bent their backs and necks. As the old adage went in that part of the world, "If you cannot cut the hand, then kiss it." They did the child minding, the washing up, cleaning, and cooking so Madame *Foulan Foulan* ("So and So") could sleep until noon, assured that some less fortunate soul would quietly carry her breakfast tray into her room. In Beirut, the moneyed crowd frequented the cafes, brothels, casinos, and racetrack, restlessly seeking entertainment. Many gambled away the profits from their inherited monopoly businesses on commodities like sugar. Meanwhile the female beggars slouched with their palms outstretched, their ragged children dozing across their laps, in between the doorways of Beirut's luxury boutiques.

My real education had happened during after-school hours, at places like the Arabian Horse Club, where I'd met the gamut of Lebanese society. Being an expatriate outsider afforded me the freedom to befriend anyone, from the scions of established dynasties, to the grooms and stable hands who lived in the refugee camps. Entire families survived in those dank rooms, watching sewage pass in the open sluices, men like the pair who had shot my sister. Some clung to the hope for a political solution to return their Palestinian homeland but others, like Ali Hassan Salameh, had given up on disassembling diplomats and peaceful means.[22]

---

[22] One more example of what fueled violence and utter despair was the Sabra and Shatila refugee camp massacre in September 1982. Lebanese Christian militia in Beirut slaughtered thousands of Palestinian mothers, wives, and children trapped

Shaking off these memories I quickened my pace, crossing the station parking lot, fumbling for the car keys in my coat pocket. Already three years old, owning this silver BMW 320i still gave me a frisson of pleasure. The irony did not escape me. Shiny things still impressed, but I wanted the chance to earn the money, and pay for them myself. Sliding inside I turned the key, listening to the growl of the engine, and eager for the heat to come on. The down payment on this car had been earned in 1979 while working in Saudi Arabia after finishing my degree at NYU. A pivotal year, those events had given me closure about Arabia, but I had believed Beirut was different.

Just landing my job with Mobil Oil and the Ministry of Information had been a test case in hiring practices. And housing was complicated, since single women employees were an anomaly. I managed to solve this primarily by house sitting for other expats away on their vacations. As an unaccompanied female, I was not allowed to stay overnight in a hotel, without a special letter of permission signed by the Ministry sponsoring my work permit. Getting to and from the office was another challenge, with women being forbidden to drive. Wearing the veil impeded your peripheral vision as the layers of chiffon covering your face, and the folds of black silk, over your head, added to the dangers of driving. On the upside, going veiled made sunglasses unnecessary, and kept the dust off, along with the ogling eyes.

Mobil Oil had assigned me an expatriate Egyptian driver. Having an unveiled foreign woman in the back seat made him nervous, and his anxiety cinched my decision to cover up. We drove to the *souk* (marketplace) where I purchased my first *abaya*. Growing up in Jeddah in the 1960s my mother, sister and I had always dressed modestly when going out, wearing sleeves and long skirts, but we had never covered our hair much less our faces. The shopkeeper showed me how to knot the ends of the folded black scarf together, and fit the two layers over my face, before drawing the floor length cloak over the top of my head. Only my fingertips and shoes poked out.

Being inside an abaya was quite an experiment. The first realization was the relief from unremitting male attention. From beneath their veils other women addressed me for the first time, inquiring in Arabic as we waited in line, "Who are you? How is your family?" Being more relaxed, I felt welcomed, although it was odd to be invisible. If someone had ordered me to cover up, I may have rebelled, but wearing those layers of black that year provided a genuine sense of safety.

Even fully veiled it was risky to be a woman alone in the Muslim holy land. Sharia law requires every female to have the protection of a designated

---

by the invading Israeli Defense Forces.

male guardian. These regulations also obligate the guardians to provide food, housing and necessities for female dependents. Mobil Oil and the Ministry of Information had granted my visa and work permit but this was hardly the same as living with my father, brother, or family as I'd previously done. Without a husband, uncle, or male cousin, to speak on my behalf, what might happen to me if anything untoward occurred like a car accident? Those were common in Arabia. Many men drove recklessly, which was a further deterrent from getting behind the steering wheel.

Tonight I rolled the moon roof open to see the starry sky while taking the curves of the Connecticut country lanes. Since leaving Arabia four years ago, my difficulties there had morphed into funny stories. One of my jobs was to compile the first Saudi government telephone directory. When trying to confirm the phone numbers, I discovered my female voice was not taken seriously, and a male coworker had to complete this task. Saudi men, even at their office desks, assumed calls from unknown women were flirtations.

On the positive side that year, I met a fellow whose help became instrumental upon my return to the US. His public relations post at the Saudi Embassy in Washington, DC gave him an enviable level of access. He played poker regularly with the president of the CBS News division and he put in a good word for me. I got an interview, which led to my hiring. His brother and sister in law lived nearby in Greenwich as befits the small world cliché.

With the car warming, I cranked up the volume on the FM radio, and sang along with Annie Lennox, "Sweet Dreams (Are Made of This)" reveling in my relative freedom. Turning off at my Rock Ridge Avenue address, the tires crunched over the gravel driveway, stopping at my parking spot beside the fine old house. I had my own entrance to the sectioned off part I lived in, and as I went inside, more practical tasks sprang to mind. What to do with this place and my BMW when departing for Paris?

* * * *

Barely three weeks later, by the end of January 1984, everything had fallen into place for my move to France. My work would be contracted on a freelance basis, program by program. I agreed to travel to the client destinations and bill the costs. My friend Lynda, from a New York publishing company, agreed to sublet my Greenwich place on a month-to-month basis. Without needing to make either/or decisions, I could add Paris on for now. Even my car could stay safely parked in its usual space until other arrangements were figured out.

Waddah had called sounding anxious. "I miss you. Can you move up your travel date?"

Although changing my reservation practically doubled the price of my ticket, I did not mention that.

The day before my return flight to Paris, I took the commuter train into Manhattan, for my final day at the office. In my purse was a gift of poetry for Mahmoud. We had arranged to meet for lunch at the United Nations to celebrate his birthday and say goodbye. After settling in my train seat, I slid the binder of poems from its envelope to peruse them once more, still unsure whether to give them to him. My third Thursday poetry group in Greenwich had seen only one poem in this collection, "His Havana Cigars."

"His Havana Cigars"

You held my hand
and now Havana hums from the fingers
a trick scent
of smoke and sweat and ash
is throbbing
like Latino music
inaudible to the ear
but I hear
rumba and maracas
when I press this palm
to my face and breathe in.

The others were private and still made me blush though our affair had ended nearly two years ago.

"We The Common Country"

Through the padded brown pipes of your fingers
I sucked the antidote to dreams.
You are my nargile
bringing back Arabia in drifts
like dunes that turn to flesh
not far away.

And, "The Temple Dendur"

Like the Temple Dendur
misses Egypt
I miss you
and the four rooms

on the Upper Eastside
where lower Egypt rules.

Where you live
behind my eyes
the camels are still
crossing the rug on
your wall, they are
heading home for Cairo
through the alabaster night
as we make love
in the dreaming light
of Nefertiti's warmed
stone head.

[Excerpts from *Measuring Distances* poetry collection]

I never hid the fact that I wrote poetry but giving it could be awkward.
Who expects to be immortalized in print? How would Moudi react to such
emotional outpourings? If I never saw him again at least he would have
these mementos. Admitting the truth of his impact and the depth of my
affections demanded a courage that refused to be shamed. Our shared
sense of estrangement from the Middle East had drawn us together but we
also understood how conflicted our emotions were towards our respective
homelands.

What cinched my decision to give the poems to Moudi was the
precedent set by my Lebanese fiancé Ayman Choucaire over a decade ago.
He had written poetry for me in Beirut and I still treasured those pages.
Returning the indigo binder to my purse, I took out a more recent effort,
which still needed editing. Though not meant for Moudi, the poem
described what it felt like to be caught between warring cultures.

"Measuring Distances"

Surely to measure is to know.
But where to begin?
Do I lay the ruler
to or from?
The went
or come?
I am neither here
nor there
so where to base my measuring?

And why, all of a sudden
in need of Direction?
For giving? For going?
For knowing?
Too long I have hung
in suspended animation
the optional illusions
Each place, each person,
presenting another choice
with its separating scale
of near or far.
…How much like men the nations are!
America and Arabia.
One the intended
the other — the lover.
pretending the heartland is the homeland
I am unfaithful to each
and may never marry.
For a past is a present
I must resolve to
run or ride
to be a widow
or a bride.
Decide…

[Excerpts from *Measuring Distances* poetry collection]

These were Lebanon's dilemmas as well as mine. Neither wholly Eastern
nor completely Western, we were third entities. Our blood had been drawn,
literally and figuratively, by the combat between implacable, overlapping
adversaries. Could their conflicts be resolved? How? And whose job was it
to reconcile them? Refolding the creased sheets of my unfinished poem, I
slipped it back into my notebook, and recalled W.H. Auden's famous lines.

"Poetry makes nothing happen. It survives in the valley of its saying…"

How depressing. Yet we must still try. With the winter scenery going by,
I rested my cheek against the windowpane, as the train barreled towards
Manhattan. Why bother to survive in this valley if not to make sense of our
suffering? All this pain was pointless unless we found some truth and
meaning in it. If life was nothing more than random chaos, we might as well
be dead. And if violence was all that defined us, future generations were
doomed to the starkest choices: be killers or victims.

As my cheek cooled on the glass I questioned my deepest motives. What
was fueling my move to France, a reckless hope, or a stubborn refusal to

accept reality? While pondering this I sensed the train's rattling vibrations penetrating my skin, intruding through my chilling cheek. This unpleasant, discordant tunelessness disturbed the very cells of my body. Each atom went on alert, resisting disruption, protecting its healthy orbit. This innermost order was proof. It was not all random chaos. From the subatomic to the cosmic, life was an interlocking series of orbits, radiating outward. And this micro battle, to maintain that order, mirrored the macro wars waging in the world at large.

Like one more human atom I was, whirling inside the global body, where so many struggled to set things right, to repair after loss and injustice, to survive destruction and war. I was hardly alone in these efforts. Though I managed to keep up a functional front, I could not rest or trust. The evidence was in the warning signs: my hyper-vigilance and my ceaseless search for the truth of what was missing. Resonance. That's what my cells craved: a return to normalcy, the resumption of an inner rhythm that interlocked with outer harmony. To function without harming others, or myself, like the natural world's organic, biological orbits.

This need, to restore coherence, was the real driver of my move to Paris. The relief and hope, found with lovers and poetry, had nurtured my persistent desire to return to that blessed wordlessness. The whirring parts of our warring world could harmonize, if only briefly. I was certain of this because my body had felt it. My cells had retained the memory of being in tune with that euphoric melody. It was real to me when loving, reading, and writing.

Lifting my chilled cheek from the window I rubbed warmth back into my skin. From this angle I noticed the reflections from inside the train were mixing on the glass with the blurring landscape going by outside. My brain tried to make sense of the two, as when past and present were superimposed. Pattern recognition. Such a primal need. Our minds often triggered our assumptions because they were so comforting to us psychologically. But assumptions made an "ass-out of u- and me" as my father often said. We had to reexamine them or fall prey to stereotyping, making those snap superficial decisions of wrong or right, black or white, which left no room for shades of grey. This was the lazy way of categorizing people, instead of entering the mysteries of individuality, and fine-tuning our perceptions.

One of my disabused assumptions had been that Americans were always the good guys. Now I wanted to know the truth even if it was awful. How else to get over the lies and reset my expectations so my decisions could be based upon what was real? That was another reason why I had to go back to Paris. I could not change Beirut's tragic outcomes, nor re-live a single day, but I could distill its lessons so as not to repeat them.

What had I assumed about Beirut? That it was sophisticated when I was not. The city and its people had intimidated and fascinated me. As a youngster I'd felt lacking, by comparison. But coming of age in Beirut was complicated by the fact that its cosmopolitan promises had been betrayed. The place of so many firsts: my first glass of champagne, my first floor show, and my first plate of *escargot* (snails) were among my formative experiences. I could remember the sensations of gaining confidence in Lebanon. Things like my new ability, to wield the special set of tongs, for prying those curving invertebrates from their oily, garlic drenched shells. Perhaps I had been too proud of myself, to assume I was one of them, those well-bred young ladies, just because I could maneuver such trivial utensils. What about the important things?

What had happened to the French woman who served that specialty? Madame Corrine. Her Relais de Normandie restaurant in Beirut was renown for its escargot, even by those who had eaten them in the real Paris, France. I knew nothing of her history. Had Madame Corrine gone to Lebanon to escape the devastation of the Second World War only to lose everything when war followed her to the Levant? I knew one of her secrets. It pertained to her preparation of those deliciously plump invertebrates. For the final week of their lives, Madame Corrine kept her snails in crates, and fed them only flour. In addition to fattening them, this treatment removed all the grit. Knowing such things had made me feel special, among the cognoscenti. And yet, I'd been dangerously close to the same captivity, of pampering luxury, raised to shed my grit, similar to those doomed snails oblivious in their boxes, eating their treat of flour and completely unprepared for what was coming.

That world vanished when the war broke out. Those who lacked such privileges smashed them to bits, in violent clashes, with those determined to preserve their advantages. Where had the middle ground gone? Although my mouth still watered to recall such meals, they were distractions from more essential knowledge. Sophistication was no defense. When order disintegrated and the Lebanese army, police, and security disappeared, people reverted to the law of the jungle with terrifying speed. As the glorified gangs took over I learned it's not the "good guys" who win.

In wartime, the winners are the guys with the biggest guns, most ammo, and armored vehicles and gasoline supplies, not those whose causes are most justified. To gain and keep their territories, the militias did whatever it took, knowing full well equally atrocious treatment would be meted out to them if captured. The war in Lebanon was a stark lesson in power, and how far people would go to get money and gain advantage. Misery was sickeningly easy to exploit. Like the smugglers, who charged exorbitant fees to take their clients to "safety" while robbing them of whatever they carried and sometimes raping the women and daughters. Having seen every trick, they knew jewelry and coins were sewn into linings and undergarments and even men hid diamonds, gold and cash inside their body cavities. Kidnapping was a big business. The militias supplemented their finances by preying upon those families or companies who still had money to extort. The most hapless were shot, point blank, at the checkpoints, just for having the wrong religion listed on their identity cards.

Whose side was I on?

There was no good answer. If you sank to the level of factions, you knew all sides committed atrocities. I had always felt more solidarity with those who struggle, than the entitled upper class, yet we expats were considered lackeys, servants to the empire builders. Most expats did not see ourselves that way. We were in an odd category. Not threatening in the way immigrants or refugees were, we did not intend to stay, or try for citizenship in the countries where our jobs took us. Even if we remained for decades, the locals knew we would leave, whether we wanted to or not. Our work visas and residence permits had to be renewed regularly. And once our work was done we could easily be deported. Our status changed only if we married locals. Although my mother had called herself a refugee, when the fighting forced my parents out of Lebanon, she had the US to return to. My parents had never been stateless. I remembered her oft-repeated phrase, "The Syrian peacekeeping force is taking Lebanon piece by piece, and keeping it by force."

As the train entered the tunnels beneath Grand Central station I put away my pen, poetry binder, and journal. Pulling on my coat, I recalled something my father had said to a friend of mine, "I think we did the wrong thing. Our kids have a foot in each world and they don't belong anywhere."

Despite all the mayhem, I still saw it as one world. To my way of thinking, dad was wrong. The entire Earth was a single unit and it was time to learn to coexist before we blew ourselves to smithereens. My generation had been the first to see the pictures of our blue marble planet beamed back from space in 1972. And my own family had facilitated that great paradigm shift in mindset, as our world went from being international (in between nations) to global. Although the term globalization would not enter the Reader's Guide to Periodical Literature until 1988, it summed up our expat accomplishments. Our work in globalizing businesses had stitched all systems tighter together than ever before: communication, transportation, and finance. Unlike former conquerors, who planted their flags and declared ownership, global corporations invaded via banking credits, consumer culture and brands. They promised inclusion, selling stock and franchises, and inviting those with resources or capital to purchase share(s) in this globalizing quest for success but the megalomaniacs could not resist temptations to rig the global game.

* * * *

At lunchtime I hailed a cab to the iconic UN building complex for lunch with Mahmoud. It was only a few blocks east from my office, but the wind and cold dissuaded me from walking. In the back of the taxi, I remembered a silly joke about diplomats and ladies.

"If a woman says no, she means maybe, if a woman says maybe she means yes, if a woman says yes, she's no lady. If a diplomat says yes, he means maybe, if a diplomat says maybe he means no. If a diplomat says 'no' he's no diplomat."

"Maybe" meant ambiguity, the space where I spent so many days of my life.

The cab arrived. After paying my fare I climbed out onto the sidewalk near the UN member nation flags. In the stiff wind coming off the East River, the colors of 159 countries snapped and crackled atop their poles, sounding like countless heel clicking salutes. There were only fifty-one flags when the UN began in 1945. The founders were still overcoming the extensive horrors of the Second World War. Over sixty million refugees were waiting in resettlement camps across Europe and Asia, and the proof of the Holocaust had begun to press its awful weight upon our collective consciousness. How could the perpetrators call themselves civilized? "Never again." Two American atomic bombs had just been dropped on Japan. Each had killed between 90,000 and 150,000 civilians. We were still contending with the arms race fueled by those nuclear weapons. Our hot wars had morphed into the extended Cold War of "Mutually Assured Destruction" and the UN was where we were supposed to talk each other down from total annihilation.

Across the street from the main hall the words of the prophet Isaiah were visible, carved into the wall.

"...they shall beat their swords into plowshares, and their spears into pruning hooks. Nation shall not lift up sword against nation, neither shall they learn war any more."

If only that were true.

As my heels tapped across the pavement towards the revolving doors of the main hall building, my eyes watered with unexpected nostalgia. I had come here often during my NYU student days and CBS years, regularly attending events like National Day celebrations with United Arab Emirates and Kuwaiti friends, and the General Assembly each autumn. I knew some leaders personally, like the Saudi Foreign Minister, Prince Saud al Faisal. Mazen had introduced us at a Waldorf Towers dinner years ago.

The son of assassinated King Faisal, the Princeton University educated foreign minister had appeared on the Sunday CBS show "Face The

Nation," and a group of us gathered at the Madison Hotel in Washington, DC to celebrate. Prince Saud brought me the first plate of food from the buffet that evening and I was so flustered, I almost refused it. Embarrassed, I knew men in the Arab world did not wait upon women, especially in public. From across the room, Mazen frantically signaled to me and I understood him just in time, to accept the proffered plate. He later explained the Foreign Minister's gesture.

"Prince Saud wanted to show the others you were not one of those ladies of the evening."

* * * *

As a journalist I had cut my teeth at the UN, interviewing sources and sometimes sitting on panels. I had even considered going to work for one of the non-governmental organizations like UNICEF. Yet truth be told, these halls were also where I lost any remaining naiveté about diplomats and politicians. The UN had failed to broker any lasting peace in the Middle East. I had lost count of the resolutions it had passed to little avail. Some UN actions had made things worse, especially the 1947 Resolution #181 that partitioned Palestine and created Israel. Although the Palestinians had nothing to do with the Nazi Holocaust, they paid the price when foreigners forfeited their land to create a home for Jewish refugees displaced by Europe's wars.

In 1967, during another Arab-Israeli war, UN Resolution #242 had called for the "withdrawal of Israel's armed forces from territories occupied in the recent conflict." But the Israelis refused to comply. Despite all UN resolutions passed since 1947, the killing and dying continued to escalate in the region.

The New York UN headquarters still emanated that paradoxical 1950s vibe, of overconfidence paired with conformity, from the days when it was built. I would miss these halls. They had given me the feeling of being part of history. Heading for the delegates dining room, I couldn't remember my first meal there but still thought its floor to ceiling windows, facing the East River, offered the best view of any Manhattan restaurant.

Mahmoud rose from a corner table as I entered. Our cheeks touched as we grasped hands in greeting. The familiar warmth coursed through me as he held out my chair. He had put on some weight. This gave an odd impression, as though the former judo champion was physically blurring, his sharp edges dissolving. That was disconcerting.

After ordering our food, we talked until the meal came.

"What's this news about Paris?" he asked with a sly look.

I had been a bit cryptic on the phone. "Actually, I'm leaving tomorrow and I don't know how long I'll stay. Maybe forever."

He blinked, "Well that's quite sudden. Why there?"

"You know how much I enjoyed my recent vacation." I paused, trying to recall if he had ever spent time in France. "I felt as if the blood was coming back into the parts of me that atrophy here in America. Even speaking French again was like using a forgotten limb, though some teased me about having a bit of a Lebanese accent."

He smiled and nodded. "I know. I don't want to go back to Cairo. But when my Ph.D. is finished, I have to return. It may take the government two years or more to give me another posting."

"Maybe you'll end up at the Egyptian Embassy in Paris," I suggested.

"I doubt it. After being here at UN headquarters, Geneva is more likely. Of course, if the government changes again, I could be out of a job, completely."

This was true. After Sadat was assassinated in 1981, Mahmoud didn't know what would happen to him or the other career diplomats. But the man who took over, Hosni Mubarak, had also served in the Egyptian Air Force like Mahmoud. Things had gone well enough for him, considering the internal politics.

Our food arrived and between bites we exchanged news about the friends we had in common. Then I circled back to my reason for moving to Paris.

"Remember Georgina Rizk?"

He nodded. "The Lebanese Miss Universe. Who could forget her? She's the only Arab woman to win. You know that contest started out as the Miss United Nations pageant?"

"Really?" Obviously I had more research to do about the history of international beauty contests, nevertheless I continued. "Remember when I told you I wanted to find Georgina and write a book about her life?"

He nodded.

"Well she lives in Paris now. On this past vacation I ran into people who know her. They've promised to help me make contact, though I'll still have to persuade her to tell me her story." From the expression on his face it was already apparent he did not approve of my plan.

"It won't be easy you know. The people she's with, they're dangerous," he cautioned. "The Palestinians don't want her talking about her husband, even though he's dead." All his diplomatic charm had evaporated.

"I know. But her story does explain what went on in Lebanon."

The mood had darkened so much I dropped the subject. Mahmoud had plenty of experience with Palestinian militants, and with journalists who pestered him for information, whether it served Egyptian interests or not. And I remembered how he still checked for bombs beneath his car.

He signaled the waiter. Time to order dessert. We decided on crème Brule.

After the waiter left, Mahmoud said more kindly, "You'll need a sponsor you know, some kind of patron."

The suggestion was sincere. I hadn't thought of it. But mentioning my idea might get it stolen and Georgina was not on board yet. Trying to sell the concept of this book to a publisher in advance seemed doubtful. Books about the Middle East were not in demand and at this point I had only published poems on my own.

Curious, I asked, "What sort of patron?"

"I don't know, someone who believes in the project and can help you. I doubt you can do this on your own."

I bristled but he meant well. "Thanks for the suggestion. If you come up with any names, let me know."

I didn't need to tell Mahmoud how patronage obligated us. In his line of work he knew all about that. Diplomacy was about those games, and in the polarized Middle East, having any sponsor meant taking sides. Obligation would taint my project and compromise the truth telling.

Our desserts arrived. Reaching into my purse I took out the envelope with the binder of poems and placed it on the table.

"Happy Birthday," I said.

He hadn't mentioned which birthday, but he was nine or ten years older than me, and I guessed he would be turning forty.

He tilted his head, questioningly, "You didn't need to give me anything."

"Well, you inspired these poems. It seems only fair to give them to you before I leave for France." I paused, "You can read them later."

Opening the binder he saw the title page, "to Moudi & Saniya," my name for him and his name for me. These were private names. (In Arabic *Saniya* meant radiant and brilliant *Mahmoud* meant praiseworthy and glorified.)

"Thank you," he replied, his smile tinged with sadness, as he laid the envelope on the tablecloth.

Had I made a mistake? I would soon have to share my poetry with Georgina as part of proving my writing proficiency. In the Arab world, poetry carries more importance than in the West. It was my solace and it had to be owned. When everything else was being written on a deadline for money, only my poems and journal entries had escaped the editors' red-penciled corrections.

That afternoon when we said goodbye in the lobby, I felt the press of Mahmoud's cheeks for a long time. Heading back to my office I wondered if we would ever see each other again.

* * * *

When crawling between the sheets of my brass bed in Greenwich, CT later that night, for my last sleep before my flight, I pondered this Paris move once more. What if Georgina refused to talk about what had happened to her and her country? Just because I thought this was a good way to tell a cautionary tale about the waste of wars, she probably had other ideas.

It still seemed worth a try, and France was an ideal location. Because it wasn't my country or Georgina's, neither of us would be bound by host or guest roles and expectations. Being a third place, Paris was a neutral zone, and this might encourage her truth-telling. The peace talks to end the American Revolution, both World Wars, and the one in Vietnam had been held in Paris. Perhaps Georgina and I would find peace there too.

I had so many questions for her. Had she approved of Salameh's murderous militancy? Was she involved in any operations? Answering truthfully would be dangerous for her and writing it down would endanger me. The embattled Palestinians could ill afford to tarnish the official versions of their martyrs' heroic lives. As I switched off the light, and laid my head down, I thought about what was omitted from official biographies. The third American president, Thomas Jefferson, had strenuously denied the truth about the children he fathered with his much younger slave Sally Hemmings, until DNA evidence proved it conclusively.

If the public knew more of the truth, would it help stop wars? Perhaps this was too much to expect. Even in the neighborhood where I slept tonight, how many of my neighbors were interested in knowing the truth about the Pequot people this land had belonged to.[23]

Sleepy now, I dozed off with the image of Lady Liberty in mind. Another kind of Miss Universe she was, a gift from the French, a universal representation of the energies and ideals of freedom, justice, and democracy. They had their own kind of beauty. And many resonated with it. Her torch aloft, over Ellis Island, this Lady Liberty had welcomed eight million refugees into America. How many had ever met a descendant of the displaced Pequot people? European settlers had treated them like they had the Palestinians in this century.

---

[23] Present day Connecticut had been called *Quinnehtukqut* "land on the long tidal river" by the Nipmuc people. This territory had been wrested from its original inhabitants rather like Palestine had been, when colonized by European settlers. A century of terrible Indian Wars had raged before the 1776 Declaration of Independence. The English and the French had armed the natives and set the tribes against each other, the old "divide and conquer" tactic. Until the bloody truth of how the United States had come into existence was faced, we would fail to master coexistence anywhere else. Our essential ignorance still plagued us. And we had carried our failings wherever we went, including the Middle East. The reservations our military had herded indigenous people onto were a lot like the UNRWA refugee camps in Beirut. The same treacheries, exacerbated by guns and explosives, had labeled all resistors as "terrorists."

Tomorrow I would cross the Atlantic, going in the opposite direction, hoping a Lebanese refugee in Paris, could shed light on the reasons why darkness had engulfed her country. It would take me a few more years to recognize how universal that darkness was when it threatened to engulf us all.

CYNTHIA F. DAVIDSON

Chapter 6

AVOIR DE LA CHANCE /
TO HAVE GOOD LUCK

It was said a long time ago that every human
being had two homelands, one's own and France.

— GEORGII ADAMOVICH

February 1984
Early the next morning Waddah opened the door to his Paris apartment. In sleepy, wordless welcome, he kissed my cheeks, my forehead, eyes, and lips. I dropped my suitcase in the hallway and he retrieved it, taking my hand to lead me to his room. The red ribbon was still where I had left it, tied above his bed, over a month ago. He unwrapped me from my clothing like some great gift. His rumpled sheets were still warm from his dreaming sleep as he lowered me naked upon them. Then he loved all my doubts away.

Later he rose to shower and dress, bestowing a final kiss before leaving to the gallery.

"Sleep now," he whispered. "We'll have dinner together this evening."

My eyelids fluttered but jet lag overtook me. My sleep was full of dreams that could not be recalled when I woke in the late afternoon. Thirsty, I padded barefoot into the kitchen, seeking something to drink. On the way through the living room, I ran my fingers over the rich red, striped Oriental fabric of the sofa sets and touched the curtains, in their pale desert sand tones. How familiar and comfortable it felt here. Was I home, at last? The small, sculpted black bird with the folded wings lay upon a bookshelf. I picked it up. The carved coolness in my palm evoked the cellular memory of the first time I'd held it during my initial January visit to this apartment. Would I fold my wings and nest with this man in this place?

In the kitchen every detail delighted me further. His refrigerator was stocked with the same things I had in my own: yogurt, cheese, olives, and grapefruit. In a cupboard over the stove was a yellow tin of loose Earl Grey tea, my favorite. Reaching for the white ceramic container beside it, I removed the wooden lid, and inhaled the cardamom-spiced mixture of finely powdered coffee grounds. A blue and white enameled Turkish coffee pot hung by its long handle from a hook beside the gas stove. I found the demitasses and filled one with water, the perfect amount for a single cup. I set the little pot over the stove's flame. While the water warmed, I added half a teaspoon of sugar, dissolving it, before adding a heaping teaspoon of the fragrant coffee grounds.

Keeping a careful eye on the mixture I stirred the lumps out and let it rise three times. Each time it rose, I took the pot off the flame for a few seconds, so the coffee wouldn't boil over and make a mess. After the third time, I switched the flame off and tilted the thickened brew into the tiny cup. The smooth head of froth made it perfect, like countless ones I'd drunk in Beirut over the years. Carrying the cup on its saucer back to the bedroom, I climbed in between the sheets to savor this taste from the past. New York didn't have any of this. What else was missing from life in America?

The coffee brought me quite literally back to my senses. My tongue recognized these flavors and it stirred up the rest of my body. What a great relief to discover that what smelled good, tasted good, and felt good to me still existed somewhere. This odd homecoming was deeply reassuring. I had missed it all much more than I realized. Like a starving person, this was sustenance I had craved.

The sights and sounds of Beirut returned like a black and white film switching to Technicolor. What a blank screen I had been when taking it all in as a young girl. The reverse was also true; I had been taken in by Lebanon. I lacked the discernment Waddah had, living there as an adult. A dozen years older, he had known Beirut as a grown man, better able to grasp its contradictions. How to sort those imprints when my own government forbid me to return? Whatever closure process there was I had to accomplish it from afar. The place which had formed me was no longer there. Even if I could physically return, the people I had known there had been scattered by the war. Waddah also needed to get over Lebanon. Would we help each other? Live together?

Having finished my coffee, I turned the little cup over onto the saucer, resting my finger on its dimpled bottom, still warm. As the sludge moved towards the brim, I swirled the upside down cup on the saucer three times in front of me, praying the answers would be legible in the grounds when they dried. After waiting a few minutes till the cup cooled, I turned it over and read whatever images had formed from the grinds. The fortunetellers did this in the Middle East, although reading your own cup was exceedingly difficult and not advised.

Just before my return to Paris, I visited a psychic in midtown Manhattan, recommended by my friend Lynda. "She told me I'd be getting a car with no effort on my part and it's already happened. My mother got a new one and my dad gave me his. You should see her."

And so I had made an appointment with Carla. The first thing the petite, red-haired, green-eyed woman said after opening the apartment door was, "I don't know what you do for a living honey, but it's over. Don't burn your bridges yet though. There's still more good to come from it. Here, have a seat on the couch."

Carla drew her chair up to the low coffee table between us and shuffled a deck of playing cards. As she laid them down, one by one across the table, every first card was some kind of heart.

"I don't know who he is honey, but he sure fell for you. It was love at first sight. Look at this."

What a relief. I felt vindicated. Waddah really did care for me.

Now in Paris, I reached into my bag beside the bed to retrieve my journal and reread the notes made that day. Right after leaving Carla I scribbled everything down in a diner across the street from her place. My journalist training had kicked in. Needing to remember everything said, I recalled her exact words.

"He's the one honey. You should marry him. There will be a child. You'd be a good mother. He's a good man, decent, spiritual. He's a mensch. He'll take care of you. He's been searching for a long time for the right woman. He knows it's you. Food brings him luck. This is the turning point for you. It's karmic. You'll be together, but not all the time. I see him travelling and you travelling. You'll stay longer in Paris than you think. It's a good place for you and so is Morocco. And Spain, something with Spain. But always lots of travels and comings and goings.

"It's not your destiny to marry an American. You don't belong here. It's not your place. The Middle East is. It all started there and it will end there.

"You are out of the prison you've been in. You're free honey. You're really out from under it. It's all coming together and going forward now. Things will be very, very good for you. You're gonna have it all kid!"

I wept.

"I see you publishing in about three years, not before," she said in answer to my question about the Georgina project. "You will do that book and it'll be a best-seller, a financial bonanza, and a play or a movie, a smash. It's needed. She will take one look in your eyes and know you're okay. And she'll eventually agree to do it. It's best to approach her directly. Just go knock on her door. You may not be able to use real names, but you will tell the story. Your writings will be translated into many languages. I see you writing about Biblical themes in modern times, interpretations.

"You know, you could become a reader like me. For sure, you will.

You're going to be a reader and a good one, even a great one someday, quietly powerful, behind the scenes, helping important people make very big decisions. Listen, I don't say this to anybody, but it's true for you. Keep in touch with me. Let me know what happens with this man and all. Call me when you get back."

When I left her apartment, I could hardly believe it was still daylight outside. Her stream of words had lifted the weight of my worries. Even her prediction of a child had given me a glimmer of hope despite my decision never to have children.

Did I want this fortuneteller's predictions to come true?

* * * *

After the workday at his gallery, Waddah returned to the apartment that evening. He escorted me to a special place, Le Paysan de Paris. Only seven tables fit into this tiny, one-room restaurant. Everyone knew the owners, and their dog Taboo. The ferocious looking Alsatian guarded the door. Various members of the family worked their culinary magic in the steamy kitchen, passing the fragrant dishes to the dining room through a hole in the wall. I asked for bouillabaisse, a seafood stew with mussels, turbot, haddock in a saffron tinged sauce. It was served with tiny vegetables alongside.

The ruby red wine we drank in accompaniment to that feast tasted like the last blast of autumn. It left a blaze of red gold smoke wafting through my brain, enhancing every other taste and texture. The label said 1969 Château Haut-Brion (Premier Grand Cru Classe) from Bordeaux, France. Waddah ordered a case of it and the proprietor assured him it was ready to take home that night. After the meal, we were offered a taste of his homemade pear liqueur. The clear liquid was poured ceremoniously into our glasses from a tall slim bottle with an intact pear at its bottom. How had it gotten in there? Months later I would learn that the bottles are placed right over the buds on the branches so the pears mature inside them.

Over this nightcap, I asked Waddah about Beirut, adding that I'd like to return someday with him.

"I will never set foot in that place again," he replied, with disgust. "*Ça me dégoûte*," he added emphatically in French.

His answer was so unexpected, it registered like a slap. The heat rose in my cheeks. Flustered and speechless, I decided not to mention any more of my silly reveries. Or how at home I had felt in his house that afternoon. We were out of step.

Instead I brought up Georgina, reminding him I might need his help in that area.

His response was even cooler than the last time we had discussed it when I reiterated that this Georgina project was my second reason for returning to Paris, as he was the first. Tonight he repeated forcefully it was not a good idea, especially in view of who her husband had been.

"Poking around in Palestinian affairs could be unpleasant as well as dangerous," he warned, as though I should know better. "But I will get you her phone number and an audience."

His friend Maurice had already given me Georgina's address and phone number, but I kept that to myself. His attitude was disappointing. Of all people, I did not want to hear such discouraging words from him. Perhaps my idealized sense of Waddah, and the sort of relationship I had envisaged, was only wishful thinking.

* * * *

The following day the skies were gray and drizzling. I had yet to see the sun on this trip while last time I had hardly seen a cloud. At Waddah's suggestion, I went to the Bonnard exhibit at the Centre de Beaubourg. On the way up the steps, I thought the place looked ugly. With its plastic exterior pipes it seemed cobbled from the leftovers of a defunct tube factory. Many of the women had a garish harshness too. While passing them on the sidewalks I regarded their black clothes and severe punk hairdos. The shaved sides of their heads, the washed out pallor of their skins, the fake leopard leggings and neon earrings screamed for attention yet pushed it away. I felt forced to look at them, against my will.

But the Bonnard paintings, with their soothing domestic scenes and softly glowing opaline colors had the opposite effect. I was glad to see them. The crowds were considerable and the attendants had to hurry the crush of people through the exhibit. I lingered in front of each canvas as long as they allowed. I purchased two catalogs in the gift shop when leaving, one a souvenir for Waddah and the other for my artist friend back in New York. At a nearby cafe I penned a letter to accompany the catalog.

Dear Lilian,

I miss you! After seeing the Bonnard exhibit today I am thinking of you and your paintings and send you this. Wish you could've been here. The serenity and grace in these happy colors, skipping and dancing in the light. He only suggests the objects, without overly defining images. There are no hard lines. He leaves the viewer to decipher the rest. I'm no art critic but I really like these paintings.

The catalog says he died in 1947, so he lived to see the end of World War II and the liberation of Paris, but he knew how destructive mankind's murderous love affair is with war and its technologies. What struck me was the total absence of any machines in his canvases. The most mechanical thing I saw was a coffee mill. This reminded me of your work too. His paintings are full of palm fronds, open windows, terraces, and views of the Cote d'Azur, cats, metal bathtubs, and nude women, bending to their after bath toilettes.

There is nothing preachy or instructive about his work, no great messages, except the love inspired by these ordinary, daily moments. Perhaps these are the most special, the small ecstasies within everyone's reach. I love his playful sense of humor: an empty flower pot, a bather stepping awkwardly from the bath, a barely discernible figure crouching to retrieve something fallen under the table, another waiting to step into the frame. He loves to surprise, with his mirrors, mauves, and orange hues. I spotted a truly banana orange cow melting into one of his landscapes.

You can almost smell the soap when standing before the bather. Oh, to hand her a towel before she shivers! Response. This magic of provoked response is Art to me. And I loved the way people fell silent before the canvases, only daring to whisper after turning away. I could've stayed all day, but so many people have come to see this exhibit they hurry you through the museum. Seeing the Mediterranean brought a shock of recognition for it's similar to the view from the hills above Beirut. But there seem to be few Bonnards in Lebanon, now anyway. I will write again soon.

* * * *

For the next two nights Waddah was out late with Saudi clients. I was not invited to join them nor did I expect to be. This was business and Waddah was "fascinated by professional opportunities," at the moment, working long hours and traveling more than ever in his efforts to secure lucrative contracts, to provide the artwork for several new ministry buildings in Saudi Arabia.

I woke in the early morning hours to find him sleeping on the living room couch, fully dressed. The second night this happened I was concerned enough to say, "I can go somewhere else. You need to rest, to sleep in your own bed."

In truth, I felt rejected, being here yet sleeping alone. Speculating on the possible reasons for his behavior I concluded he must be tired and conserving his energy. But by the third night, I was genuinely upset, to find him out on the sofa yet again.

"What is wrong?" I pleaded.

He wouldn't say anything beyond mentioning, "It has nothing to do with you. It's just bad timing. I am under a great deal of stress at work, as you know."

But this explanation didn't satisfy me. In reviewing his behavior and our recent lunch conversation at Le Bar Americain near Montparnasse earlier that day, I realized he had not touched my hand or looked at me as often as before. He had less to say. As tempting as it was to believe his excuses, intuition nudged me to look for the message contained in his silence and withdrawal. Perhaps my expectations were the problem.

In an effort to get my bearings, I prodded him into a discussion he was reluctant to have. "Listen Waddah, if we have made a mistake, if I have misjudged the situation, and this is not going to work out, we can just stop."

"No," he protested, he did not mean that. He explained, "It is a matter of degree, gauging the right degree." Adding, "Maybe it's not good to try to mix love in, where one lives and works."

Hearing this, I felt crushed but also relieved. Dealing with reality, as he saw it, was preferable to not knowing. Although this was hardly the reply I had hoped for I suggested, "But aren't people in love supposed to stick together and share the good times and the bad?"

"I would not wish that on my worst enemy. You don't know what I've been through. A very complicated life can't just go simple all of a sudden," he said.

"Maybe what you really need is something simple and strong in your life," I replied, defending my affection and myself.

"Ah, there is the ideal, and then there is the reality. It's like trying to grow a tree on shifting sand," he said with that tone of resignation creeping into his voice.

"Maybe you shouldn't try to grow a tree," I said, thinking of the ribbon tied above the bed that was supposed to have sprouted roses by spring.

"Maybe a small lawn," he said. "With a few flowers on it," he added without conviction.

Earlier that afternoon I glimpsed an elegant terrarium in a flower shop on Île Saint-Louis. An apt metaphor for what I had hoped we could create together in Paris. I wanted to buy it for Waddah. Imagining us sheltered beneath our bell jar of love, protected from the storm of wars, tending our tiny Eden under glass. Could we inhabit a little slice of paradise in this unrelenting world of harshness? For a good while I stared at the gentle moss, curling ferns, and bonsai palm within the terrarium. Priced at over $200, I resisted the urge to buy it though it conveyed what words had not. Everything was so uncertain. I would need my money for a hotel room if the situation did not improve and I had no idea how long it might be before I would work again.

Over lunch I hinted, "Perhaps I should go stay with my friend."

"No, if I meant for you to go, I would've told you that. No. Stay. I want you to stay," he argued.

Maybe he was saying this to be polite, feeling guilty after asking me to come back to Paris. But I need more to go on. I would not stay with a man just because it was practical.

That evening when he went out and told me not to wait up, I had fallen asleep on the couch in his place. He came home to find me there. Trying to make him speak was futile. He just got angrier.

My lip crumpled and I blurted out in frustration and confusion, "Why? Why?"

His eyes flashed. He pulled his jacket back on, picked up his keys from the table, and went out the door into the 3:00 a.m. darkness.

I sobbed loudly, "I can't believe this, I can't believe it!"

Returning to the bedroom I sank onto the bed, crying until the tears ran dry. In the bathroom I examined my puffy, red-faced reflection. What a mess this whole thing was. Turning on the cold water I rinsed my face. Trying to sleep again was hopeless so I made a cup of tea, took it back to bed and reached for my journal. Writing always steadied me.

How ironic! One month until my thirtieth birthday. Shouldn't I be wiser by now? I feel like I have crashed and burned. After being so happy to come here, and flying so high, I feel so totally mistaken now. How could my own feelings betray me like this? Can I be so wrong when I felt so right about everything such a short time ago?

Can this be the same man, who asked me to come spend the night, a scant month ago? And whose note with three dozen roses said, "And I love you infinitely?"

What went wrong? What is he thinking now? What does he expect me to think? What's the truth? Is there any truth?

God! I wish I could've left this house when he did! If only I had called Zemira the other day, I could've gone to her place now. I can't just sit here, like a condemned woman. Is it my fault? Am I acting like a teenager? Is it stupid to believe in love and feelings? This time I wanted so much to believe! Have I let my own feelings dupe me?

Waddah. Beirut. Paris. Romance. Ha.

And everything that psychic said?

What's wrong with me, with him, with the world?

Well, these tears are real enough. Waddah is gone and I'm alone again. He leaves tomorrow for a two-week trip to KSA (Kingdom of Saudi Arabia).

Now what? Love? What a hoax!

After the sun came up, feeling a little better, I washed, dressed and left the apartment for some fresh air. Heading for the cafe in the Place des Vosges I knew a grand crème with a croissant breakfast would cheer me. Taking out my journal afterwards, I finished the entry I had begun at 3:00 a.m.

Waddah had not returned by the time I left this morning at nine. It's over. I won't be treated like this. I'm through. There's nothing wrong with me. If it is wrong to believe in love, I'd rather not live.

I reread that line before continuing, pressing harder with my pen.

I can pick myself up and dust myself off and go on from here. If he's not the one, there are other fish in the ocean.

The phone was ringing when I returned to the apartment. It was Waddah.

"Did you sleep well?" he asked.

"On the couch," I answered coldly.

"Listen, let's have a quick lunch, before I leave for the airport."

"It's not really necessary," I said. I could hear the anger coming through his teeth as he struggled to get the next words out.

"Call me at the gallery later if you feel like it."

After the longest pause I responded, "Okay, let's do it."

He made me repeat it, saying he couldn't hear me. We hung up.

* * * *

I looked at my watch. Not quite ten o'clock. If I went in person to hand-deliver the second letter I had written to Georgina yesterday, perhaps I could catch her at home, and speak with her. Gathering my letter and sheaf of my poems as a present, I left Waddah's place. The rain was coming down hard. In my single-minded determination, I had forgotten to grab my umbrella. Out on the corner trying to flag a cab I was completely drenched by the time one stopped for me.

As the driver negotiated the crosstown Paris traffic, I stared at the rain streaked window, shivering. "It's black or it's white," I thought. Either Waddah loved me like he said or else he didn't. I could accept either verdict but I had lived too long in the gray zone to stay there anymore. Denying the need to love, to feel, and be loved was a walking death. It had to be all or nothing. I could no longer settle for less. What did Waddah mean about "gauging the right degree" of our relationship? Either we had one or we didn't. I wanted to live for love. Maybe he didn't. That was the problem.

Reaching this conclusion provided some relief. The taxi pulled up in front of Georgina's building. I asked the driver to wait as I got out and rang the bell marked Rizk. I gave my name, just like last time, to the Filipino maid, who buzzed me into the building. Climbing the wide stairway to the door on the second floor, I asked the young servant if Madame was home.

"Yes but she's sleeping."

"Did you give her my last letter?"

"Yes. Madame has been traveling. She came back only two days ago."

Oh that explained it. No wonder I haven't heard from her. "Please give her this, and ask her to call me, as soon as she can. I may have to go back to New York. The phone number is inside."

Passing her my package, with another note about the book proposal and more poetry samples, I did what I could. Now I had to hope Georgina would call me before I left Waddah's place and my number changed. After thanking the nodding maid, I dashed back down the carpeted stone steps and climbed into the waiting taxi for the ride back to Waddah's.

On the drive back across town, I made up my mind to call the Burkes this afternoon after Waddah departed for Saudi Arabia. I would take up their offer to use their Paris home as my starting base.

The cab stopped at a red light and I glimpsed the newspaper headlines at a corner kiosk. The Herald Tribune's front-page banner said, "Last Marines Leave Beirut."

* * * *

As soon as I reached the apartment, I started packing my things. Waddah called again saying he would pick me up for lunch, as it was still raining.

"I know. I've been out. Over at Georgina's." I meant to sound triumphant, having never told him his friend Maurice had already given me Georgina's address and phone number during my January vacation.

Waddah said nothing except, "I'll be there between one and 1:15."

After hanging up the phone I went back into the bedroom to continue packing. Hearing his voice made me angry. Seeing the ribbon on the wall above the bed I decided to take it down and cut it into a hundred pieces when I left.

Getting that angry actually helped to calm me down. I stopped folding my clothes and sat on the edge of the bed realizing how melodramatic that gesture was. Cutting up that ribbon would end everything, branch broken, bridge burned. Perhaps he was as disappointed as I was. I still wanted to believe Waddah had it in him, to love, and our relationship might have a chance.

But I also needed to know if we had no chance. No matter how lovely they are, illusions can't be rescued. He wouldn't say why he already abandoned me, physically speaking. How sad. Despite this cynical world, I had found the courage to declare I'd live for love again only to be struck down so soon.

Don't let me strike out with Georgina too I reckoned. Something good must come from all of this.

Waddah was late. There was no time to go out to eat before he had to leave for the airport. I pulled food from the fridge and put it on the table. When he came through the door he hugged me, then regarded me like a petulant child as if he was the father, determined to scold. His expression made my blood boil.

"Look," he said, "it isn't a tragedy. I'll see you in America. I'll write to you. I'll call you after the weekend, to find out your program." Then he started throwing his clothing into a suitcase.

"Damn you," I thought. He expected me to be gone by the time he returned. Did he ever intend to see me again? And for this I spent twice as much to come to Paris earlier than originally planned. He did not need to instruct me about my feelings. Only the guilty belittle their deception by declaring, "it's not a tragedy." It's worse, because this one could have been prevented. He had caused this pain.

All I said was, "Why are you confusing me? Don't you remember what you said to me?"

"Well, I don't have a 64 byte computer brain, but I am a pretty quick thinker," he replied.

I thought, "I love you" is only three words and not too hard to remember, but I said nothing. Now I just wanted him to go. Leave me alone to think. Soon enough he went out the door, pecking me on the cheek, saying he'd call from the Kingdom. The rooms settled back into their beautiful stillness once he was gone. Overcome with fatigue, I laid down and was soon fast asleep.

Waking early the next morning, I resolved to get out of the apartment and get on with my plans. Despite the drizzle, I walked to the same cafe Ma Bourgogne in the Place des Vosges for breakfast, remembering to bring my umbrella this time. The waiter recognized me with a nod. This could become my neighborhood. Why not? If only the sun would come out! The low gray sky was pressing me down.

Staring out the cafe windows at the passersby hurrying to their jobs and offices, I ordered a second cup of coffee. The rain fell in sheets now. From my purse I took out a half-finished letter to Lynda, the friend who had sublet my Greenwich apartment. While waiting for the rain to cease, I could at least get something done.

Dear Lynda,

Well, here I am in Paris, wishing things were going better. I have no more answers than I did before coming back. Tomorrow I'll take a third letter over to Georgina unless she calls me today. I am trying humor, patience, and everything short of threatening her. It is useless to hurry an Arab, that much I know. And no one can be forced to talk about their life when not ready to.

Maybe she has to get me checked out by some PLO higher ups. Since her husband's death, she's probably still on their payroll. She keeps irregular hours and doesn't seem to have any job here to support herself. Twice I've gone to her place but only got as far as the Filipino maid. So much is out of my hands, and up to some sort of luck, I suppose. It's a bummer to wait around all day, hoping she'll call, and even agree to see me, much less agree to collaborate.

Remember that psychic you told me about in New York? I saw her before coming back here. She told me a lot: that Paris was a good place for me, and that I would stay here longer than first thought. She predicted Georgina would agree to do the book, and that it would be a smash success. Ha ha. I would like to believe it, but it's hard to have hope when she won't get back to me.

There is a new man in my life, the one I mentioned meeting here while on the January vacation. Our romance is at the frustration stage, and has yet to define itself. What a dreamer I am! "Starving artist in Paris garret…" What a cliché! Don't worry too much. I won't do anything too foolish. There are realistic alternatives, like finding a job here, etcetera.

Despite the other headaches, it's wonderful to be back overseas. And Paris is as good a place as any to be an expat. I feel like only half of me existed in New York, and now I'm whole again, my languages and limbs no longer atrophying.

The US will always be there to go back to. While still young, without major responsibilities or dependents, I prefer being out in the world. It's a little scary to think, "You can do anything you want now…so, what will you do?" We are more accustomed to feeling hemmed in by limitations, but I've no mortgage or car payments left to make and only myself to feed for now.

Sorry if I'm babbling on but there are only strangers in this Parisian cafe at present. When do you plan to come visit? I will write again when the fog about my future lifts. The literal weather is damn awful too. Please write soon now you've got my new address, care of Waddah's galerie.

Much love, Cyn

PS Today is the 29th of February, a leap year. Isn't that when the girls can ask the boys to marry? Wish I knew a worthy candidate.

The rain did not look like it was going to let up any time soon. Walking back to the apartment I bought the Herald Tribune. While waiting for Georgina to call me I could read and write to keep busy. On the front page of the newspaper was a picture of a Lebanese couple, running from the scene of a car bomb explosion the day before in Beirut. An armed man in camouflage fatigues was off to the left and behind him, the grim faced man pulled his sobbing female companion by the hand. The scene was too familiar. It is what terrorism looks and feels like. Smoke billowed from the burning cars behind them. Beneath their feet, the pavement was littered with bits of metal, wood, and stone.

I stared at the picture for a long time.

How dare I complain about waiting for Georgina. People are dying every day in Beirut! How dare I be afraid here in Paris to do what must get done. I ought to be ashamed of myself.

I tore out the picture and put it into my journal, to remind me, every day. And then I drafted my fourth note to Georgina, trying for right the tone, urgent but not too bossy.

* * * *

110

March first dawned, cloudless and sunny. I rejoiced, throwing open the window shutters of Waddah's place. At last, it's bright out! I jumped into my clothes and went out for breakfast coffee. Time for a nice long walk. Following the rain-swollen River Seine, I wondered how deep its murky dark green waters were. The ancient gray stone quays inspired me to imagine boats of the previous centuries pulling up at these landing points. Women in hooded cloaks and billowing skirts disembarked to climb these rock-hewn steps, on their way to secret rendezvous. Undoubtedly some were disappointed or deceived. How many women had thrown themselves into these waters to end the pain? I shivered and glanced up at the round towers of the Conciergerie, where Queen Marie Antoinette and her King Louis XVI had waited to be fetched for their final trips to the guillotine. Somehow Paris had survived the pendulum swings of its history, from excess to revolution, and violent bloodletting to arrive at relative peace. Would Beirut survive the same?

My steps had carried me to Pont Marie and Île Saint-Louis where Waddah had brought me for ice cream at Bertillon's two months ago. On the bridge I paused where we first held hands and shook my head ruefully before continuing. This time I paid more attention to the surroundings. Obviously tourists came here. The island's center street had deliberately charming restaurants and pricey boutiques. At its tip was a footbridge connecting Île Saint-Louis to its larger sibling, Île de la Cité. Here rose the backside of Notre Dame cathedral, with its jeering gargoyles and Gothic spires. Dedicated to Our Lady the Virgin Mary, the building was eight hundred years old, and still massively impressive despite being black with grime, soot, and car fumes. Among the other historic events held within its vaulted space was the ceremony to crown the upstart Corsican General Napoleon, who had himself made Emperor in the post-revolutionary era. He had his former Caribbean mistress Josephine, now his wife, crowned too, although once he realized she could not bear him an heir, he cast her aside.

Nestled behind the cathedral was a quiet triangular park. I let myself in through its low metal gate. After wiping off the pigeon droppings with my gloved hand, I sat on the slatted wooden bench to rest and take it all in. The dark branches above were starting to send forth their tiny green nubs. These flags of spring would soon unfurl. The seasons keep turning and likewise, I must go on. Spring will help me remake things.

Shutting my eyes, I lifted my face to the sun, grateful for this change of weather. As the golden warmth penetrated me, I asked it to drive out the disappointments of February. I remembered sitting on similar benches at the train station in Greenwich, Connecticut, waiting to board my commuter train to Manhattan. How much I had desired then to leave it all behind, I would not go back now. Fumbling with the top buttons of my coat, my fingers reached inside to feel the familiar bump of my Ayat al-Kursi amulet, on its gold chain. The rough equivalent of a Catholic Saint Christopher's medal, Muslims believed this "Verse of the Throne" protected Muslim travellers, wanderers, and seekers. Wearing one had been a source of reassurance to me for over a decade already.

I slowly recited the Arabic words of the Quranic prayer from memory, as my Lebanese fiancé Ayman had taught me to do:

Allahu la ilaha illa Huwa, Al-Haiyul-Qaiyum La ta'khudhuhu sinatun wa la nawm, lahu ma fis-samawati wa ma fil-'ard Man dhal-ladhi yashfa'u 'indahu illa bi-idhnihi Ya'lamu ma baina aidihim wa ma khalfahum, wa la yuhituna bi shai'im-min 'ilmihi illa bima sha'a Wasi'a kursiyuhus-samawati wal ard, wa la ya'uduhu hifdhuhuma Wa Huwal 'Aliyul-Adheem.

اللّٰهُ لاَ إِلَـهَ إِلاَّ هُوَ الْحَيُّ الْقَيُّومُ
لاَ تَأْخُذُهُ سِنَةٌ وَلاَ نَوْمٌ
لَّهُ مَا فِي السَّمَوَاتِ وَمَا فِي الأَرْضِ
مَن ذَا الَّذِي يَشْفَعُ عِنْدَهُ إِلاَّ بِإِذْنِهِ
يَعْلَمُ مَا بَيْنَ أَيْدِيهِمْ وَمَا خَلْفَهُمْ
وَلاَ يُحِيطُونَ بِشَيْءٍ مِّنْ عِلْمِهِ إِلاَّ بِمَا شَاء
وَسِعَ كُرْسِيُّهُ السَّمَوَاتِ وَالأَرْضَ
وَلاَ يَؤُودُهُ حِفْظُهُمَا
وَهُوَ الْعَلِيُّ الْعَظِيمُ

Allah! There is no deity save Him, the Alive, the Eternal.
Neither slumber nor sleep over taketh Him.
Unto Him belongeth whatsoever is in the heavens and whatsoever is in the earth.
Who is he that intercedeth with Him save by His leave?
He knoweth that which is in front of them and that which is behind them,
while they encompass nothing of His knowledge save what He will.
His throne includeth the heavens and the earth,
and He is never weary of preserving them.
He is the Sublime, the Tremendous.
[Surah al-Baqarah 2: 255]

I had never understood all the words. Nor did I feel the need to. The Unknown was part of its magic, that paradoxically familiar feeling of being a foreigner, under a spell, and more comfortable with not knowing.

On my way back to the apartment, I bought groceries from the shops and the vendors on Rue Saint Antoine. Standing in line with everyone to buy a fresh baguette — a half one as I'd just seen the woman in front of me do — I felt deeply contented. In some small way I belonged here, even momentarily, because I was willing to pick up the rhythm of daily life in this place, where an alternate universe existed. Chewing a hunk of the crusty warm bread while walking back to Waddah's empty apartment, I began to believe life on my own in Paris was equally possible, even preferable.

After fixing myself some lunch, I cleared the table and took out a card purchased from a newsstand for Georgina. Crafting my words carefully for this latest salvo, I pled my case in my best handwriting. I sealed the envelope as soon as I finished before my mind could change. Tomorrow I would return to her place on Rue Georges Ville. Had she chosen that street on purpose for its name?

I took out my file on Georgina, which had grown over the years. I wanted to refresh my memory about major events and dates to prepare key questions for when she called me back. One of my first questions for Georgina was about how she'd met Salameh and when. Who had introduced them? Public sources claimed they got together in 1976 five years after she won the Miss Universe contest in Miami, Florida. Between the manila folder covers were several pages torn from my copy of the 1982 book *The Red Prince*. Two Israeli journalists, Eitan Haber and Michael Bar-Zohar, had written it after Georgina's late husband Ali Hassan Salameh was killed in 1979. Much of what they said had to be taken with a proverbial grain of salt since they came from "the enemy" side but not much else was available on Salameh's life. One author, Michael Bar-Zohar also wrote spy novels, under pseudonyms like Michael Hastings and Michael Barak. Their information might be untrustworthy propaganda, yet my only other sources were press cuttings in English from Beirut newspapers and magazines. At least the Israelis cared enough about their Arab adversaries to record the details of their lives. The deeds ascribed to Ali Hassan Salameh were quite awful if true but many paragraphs lacked the objectivity we journalists were supposed to cultivate.

On page 212 for example,

…although years have passed since the Munich Olympic massacre, Mossad's bloody accounts with him have not been settled. Salameh had been, and still was, one of the cruelest enemies Israel has ever had. After what he had done in the Olympics and in Lod, at the (Israeli) airport massacres, Salameh could not escape unharmed.

The last sentence referred to the horrific events in 1972, during which the mistakes of the German police turned a hostage exchange into a bloodbath. No mention was made of the original Israeli cruelties, which motivated the revenge-seeking Palestinians. For the whole truth you had to go further back in time and consult multiple sources, but how many did? Choosing sides was easier than studying the complicated history. How much did Georgina know in those days about the man who would become her husband five years later? 1972 was one year after Georgina won the Miss Universe contest, and the year I turned eighteen and graduated from high school in Beirut. That year more than a dozen incidents had occurred, practically one a month. Taken together they demonstrated how one thing led to another in the region and I reviewed them.

In February 1972 a Lufthansa plane was hijacked to Yemen. The hefty ransom paid for the 182 passengers and crew helped finance Salameh's other operations that year. The BBC reported five million dollars was paid by the West German government to the PFLP (Popular Front for the Liberation of Palestine), the biggest ransom ever paid for an aircraft. Others later claimed the real amount was $500 million. The Yemenis were reportedly paid a million dollars too, to allow the Lufthansa plane permission to land in Aden.[24]

Three months later, on May 8th 1972, Salameh sent a handpicked team of hijackers to Vienna, Austria with a mission to seize the hostages he needed for negotiating the release of other Palestinians from Israeli jails. The four commandos, two men and two women pretended to be couples although they'd only met the day before. One of them, Theresa Halsa, was only eighteen. An Arab Christian, she was a student nurse born in Israeli held territory. The other woman was Rima Tannous. They'd received tactical military training, with handguns and explosives, in clandestine camps in Lebanon. The men, Taha Abu Snina and Abed al-Aziz Atrash, were experienced hijackers and Salameh chose them because of their success in prior operations.[25]

Using forged Israeli passports, Salameh's team boarded the Belgian owned Sabena Airlines flight 571. Twenty minutes after taking off from Vienna they took control of the jet. Brandishing handguns, grenades, and explosive belts from their carry-on bags, they told the pilot to fly to Tel

---

[24] One of the hostages on that hijacked flight was Joseph Kennedy, the nineteen-year-old son of Senator Robert Kennedy. RFK had been assassinated four years earlier by a Palestinian Christian, a former stable boy, with a Jordanian passport. Sirhan Bishara Sirhan shot RFK because, "He did not keep his promise to send us fifty fighter jets after the 1967 war." Sirhan was triggered by the sight of American Jews celebrating their victory on the anniversary of the 1967 Arab-Israeli war.

[25] Hundreds of planes were hijacked during the 60s, 70s, and 80s. Hijackings were popular because of what they accomplished when successful. The only El Al plane ever taken was also the longest lasting commercial airline hostage situation, taking place over a period of forty days. In the end, everyone was released unharmed in exchange for sixteen Palestinian prisoners. This emboldened the hijacking business, not only in light of the people exchanged, but also for the profits made as well.

Aviv. Once there, Salameh hoped to trade the 90 hostages for over 200 Palestinian prisoners. But the Israelis outsmarted the hijackers. They killed both men, captured the women, and rescued all the hostages. The women were eventually traded in a prisoner exchange after the 1982 Israeli invasion of Lebanon. The Israeli soldiers participating in the counterattack included Simon Peres, Ehud Barak, and Binyamin Netanyahu. All of them would become future prime ministers of Israel. Like them, Salameh intended to become a future prime minister of Palestine, and he was following in the footsteps of former Jewish militants, who had also used violence to wrest control of the territory that became their country. The pushed out Palestinians conducted hijackings and used any other means they could in their attempts to regain the same territory, and so the terrible cycle continued.

Later, during that same month of May 1972, in revenge for the failed Sabena operation, another attack was planned by a fellow Palestinian commando George Habash, leader of the PFLP (Popular Front for the Liberation of Palestine). He recruited three sympathetic Japanese Red Army operatives because Asians were less likely to raise Israeli suspicions. They boarded an Air France flight from Paris to Tel Aviv's Lod (Ben Gurion) airport. Inside their checked luggage was an arsenal of guns and grenades. After retrieving their suitcases and weapons in the baggage claim area, the three Japanese men dressed in business suits, shot everyone who moved inside the arrival terminal. One even fired at disembarking passengers from another flight. As planned, one Japanese attacker managed to blow himself up with a grenade. Another was shot dead by security police. The third recruit was captured alive and confessed everything, explaining who'd sent them and why.

The operation left over eighty wounded and twenty-six dead, among them seventeen Christian Puerto Rican pilgrims. They had nothing to do with the Palestinians or the Israelis and had merely gone to visit the Christian and Jewish Holy Land. Few tourists traveling to Israel realize their commercial airplanes are landing on the rubble of a former Palestinian town, Lydda. Renamed Lod by the Israelis who occupied it, it was once the home of the man who planned that May attack, George Habash. His family had lived there before the fighting in 1948 turned them into refugees after Habash's sister was shot. Unlike my sister, she did not survive.

Due to all these events, Georgina, the first Arab Miss Universe, was deemed persona non grata that May 1972, and refused entrance to the US. When did she find out her future husband's activities prevented her attendance at the next Miss Universe contest? Traditionally the previous year's winner places the crown on the newest one, but Georgina had to stay home. The woman who had crowned Georgina in 1971, Marisol Malaret, was the first Puerto Rican to win the title and her victory inspired the idea of holding the pageant in the unincorporated Caribbean territory of the US.

However, Georgina's absence failed to prevent violence from occurring at the 1972 Miss Universe contest; Puerto Rican protesters, seeking independence from the US, set off two bombs near the El Dorado Hotel in San Juan during the contest week.

Georgina had yet to meet Salameh who was orchestrating his next operation that September 5th and 6th, the Israeli hostage taking at the summer Olympic Games in Munich, Germany. Salameh's code name for this plan was Iqrit and Biram, the names of two Palestinian Christian villages, whose inhabitants were expelled by the IDF during the 1948 Arab-Israeli War. The villagers had been told they could return in two weeks but they ended up in refugee camps in Lebanon. Salameh intended to trade the eleven hostages, Israeli coaches and athletes, for over 200 Palestinian prisoners in Israeli jails. But the botched German rescue attempt foiled these intentions. Most were killed, all eleven hostages as well as five of the eight Palestinian commandos. Three perpetrators were captured.

The following month, in October, another Lufthansa flight was hijacked to force the release of those surviving Palestinian commandos from West German jails. That hijacking succeeded without any bloodshed. All of these events had happened in just a single year.

Could this endless looping insanity be stopped? I pushed aside my notes and rested my head on my crossed arms, atop the table. What good did it do to remember all these details? It was too much to take in. Yet others in the Middle East dealt daily with far greater despair. They didn't have the luxury of reading and writing books.

I thought of Georgina's father-in-law, Sheikh Hassan Salameh. She had never met him. He had died in the fighting during 1948 when her husband Ali Hassan was only eight years old. Like other Palestinians, Sheikh Salameh had taken up arms, trying to rid his land of Ottoman occupiers, only to see them replaced by the British colonial army. As Hitler rose to power, more desperate European Jews arrived in Palestine every month, a direct result of the *Nazis Endlösung der Judenfrage* ("Final Solution to the Jewish Question"). In addition to the pressures created by Germany's extermination policy, a modern Zionist movement[26] was capturing the imagination of Jews seeking to escape the historic European prejudice and persecution, endured during ethnic cleansings in previous centuries.

---

[26] Theodor Herzl, an assimilated German speaking Jewish writer and political activist, born in the now defunct Austro-Hungarian Empire, had begun to doubt assimilation was the answer. After his experiences with anti-Semitism in France, he wrote in his diary in the summer of 1895, "In Paris...I recognized the emptiness and futility of trying to 'combat' anti-Semitism." The following year he published a book *The State of the Jews* promoting return to the historic land of the forefathers. The Zionist Organization was formed in 1897.

Before the European Jewish nationalists and war refugees arrived, the local Jewish population, Christian minorities, and the Muslim majority had lived in relative peace. The shared Semitic origins of the Arabic speaking Sephardic Jews and Muslims went back 4,000 years. Even their languages were similar. For example, Hebrew-speaking Jews said *Rosh Hashanna* for their New Year greeting while Arabic speakers said *Ras el Sanah*. But the Ashkenazi European Jews, who fled the Holocaust, were very different. They spoke Yiddish, a German derived language, and many were profoundly traumatized by the war. Their ideas about nationalism, socialism, and communism were not traditional and their kibbutz settlements were a prime example. Some Ashkenazi even looked down upon their fellow Sephardic Jews, because they were not Germanic European, and they spoke Old Testament/Torah Hebrew, or Ladino, the Spanish derived language from the Golden Age centuries, before the expulsion from Spain.[27]

These divisive tendencies were plentiful among Christians too, who discouraged marriage between Catholics and Protestants for centuries. Muslims were also prone to separatism. Born Christian I had never seen the Muslim Holy Cities, though I had lived near them for a decade, since non-Muslims are forbidden to enter. Out of respect, I obeyed the prohibition. Although my Saudi friends had invited me to visit Mecca, it did not seem worth the risk to all of us. I did know you had to recite the *Shahada*, profession of faith to enter Mecca:

لَا إِلَهَ إِلَّا ٱللَّٰه مُحَمَّدٌ رَسُولُ ٱللَّٰه

There is no god but God. Muhammad is the messenger of God.

I knew it by heart for its curving white Arabic script was above the sword on every emerald green colored Saudi flag. The Jews had an older equivalent, called the *Shema*, "Hear, O Israel: The Lord our God is one Lord."

My thoughts returned to Paris, and Waddah's apartment where I was still sitting at the table with *The Red Prince* book laying open to black and

---

[27] The origins of monotheism, the One God notion, went back to the Jewish Torah, and the Old Testament herder of flocks, the patriarch Abraham. His name in Arabic was Ibrahim. Because Sarah his wife was barren, the couple took an Egyptian handmaiden, Hagar. Her name means "she who flees" or "one who seeks refuge." Hagar, the domestic servant and second wife, bore Abraham a son, Ishmael or Ismail in Arabic. But when the aged Sarah finally conceived, and bore her own son, Isaac (Isḥāq in Arabic), she no longer wanted Hagar and her son. Banished to die in the desert, Hagar prayed for divine help. The story says *Hashem, God, Allah,* saved her and Ishmael, making a spring appear, miraculously. This well called *Zamzam* still flows today, in Mecca, Islam's Holiest City.

white pictures. One showed Ali Hassan Salameh and Georgina Rizk cutting their wedding cake in 1976. The other had been taken of Salameh, with the Lebanese president elect Bashir Gemayel. Both men had been assassinated but Georgina was still alive. I reread the book's epilogue.

In the morning hours of May 15, 1979 on the thirty-first anniversary of the creation of the state of Israel, Georgina Salameh gave birth to a son…

In her hospital room, surrounded by armed guards, Georgina said, "Today I am a queen again. Ali is back. Ali was the spiritual son of Arafat. They are both sons of the Revolution. Ali's sons: Hassan and Ussama (both from his first wife) and my baby are also sons of the revolution. They will fulfill their commitments, and that makes me happy."

Of course Georgina would name her fatherless son Ali Hassan Salameh. That boy would be five years old in two months. Janet Burke had seen him in the lobby of their building where he lived with his mother. According to Janet, the Filipino maids looked after him for the most part, since Georgina often traveled.

＊ ＊ ＊ ＊

The phone rang. It was Maurice, Waddah's friend, calling to say he would pick me up for dinner, around eight o'clock.

"Would you mind passing by Georgina's place, on the way to the restaurant?" I asked. "I want to drop off another note to her."

"Sure, happy to help," he replied.

"I am glad to hear you say that Maurice. I feel like this book project of mine is getting nowhere."

"We can talk more about it tonight," he assured me.

While getting dressed I realized it was a Thursday night. Back in Connecticut the poetry group would be meeting. If I had stayed there, would I be seeing those women this evening? We had shared so much, especially the ups and downs of our emotional lives, recorded in our poems. The group had served a good purpose but it seemed to be winding down. If I stayed in Paris, they would be what I most missed about Greenwich, Connecticut. I vowed to send them each a postcard tomorrow.

Maurice knocked at the door. His eyes were shining, "I'm so glad you came back to Paris," he said, taking me by the shoulders and pressing his cheeks to mine warmly. The two kisses, one on each side, traditionally acknowledge the Guardian Angels sitting on our shoulders.

He offered me his arm as we walked to the car and I took it. Some of my original enthusiasm for Paris was returning, though it was tempered now, by the realities of my last trip. We stopped by Georgina's building.

When no one answered the bell, I dropped the card through the mail slot hoping it would reach her.

Maurice and I decided to eat light, and drove to a Japanese sushi place off the Champs-Élysées. Toasting each other with eggshell porcelain cups of warm sake, we talked about Georgina and Beirut. Maurice had another tragic tale, having lost everything during the war. His Ras Beirut showroom had been blown up and his uninsured warehouses full of furniture stock for his business, all looted. He had to start again from scratch. By touring Persian Gulf countries with sample photos and letters of representation in his briefcase, like one of his own junior salesman, he managed to carve out a new financial foothold. But the ordeal had instigated a heart attack.

His tone changed as he recounted the details of his operation.

"An interesting thing happened, just before my open heart surgery. I am not much for religion anymore, not since the war experiences in Lebanon. I wasn't even sure I believed in God, but I do now. On the way to the operating room, my dead mother appeared to me, in a vision as clear as day. She assured me that everything would be fine, and that I would survive the surgery. It was amazing. Nothing like that has ever happened to me before.

"Well, that probably saved my life, having so much faith, because after the operation, the hospital gave me the wrong blood, not my type A+. I saw the label on the transfusion bag, and tried to tell them, but I was still too heavily sedated to make any sense to them."

His brother managed to get the bag of blood switched to the right type in time to save his life.

The account gave me goose bumps and I decided then to tell him about Carla, the psychic I had visited in New York. The details tumbled out, especially those concerning Georgina and the project.

"Well then, don't you give up!" he exclaimed.

He confessed he'd also visited a psychic.

"She told me, 'You will marry a woman named Farah.' When I met an American woman named Joy [the English equivalent of the Arabic word Farah] I married her."

After dinner we returned to the Avenue Wilson apartment for a nightcap. Once there and settled on the sofa, Maurice recounted his recent adventures in Abu Dhabi. He'd gone there chasing a furnishing contract for a new palace the ruler was building, Sheikh Zayed Al Nahayan, the president of the United Arab Emirates.

"How much we have in common," I said, relating a few of my own stories about Sheikh Zayed. I had met him, and his wife Sheikah Sheikah in

London, more than ten years ago while working at the UAE Embassy. Once again, expat connections in Beirut had provided a safety net and my sole contact in London, Astrid Arabian. An Armenian secretary, Astrid had once worked for the Swedish Volvo representative whose wife and daughters became good friends of mine. I'd met the Gorrel family at the Arabian Horse Club where we often rode together during my boarding school days. Tracking Astrid down in London was complicated because the "Trucial States Office" no longer existed. By then the seven Gulf emirates had morphed into the United Arab Emirates, having finally gained their independence from the British, in 1971. When I managed to locate Astrid's renamed office, she had just departed on maternity leave. As fate would have it, they gave me her old job, which is how I ended up working in the Visa department of the UAE Embassy.

After recounting that tale, I showed Maurice a ring I was wearing. As he examined the interlocking triangles of emeralds, sapphires, and rubies mounted in a gold setting, I told him the story of the woman who had given it to me. One of my many duties at the Embassy had been to escort visiting Bedouin ladies from the Emirates to private Harley St. physicians, for prenatal exams, checkups, and various medical procedures. They were not shy about lifting their skirts for examinations but refused to remove their veils. One elderly lady had been given her test results. The news was not good. She was dying of cancer. I had walked her to her seat on the plane, settling her in for her final return to Abu Dhabi. She thanked me by putting the ring on my hand while saying goodbye. So many stories like that and there had never been anyone to tell them to.

But Maurice wanted to hear them all, so I recounted another one I'd never told. "The last time I saw Sheikh Zayed was five years ago, in 1979. That day was also the first time I saw Queen Elizabeth in person. We were all at the King's Camel races, outside Riyadh. The Saudi King Fahd (at the time) had invited Sheikh Zayed and the other rulers from the nearby Gulf States to see the British Queen who was making a state visit to Saudi Arabia.

"Knowing the Queen was a racing devotee, several rounds of camel racing had been arranged for the morning's entertainment. At noon, it was time for the Zuhr prayers. Sheikh Zayed rose from his seat and went down to a patch of sand, where the rugs beneath the reception tents ended.

"He knelt on his *bisht* (cloak) and began performing the pre-prayer ablutions, with sand and the smooth stone, as the Bedouin do, in the absence of water. Seeing him do that really impressed me.

"It greatly embarrassed the Saudis however. Perhaps that's what he'd intended. These 'keepers of the holy places of Mecca and Medina' seemed in such a hurry to impress the Queen of England they appeared to forget the basic duty of Islam. It had taken the Emirati people several generations to rid themselves of British rule, as you know. I thought it a powerful demonstration on his part, much better than saying anything. Eventually some men hurried over to guide him to where there was water set up for washing and a proper place to pray."

"Why didn't I meet you at ten or fifteen years ago?" Maurice asked, regarding me with unabashed fondness.

I shook my head wistfully, "I wish I knew."

We talked long into the night, trading stories about people we had known and heard of, including Kamal Adham,[28] the brother-in-law of King Faisal, and former CIA station chief, Ray Close. Word was when the American spymaster's cover had been blown in 1977, he had left the Agency to work for Kamal Adham, the founder of the Mukhabarat Saudi intelligence. I had met Kamal Adham, the white haired bon vivant with the Van Dyke goatee, here in Paris seven years ago.

Tonight had been quite an evening, but it was time to go. I looked at my watch, the universally accepted signal for goodbye.

"You are welcome to stay here. We have four bedrooms," Maurice said, waving his hand in their general direction.

"Thanks, that is sweet of you. Not tonight, but I might take you up on it another time," I said, thinking of my housing situation, and the uncertain state of affairs with Waddah and Georgina.

"Okay. I'll drive you back to Waddah's then. Can we have dinner again tomorrow night?"

"I suppose so," I said, as he held out my coat. Here I go again, on this merry-go-round of men.

Later that night, laying in bed alone in Waddah's apartment, I could not sleep. Too agitated by the wide-ranging conversation with Maurice, I reconsidered my road not taken. In my early twenties, I had not grasped the scale of what was going on with Kamal Adham, nor their recruitment tactics, but I had known I was out of my depth. The night Mazen took me to meet this head of the Saudi secret police, he had been determined to have me make a good impression. For the occasion Mazen had taken me shopping at the couture House of Nina Ricci. Decked out in the most expensive clothing I had ever worn — a ruffled, floor length black silk Nina

---

[28] The Turkish born spymaster Kamal Adham, (1929-1999) attended Cambridge University before his half sister Iffat married Prince Faisal ibn Abdul Aziz in 1932. At the request of his brother-in-law, now King Faisal, he founded the Al Mukhabarat Al A'amah, the Saudi secret police force, in 1965 (later renamed General Intelligence Presidency and served as its chief until his dismissal for failing to forestall the Mecca Mosque incident in November 1979.

Ricci gown costing several thousand dollars — I became suspicious of another agenda when Mazen presented me to Kamal at his Paris apartment. Had something similar happened to Georgina?

As things turned out, my decision proved providential, once the corruption came to light. Despite all his informants, this chief of Saudi internal security, and his organization had already failed to prevent the 1975 assassination of his brother-in-law, King Faisal. And the November 1979 Mecca Mosque incident[29] would be the final straw.

These seminal events had cost Adham his prestige, power, and post. Then came all of the negative publicity and criminal indictments, following the exposure of the corruption Adham and other has been involved with at the Bank of Credit and Commerce International (BCCI).[30] Mazen's brother Ghaith Pharaon[31] (1939-2017) was also one of the criminal defendants in this scandal, which landed him on the FBI's Ten Most Wanted List.

Not interested in selling myself to the highest bidder, or collaborating with any government agency — Saudi or American — my personal agenda was embarrassingly simple. Instead of becoming a pawn in their games, my aim was to live long enough to see how it all played out, and someday write it all down. My independence had proven its value as these players self-destructed. Freedom of conscience and personal agency were worth more to me than all the gold or glamour in the world. I had begun to suspect Waddah may have gotten wind of my former friendships, and their politics might have cooled his ardor.

I would have liked to have met Kamal's half sister, Queen Iffat Al

---

[29] The violent, two-week takeover the Great Mosque in Mecca started on the Hegira Islamic calendar's dawn of the new Islamic century 1400. The leader of the rebellion, Juhayman Al-Otaybi, had previously been detained for advocating an even stricter return to Islam, including banishing all non-Muslims from the Kingdom. His message resonated with those who considered the ruling Al Saud family too corrupt, too ostentatious, and too Westernized. Of the four hundred resisters, over one hundred were killed in the siege. Many pilgrims taken hostage, also died. The sixty some attackers who surrendered were publicly beheaded in eight Saudi cities.

[30] Kamal Adham teamed up with a Pakistani financier, named Agha Hasan Abed, founder of BCCI. They spent the money of depositors as if it was their own. The bank defaulted on its debts and regulators closed it in 1991.

[31] Ghaith Pharaon, Mazen's younger brother, was on the FBI's Most Wanted list after his company REDEC, the Saudi Research and Development Corporation, suspended its debt payments to 40 international banks in 1985. The bitter legal wrangles involved several American bankers and politicians and millions of dollars in loans that were never repaid.

Thunayan.[32] Iffat had been born in Istanbul in 1916. She married Faisal bin Abdulaziz Al Saud in 1932, three decades before he became king. The two had met when Iffat made her Hajj pilgrimage. As King Faisal's favorite, most educated wife, she became the most well known. They had nine children together. Having grown up in the Ottoman Empire, Iffat had earned a teaching degree and remained an outstanding advocate of education. Her sons went to Ivy League colleges Princeton, Harvard, and Georgetown. By contrast, fewer than ten of her older brothers-in-law (of King Saud's 100 plus children) even finished high school. Iffat made sure her daughters were educated too, and she founded several educational and welfare institutions to ensure progress for women. Her motto was, "The mother can be a school in herself if you prepare her well." I had only known one of her five sons, Prince Saud, a Princeton graduate, who became the world's longest serving Minister of Foreign Affairs, from 1975 to 2015. As I drifted off to sleep tonight in Paris, I thought about the differences between my formal classroom education and what I had learned outside those institutional walls. More than one of my fellow classmates had ended up working for government agencies, including the CIA, but what I had already seen of their corruption made me wary of them all.

* * * *

The next day I bought the Herald Tribune newspaper and noticed a job offer in the employment section. "International publisher seeks editor-writer-researcher. Must be able to do bright copy and comment on world news and politics, etcetera."

A perfect job for me. The company's address was on Île Saint-Louis. I had seen the street name during my long reconnoitering walk. Sitting down at the typewriter in Waddah's apartment, I immediately wrote a letter, addressed an envelope, and enclosed a copy of my biographical sketch. Grabbing my coat I hurried out the door, to walk to Île Saint-Louis and personally deliver my letter. I found the offices and put my envelope into the company's mailbox. Walking back to Waddah's place, I thought, today is Friday. Maybe I would hear from them on Monday. Maybe I would even get the job, maybe…maybe…maybe.

While strolling the Paris streets I hummed an old tune, "What a difference a day makes, twenty-four little hours, and the sun and the flowers, I am glad there is you…"

---

[32] Her great-grandfather was governor of Riyadh during the 1840s. Her grandfather was taken to Turkey as a prisoner of the Ottoman Empire following the collapse of the First Saudi State.

Chapter 7

AIMER À LA FOLIE /
CRAZY LOVE

A coeur vaillant rien d'impossible.
For the valiant heart, nothing is impossible.

— FRENCH PROVERB

March 1984
Journal entry:

Well, well, maybe it was meant to be Maurice all along! Not Waddah! We have fallen in love! Like two teenagers, we can't keep our hands off each other. My lips are chapped from thirty hours of kisses, and I am bursting with all the details we discussed, from finances, to my future in France, to our future. I spent the night there...he knows me.

It is so good, and so easy to be with him. Our lovemaking is a dream come true. There never needs to be another man. Wait until I tell Carla the psychic how things turned out. For once, writing seems superfluous. What words can convey such feelings?

He kissed me for the first time in Calvados, a little piano bar, near the George V Hotel, where we went after a big fresh seafood dinner at Chez Francis. Tender kisses, all around my mouth, like bees loving a flower. We were listening to the black American singer pianist Joe playing "Strangers in the Night." I'll never forget it. This changes everything. Too bad he's married...

I put my pen down and looked around Waddah's bedroom. Time to bid adieu to what had looked so promising but came to naught. Since his departure Waddah called, as he said he would. Over the weekend he explained, "I have bad news. My brother will be coming from London this Thursday, and he'll need the apartment."

So by this Thursday at the latest, I had to find another place to stay.

125

Maurice said the maid might talk about us to his wife. In a month she'd be coming to Paris, so there was no point in staying there. Besides, Maurice was leaving for London Tuesday on business. I telephoned Mr. Burke's office. His French secretary explained they were still in the US and gave me a number where they could be reached. Though I hated to ask for help, even though Janet had explicitly offered it, I dialed her. "Would you mind if I house sat for you, until your return?" She assured me I was more than welcome to stay there.

That Monday Mr. Sigal, the director of the company where I'd applied for the editor's job, called, interviewed me and offered me the job. After promising to get back to him by the end of the week, I starting making calculations. Was the salary enough to live on in Paris? What did apartments rent for?

I returned to Georgina's with my latest note. The maid let me in this time as Madame was at home. On the other side of the living room wall I could hear Georgina on the telephone, in her bedroom at one o'clock in the afternoon.

She told the maid, "Tell her I can't see her now. I will call her. Tell her to leave her number. No I have it." Her voice was husky. Did she smoke? The maid relayed Georgina's message exactly.

"I'll be staying here at my friends, the Burkes downstairs starting at the end of this week," I explained, giving her my new number, and motioning that their apartment was right beneath. "This will make it easier for us to arrange a meeting, anytime."

Later that week, I carried my luggage to the door for my move to the Burkes. Before leaving Waddah's apartment for the last time, I went back into the bedroom to retrieve the red ribbon from my blouse. It was still on the wall above Waddah's bed. Untying it carefully, I let this be a final ceremony for the sake of closure. In the backseat of the taxicab, on the drive across town to Rue Georges Ville, I drew the ribbon from my pocket and ran it through my fingers, musing about its meanings. This was the red thread of passion, connection, and the blood throbbing in our veins. It symbolized life continuing. I had left a thank you note on Waddah's desk for him to find upon his return. My wish was that we could remain friends. I mentioned my new job and left the Burkes phone number, "If you want to keep in touch." Had he and Maurice spoken to each other about me? I didn't know.

Putting the ribbon back in my pocket, I took out an advertisement torn from today's issue of the Herald Tribune, which I purchased on my morning walk. It described a "charming" studio apartment, on Île Saint-Louis, one street away from where my new job would be. I had hesitated to make the phone call, hardly able to believe in such luck, but the rent sounded manageable with what I would be making.

After stopping at Mr. Burke's office to collect the key from his secretary, the taxi continued to the apartment. Soon I was settled in the Burkes guest room. Then I sat down to call the number of the rental ad. The man who answered was the owner, Monsieur Masclet. His English had a French accent. He agreed to show me the place the following afternoon.

* * * *

The following evening, I wrote to Lynda thanking her for taking over my old Connecticut place, and filling her in about my new Paris apartment.

Dear Lynda,

Where do I begin? So much has happened on every front, except the Georgina one. I have a job, as an editor-writer. Work starts next week. This afternoon I found a place to live. You have to start thinking about when you can come and visit!

It's a studio apartment in a seventeenth century building, in the fourth arrondissement, on the Île Saint-Louis. The minute I walked into the courtyard, I knew I wanted to live there. It's the only place I saw but I felt so sure about it I'm not going to look anywhere else.

You enter through a massive red wooden gate, with a door inside it that opens onto a cobblestone courtyard. Horses and carriages used to clatter into the stables on the ground floor, what they call here the rez-de-chaussee. The building has been classified as a historical monument. Nothing can be done to alter it, without permission from the government, so it retains its original character. The French call this kind of place a "hôtel particulier."

The landlord Mr. Masclet lives here and owns several apartments. He's a wine merchant in his forties and his wife Selma is an American from California. The painter Matisse's grandson owns one of the buildings in the back of the courtyard. After you come through the red door, the wide stone staircase on the right takes you up to my apartment on the second floor. The famous volcanologist, Haroun Tazieff and his wife, live on the next floor above me.

The place is fully furnished. The entrance foyer doubles as a dining room. The table beside the window opens up to seat several dinner guests. The ceiling has been painted blue, like the sky, with a few puffy clouds. The right side of the apartment faces eastward towards the courtyard. Those tall French floor to ceiling windows let the sunlight shine into the rooms. The salon, sitting room, is on the left. A small wooden staircase built into the wall leads up to the loggia (balcony) above, where the big bed is hidden from view.

You can imagine how high the ceilings are to have enough space for that. The large stone fireplace in the salon has been fitted with a modern heating unit, and the gas casts a nice flame. All the furniture is French, and the things just belong there, including a large antique wooden desk for me to write on.

What perfect luck! A cozy, quiet place, on an island, in the middle of Paris. And my job is only a few doors away. It all seems maktoub. Everything about Paris feels that way.

Don't laugh, but I've already changed boyfriends. The new one is Maurice. I met him on the same January vacation as Waddah, on nearly the same day. Only problem, this one is married.

After finishing the letter I laid my pen down. Feeling queasy, I looked for something to eat, to settle my stomach. Low blood sugar perhaps, or nerves, after so many changes in such a short time. The Burkes apartment had a proper modern kitchen. By comparison the studio one was tiny, and truly French, but manageable. The only real drawback was the shower stall in the little bathroom of my soon-to-be home studio. No tub. I love taking baths. Oh well. Opening the fridge at the Burkes I searched the contents but nothing appealed. This nausea might be from overdoing it, after all the recent restaurant meals with Maurice. He jogged every day as part of his post-op routine. Getting fat in France would be easy to do if I didn't start exercising soon.

* * * *

The following week, on my second day of work, I still felt slightly ill and Georgina had yet to call. Soon I would be moving again, into my own studio much further away and decidedly less convenient. By now I had hoped to make some progress with her, yet I also knew how much patience was required when dealing with Middle Easterners and Georgina's situation was complicated. If she was still on the PLO "payroll" she would need Arafat's agreement before undertaking any such project. Her martyred husband's reputation had to be finessed.

They also had to check me out. What might disqualify me in their eyes? How long would that process take? Here in Paris I was an unknown entity. Had Georgina kept in touch with our common friend Mazen? Would he put in a good word if asked about me? "My people talked to your people..." So much depended upon who you knew. Some of my contacts might be considered disqualifying but there was nothing I could do about that.

Maurice was due back from his London trip tonight. Our plan was to spend as much time as possible together before his wife, son, and daughter arrived near the end of the month. Despite his nonchalance about being married, the situation definitely bothered me. Why repeat the lesson I had learned from watching my father's infidelities as a child? Nevertheless our unusual similarities drew me in and I didn't want to stop myself.

128

From London, Maurice called often, using his nickname for me, Pistachio, due to my "cute little nose."

This made me laugh. Growing up in Arabia, my small nose had made me feel inadequate. Everyone else had prominent, distinguished "family" noses. By contrast, mine seemed even less significant. As an adolescent, I stood in front of our bathroom mirror in Jeddah, pulling on the cartilage trying to elongate it, and encourage a downward curve at the end, like those of the people who surrounded me. Maurice had howled with laughter when hearing me explain this on the phone. Another thing I had never told a soul till now.

It was so reassuring to exchange such confidences. I felt deeply recognized by this man, who had so much in common with me, and could validate my experiences as I validated his. Part of me could scarcely believe it could be like this. Upon his return, we enjoyed a tender reunion, and stayed in that evening, eating a simple meal at his place. Lying abed, we talked and talked. Never had I felt so freely adored before. Such compatibility. He could finish my sentences, as I could his. Yet I scolded myself. Don't love him so much! You know it can't work out. But in my skin it felt so right. I couldn't help it, and Carla's positive predictions gave me hope.

* * * *

The next day my monthly was due but there was no sign of it. Uh oh. What if I am pregnant? Carla had predicted a child. Had I been careful enough about birth control? Opening my agenda book I counted the days, noting the fertile ones. If I am pregnant, what will I do? I didn't want to believe it was possible, nor did I want to breathe a word about it to Maurice. No sense worrying him unless I was absolutely certain.

All day at work the nausea stayed with me, a strong indication of what I didn't want to contemplate. The signs were familiar. Having been pregnant before, I could recognize them. Seven years ago in my student days, it had been out of the question to keep a baby. At New York University's teaching hospital, I had the procedure done, relieved that it was safe and legal. I told the father nothing until afterwards and he agreed I'd done the right thing.

Twenty-two at the time, I had only dared to confess the truth in my journal, in French. "*Je suis enceinte.*" Though I'd discussed it with no one in advance, I never regretted my decision. My vow not to bring children into this world had been very clear. No innocents should suffer the stupidities of incompetent adults. Peace and security ought to be the pre-conditions for raising families. Otherwise, we practically guaranteed more wars. This time though, I thought I was in love. Not yet able to see my sudden affections as the symptoms they were, of my psychological vulnerabilities after so many

129

stressful events, I was slowly warming to a new belief in the natural process and a more regular life, even if it was with the wrong man. Our harmonizing physical chemistry, interlocking experiences and strong emotions, had taken the edge off my old certainties about having no children. This month I would be thirty. Being a single mother was never easy but seemed more viable now. How to make the best decision? When the time was right I would discuss it with Maurice. That in itself was already a big change for me.

The following afternoon, after work, Maurice came with the car to help me move from the Burkes apartment to my own place. As was the custom with Middle Eastern men, whose women judge them by their generosity, he gave me the security deposit and first month's rent on the furnished apartment, although I promised to pay him back. We stopped to buy towels and bed linens, which was all the place needed.

We ate lunch with a French lawyer friend of his, Catherine Genis, who examined the rental contract. There was nothing frou frou about this woman, with her stout frame, frizzy hair, and lack of makeup. Extremely competent, I liked her right from the start. In the coming months, she would become another dear French friend. I would be blessed with several.

Meanwhile Maurice was being so caring and communicative, I just let him spoil me, and did not mention my suspicions. We might as well enjoy whatever time we had left to be together. Being married to an American, he was based in Virginia, and traveled through France on his way to the Middle East for business. Remembering Carla's predictions provided some comfort. She said we would not be together all the time and that both of us would often travel.

My new landlord had left a bottle of champagne cooling in the fridge as a welcome gift. I opened it and poured two glasses. "A toast, to a new life, for us both." I did not mention the potential presence of a third life. Instead I recalled Monsieur Masclet's words when first showing me the studio, "I hope you have nothing against marriage, because everyone who has lived here has ended up getting married. It is a real love nest."

The next day during my lunch break from work, I went to a nearby pharmacy to purchase a pregnancy test kit. I had to be sure. Knowing the truth was important in all things. If the test was positive, I would not tell Maurice until after his wife left. My worrying was bad enough, but he had a heart condition, and financial insecurities. Why tell him any sooner than necessary?

On our last night before our temporary separation, Maurice was very sweet, yet he stressed the point that he was not the jealous or possessive type. "I want you to feel free, to see and date others. I sincerely hope you will meet a nice young man and get married and have a family and all that."

I bit my tongue. The test that morning had proven my suspicions correct. I was definitely pregnant, and here he was, telling me not to get too attached. Was I the jealous or possessive type?

After seeing the positive test results, I wept in the shower, with the water streaming over me like tears from the sky. Having to choose yet again, between keeping an actual child or giving it up, was easier when the choice was abstract. I used to be so sure, but my former resolve had weakened. Maybe it was the hormones, I speculated while toweling myself dry. I decided then I could have a child if and when I was ready. And truth be told, this was still a rotten world, not a decent place for raising healthy children who deserved to be wanted, planned, and well loved.

* * * *

For the next two weeks, Maurice was with his wife and kids. On my own I took long walks after work and on the weekends, avoiding my new friends while mulling things over. Never before had I noticed so many babies and pregnant women in Paris. They reminded me that I did not have to be alone forever. Would things be better if there was more than just a man to love and myself to live for?

Reality pressed upon me. Where to get this procedure done in Paris? How much would it cost, to undo this mistake, versus letting things take their natural course? I considered both alternatives for as long as I could bear it. Meanwhile, I felt sick all the time, not just in the mornings. Perhaps there was a complication? I was eating well and hungrier than usual for meat. At night in bed alone, I folded my hands over my belly and wondered what it would feel like, to let it keep swelling for nine months. Adding up those months, I calculated that this baby would be born in late November. My parents' birthdays came at that time of year. How would they react to the news of such an event? They'd never known about my previous pregnancy. Whatever I wanted to do, no one else's opinion would stop me now either.

What a strange thirtieth birthday present. This is not why I had come to France.

That Sunday afternoon, I had a little housewarming party, and invited the people I knew, including some from work — Maurice's French lawyer Catherine, Hugette, my friend of Zvoni's from Air France, Freddie (Frederique) the proprietress of the hair salon, and Zemira. My little apartment lent itself to entertaining and this event inaugurated many more get-togethers within its walls. I bought cakes and other goodies, happy to have the company of new friends. Their compliments on the apartment helped me understand what a coup it was to have found a place on Île Saint-Louis. The address had a cachet I had not realized. Beginners luck. I had simply taken the first place I had seen because it felt so right. Waddah had accused me of "being an impulsive girl," but impulsive or not, I trusted my own instincts. They were a kind of truth even if others were not truthful to theirs. What other guidance had I been able to count on?

Not burdening anyone else about my pregnancy, I knew I'd soon need help with referrals and finding a doctor. After everyone left I sat at the writing desk and wrote to Lynda about it. Telling her the truth gave me some respite. In her latest letter, she'd replied to my news about Maurice, "I hope you know what you're doing. I just don't want you to get hurt."

I also wrote a fifth letter to Georgina to mail on my way to work the next day. As I penned the news of my move, new address, and permanent phone number, I thought of how a baby might affect this project. Georgina had been four months pregnant when her husband was killed by a car bomb. What had it been like to become a mother so soon after becoming a widow? Surely it was worse than what I was facing.

That week I wrote a lot: to family, friends, and my old consulting company, giving everyone the news of my move and my change of address details, explaining my decision to stay in Paris. To my prior employer I reiterated my offer to continue our contractual arrangement. If they could promise me five or six programs in a row, we could split the airfare from Paris to New York, and I could do jobs for them in the US as well as overseas.

My Paris job was growing complicated. The American director was encountering tax and legal problems in France. It was also a full-time commitment, which I had promised to avoid when moving overseas. Forty hours plus per week left me too exhausted to write, to fulfill my *raison d'être*. That week I submitted several poems to expatriate magazines in Paris. "You are not legit if you don't submit" is the writer's code.

* * * *

Around seven o'clock one evening, Maurice called unexpectedly.

"I am in the neighborhood, with my son in the car, hoping to catch a glimpse of you walking home from the office. I miss you so much," he said.

The tears came after I hung up the phone. I kept my resolve to not bring up the pregnancy.

March 27, 1984, my thirtieth birthday dawned, gray and wet. Pressing a mug of warm tea to my midriff, I faced the long window wanting to cry. In the courtyard below, the cobblestones were soaked and dark. Rainwater streamed down the outer walls of the building. While dressing for work, I felt heavy and sick. On the short walk to the office in the cold wind, my umbrella blew inside out. This too was Paris, I reminded myself grinding my teeth.

Fiona, the English woman who ran Waddah's gallery had called to invite me to a *vernissage* (opening) at a small gallery on the island tonight. That was something to look forward to. Tomorrow night, Zvonimir's friends had planned a *raclette* dinner. Having no idea what raclette was I was keen to go. Keeping busy would pass the time until Maurice and I were together again. Moping at home served no purpose. In my purse was a ticket for a concert at the American church this coming Friday evening. A young American woman would be singing her own songs, in French and English, with her band. Yet to find anyone free to accompany me, I vowed to go alone if I had to.

At the office, I worked on a subscription promotion plan. At four o'clock my coworkers surprised me with a birthday cake. Barely there a month, I had not expected anything. Blowing out the candles, I wished for happiness with Maurice and success with the Georgina project.

The evening turned out well. I saw Fiona's artist beau again and met more of her French friends. A gregarious, talkative bunch well connected with the Paris art scene, they invited me along to dinner as we left the gallery. While walking to a little place on the island, I recalled Lilian's opening in New York and how meeting Zvonimir that night had catalyzed my coming here. On a corner of the paper tablecloth, one of the artists Serge, drew me a birthday cartoon. I tore it off for a keepsake when leaving. Returning on foot to my studio, I was lightheaded with the Brouilly Beaujolais. Before crawling between the sheets of my loggia bed, I slipped the impromptu birthday sketch in the pages of my journal. Things could be worse.

Fiona had told me, "Waddah sends you his best wishes. He will be here for a week now and said he would be calling you." My response was something between an eye roll and a smirk.

My soon to be twenty-five year old brother called from the US to wish me a happy thirtieth.

The following night at Freddie's, I met more people, and I learned all about raclette cheese, cooking my own wedges on the heating apparatus, placed in the center of the table. Along with everyone else's, mine melted beneath the broiler coil in its individual metal dish. When liquid enough, we poured it over the small boiled potatoes, "in their jackets" or "nightshirts," *chemise* as the French called these unpeeled spuds. It was fun, and my French was holding up, although spending entire evenings in the language took double the energy. At dinner, I met a woman from Nice, in the south of France and her younger companion, who came from Biarritz. They explained this was a poor mountainous region near the Spanish border. I had already noticed the French habit of asking the same questions during first meetings. Where you were from, and where had you last vacationed, were always mentioned. The replies satisfied the need to peg each other's status.

I had met few born and bred Parisians. How long did it take to become a true Parisian? The real ones had a discernible accent. Freddie's friend was in her forties, with a slim, energetic body and close-cropped black hair. Divorced and well preserved, her boyfriend seemed twenty years younger. Though I had often seen this age disparity between men and their younger girlfriends, this was the first time I'd seen the reverse. Handsome in an elemental way, was it uncharitable to think he might be a gigolo? The woman was clearly the provider and the one with the power.

The fellow worked out, proud to be in good shape, with his short-sleeved shirt rolled up to display his muscles. His face was scarred, with a few nicks around his mouth. They made the fullness of his lips more noticeable. The marks from cuts and stitches gave him an air of defended vulnerability. I asked about them.

In his strong regional accent, he replied, "I had a run-in on the Champs-Élysées with a gang of angry Arab youths. They were taking revenge for one of their comrades by beating up the first French kid they could get their hands on." At least they didn't have guns I thought, like the Palestinians who exacted their revenge on my sister.

His matter-of-fact attitude made me conclude these squabbles were a regular occurrence between the French and the immigrants from former French colonies in North Africa. The tensions were worse in some cities. The fellow had a curious habit of sucking the air in through his lips and teeth, whenever he said "*Oui*," or when something impressed him. I kept asking questions to encourage this while watching his sensuous mouth.

The wine had loosened my inhibitions and his attention excited me. At one point during dessert, while the others were chatting, our eyes embraced. We did not allow the mutual attraction to show again until saying goodbye a tad too warmly. As the evening ended our cheeks pressed together twice on each side. This *bizoux* was customary in southern France.

Alone in bed later, remembering his strong, well-shaped hands, I recalled the strangely-shaped tip of his right ring finger, mangled by some machinery he explained. A fantasy began as I imagined those hands touching me everywhere. Surely he was the sort of lover who knew how to please a woman. Perhaps I was not such a lovesick puppy after all. Maurice and Waddah had not managed to monopolize my psyche. Meeting this man inspired me to appreciate my freedom, the thrills of seduction, and the fact of my own agency. The whole interaction revealed something about desire and desirability, mine as well as his.

Romantic love, seduction, and pleasure seemed low on the list of priorities for American men. Those I'd met were focused on money making, drinking, and scoring in sports, and bars. As for games, I'd rather play than watch. With my pregnancy hormones on overdrive, and my swollen breasts, I felt intensely feminine. Paris was summoning forth both inner goddess and devilishness.

Centuries of women had survived here in the past. Living by their wits, working their wiles, traveling to their assignations, right where I was on Île Saint-Louis. For a moment I pretended I could have any man I set my sights on. If I looked at him, long enough in a certain way, he would follow me. And yet the one I thought I wanted was sleeping across town tonight with his wife. Having didn't mean keeping.

* * * *

That Friday evening on my way to the concert at the American church, I took my sixth note to Georgina's place. When the buzzer went unanswered, I slid the envelope through the mail slot. Grimly I decided it was time to take another tack. In my latest letter, I said I would return the following evening at six o'clock, unless she called to cancel. Waiting for her to call and make an appointment had not produced results.

Before the concert started, I walked down Avenue President Wilson passing Maurice's place. The desk light was on in the third floor window of the room used as an office. Maurice was sitting there. Only the back of his head and shoulders were visible. One more night and we would be together again. He was on the phone. A young girl, possibly twelve years old with chin length hair, stood beside him. A little boy, not more than five, was playing with the telephone cord on the other side. I stood in the cold drizzle below for as long as I could bear it, looking up at the bright-framed window square with its family tableau as the daylight faded over the Paris rooftops.

* * * *

The following evening at six o'clock sharp, I arrived at Georgina's apartment building as promised. Through the intercom her Filipino maid informed me, "Madame just left, before ten minutes, looking very beautiful."

Her emphasis was on the word "very." She must be *very* proud of her mistress.

"Will she be coming back soon? I can wait," I offered, feeling my despondence rising.

The maid answered, "I don't think so Madame."

I added, "Well, please tell her I was here. Don't forget." What else could I do? I turned and left.

Trudging back along the Avenue Georges Ville to the Metro stop at Place Victor Hugo, I remembered something Maurice had said, when he'd called today to remind me of our dinner date for tomorrow evening after he saw his family off at the airport. He repeated some gossip heard in London, about Georgina currently dating some Christian Lebanese guy, who lived there.

"He is no good. He's a real playboy." Maurice said. "He used to date someone else I know."

What was Maurice being called behind his back? I was not his first extramarital affair. It struck me with a pang that Maurice was a lot like my father, and I was playing the part of the women he regularly took advantage of. The last thing I wanted was to be another victim. There were plenty of unsavory vocabulary terms to describe this behavior. The heels of my boots drilled into the sidewalk even harder with this realization.

At the steps leading into the metro, I changed my mind and turned defiantly toward the cafe on the corner instead of proceeding home. I took a seat and ordered a Campari and soda. Rummaging in my handbag for paper and an envelope to write Georgina yet another note, a rueful smile lessened the sting of shame. My common sense was questionable but I was never out of stationary or writing instruments. Endlessly filling journal pages and dashing off letters, I had little to show for my efforts except too many mistakes. Yet I persisted, composing my seventh or eighth note to Georgina in a huff.

"If you do not want to see me, or speak to me, please let me know, by phone or by letter, and I will stop bothering you. I just don't know how to interpret your silence."

With a touch of vengeance I added, "I intend to do this book in any case. I thought it only fair to tell you about it, and to offer you the chance to collaborate, and share in any profits."

If the last phrase did not get her attention, nothing would. After draining my Campari, I paid for it and walked back to her building to drop my latest missive in the mail slot.

At home later, Zvonimir called from the US to see how I was doing. He was planning a trip to Yugoslavia, via Paris in May, and wanted us to be together this summer.

"I will come again in June. I want to bring you to Yugoslavia then. You must come and see my country. We will take a boat and tour the islands. You will see what I paint."

He reminded me of what he'd said a year ago, "Remember? My hope is that we will see each other at least once a year for the rest of our lives."

As romantic as this sounded, I had no idea what might be happening in my life by June and said so. "Perhaps I will be in the US working. It's our high season for training programs. Expatriating executives relocate their families during the summer, so the kids can start the school year in the new countries. I need to go back and earn some money. I don't want the full-time job here anymore. It leaves me no time for writing."

He asked how things were going with Georgina and I shared my disappointment. He urged me not to give up. As for the summer, we could leave things open for now. When he came through town we would talk again. I climbed into bed thinking about what I had not told him, about Maurice. Tomorrow I had to tell him about the baby. I also decided that at the end of the week, when I received my paycheck, I would give my notice to leave that job.

CYNTHIA F. DAVIDSON

Chapter 8

C'EST VRAI OU DÉSOLÉ /
IT'S TRUE OR IT'S TRAGIC

The future is made of the
same stuff as the present.

— SIMONE WEIL

April 1984

The next day we had a sweet reunion. Maurice took me back to Tse Yang, the restaurant where we met, a scant four months ago. We ate the same sesame seed caramel apple dessert, poured into ice water at the table. Later, after making love, I told him I was pregnant. Crying a little, I admitted I thought about keeping the child, but Maurice was quite firm.

"No, you mustn't keep it. My wife has had three abortions, the last one eighteen months ago. I do not want any more children."

That confirmed my previous certainty. This world did not deserve any children of mine.

For the next three days, Maurice never left my side. We even showered together. It was April, yet snow was falling on Paris.

* * * *

A week later I was gently wheeled back to my room from the operating theatre. Maurice had taken me to the clinic, and stayed with me throughout, insisting on paying for everything despite my protests. Still heavily sedated, I struggled to pronounce the words as I reached for his hand. "I love you. I know I'm not supposed to, but I do."

Around sunset, when fully awake, I stood at the window of my room and noticed a tree at the center of the clinic's inner courtyard. Its smooth boughs held a tiny, empty nest. Plenty of birds gadded about, chirping happily, taking flight, and landing, their splayed tails flicking. Today I am the emptied nest. Yet the birds still sing. Life goes on. I have sent this small soul back, to wait until I am ready to be its proper mother, if that day ever comes. Children don't ask to be born yet they often bear the blame. Hadn't I?

For more than a week after the abortion, my dreams were full of blood. I wrote them down in my journal.

Men were committing "sepuku," the Japanese ritual suicide, by sword. A line of men were kneeling on the ground in front of a building I was passing. They were disemboweling themselves, one at a time, with great deliberation and great dignity. They all used the same knife, which they passed on to the next man, after cutting their own abdomens open.

In another dream I remembered distinctly a woman holding an infant in her arms. Also kneeling, she leant forward to rest her bare throat upon the point of a long sword. Suddenly she pushed forward, and the sharp blade passed clear through her neck. The baby flew out of her hands, and landed in the arms of another person standing by. This man caught the child.

After such nightmares, I took it easy for a few days. Relieved to have already given my notice, I no longer had to rush and dress for the office job. I laid in bed for as long as I could. After an extra cup of tea, I looked through the pile of letters the concierge had handed me when Maurice brought me back from the clinic. Before delving into my correspondence, I thought about the concierge. Had she ever had children? A thin, grey-haired French woman, she occupied the ground floor rooms nearest the thick wooden gates of 15 Quai de Bourbon. We had never conversed about anything remotely personal. She referred to me in the third person, saying in French, "Madame, she will be coming back later today?"

This form of address was a holdover from before the 1968 student uprisings, which eroded some practices of Europe's rigid class system. The use of the formal "*vous*" (you) instead of the familiar "*tu*" form of address was one way the French language maintained distance in hierarchy and status. My concierge was the only person who maintained this extreme third person form with me. Unsure of how to respond, I would reply "*oui*" for the most part, rather than attempt to describe myself as "she."

Paris had punished me but she was also broadening my perspective. What were my little troubles in the context of such a vast history? This Quai de Bourbon building itself was older than my country by over a century. Since moving to #15, I'd discovered a former French Finance Minister, Count Jean Charron had built it in 1637, the year after the Puritans established a colony in Connecticut and clashed with the Pequot colony. A stone plaque on the outer wall said the building was first called the Hotel Le Charron. The term "hôtel particulier" was for the private homes of the wealthy, not "hotel" in the modern sense of the word, though the rooms may have been sectioned into private apartments later on.

The name Bourbon referred to more than a brand of whiskey. The Bourbons of Quai de Bourbon could be traced back to 1272, when Beatrix of Bourbon married the sixth son of King Louis IX of France and bore six children. The Bourbon family was a window into French and European history. Legitimate Bourbon births had produced the most famous kings of France, who ruled from 1589 to 1792, mixing their blood with most of Europe's royal families. And there had been plenty of illegitimate children, Bourbon and otherwise. Abortion had only been legalized in France in 1975.

Returning to my pile of correspondence, I found a letter from my previous employer confirming our recent telephone discussions. They were officially contracting my services for a series of training programs to begin in the US at the end of this month of April. The first would be in Dallas and Fort Worth, Texas for General Dynamics. This change of pace was definitely needed. After my failure with Georgina and these disastrous love affairs, I had to collect my wits, and some income, to continue living in Paris.

Maurice also planned to depart for the US in the middle of April. The following week, a relative of his came to visit and the three of us went out to dinner. This cousin was young and single, living the fast life in Florida with plenty of "wine, women, and song," if one believed his tales. His easy come easy go attitude exacerbated tensions between Maurice and me. We had our first quarrel, aggravated by the prohibition against lovemaking. The doctor had insisted on two weeks rest and recuperation, and I was in no hurry to jeopardize my body or my mental health.

On a rare, sunny day, as we strolled arm in arm one afternoon, Maurice reminded me in a chilling tone, "Don't get too emotional about me."

His words stung. "I hear you Maurice. We have been through a lot but I understand the terms of this relationship very well. While you are here, let's enjoy ourselves. When you are gone, you will be gone."

He needed to hear himself say those words, fearing he'd become too emotional and too attached. Despite what he said, his eyes, his voice, and his hands showed a man still in love. Saying he did not want to hurt me was really about him, not wanting to be hurt. After what had transpired, I'd regained some objectivity, able to remind myself, he is far from perfect and I am not a willing victim. I must prepare to get over him. He was not the first man nor would he be the last.

Over the next few days my body righted itself hormonally. My strength and energy returned. I no longer felt nauseous, although the birth control pills the doctor prescribed took some getting used to. They would prevent unwanted pregnancies more effectively than the despised diaphragm. Maurice went to London for three days and this gave me time to reconsider our situation.

In my journal I wrote:

I shall defend the dignity of my feelings. If Maurice cannot do the same I must let go of him. I believe in love. He loves me, yet he's afraid of what that means. The changes...

Rereading the lines, I thought this sounded awfully high and mighty.

He had admitted, "I have never gotten this involved, in sixteen years. I have told you, I am already committed. I don't know how long I've got left. I even told my wife when she was here to go out, to see other people, and enjoy herself."

Maurice had begun to look older than the dozen years between us. Regarding his features for a long time, I questioned my own emotions. A change of heart? Regret? Withdrawal? What welled up was an infinite sense of tenderness. This brought an odd conclusion. Since I had loved him, and he had loved me, things had equaled out. I could let him go. I did not want him to regret knowing me, nor did I want to regret having known him. Why persist just to watch it all sour? If things had to end now before degenerating, so be it.

I penned a note to give him upon his return from London.

Dear Maurice,

Before we part, let me say a few things. You said you do not want to hurt me, nor do you want to be hurt. The best way to prevent hurt is to know where it comes from. Perhaps we are confusing things by not stating clearly the truth about where the danger lies.

I am not the issue Maurice, your fear is. You are afraid of love, not me. It comes out looking like anger sometimes. It is really defensiveness. Your real struggle is inside you Maurice, not outside, with me.

If we never see each other again, you still have to decide how to live your life. Since surviving the war in Beirut, and your open-heart surgery, your life has widened and deepened. You have been given a second chance, a second life. Your challenge is how to honor that. You can live more fully and truthfully now, because you no longer fear death. You have experienced your own spirituality. So I ask you, how can such a man be afraid of love?

You said you are "a man of ideology," and I admire that. Love is also a form of ideology Maurice. It exists only as a belief. Like nationalism, love is above all a belief in the power of a feeling.

Only recently have I come to believe in love myself. I am still discovering what it means to have this belief, feel these feelings, and endure these truths. Love is not an easy faith to have. But you believe in it or you do not. It's like being pregnant, you are or you are not. The battle you are waging is with your own heart. I wish you all the love in the world.

And I signed it, knowing it revealed a lot about me too.

* * * *

Maurice read my letter upon his return. We discussed this idea, about the fear of love. He insisted he could stop himself, that he was not going to stay in love with me.

"I have stopped myself before," he insisted.

I thought of how I had stopped myself too, pulling my emotions back so recently, with Waddah. But Maurice held my hands and kissed my face and lips constantly that whole day. The sunny warmth enchanted us, as we sat upon a bench in my favorite park beside Notre Dame Cathedral.

He told me then, "I want us to have an unusual friendship."

Zvonimir had said something similar, suggesting we see each other every year for the rest of our lives. Was this my destiny? Having not been able to envision a natural future, of marrying or bringing children into this world, what other options were there for me?

A line of Sufi poetry came to mind: "Lovers do not finally meet somewhere. They are inside each other all along." The inner voice was saying, "Don't fight this. Let him say it is not love, though he doth protest too much… you would win a battle (of semantics) and lose the war by insisting that what he feels is love."

At one o'clock in the morning, he finally left my little studio. We had spent the entire day and evening together, still unable to make love till my healing was complete, yet he was calling me "Love."

Either I am a fool, or I'm becoming wiser I thought, and it is too early to know for sure which one it is.

He flattered me, saying, "You are so strong and so soft at the same time. It is beautiful, intellectually and emotionally. You are so wise, I knew it, but now I know better. You can have anyone you want. You are going to have it all. I know it, and I will be so proud. I will see your work published and be able to say, I know her. And when you get married, I will send you the biggest bouquet anonymously."

* * * *

During the next four days Maurice traveled to Italy and toured furniture factories in Milan. Waddah was also traveling constantly, his professional opportunities holding even more fascination for him. My days were equally busy. Often out, I wondered if either had tried to reach me, and resolved to purchase an answering machine, so people could leave me phone messages. Only two days remained for us to be together when Maurice returned. We celebrated with lunch at an Indian place. Over the lamb biryani I sensed the four-day separation had resolved his emotions as it had mine. Yet he wanted us to spend the night together. My body was finally healed. We would make the most of it.

In the late afternoon, we went back to my studio. Tenderly he guided me upstairs to my loggia bed, the one where I had spent too many nights missing him. With great care he undressed me, and the slow kisses began, with my "Pistachio" nose. Down he continued until he had spread me like some pink petalled rose upon the yellow sheets. Kissing, licking, and sucking my flesh, calling me his goddess, he worshipped me until I became a blaze of glory.

It was to be our final coupling.

The following day Maurice left France. I teetered between twin desires: to stay alone in my darkened apartment, grieving and sinking into depression or to get back into the flow of life — put myself back out there. Circulate. Don't refuse to live or refuse life. My newspaper horoscope read, "That mythical tall dark stranger could actually turn up in your life, or it could be that you decide to live your life as though the romance of your dreams is just around the corner, good idea!"

Ha, I thought bitterly, my eyes still swollen with tears. Would I ever see Maurice again? Half of me wanted to wait and be true to him only. The other half knew that was sheer folly. The best I could do was to preserve what was positive about our experience, and go on to the next goodness.

Joanne, another expatriate girlfriend I'd known in New York, had written to insist I look up a friend of hers in Paris. An Australian herself, Joanne had met a Frenchman during his vacation in the US. After striking up a conversation in Manhattan's Central Park, she and Bernard had a passionate affair. Although I had misgivings about complicating my life with another man, I decided to meet him. I could make up my mind afterwards. Perhaps my problem was not boyfriends per se but Arab boyfriends, and the married ones. I thought of Georgina and how she had the courage to go on after her husband was killed.

I had already forwarded a copy of Joanne's letter to Bernard and suggested he give me a call. While Maurice was in Milan, Bernard phoned. We arranged to meet at a cafe in Place St. Michel.

"How will I know you?" he asked.

"I will wear a red scarf."

That afternoon, standing in front of the mirror draping the red shawl over my black cape coat, I told myself, "You must do it. Get out of this apartment. Go and see. Get over Maurice. Don't give into sadness and drown."

Three hours later I was back in my studio writing in my journal:

I am scared. It's the man I've just met. He's a devil. I can feel it. A handsome plastic surgeon, he twice used the word "violent" to describe his after work activities. Did he only mean sports? From his lanky body one can tell he's the hard exercise type.

I am picking up something else though. I can't even make up my mind whether I'd like to take him as a lover, or never see him again, to finish with this tension. I know I'm off-balance. I've barely left the last night of love with Maurice, who is so easy, compared to this hard, unmarried man.

This one is a hunter, restless, and questing. He would not be satisfied, even after the kill, when standing over the bloody carcass. He didn't ask me if I wanted a lift, he told me he'd take me, to the bookstore where I had planned to go to afterwards. Something seemed insincere, forced, or too practiced in his laughter and smiles. This wasn't the awkwardness of a first time meeting.

He was sizing me up and making judgments, ticking off boxes in his brain.

He wanted the facts, information about where I live, if I'm alone, my schedule and plans, how long I'll stay in Paris, money, other friends, etc. Like the surgeon he is, his questions resembled incisions. He's not one for niceties. He wouldn't pamper me like Maurice has. Do I need something very different like this to cure me? I am not really drawn to blond men with their pale eyes...

This man probably goes through women the way a rabbit goes through fields of carrots. He's beautiful to look at, with the fine hands of an artist, yet inside him I sense something less beautiful. His core is loose, the seed of him shrunken by some ennui or unresolved pain, which rattles around inside him.

At least he's well traveled. He's even been to Beirut, about 10 years ago. He liked it enough to have considered staying on for a year with the medical mission.

I think he's judging whether I'd be convenient, and fit into the scheme of his life for the moment, as though it's a foregone conclusion that I would agree if he decided to invite me in. Would I say yes?

He smoked one long thin cigarette with his cup of tea. He touched my arm briefly at one point and shook my hand goodbye in his car, very lightly, hardly clasping at all. He invited me to dinner next week, "I'm not going to cook, but I have other people, and someone to cook for me" Odd.

I guess I'll go along and see if only to confirm my suspicions.

Chapter 9

COUP DE FOUDRE /
THUNDERBOLT

Paris is the keeper of the world. It doesn't belong to itself,
it doesn't belong. This is why it is circular...it is living in
one's mind, like the turning center of everything that is.

— GERTRUDE STEIN

Three days later, on Good Friday, I went to the Burkes for dinner to celebrate their return to Paris. Georgina had never answered my last note, so I left another one under her door. Was this the tenth? I had lost count. At least it was safe to vent my frustrations with the Burke family. In turn they filled me in on their observations during the last few days.

"Things upstairs have been very quiet," Janet said. "The little boy, Ali Junior, comes and goes to school with the Filipino maids."

So, there were two of them, I noted.

"Georgina seems to be off on another one of her trips."

"What good little spies you are," I joked, thanking them again for their help.

After the meal, everyone wanted to go out. "Where can we go in Paris that's appropriate to take our eighteen-year-old daughter?" Tom asked. She was visiting from the US.

I suggested, "How about some live music, at Calvados? Joe Turner plays jazz and blues tunes and he sings in English." That cinched it. I knew the place because Maurice had taken me there and the American musician was a good entertainer.

We set off, walking to the piano bar. Arriving just before midnight as the place started to fill up, we got a good table, near the front of the room. When Joe played the opening chords to "Strangers in the Night," a lump formed in my throat. Leaning my head against the wall, I remembered

Maurice's first kiss, right here while those same notes had played. Yes, it all seemed sappy now but it hadn't then.

The bar grew smoky and mellow. The Burkes sang along with the songs we all knew as we clapped our hands and snapped our fingers at the more raucous ones.

A tall dark-haired man came in. Handsome, in a suave, striking way, he was elegantly dressed in a navy blue suit that fit him well. His dark eyes flashed as he searched for whomever he had arranged to meet.

I guessed he was not more than thirty-five, if that. He spotted his friends and made his way across the room to a table where three women waited for him. They looked like sisters or relatives. The greetings were in that familiar mixture of French and Arabic. Were they Lebanese?

Though I tried to follow their conversation, the noise and music prevented my eavesdropping. For the ensuing half hour, I glanced his way often. He noticed and took a long look of his own, despite the efforts we both made to conceal this, from those we were with. Suddenly he rose to leave, and followed the three women out the door. As he passed our table, he winked and smiled at me.

There goes the best thing I've seen in ages, I thought, already pining for this "tall, dark, handsome stranger" as that silly horoscope paragraph had predicted.

Less than twenty minutes later he returned with another man and my spirits rose. He chose to sit at the closest available table, facing me. "*Helwa, helwa*" (pretty, pretty) he said to his friend in Arabic, indicating my direction. This emboldened me, despite my blush reddened cheeks. Returning his gaze was harder now. Inside me a silent argument began.

"Well, he walked out the door once already. Will you let him go again and do nothing? What can I do? Think of something woman! You may never get another chance. And you'll regret it if you just sit here like a bump on a log."

I stared at the damp napkin under my Campari and soda glass with its melting ice. Carefully tearing off a dry corner, I found the pen in my evening purse and wrote my name and phone number on the scrap of paper. Folding it into a small square, I put away my pen and glanced around the table. No one had paid any attention to what I was doing. They were busy watching Joe Turner and talking to each other. The people at the next table were leaving. It was three o'clock in the morning. The Burkes had decided to call it a night and go home to make us all breakfast at their place.

While Tom Burke signaled the *vestiaire* (cloakroom clerk) for our jackets, I looked at the folded napkin still in my palm.

"Do it," prompted the inner voice.

I had never done anything like this before. At the time, I didn't see it as a reversal of roles. Although I had much to learn, I'd finally taken the predator's initiative, after being the prey for so long.

Hanging back to leave last, I dawdled getting my jacket on. As the others threaded past the tables, heading for the exit, I quickly leant across the empty table separating me from this compelling stranger, and slid the note across in his direction.

Not daring to look back until I reached the door, I turned to see his eyes following me. With a tilt of his head, he silently inquired whether the note was meant for him. With a nod, I left the club, my inflamed cheeks slapped by the cold night air outside. Shocked back into my senses, I confessed what I had done, as we walked back to the Burkes hungry for scrambled eggs and bacon.

Janet was the most surprised.

"He probably thinks I'm interested in him," I fibbed. "Won't he be disappointed when I ask him if he knows Georgina!"

To be fair, the competing desires — for love and truth — were moving me so fast, I could barely keep up.

Before crawling into bed that morning, I pulled the heavy drapes over the long French windows, to keep the sun out. After being so desperate for sunlight this winter in Paris, there was now a surfeit of it. Lying awake I wondered what would come of this, if anything. Would the stranger call? Would Maurice? And Bernard, what about him? It was Georgina's call I really wanted! Could my brashness at Calvados be blamed on that horoscope prediction?

This new man was far more to my liking than the blond Bernard. I giggled under the sheets. What will I do if this stranger calls? Having never taken the initiative like this I was out of my depth. But reviewing the day as a whole, I was glad to have gone out and had fun with my friends. Instead of succumbing to the sadness lurking beneath the surface, normal things had excited me.

* * * *

The next night, as I undressed for bed the phone rang. It was the stranger from Calvados. For twenty minutes we chatted in French. As soon as we hung up, I wrote in my journal:

In less than five hours I have to get up for the Easter sunrise service at the American Church with the Burkes but I am too excited to sleep. The man I gave my number to last night just called. His name is Omar Chaker. He's not Lebanese, he's Tunisian. He said he was calling from the Hotel George V. Hum.

He said he works for the Saudi prince, Mishari bin Abdul al Aziz, one of King Fahd's brothers. Haven't I heard of him before? Will double check. We even have Saudi Arabia in common. I liked his voice very much, and his well spoken French.

He handled the conversation well, not too slick, just nervous enough, but with an underlying confidence about handling women. My French is better when I'm not so unnerved. We arranged to meet Monday afternoon.

I hope he's not a pimp for the prince. Or a gigolo.

I have to find out as much as I can about him and whether he's married or not. Ugh. No more married men after Maurice.

We explained about ourselves. He's been coming to France for fourteen years. I asked if he'd ever been to the US. No. I doubt he speaks any English.

He said he was impressed by how discreet I'd been. He liked that. How curious and exciting all this is. Am I ready for another adventure?

And Maurice? Well he hasn't called, that I know of, since he left for the US. I have the feeling we will never see each other again.

I'd like to look into the eyes of this Omar and study his face, to discover why I find him so attractive. What are the actual ingredients? He was charming when I said I was new to Paris. He wants to show me around. I can hear my own heartbeats in my chest now, thump thump. The phantom lover, what every woman wants, "a tall dark handsome stranger." What a silly girl.

I closed my notebook and wrapped my fingers around my Ayat al-Kursi amulet on its neck chain. Something had to protect me during such reckless times. We had already agreed to meet on Monday afternoon. I slept dreamlessly and deep.

When the alarm rang, it was still dark out. I rose and dressed quickly, taking the stairs and crossing the cobblestoned courtyard to let myself out the big red door as quietly as possible. The black sky was shedding its inky depths. At the eastern edge a pale brightness was peeling the blackness back. On Pont Marie I stopped to regard the River Seine. At this hour the waters were calm. Fish rose to snatch bits of flotsam from the dark surface, like feeders from the subconscious, nibbling at the dregs of a dissolving reality.

Looking back up at the massive stones of my 15 Quai de Bourbon home, I craned my neck to see the window I had looked out of so often lately. During the recent string of sunny days, I had parked myself at the dining room table beside that window, writing for hours, working on my poems and questions for Georgina. In that calm place, peace was palatable. I faced an inner courtyard protected from the clamoring, warring world. Surrounded by the waters of the River Seine, my island was accessible only by bridge. Île Saint-Louis was just what I needed, though I had not consciously asked for these elements. My innermost urgings had brought me here and provided what was required. Once again I had "floated up" into what was right. Logic alone never would have steered me here.

But I couldn't hide on my isle and keep the world at bay. How to go forward and balance these forces of intuition and intellect? One focused inward and the other outward. What synthesized them? From inside my studio I had looked out over the Paris rooftops, with their punctuation of black chimney pipes, remembering the deeper truth of the stones beneath. They supported everything making a solid foundation. That's what I wanted, the bedrock of solidity, as decisive and enduring as the cobblestones of this city's streets and courtyards. Standing on Pont Marie, I leaned against its ancient side, realizing stones also built bridges.

And what do bridges do? They join what is separate. They convey goods and people back and forth. Paris is a bridge and living here will teach me to bridge what's broken inside me. Until now I had thought Georgina was my bridge back to Beirut, but both of us were here in Paris trying to bridge the gap between our ruptured former lives and whatever the future held. Though I had yet to hear from her, my stubborn trust in the workings of the universe still buoyed me. Things had unfolded since my move to Paris. Despite the sad costs, I was intact, enough to feel both ecstasy and pain. The darkness had not numbed me nor snuffed out my light. Remaining a lonely island would not help me persevere. These waxing and waning cycles had been endured like the moon and its phases. Georgina, Waddah, and Maurice had their own decisions to make. It was not my place to force anybody to change though I believed we could. And since things rarely go our way, what we do when they don't, makes all the difference. Releasing former desires makes room for new ones.

The waking birds began to chirp. The April air smelled morning fresh and I breathed it in deeply before Easter holiday traffic could taint it. The slanting light of the rising sun encouraged my surrender of the wintery Paris grey. How familiar this streaming spring light was. It was Mediterranean, the same azure brilliance that illuminates Beirut, Nice, and Athens, and the ruins of former Roman, Greek, and Phoenician civilizations. The sun's light was not the same in New York. Here it glanced off seven hundred year old walls made of pale granite as ancient as the Earth Herself. I invited their reflected endurance in, to soften and strengthen me as I leant towards the light streaming across Pont Marie. This sunlight, this river water, and this quiet were the medicines my soul had pined for. The bird songs perfectly accompanied the swelling April light.

Later that day, after the sunrise Easter services and a holiday meal with the Burkes, I went home to my island studio. Flinging the windows open to the church bells ringing out all over Paris, I celebrated the Resurrection. Having never heard such sounds before, my body quivered with the joyful clanging as it echoed throughout the city, sensing the possibility of new beginnings for me too.

That Monday morning I could not make up my mind about a single thing. Whirling around my little apartment, grabbing pieces of clothing out of the closet, I couldn't decide what to wear or even how to fix my hair. A mixture of hope and dread regarded me from the mirror as I brushed my teeth. My stomach roiled with anticipation. Something else was vying for my attention. Was common sense trying to warn me? At two o'clock in the afternoon, a total stranger, this man Omar would be coming here, where I live alone.

Why am I taking such risks? What's propelling me? I pushed these concerns out of my mind and focused on immediate practical considerations. What shall I say when I open the door? Should I offer my hand? Or let him kiss my cheeks? Was he more Arab or French at this point? Would we sit on the couch? Should I offer him a chair? Which refreshments? Did he smoke? Or drink? Would he hold my hand? Would I chatter too much from nerves?

How far would things go? If he kisses me I'll swoon. It will never stop there. One touch and I'll be a goner.

It was both thrilling and alarming to realize this. He could be an axe-murderer, a drug smuggler, or anything else. Finally settling upon a lavender blouse and a skirt and jacket ensemble, I braided my hair and slid the pair of crystal-decorated combs Zvonimir had gifted me in January as the final touch. Don't lose your head. Remember the results of other adventures. Various scenarios jumbled my thoughts.

At two o'clock he called, saying he'd been up till past five in the morning, but he had just finished showering and dressing, and would be right over, in fifteen minutes.

I took out my journal to steady myself and wrote at the top of a fresh page:

April 23, 1984.

Two hours later, I scribbled in a great rush:

Omar just left. Everything happened as I imagined. He even used the word "phantom" more than once. My god, what will happen next?

He wanted nothing to drink. He kissed me on both cheeks upon arrival and then sat on the sofa. I flitted around the room for a while. Eventually he invited me to sit beside him on the couch. We talked for about an hour.

He noticed there were no ashtrays and asked if I smoked.

"I never have."

"Me either," he replied.

I added, "To kiss a man who smokes is like kissing an ashtray".

With that he pulled me toward him and kissed me for the longest, loveliest time, with those full dark lips and that insistent masterful tongue. No turning back after that.

I slid onto the floor on my knees between his legs and looked and looked at his face, studying those beautiful eyes. A scar on his left brow. I will ask about it next time. His face has quite a lot of flesh on it, but it is all in the right places. He has real cheeks. The mouth is…deadly. I remember undoing my braid, and removing my earrings and hair combs while he kissed me.

"It's too hot with your jacket on, non?"

He stood up to remove it pulling me up as he rose from the couch. And then we were pressed together, our full lengths in a long embrace. After the jacket had come off I helped him out of his shirt. The clothing was all very fine; a double-breasted silk blend suit with grey, black, and perhaps a line of blue woven into the Italian made fabric. The tie was grey silk and the shirt polished cotton. How tart and male he smelled as I slipped his arms from his sleeves. This is what they mean when they say, "It's chemistry."

And then we went up the steps to my bed in its alcove. Everything was heavenly, just the right mixture of tenderness and force. Oh the wonder and delight of pleasure. And this afterglow, feeling swollen and plush. Grateful to be on birth control.

I put down my pen after scrawling this, remembering the sight in the mirror afterwards, as he stood behind me knotting his tie.

"What have I done?" I said in French, regarding our reflections.

"I can tell you don't do this all the time," he said, smiling as he wrapped his arms around me, watching my reflection, my face reddening.

Then he had to leave, back to the Hotel George V for some reception. He said he'd call.

What happens now?

I didn't know what to do with myself after he left, unable to concentrate, read, or write letters. All I could think about was Omar. He had said I was so *douce* (soft) and I had told him he was so *beau* all over. He speaks no English.

Turning on the television failed to distract me. Only one week remained before I had to leave Paris for work in the US, for a month or more. What would happen with this Omar in my absence? Since I could not bear being alone in my apartment after he left, I took a brisk walk around Île Saint-Louis, determined to calm myself down by wearing myself out. As my footsteps covered the pavement, I reviewed our conversation topics, remembering I had asked him about Georgina.

He did not know her but he had a rich Lebanese lady friend who might be able to help. I bet he has a lot of lady friends. He had made a comment about how "women always get what they want."

As I strode along the now familiar quays I thought yes, sometimes we do.

We talked about how we both knew this would happen, in that first moment at Calvados, when seeing each other. He related a similar incident, with a princess from one of the Gulf countries, about a year ago. She'd noticed him in another Paris hotel. Being veiled, only her eyes were visible to him, and her teeth shining from behind the gossamer thin black fabric. This had excited him, a powerful reminder of his boyhood in Sfax, his Tunisian hometown, when the sight of an ankle, much less the knee of a woman had thrilled him.

The next afternoon a black servant woman from the princess' entourage passed him a note while he bought a newspaper in the hotel lobby. The only thing written on the scrap of paper was a room number. He went straight to that room and knocked on the door.

She was waiting for him, alone, unveiled, and very beautiful. They made passionate love the entire afternoon, knowing they would never see each other again as it was too dangerous. In Islamic countries governed by Sharia law, such behavior still carries a death sentence.

He also explained the reasons for his erratic schedule, speaking of what it was like, working for a Saudi prince. After living there, I could fully imagine his situation. I knew how Saudis were, especially the royals, who expected you to be at their constant beck and call. There were no established working hours. You were at their disposal. If you did not understand and accept this, it was impossible to work with them.

Omar said he would have no real private life until the prince left Paris, which would not be too much longer. He assured me we would make up for lost time before he returned to Tunisia where he was furnishing his house and planning to ship a car back.

Arab men were expected to have a furnished house ready to bring a bride home to. Most self-respecting Arab fathers insisted that their daughters marry men who could provide this much for them at least. Omar is sure ripe for wedding if he hasn't already. He'd denied being married when I'd asked him.

I loved the sound of his name. The fact that it had no previous personal connotations was a relief. In Arabic, Omar meant eloquent speaker. Was he a "silver tongued devil?" Of course there was Omar Khayyam (1048-1131) the great Persian Muslim poet who wrote "a loaf of bread, a jug of wine, and thou beside me..." and Omar Sharif, the Egyptian actor. Wasn't there a famous, Caliph Omar II, who transformed Islam into an imperial power? My Omar was probably named after a relative, I guessed.

Love drunk, lust drunk. As we made love, I whispered his name over and over as though chanting a spell. "Omary, ya Omary," I said, adding the "y" to make him "my Omar." Close Arab friends had continued to call me "Cyndy" long after I insisted everyone else call me Cynthia. So much of my love life had not been in English.

At the doorway, when we said goodbye, I told him, "*Bayti zay batik.*"

This meant "my house is yours" in Arabic, inferring he was welcome here any time. I understood our trysts would be on a "catch as catch can" basis until the prince left town: stolen hours, on short notice, like these first two this afternoon.

He said he would come and go *comme un fantôme* (like a phantom).

Recalling this made me shiver for it was exactly what I'd imagined him to be.

Returning from my walk, I heard the phone ring while climbing the wide stone staircase, and hurried to my door, pulling out my key. It was Omar, asking how I was, telling me he missed me already. He asked for the downstairs door code. No one could pass the heavy red wooden gate after eight when the concierge shut it for the night.

I hesitated. This was dangerous. Although, I could still refuse him entry at my door once he had crossed the courtyard, if I didn't want to let him in for whatever reason.

But hadn't I let him in already?

A bit late now for second thoughts, yet I knew this step would put me at his convenience. It gave me pause. Some of my wits were left, even if I didn't want to listen.

I intoned the sequence of letters and numbers once. He said he had to go for now.

As my hand dropped the telephone receiver back into its cradle I asked myself, what do I really know about this man? We have yet to discuss the regular things, like our ages and our families. I have no idea where he stays in Paris when not at the hotel with the prince. Does he have relatives here like so many North Africans do?

Had he ever been to university? What other kinds of work had he done? While mentioning the places I'd lived, I had asked him about Lebanon.

He'd said he had never been there. On the heels of that exchange he had asked me if I had ever been *déçue*. In French this word conveyed more than the English translation "deceived" or "disillusioned."

"Yes," I'd answered immediately. "J'étais déçue par Le Liban," (I was deceived by Lebanon). Had he expected me to name a person? One was not generally deceived by something as abstract as a country. Deception was personal, not symbolic.

I had fallen for Lebanon's beauty and its glamor. A bit like this Omar I reflected wryly. Yet I had been so wrong to fall in love with a place where so many terrible things had happened. Where "friends" had degenerated into killers. Where I'd almost lost my own family.

Some called Beirut, the "sunny place for shady people." A beguiling, belly dancer of a city, displaying its brazen charms, it relished witnessing our capitulation. It had fooled so many. Perhaps this has something to do with our unacknowledged psychological shadows?

Maybe Omar was the deceiver. Something had prompted that question. His beauty enchanted and motivated me to a new degree but now that my daring note had beckoned him, I did not know how to take the lead. Normally we women did the attracting and spun the charming web. We were the targets. We didn't shoot the arrows. Georgina knew this. Had her beauty deceived or betrayed her or others? Beauty inspired projections, predators, and possessiveness. The opposite of beauty was ugliness, the horror of random chaos, the indiscriminate violence committed by human beasts devolved to utter baselessness.

When I laid my head on the pillow that night the memories welled up. *Beyrouth*, that doomed city, of so many spellings and incarnations. An impressionable eight-year-old when first seeing it in 1962, I remembered checking into the brand new Intercontinental Hotel The Phoenicia. As we drew up to the entrance, white-gloved doormen in uniforms opened the door of our taxi from the airport. They held the plate glass doors open as we strode in to cross the polished stone floors of the expansive lobby. Four hundred and fifty rooms were arranged around its open white square interior, its architectural design inspired by the Moors AlHambra in Spain. The fretted stone balconies invited the Mediterranean breezes to pass through. An oval swimming pool graced its center, with intricately tiled mosaics in a chartreuse and azure color scheme. At the deep end, an underwater bar. The word Phoenicia held magic for me, though now the once magnificent hotel was a blackened bullet-riddled hulk, frequented by snipers with telescopic rifle sights these days.

The Phoenicia was named after the ancient Phoenicians who had ruled an extensive trading empire when Europeans were still cutting their clothing off once a year to take a May Day bath. Beirut was thriving then, as a commercial hub, known to the Greeks and Romans centuries before Paris was settled and France became a nation. Famed for their maritime skills, and their monopoly of the purple dye used for royal clothing, the Phoenicians developed the first phonetic alphabet, a contribution that lives on in the languages we use today.

As a kid I knew none of this history, yet the Beirut of the 1960s had enchanted me. Before moving to Lebanon for boarding school in the summer of 1970, I had often gone there for dental and doctor visits as well as vacations. Escaping the restrictions of the Arabian Desert, we relished the sophisticated Levant with its freedom of choice in music, fashion, and movies. Beirut was the place of so many firsts: my first taste of vichyssoise and my first fiancé but it was also where I had my first disillusionments and deceptions, and seen the truth of man's murderousness.

I remembered Salim El Lawzi, the well-known Lebanese journalist and publisher, last seen alive in Beirut. We'd met at a New York dinner party with UN delegates during my journalism school days in 1978. In 1980, while making a risky trip back to Beirut for his mother's funeral, he went missing. Days later his mutilated corpse was found in a ditch. His fingers had been burnt off with battery acid. What had he known that was worth doing this? His severed penis was stuffed in his mouth. Who did such things?

Carolyn Forché, the poet had written, "There is nothing one man will not do to another." When hearing her read her war poems aloud in a university hall, the tears ran down my cheeks. In her book, *The Country Between Us*, she bore witness to the atrocities committed by government goons in El Salvador. One of the generals there had invited her to dinner. After the meal, he dumped a bag of dried human ears onto the table to show off his trophies. Dropping one into a glass of water, she'd watched it swell as if still capable of listening. Strangely it had been a great relief to me, to know someone else understood these horrors. And, she had found a way to respond to them, and survive without becoming another victim or victimizer.

Tonight in Paris, as I drifted towards sleep, the image of the old whore bubbled up again. Dangling from the electrical cord, she hung in an empty Beirut apartment. The windows were open or missing and the wind gusted through, tainted with the unforgettable stench of burnt flesh. Spent, like Corniche Mary, who had plied her trade near our boarding dormitory, with her paunchy powered cheeks and smeared lipstick.

If I had stayed would that have been my fate? Or Georgina's? Did the world in general reduce women or was it Beirut in particular, warning me?

* * * *

The next day while doing my grocery shopping, I compared the real Paris, France with the "Paris of the Middle East." Their geographies had determined their fates. The French called their homeland the Isle de France with Paris at its heart center. Though landlocked, the city straddled the fluid River Seine. By contrast, Beirut is a seaside port, hemmed in by mountains. Built at the desert's end, Beirut edged Europe, laying across the same Mediterranean Sea, whose waves lap the southern shores of France. Both cities had been pagan, centuries before labels like Jewish, Christian, or Muslim existed. And since their conversions to monotheistic religions, they had endured more than a fair share of violence. Capitals of empires, both had survived successes and starvations, as their fortunes rose or fell. The same marauding Roman, Mongol, and European troops had invaded their territories and both dealt with terrorism, refugees, and corruption today.

"The French would sell the gold from their grandmothers teeth," my father had declared more than once, though I could not remember him citing a single example to support this declaration. What rankled me were the French collaborators, who bowed to the Nazis, once they rolled into France in 1942. Three years later, after the defeat of Germany, many claimed to have been in the Resistance. Yet during the Vichy regime of Marshal Philippe Pétain, almost 80,000 Jewish refugees and French citizens had been rounded up, and sent to concentration camps. The city would have been destroyed however if Paris had been fought over, street by street like Beirut had been. I had to wonder what would happen to the US, if a tyrant took over. How many Americans would collaborate or choose to resist?

Every country sought to maximize their advantages, and leverage their assets, geographic and otherwise. The Lebanese had no oil wells or diamond mines and few natural resources beyond their strategic locale and their cedars, so they became traders. Their mountain forests had provided the lumber prized by Phoenician ship builders and was used for building the first Jewish temple in Jerusalem. The cedars of Lebanon are mentioned more than a hundred times in the Bible. The Crusaders had passed through Lebanon on their way to and from the Holy Land. Like most small nations, servicing the needs of empires, the Lebanese excelled at playing two (or more) sides against each other. Playing the middleman role for centuries, they were relationship experts and expediters who owed their survival to their skills at exploitation.

Anything could be arranged, for a fee. Without asking too many questions, they provided banking services, luxury apartments, or a wink from airport customs officials. Kalashnikov machine guns, missiles, hashish, boys, women, or bogus identity papers were easily procured. Had opportunistic venality destroyed Lebanon? Corruption existed in France too, but so did the Napoleonic Code of 1804, which banished the most egregious privileges of nobility and instituted civil law and a meritocracy. In a kingdom of vying middlemen, everyone was on the take, obligated to do favors, and offer preferential treatment in the absence of impartial judges who held the law above personal relationships. When everything and everyone was for sale, no one could be trusted.

Even the great French General De Gaulle had confessed, "I left for the complicated Orient with simple ideas," when he ordered the withdrawal of his troops from Lebanon in 1946.

I was struck by the fact that the seals of both cities featured ships. The motto of Paris was *Fluctuat nec mergitur*, Latin for "tossed but not sunk." And Beirut's motto? I would have to find out.

Browsing the shelves of Paris's best-known English bookstore, Shakespeare & Co. later that day, I found the answer. Also in Latin it was, *Berytus Nutrix Legum*, meaning the Mother of Laws. What to make of this?

Back at the apartment, engrossed in a deeper study of Beirut's history, my phone rang. Bernard's voice brought me back to France.

"I've been trying to reach you," he said, peevishly. "But you never seem to be home."

"Sorry. I have been out quite a lot lately," I replied.

"The dinner party I am planning had to be postponed to the coming weekend. Can you come?" he asked.

As I listened, my impression of him, from our rendezvous at Place Saint Michel returned. I told him a little white lie. "I'd love to come, but I'm leaving for work in New York this Saturday. Maybe another time, when I return in a month or two."

I hung up. It was almost true. I would be leaving, but not until Monday. In the meantime, I'd rather be free to see Omar. He seemed more familiar. Conditioned by life in the Arab world long before we ever met, I felt as if I knew him. And we were both foreigners in France, this third place, in between our cultures of origin.

Readying for bed that night, I wondered if my phantom would ever visit again. Would I tell anyone about him? Imagining reactions to this news, I recalled how my parents had never liked anyone I'd been attracted to. It was far too early to mention Omar. Their preconceptions would blind them to the actual man. Since leaving Lebanon, my mother regularly said, "Arab is a four letter word."

Ouch. And this one doesn't even speak English.

Waddah, Maurice, and now Omar. Which was the one? None? Were these men consolations or deviations? My goal was to work with Georgina. Had she dated much since her husband's demise? I decided to call Carla upon my return to the US. Consulting objective feedback from the universe — aka intuition — was one way to allow for corrective instructions.

* * * *

Riding the metro back from a poetry reading the following afternoon, I marveled at how Paris felt like home already. No longer a tourist, I had rent to pay, phone, electric, and gas bills too. I wrote *cheques* on my own French franc account, and knew exactly when the sun came through my windows, and where to buy pink grapefruits and better bread for the same price. Melting into the streams of people flowing through the underground tunnels to and from the trains, I felt a sense of belonging. What a relief from the intractable loyalty contest between America and the Middle East. Among these third place multitudes, I was not an oddity. The variegated bouquet of nationalities, with their lively, alternatives were energizing. The African women sitting near me, with artfully wrapped turbans of brightly patterned cloth, had just finished their shopping at the same open-air market. Each of us going home with our goodies, small sweet melons, and bulbous *aubergines*. In the metro's fluorescent lighting, their generous flesh glowed purplish, the same hue as the skins of the eggplants.

I loved riding these trains and popping up anywhere in this delectable city. The metro opened in 1900, the year my grandmother was born. Here we ride on rubber tires. None of the horrible screeching of metal wheels on metal rails like New York's subway. These doors open only when necessary, avoiding the senseless automated clanging of every door at every stop. First and second-class car distinctions are waived after 7:00 p.m. Without them, class-conscious Parisians may never have agreed to try public transport. Free from the French pecking order, I'm delighted when French strangers ask me for directions.

But I felt quite different recently when accosted by an American, with a noticeable Brooklyn accent, while passing through my favorite tiny park, behind the Notre Dame cathedral.

"Where's the entrance to this place?" she demanded, with no preamble.

I responded in French, *"Je ne sais pas madame. Je ne peux pas vous aider."* Afterwards, I regretted my refusal to help, as it probably reinforced her impression the French were rude, yet she was the one who had not been polite. "Excuse me? Please? Can you help me?" Those words are far more likely to inspire assistance than acting as if everyone in Paris is standing around waiting to be a tour guide.

Occasionally, when turning a corner on my long walks, it suddenly felt like I was back in Beirut: the scale of the buildings, the architecture, and the balconies. In America the cities are so utilitarian. Some don't have sidewalks anymore, like Houston, which was built for cars. I did not miss mine, with parking practically nonexistent on Île Saint-Louis. How often had I lingered in a cafe in America? Rarely. In my experience, Americans seemed to prefer watching television instead of each other. Leaving the metro I noticed a real dandy. He sat outside, sporting a jaunty hat, a cane, and pinky rings. Smartly erect, he took in the ladies, without ogling them. Ah, the romance of Paris, where half the population are lovers and the other half are looking to be. Ingénues soon lose their naiveté in this city, overflowing with men and women eager to indulge, or take advantage of them.

Chapter 10

MON FANTÔME /
MY PHANTOM

There was a door to which I found no key:
there was a veil through which I might not see.

— OMAR KHAYYAM

On Friday night Mon Fantôme Omar called, to say he might be able to visit on Saturday. "But not till after midnight at the earliest, when I finish with the prince."

Hoping we'd brunch together in the morning after a night of love, I stocked my fridge with treats. With fresh flowers in the vase, the scent of furniture polish lingered in the air, after my housekeeping exertions. At 3:00 a.m. perfumed and prepared, wrapped in a turquoise negligee, I fell asleep, after straining to hear the familiar click of the big, red wooden door opening and the measured footfalls of this particular man, crossing the cobblestoned courtyard before climbing the steps to my door.

How does one summon a phantom? Can I will him to appear?

When the doorbell rang I woke instantly and bolted down the stairs from my loggia bed loft. A glimpse of my wide-eyed self in the mirror, my loose hair flowing like a shadowy cloak.

Omar took me in his arms with a grin, explaining how he'd just gotten away from them. "The Prince and his entourage dined at one of the Oriental cabarets." The belly dancers gyrate till dawn in those places, as long as there are customers. His hair and clothing stank of cigarettes.

"What time is it? I fell asleep."

"It's 4:00 a.m." he replied, his eyes bright as he pressed me harder to him. As I melted, he stiffened in anticipation. A quick visit to the bathroom and then I climbed back up the steps to my bed. Omar was already undressed and lying there, holding the sheet open to welcome me between

161

the covers.

Sliding in, I wanted to feast my eyes on the sight of this phantom, unable to get over how powerfully his presence affected me. For sheer maleness, only Moudi ever came close to this.

"I missed you," he said.

Down I descended into the depths of his eyes thinking this is what magic is. Words only break the spell.

"It's as if we've known each other for years," he said gathering me to him as the kisses began.

As the fever of our movements mounted I gasped, "I'm a little afraid of you...you're so strong."

Breathing heavily, he answered, "But you like this. I want to be a little savage with you, to hurt you a little."

How different these words sounded in French. He bit my cheek and rolled me over to take his beautiful brown weight.

Afterwards, we went to wash, and then returned to bed with chilled feet and little shivers. He warmed me, kissing my ears and neck. I lifted the covers again to appreciate his beauty. I wanted to remember every detail, to absorb the why of this mystery. I stroked his belly, his hipbones, and his smooth chest. My finger traced the upper muscling of his arm, traveling down to the bend in his elbow, marveling all the way. What part of him will become my favorite spot? The hollow between the neck and curve of the collarbone had been my special place on Moudi's body.

"Omary, Omary, Omary," I whispered, closing my eyes and nestling against him. Gently he turned me on my side and curled his body around mine, his hand cradling my cheek. We slept like silverware in a drawer.

In the morning his erection woke me pressing against my buttocks. Through the drawn curtains, the sunlight made a weak attempt to enter the room as he took me again with a force that left me dizzy. I cried out, grabbing the pillow to muffle my pleasure, lest the neighbors hear the sounds of a phantom possessing me.

That morning while he showered and dressed, I fixed a demitasse of Arabic coffee and set out some brunch. Words seemed superfluous. Nevertheless I had to tell him I was leaving the following day. Somewhat shy with each other now, as we sat in daylight at the table, I broached the subject.

"I have to go back to the US for a month or more to work. Could you come meet me in America, while I'm there? I'd like you to see my country."

"Pas maintenant" (not now), he explained, reminding me of his plans to return to Tunisia, with the shipment of furniture for his house and a car. "Why don't you come to Tunisia instead?"

Then I asked him, "Are you married?"

"No, but I hope to be someday. I want to have a family. You know the

Oriental mentality."

Yes, I do. He says he is thirty-three and his birthday is in May, when I asked those questions next.

"Guess how old I am?"

"Twenty-six, twenty-seven?" he smiled.

"Thirty!" I said, "And proud of every year!"

We were still laughing when he rose to go. He held me tight again, pressing his body to the length of mine, swaying slightly. This made me want to dance naked with him. Maybe next time. My eyes were closed. Tenderly he kissed the lids.

Dreamily I asked, "What would you like me to bring you from America?"

"Nothing, except you, returned to me in a golden wrapper!" he said, hugging me harder.

We kissed intensely for a final time before letting go. Holding the door open, I watched him descend the curving stone steps until he was out of sight. Running to the window, I watched him cross the courtyard below. He looked up, saw me, and smiled, lifting his fingers to blow me a kiss.

Returning to bed, I held his pillow to my face, my nostrils flaring with the effort of catching one more whiff of him before falling back to sleep. Upon waking I carefully gathered the few strands of his hair from the yellow bed sheets. Taping them into my journal before beginning the next entry, I admitted with my pen, "I am totally besotted with this man."

* * * *

As my Air France jet took off the following day, I watched Paris shrink through the oval Plexiglas of my window seat. Loath to be pulled away from Omar and this city, I thought of how he had called me *Iyuni* (my eyes in Arabic) when he phoned to say goodbye. During our last encounter he used the term *Hayati* (my life). How many years since my heart had warmed to those endearments?

My Lebanese fiancé Ayman had whispered them. My first man. Had he spoiled me or taught me well? Six months he had waited, just to kiss me. Still a virgin at eighteen, it sounded silly to say "I gave him my virginity" or he "took it," as if something had been lost. In truth, I gained so much that day. Initiated into this realm of lover's worship, my entire being had glowed when I returned to my school dormitory. After sharing that experience, I deeply valued shared ecstasy and its transformative powers.

As the plane climbed to cruising altitude that afternoon above the Atlantic Ocean, I remembered how my old Ayman differed from this new Omar. My former fiancé had been only twenty-two. How had he learned to revere the feminine? His Druze religion set him apart. A somewhat secretive sect, their mystical version of Islam forbade polygamy, slavery, and circumcision. They also advanced equality for women, and the separation of church and state, quite unusual for the Middle East. But being a Muslim minority had cost the Druze a thousand years of persecution. Ayman explained he had yet to learn about their faith practices because adherents are not fully initiated until they are in their forties, and mature enough for enlightenment and spiritual ecstasy. If we had married, what would have happened to us?

Remembering what we had shared reconnected me to the transformations those experiences inspired. Safely stored in my memories were the trips we had taken to the old stone house in Arsoun, a Druze enclave some twenty-five miles outside Beirut. The Choucaire family's ancestral land and terraced orchards spread out over the mountainside. Equally vivid in my memory were the rooms of his parents' apartment in Beirut. Georgina's Rue Verdun place was nearby in the same neighborhood. Had Ali Hassan Salameh initiated her into transformative states of ecstasy? Is that why she'd chosen to remain with him when she could have had most anyone else?

The afternoon when we sealed our bond in 1972, remains inscribed in myriad detail. We had gone to the Beirut apartment after his senior year classes at AUB that day, and my senior year classes at ACS. His mother had asked the maid to prepare my favorites: *fattoush*, a green salad with bits of toasted Arabic bread and lots of lemon juice and *rizer halib*, a delicious rice pudding, with *snobar*. I would not learn the English word for pine nuts for another decade. Jamila, the woman caretaker of the Arsoun mountain village home had shown me how to harvest them, carefully, from the cones. When the Syrian Army came over those mountains to occupy Lebanon, Jamila had been raped and killed.

Was ecstasy the only way to balance out all the trauma?

I refocused upon Ayman and his mother. A dark-haired, dark-eyed woman from Damascus, petite and plump she was still attractive in her soft way. Always polite and kind to me, I doubted I was her first choice for a daughter-in-law. Ayman was her only child, despite her attempts to have others. His parents may have been disturbed by the idea of their sole child marrying an American foreigner from outside their faith, yet as far as I knew, they had never actively opposed our relationship. Perhaps they expected our affair to run its natural course or thought it might be useful to have an American in the family in the future. Neither parent spoke a word of English. I spoke French with them. They had never been to England or America although they were sending their son to AUB.

The diploma of Ayman's father Chawkat was from Saint Cyr, the

French military academy, and was proudly displayed on the wall of his book-lined study in Beirut. Chawkat Choucaire still possessed the intimidating posture of an officer and spoke the fine French of the well educated. An urbane, dapper man in his late fifties, he often invited me to join him in his study while he drank coffee, smoked his pipe, and debated with his son. A life-sized photo of a smiling Gamal Abdul Nasser, the recently deceased Egyptian President also hung on the wall, along with a colored map of the Middle East, and another of the world. Chawkat greatly admired the charismatic Egyptian president and had served in his cabinet as Minister of Defense, when Egypt united with Syria to create the first United Arab Republic in 1958.

In that room, I met another politician the late Kamal Jumblatt and his son Walid. The tall, ascetic father Kamal was the leader of the Druze and a genuine mystic. The leading family of Syria the Assads were Alawites, another Muslim minority dating from the ninth century. The American government had judged Jumblatt's Progressive Socialist Party "too leftist" because of his non-alignment policy. Gazing out the window at the clouds below our plane today, I remembered his murder in the spring of 1977, five years after I'd shaken his hand. Everyone believed the Syrian dictator Hafez el Assad had ordered the hit. Rifaat el Assad, brother of Hafez, and the former vice president now lived in exile in Paris. A despised butcher of dissidents and opponents, Rifaat was no longer trusted by his own family, after planning a takeover when his brother was ill.

A series of coups had brought the Assad family into power in 1971 and they ruthlessly rid the country of alternatives afterwards. Power changed hands unpredictably in the Middle East. Ayman's father Chawkat had given up on the dream of a United Arab Republic when Nassar died suspiciously of a heart attack at age fifty-two. Once the Assad family seized hold in Syria, Chawkat departed Damascus forever, and retired from military life. Returning to Arsoun, he intended to spend his remaining days cultivating his olive and fruit trees on the parcel of mountainous land granted to the Choucaire family for previous service to the Ottoman Empire.

Ayman's ideas about power in his student days were evident in the posters of Fidel Castro and Che Guevara that hung on the back of his bedroom door. He'd even named my breasts Lenin and Trotsky, which was preferable to Stalin and Marx. On the day he had "rung the big bell," we had lunched with his parents, before retiring to the bedrooms for our siestas. I could still recall Ayman's heavy, wooden bed, with its dark carved headboard, hand embroidered sheets, and the long French pillow. I had wept in his arms from the sheer joy of sharing such wonderful pleasures.

Tiptoeing to wash in the bathroom afterwards, I'd taken care to be quiet, as his parents were still napping on the other side of the tiled wall. After straddling the white porcelain bidet I noticed the little cake of soap in its recessed wall holder, and the small white towel hanging conveniently near my knee and wanted to weep again.

Such great tenderness overcame me, for the woman sleeping on the other side of that wall. I felt happy to share these intimacies with her: this secret of ecstasy, this son, and even these porcelain fixtures. The memory bubbled up of when I had asked my mother about this extra plumbing the first time I'd seen a bidet in Cairo, Egypt. She said it was for washing your feet. Had her answer been in ignorance or reticence with me, her eight-year-old daughter? In our subsequent homes in Jeddah and Beirut, my mother had used the bidets as magazine racks or stuck plastic flower arrangements in them. I glanced around the airplane cabin now, recalling my father's tale about the Saudi King Khaled's personal Boeing 747 jet. An extra $250,000 had been spent to redesign the hydraulic system so it would provide enough pressure for powering the gold plated bidets on his private plane.

Although my initial introduction to womanhood had not gone so well, it had been a happy day when I went all the way with Ayman. Making love so delicately, bending his head between my thighs, there had been exquisite pleasure instead of blood and pain. I felt as though I'd entered another dimension. Had Ayman spoiled me? Or was this a right, to expect equality not shame, when sharing pleasure? That capacity for ecstasy had certainly seen me through many sorrows since. Omar had not yet worshiped at the fount of me, I thought euphemistically. My father's crude statements about such things had made me cringe as a teenager, yet there was some truth to them. I recalled my father's comment when my sister announced her engagement, "Does he ring the big bell?"

"Daddy! Really!" she had said, shushing him with exaggerated embarrassment.

* * * *

After chasing the afternoon sun across the Atlantic, our flight landed in New York. I hurried through immigration and baggage claim to catch another flight to Houston, Texas. There I would run a three-day program for General Dynamics employees on their way to live in Beni Suef, Egypt. They were part of the Peace Vector project, which had followed the historic Camp David agreement between Presidents Sadat and Carter. In the transit lounge, a man walked by carrying a bag with the familiar decals of Middle East Airlines MEA and SDI Saudi Arabia Airlines. Tears came to my eyes. For twenty-one years our lives had depended upon those two companies and the hooks of those decades were still deeply embedded in me.

After the training program in Texas, I flew back to New York to spend the weekend in Connecticut at my old place where Lynda now lived. Nothing had changed there: the brass bed, the yellow coverlet, the rugs, and other houses and streets were all where I had left them. But I felt different, no longer the same woman, though I could pretend to be.

* * * *

On my old commuter train to New York City that Monday morning, I wrote Omar a postcard, care of the Hotel George V. It pictured cowboy boots and the flag of the Lone Star State. At the office, I wrote another card to Georgina and tackled my phone call list. Next week I'd be running another pre-departure program on Egypt in New York, so I called my old beau Mahmoud to invite him to participate as a resource person again. Our office had already tried to reach him without success. When I dialed his home phone number a recording said it had been disconnected.

I tried his UN office and was told he was no longer in that department and there was no forwarding information. That was odd. Finally I tracked down our mutual friend, the man who had introduced us.

"He had his phone disconnected last week to get rid of the reporters. The press just wouldn't leave him alone."

"Why? What's happened?" I asked, panicking.

"You don't know?"

"No. I've moved to Paris. I'm only here on a visit."

"Oh. Well, his nineteen-year-old nephew committed suicide in his apartment. He got hold of Mahmoud's gun and shot himself in the head. Blood all over the place. I know. I saw it. He called me before he called the police."

My heart sank. "I can hardly believe it! Why? Why?"

"The kid flunked some qualifying test at a computer firm in New Jersey. He had a big fight with his father and left Cairo to come here and make his own life. He was a computer whiz back in Egypt and thought he would show his father. I don't understand the whole story but he did not do as well as he expected and was having trouble getting a job here.

"One afternoon while Mahmoud was at the office, his nephew found the gun, fired a few practice shots, and then shot himself."

I could vividly imagine the scene. Having seen that snub-nosed .38 special many times, I knew just where Moudi laid it down, on top of the bedroom dresser, each time he removed the revolver from its leather underarm holster. He had needed a gun for protection from Palestinians and others who wanted revenge after Egyptian President Sadat signed the US Peace Accords in 1978. Sadat had visited Israel in 1979 while I was working in Saudi Arabia. In the streets of Jeddah I had seen other Arabs spit upon Egyptian civilians because of what their leader had done. I recounted these details in my training programs about Egypt and other Middle East countries. Few Americans understood the risks Arabs took when "befriending" America or Israel. Perpetual war was more profitable. If we had wanted peace, the US might have had it long ago.

Mahmoud's pistol had lain beside an old June 1967 issue of Life magazine. For almost twenty years he kept that magazine on his dresser as a reminder of the humiliating defeat Egypt had suffered during the 1967 Six Day War with Israel. The cover story recounted the events of that June 5th morning. Mahmoud had been in the Egyptian Air Force then. As the Israeli jets arrived, he ran towards his Russian made fighter jet. Flying in below the radar, the Israeli pilots were not detected in their initial operation of that short and deadly war. They had strafed the airfield, buildings, and equipment, decimating Egyptian defenses. Using specialty bombs, designed by a French/Israeli company, they ripped the runway surfaces to shreds. This ensured no Egyptian fighter pilots could take off, if they and their planes had survived the three waves of air attacks. As bullets pounded his parked Russian MiG fighter jet, Moudi fell to the ground. This probably saved his life, though he had judged himself harshly, for lying in the sand pretending to be dead. The Israeli pilot had made one more pass over him to verify his demise.

Over 450 aircraft were destroyed at their bases across Egypt during the Six Day War. More than a hundred Egyptian pilots were killed along with many Egyptian Army soldiers fleeing the Sinai in trucks. Under the command of a female prime minister, Golda Meir, the IDF, and the small but nimble Israeli air force, also reduced Syrian and Jordanian air forces to rubble, winning a decisive victory, and more territory, via air superiority.

Six years later, during the Ramadan/Yom Kippur War of 1973, the Egyptians wreaked a terrible revenge upon the Israelis for those 1967 humiliations. As far as I knew, Moudi kept no souvenir of that victory, just the one detailing the prior shame.

"Where's Mahmoud now?" I asked our friend. I wanted to comfort him. How terrible to come home and find his nephew like that. His brain tissue, bone fragments, and viscera all over the walls. Reality is far worse than the special effects of films and television shows, which never capture the accompanying smells nor the way the bile rises in your throat and your body shakes in front of the actual carnage.

"He has gone back to Egypt, to take the body home to his uncle for burial."

I thanked him and hung up the phone. I got up, then sat down, with tears rolling down my face. Hunting for a tissue in my purse, I daubed my face, unable to sit still. I walked to my office window, my chest and throat burning with waves of rage, anger, and despair. The sheer waste of all the dying threatened to engulf us all. Looking down at the traffic on Lexington

Avenue, I remembered Khalil Hawy, the Lebanese poet. He'd jumped to his death from the cliffs at Beirut's Pigeon Rock in 1982 as the Israelis invaded his country. I had felt the same overwhelming desperation to escape such awful irreconcilable pain, the sort that made you lash out, pull a trigger, jump, or blow yourself up. Exploding was better than those unbearable feelings.

I remembered wanting to die even before the war. My despair over the unfairness and injustice in my own family, as well as the world made life seem hardly worth it. Why stay alive if only to suffer more of the same? One evening, I overheard a conversation Amal and my parents were having about me. Amal was the half Turkish, half Lebanese stewardess my father had been sleeping with for years. How could my mother not know this? Was she oblivious or just pretending to be? The three of them were sitting on the living room couch in our Rue May Ziade apartment in Beirut, discussing my relationship with that "Commie boyfriend" Ayman. Instead of facing their webs of deception, they were talking about how to punish me, because I had dared to continue meeting my fiancé in secret after my father had forbidden me to.

Listening undetected on the other side of the wall, I heard the full extent of their betrayals. At my father's urging, I had accepted Amal as a friend and co-worker. The two had taken me into their confidence, and I'd even visited their love nest with its animal print bedspread. I never breathed a word of this to my mother, who never took me into her confidence, or asked me anything. She never confronted dad about his drinking or philandering. Denial was her way. So I said nothing, incensed at them all.

Amal had pretended to care about me to gain my confidence. Meanwhile she reported everything I said about Ayman to my father. As heartbreaking as it was to hear Amal betray me, what compounded the felony was knowing my father was betraying my mother with her, and both my parents were conspiring with this poisonous third person to betray their own daughter. The three were determined to break my engagement with Ayman "once and for all."

Compared with their relationships, mine was clean and good and natural, a first love. How dare they attack me, the only person in a healthy, reasonable partnership! And were they really blind, or just turning a blind eye to their friend Mazen's long-term affair with my underage sister? Which was worse? My father's adultery? My mother's complicity? Or their pedophile friend, who had also tried with me?

So much dirt and deception! Who were they to judge me? Their slime threatened to engulf us all. Mazen had started with my sister Karen when she was fourteen, and never had any honorable intentions towards her. I had already gone off to boarding school by then, and he had just married Fatin, the Syrian bride his mother had chosen for him. His parents had insisted it was time for their eldest son to produce an heir. When he had wanted to marry his German girlfriend during his university days, his parents had threatened to disinherit him, and he'd succumbed to their pressures. After he told his girlfriend it was over between them, the German woman had stuck her head in the oven. Her death seemed to have killed something in Mazen too.

If this was how the rotten world worked, I wanted no part in it. I would rather check out. The betrayals had cut so deeply, I was hemorrhaging emotionally. Inside was a deepening pit of shattered trust, and I couldn't take it anymore. I had run out of options, and decided the pain would stop if my life did.

When I entered the living room my father lit into me, "You'll marry an Arab over my dead body!" Then he bellowed, "Have you slept with that creep?"

My "yes" practically blew the roof off of their Beirut apartment.

As the words and images of that day, a dozen years ago, rushed back, I could feel the cool ceramic tiles of the bathroom floor beneath me, for I'd gone there to escape the scene. After locking the door, I knelt beside the tub with the razor blade in my hand, not wanting to make a mess. I turned the spigot on and put my arms in the tub. With the water running, I got ready to cut across the skin of my left wrist, but paused. Which wrist to cut first? Being right handed, would my left have sufficient power to slice through my right wrist deep enough to do the job?

What saved me? My refusal to unlock the bathroom door that night meant my father had to break it open. But by then the crisis had been resolved for me. For the first time I heard it, the still small voice that came from within. "Don't do it. You don't have the problem. They have the problem. Just get out of here and everything will be alright." I dropped the razor blade just as the doorframe splintered.

My crumpled body was hoisted off the bathroom floor and put into bed. My mother came in afterwards to hiss at me. "Don't you know every father's daughter is a virgin until she marries? You shouldn't have told him."

"If he didn't want to know the truth, he shouldn't have asked," I replied.

Shortly after this, Doctor Amin Mousalli arrived at our apartment, summoned by his sister, Amal. This was the first time I had seen or heard about him. Opening his medical bag, he readied a syringe to give me an injection.

"You will sleep now, for about twelve hours. When you wake up, come to my office. Here's my card. We need to talk. You have to get out of here." Though we had never met before, I decided to follow his instructions as the sedative took effect.

That had been my last night in our Rue May Ziade home. More

deceptions were yet to come, but none so bitter as that night, early in my nineteenth year. Looking back, I saw more clearly how my fiancé Ayman and my father set up a false contest, trying to force me to choose between the two of them. This was about patriarchy, and two men squaring off, not what might be best for me. Ayman's father Chawkat met with my father and assured him of their positive intentions concerning marriage. They would accept me without a dowry (as was the custom) and agreed to pay my college tuition.

Dad refused, and recounted these details after the fact. I was not consulted, not permitted to speak for myself, not even present when they discussed my potential future. My father's preference for resolving issues by creating a crisis had always given him the upper hand. During the chaos his strategy caused, he retained the advantage. But forcing me to choose between Ayman or him backfired. To their surprise, I chose neither man. Instinctively I knew there must be another way, a third choice. Of course neither man had suggested this option. Perhaps they failed to imagine I would choose the freedom to live my own life.

Two years after that fateful event, on the night I turned twenty-one and my father shared his side of my conception story, he also complimented me.

"You know, I hated like hell to hear it, but if you had lied to me that night (about Ayman), you would still be a child in my eyes."

* * * *

Looking west across at the jagged Manhattan skyline, from my office window, I thought of how withdrawn and passive I had been over a decade ago. Rather than shout about their lies, and throw their betrayals in their faces, I kept quiet, never raising my voice to say what I knew to be true. Why? How did you defend yourself against a pack of liars? These people were supposed to protect and defend me, yet my parents had become my enemies. Their betrayals went the deepest. No words they might say would ever change the fact that they were not allies to each other, much less to me. They did not have my best interests at heart. The entire incident had stunned me into stoicism. This survival tactic had been my stance since childhood, when my father beat me with his belt. I held my emotions in, closed as tightly together as my lips, unwilling to give the bastard the satisfaction of seeing me cry.

The day after contemplating suicide, I moved in with Doctor Amin Mousalli and his Swiss wife, Francine. At their apartment, Amin filled in the missing details, about how long my father had been involved with his sister Amal. The affair had started in Jeddah, when Amal was a stewardess with Saudi Arabian Airlines and their relationship was the reason my father had taken the job in Lebanon. Another Mousalli sister was married to a Bin Laden, who provided Amal with a visa to live and work in Saudi Arabia. This wealthy Saudi brother-in-law had bankrolled Dr. Mousalli's gynecology and obstetrics clinic in Beirut where I worked as a receptionist. Among the patients were Saudi princesses, and other women, seeking to be remade into "virgins" before their weddings. There I also saw my first abortion. The woman was a Palestinian refugee from the camps who worked cleaning the clinic offices and the Mousallis apartment. She already had six children. I held her hand during the operation, performed by Dr. Mousalli, without anesthesia. He drew the line at some procedures however. One of his Bin Laden sister-in-laws asked him to surgically remove her young daughter's clitoris. When he told me he had refused, he said some old woman would probably do it with a razor blade in less than sanitary conditions and possibly cause an infection that might kill the child. Either way it would ruin her life. Female genital mutilation was not yet a household word but I would learn more about it by reading the 1977 book *The Hidden Face of Eve* by Egyptian doctor and first female Minister of Health, Nawal el Saaddawi.[33]

A few weeks after I moved in with them, Dr. Mousalli's Swiss wife, Francine, gave birth to their son Philippe. The delivery was difficult, and I became the nanny/au pair for the infant while his mother convalesced. Francine also had breast reduction surgery after giving birth and contracted a stubborn infection that refused to heal. Rather symbolic of the sickness of the whole situation, her husband, the doctor, took advantage of me then. This may have been his plan all along, for this was one way to get back at my father, for the adultery with his sister Amal. As far as I knew, Amal was still sleeping with my father, though I was no longer in touch with my family at that point. In the fresh bout of despair triggered by all this, I swallowed a bottle of pills. Dr. Mousalli pushed a tube down my throat and pumped out my stomach.

When my Lebanese residence permit ran out I got away. Leonie Farajallah's letter of recommendation secured my acceptance at a riding stables in Hertfordshire and I left for England to start my own life.[34]

---

[33] **Born in** 1931, Nawal el Saadawi is an Egyptian feminist writer, activist, physician, and psychiatrist who campaigned to outlaw the practice of female genital mutilation, which she underwent as a six-year-old. She has written many books on women in Islam, and was imprisoned in Egypt for her work. Many describe her as "the Simone de Beauvoir of the Arab World."

[34] I'd hear the rest of Leonie's story thirty years later. Another Beirut tragedy, the violence during the war had forced her to leave everything except her sons. She'd taken them to Sweden and divorced Kamal. All the horses had been shot dead in

For the next two years, I did not speak with my parents. Eventually moving to London, I found work at the United Arab Emirates Embassy, and was relieved to be earning my own living. Only after my independence was fully established did I agree to see my parents again. After my father's revelations about my conception, and my mother's silence, I often wondered about her resentment towards me. Did she get pregnant with me by mistake or on purpose? Knowing which might explain why our relationship had often been so strained. Since I am not sure if she would tell me the truth, I never asked her. After all, in those crucial moments when I was nineteen — the same age my father was when he married her — my mother had rebuked me for not lying.

Our rift remained, only partially mended. The war had further eroded my trust. No wonder I needed the truth so badly. I turned from the window to the work files on my desk. That pre-departure program still had to be staffed. "Duty calls" as my father would say.

* * * *

The next day at the office, my colleagues invited me for drinks after work. They wanted to hear about Paris. What was life like over there? What could I say? They harbored such romantic notions of the place. Describing my apartment and detailing my days could not convey the effects Paris had wrought inside of me. The importance of Paris was not how the city looked but how we responded to what it stimulated in us. I tried to explain how Paris had brought more of the real me to the surface. Recounting the night at Calvados when I had slipped that note to Omar I added, "I never would've done such a thing in New York." I omitted mentioning Waddah, or Maurice, and the child I had chosen not to keep, but spoke of my ongoing difficulties with Georgina, "which means I have to spend more time in Paris."

Paris and Georgina. Paris and Omar. While commuting that week I tried to imagine what might happen next. Would Georgina ever sit down and do the interviews with me? It looked less and less likely. And Omar? In my mind there were two extremes: never seeing him again versus marriage and children. Why had I changed my mind about having a family? Was this love? Infatuation? Or some deeper healing? "You'll know when you want to have his baby," goes the old saying. My intuition had shown me a curly

---

their stalls. As difficult as it was to take these facts in, it was even harder to accept who had killed them. Rather than leave them to suffer, locked up without food or water, when no one could care for them, or turning them loose to be injured, maimed, and terrified in the city streets full of ricocheting gunfire, Leonie had put a single bullet to their brains because she cared.

headed child, playing near Omar's knees. How to interpret that?

I was strangely proud of acting upon my desire the night we'd met. By writing him that note, my actions had turned a fantasy into reality. I was still waiting for this to happen with Georgina. For once I had done the choosing with a man and he had responded to my beckoning. Knowing what we want was the prerequisite to getting it. Propelled by desire, both of us obeyed what steered us towards each other. Omar inflamed my imagination but had not quite fulfilled it. Now I craved him, sitting on a train, in another world entirely. Closing my eyes I summoned him in a still luxuriant memory, watching his shirt slide off his beautiful brown shoulders, the smell of him rising as he gathered me to him. The beauty of this man was like Georgina's beauty. Compelling, at least for me. What truth was there in beauty? Was I ready for passion to consume me?

Reaching for my pen and journal, I started writing. The words came like divine dictation demanding to be recorded.

"Mon Fantôme" poem in French and English

Mon Fantôme
il n'y a rien a dire
qui peut t'expliquer
qui peut m'expliquer
comment tu m'as trouvée
comment tu m'as prise
avec un regard.

Comment t'es arrivé
dans ma vie, comme
la première nuit
qui a enveloppé la lune
pour lui faire plaisir.

Tu m'as trouvée et
tu m'as libérée
de ma peur
de la nuit –
de ma peur
de l'inconnu –
de ma peur
de la vie
de l'amour.

Tu es un vrai fantôme

conjure d'une moitie
d'ombre et de désir
tu es un vrai fantôme
qui m'as laissée penser que
c'était moi qui ai choisi.

Tu es un fantôme pour le vrai
qui possède le pouvoir
de me faire comprendre
le pouvoir de la passion,
car j'ai eu peur de comprendre ca,
sans quelqu'un qui peut me faire croire
que c'est plus que possible –
que c'est la vérité, la plus belle.

Tu as cassé toutes les règles
tu as prouvé que
l'exception existe…
que les fantômes existent.

Tu m'as donnée le désir
d'être une fantôme aussi
qui peut t'offrir
des cadeaux
aussi profonds
aussi beaux.

English translation:

My phantom
There is nothing to say
that can explain to you
that can explain to me
how you have found me
how you have taken me
with (just) a look.

How you have arrived
in my life, like
the first night
that embraced the moon
to give it pleasure.

You have found me and
you have freed me
of my fear
of the night
of my fear
of the unknown
of my fear
of the life
of love.

You are a real phantom
conjured half
of shadow and desire
You are a real phantom
who has let me think
that it was me who chose.

You are a phantom for real
who possess the power
to help me understand
the power of passion
for I was afraid to understand this
without someone who could help me believe
that it is more than possible
that it is the truth
most beautiful.

You have broken all the rules
you have proven
that the exception exists
that phantoms exist.

You have given me the desire
to become a phantom too
who can offer you
gifts
as profound (and)
as beautiful.

[Excerpt from *Measuring Distances* poetry collection]

That Thursday evening I took five copies of this new poem along to share
with the women in my old poetry group. They were no longer meeting like

they used to, but we gathered at Bonnie's house for old time's sake, to catch up with each other. After sharing the poem, I tried to convey what life was like in Paris, but this attempt felt as futile as trying to explain it to my co-workers. Maybe Europe and America were impossible to put together, except inside of me. Leaving Bonnie's place that night I felt sad, knowing we might never see each other again. Losing these women would be hard but I was already a bit unreal to them. Our choices were so different. A gap had formed that resisted bridging. Will they continue to write? Would any of them take up my offer to come to Paris and stay with me? If they did not believe in those possibilities, I could not make them.

Andrew "Andy" Fetterolf, Cynthia's dad, 1961 in Jeddah, Saudi Arabia

Fetterolf family in Beirut, 1967

Cynthia & her father in Jeddah leaving for Swiss boarding school, 1969

Andy & Lynn Fetterolf, Cynthia's parents in Jeddah 1963 with Daoud Al Rumeih, Royal Saudi Air Force & Yusuf AlTawil

View of Beirut, Lebanon from
Phonecia Intercontinental Hotel, 1970

Lebanese Residency Card

Cynthia & Dr. Amin Mousalli
in Beirut nightclub, 1972

Cynthia nineteen-years-old
in Beirut

Saudi Ambassador to the US
Ali Alireza & Cynthia in
New York, 1978

(left to right) Craig Fetterolf,
Lynn Fetterolf, Mazen Pharaon,
Karen Fetterolf in Beirut, 1971

Cynthia in 1979

Cynthia at home in Paris

Cherifa and Sylvie

Catherine Genis

Cynthia's thirty first birthday
at Paris home

French travel card

Frédérique & Darius

Omar Chaker

Cynthia thirty-two-years-old
in Paris

(left to right) Cherifa, Cynthia's
grandmother Hattie Trout,
Janet Burke & daughter

Fiona Dunlop

CYNTHIA F. DAVIDSON

Chapter 11

A QUOI BON? /
WHAT'S THE USE?

Of all our games, love's play is the only
one which threatens to unsettle the soul.

— MARGUERITE YOURCENAR

May & June 1984

Ten days later, after more work and travel, I went to Washington, DC for
the annual SIETAR conference, the Society of Intercultural Education
Training and Research. Most of us in the cross-cultural education field
belonged to this professional association. I arrived a day early to spend
some time with my friend Nadine, the Peace Corps director. We had done
screening and selection work together, and I'd run programs for her people
before their overseas assignments. She invited me to stay at her home and I
gladly accepted her offer after too many nights in sterile hotel rooms. On
my free day, after Nadine went to work, I decided to call Maurice, who
lived not far from the capitol. Perhaps we could share a meal or meet for
coffee as friends. While dialing his number, my fingers trembled.

His daughter answered and then her mother came to the phone. Surely
my nervousness showed in my voice.

"Cynthia?" she said. By her manner it was clear she'd heard my name
before.

"Yes, I'm a friend of Waddah's, staying in Washington, DC for a few
days. Is Maurice there?"

"No, he's out at the moment."

"Can I leave a number for him to call me back?"

She took it and I hung up, sweaty with a bad premonition.

Maurice called back about an hour later. We hardly said hello before he
launched into his travel schedule, "New York, London, Abu Dhabi..." He
was leaving tomorrow and couldn't see me. His voice was cold.

"What's wrong?" I asked.

"I met an old suitor of yours, who knew you in Beirut when you worked for that doctor." His words dripped with venom. "He told me you were in love with him."

I felt faint, and sat down, shifting the receiver to my other ear. I wasn't sure which old suitor he was referring to. Could that terrible time still hurt me after all these years?

"I daresay, the doctor was in love with me." My words lacked conviction. I fell silent. It was pointless to defend myself against all those lies when someone you cared about preferred to believe them. How to explain such dark days to another when I could barely tolerate thinking of them myself? Back then I'd been fought over like a carcass: by Ayman, by my parents, and then by Doctor Amin Mousalli.

The sins of the fathers. So many opposing forces had clashed over and around me. They'd presaged the coming war that would tear everything apart. To get from one day to the next, I had struggled to transcend their either/or choices. I wanted to evolve, to spiral beyond those restricting choices, and come up with something better on my own. When father and fiancé had forced me into their classic patriarchal contest, I'd rejected them both, refusing to return to daughterhood or go on to marriage and motherhood with Ayman. Faced with two unsuitable alternatives, it was best to keep going. Defiance did not need to be self-limiting. I thought of the good work I had done at the doctor's, caring for a brand-new baby, and his mother, who had almost died, but the roof over my head, the food I ate, and the shelter from the storm created by the men in my life, had certainly cost me. The price had come out of my hide, literally. Another Beirut episode.

But none of it mattered anymore unless I let it. Maurice was still on the line. I had almost forgotten him in this flood of ancient anger. Was this how he'd justified his decision to get over me, to stop himself, as he put it? Why fight him? Frankly I thought, as I took a deep breath, if Maurice and Omar were standing side-by-side in this room right now, I'd choose Omar. Maurice represented everything I wanted to be done with, the tawdry side I had seen of Beirut. My history could not be altered but it could be overcome. Omar was my fresh start, a new story, some healing beauty.

"Well I am sorry you prefer to listen to your friend. You sound like you've already made up your mind. Too bad Maurice. What we had was so lovely. Goodbye." I hung up before he could say anything or I could take anything back.

Still shaking I rose from the chair in Nadine's house and gazed out the window. By now the sun was going down behind the nation's bulbous white capitol. An incredible weariness came over me. I sank onto a blue sofa and stared at the ceiling fan twirling gently. The curling discs of the colorful South American mobile suspended from it sent forth a tinkling music as twilight descended. Instead of crying, a quiet resolve arose within me.

Like the doctor, Maurice could only hurt me if I allowed them to. The scale was different here, intimate and personal. I had the freedom to choose how I reacted. Unlike the massive scale of the war's violence, this issue was in my power to do something about. I decided to treasure what was good and memorable, the moments of insight and ecstasy. As the stupidity of war ground everything else to dust, I would salvage what was worth collecting.

An image came of doves and pigeons being gathered in Beirut. Their owners would stand on their rooftops, holding long sticks overhead, tipped with fluttering cloths, and wave them near the dovecotes. Round and round those flags would go, and the birds would see them, and move in flying in wide rhythmic arcs, from all over the city. Each bird joined their own flock and returned to their respective coop. I was also summoning my entire brood of cooing, whirling memories, in every shade of emotion and color. Remembering my attempts with Georgina, I decided my efforts must be for the best, since seeking her had brought Omar into my life.

* * * *

At the opening of the conference the following morning, I greeted old colleagues and met new people. During the lunch break, friends introduced me to a Romanian fellow, a partner at a Paris-based consulting firm Intercultural Management associates. Their work was similar to mine at my previous employer's. Indrei gave me his business card and we agreed to meet for lunch the following week in Paris upon our return to France. Intuition nudged me to follow up on this as it would allow me to continue my cross-cultural work.

That evening I told Nadine about this latest bit of luck. "My theory is, if you really want to do something, a way always opens up. Never allow money worries to stop you. Like Machado said, 'You make the path as you walk.' But you must want that one thing long enough and hard enough, without giving up."

Nadine, a diplomatic hostess and a good listener, concurred with a smile, promising to come visit me to France (and she did later that year).

During a conference break the following afternoon, I went to a phone booth to dial Carla's number again. Since arriving in the US, I had tried to set up another appointment, leaving messages on her answering machine. But my work kept me moving constantly from one city to another, and Carla had not managed to catch up with me before I'd traveled on.

This time she answered the phone.

"When are you getting married?" was her first comment.

"I don't know! No one's asked me yet."

"Don't worry. They will. How's my favorite *shiksa*?" (A Yiddish term for a non-Jewish woman).

I blurted out something about Omar, and asked if I could see her before my return to Paris. We agreed to meet in Manhattan on Memorial Day, at three o'clock in the afternoon.

* * * *

That evening I copied the "Mon Fantôme" poem onto a card, calculating it might arrive just before I did, if I mailed it to Omar in the morning, care of the Hotel George V. Falling asleep that night, I felt a sense of peace returning, although the hectic work trip had worn me out. Some unscheduled days with Omar were just what I wanted. At the conference, I noticed everyone was in a rush, talking fast, walking fast, and getting right to the point. Being so hurried left little time for feeling anything deeply. Too much competed for our attention as people and events went by at seventy-five miles an hour. Having lived that way, I recognized the pattern.

In Paris, some days I didn't get dressed until one in the afternoon. No longer bound by office hours, I woke to make a mug of tea and take it back to bed with me. My days started with reading, writing, or contemplating. My general rule was no radio, television, or newspapers until later, preferably after six o'clock in the evening. Balancing all the outer stimulus was important. Time was required to think my own thoughts and draw my own conclusions. Journaling helped me tune into intuition. Since creating this womb of privacy, I had roamed through my own mind and discovered my true ambition: to become a wise old woman. Not exactly sure how to go about this, I knew it was not about the number of dollars I earned per year, or what sort of house or car I owned although it was connected to my search for the truth.

From the guest bedroom of Nadine's suburban home, I thought about the neighbors working to keep up with the Joneses and concluded I was willing to trade all the SUVs, Cuisinart machines, and microwave ovens just to have this precious free time. I wanted wisdom. Who had that? It was not a consumer item. I did not have it yet but at least I knew what I wanted and I was willing to do the work to find it. To get wisdom you began by separating truth from lies. This took my thoughts back to Paris, Georgina, and my current quest. Omar. Mon Fantôme. His deep, dark eyes, so slow and savoring. Perhaps he was part of my foolishness, for one had to be willing to pass through whatever it took on the way towards becoming wise. I chuckled, too sleepy to think straight, as dreamland approached.

On Memorial Day morning, Carla called to cancel our appointment. "Neither of us should risk this holiday traffic," she said. "Besides, you'll be back in about a month and I'll read for you then. Don't worry. Everything is going to be just fine."

She sounded so sure, I believed her.

The next evening I flew back to Paris.

* * * *

Out of breath from carrying my suitcases up the stone steps to my door, I heard the phone ringing inside as I fumbled with my key.

"I was afraid you had disappeared," Omar said. Uncanny.

I'd also been afraid he had disappeared, like phantoms are prone to do. After being separated for more than a month, I'd forgotten how much I loved his voice, and his French.

"Where are you? When can you come see me?"

"Around seven but I will have to leave by ten tonight," he explained. "I wasn't sure if you were coming today or tomorrow, so I promised the Saudi fellow I would see him tonight."

"I'll be waiting for you. We'll take whatever time we have." My hands caressed the phone as I replaced the receiver. Omar. He was still real. There was just enough time to take a nap and catch up on the lost sleep from flying overnight. Then I would make myself as beautiful as possible and be ready for him when he arrived.

Just after seven, from my open window, I watched his tall, dark form crossing the courtyard. The bells were ringing, from the nearby towers of Notre Dame and elsewhere. Why? It was a Wednesday. Standing there in the late May evening air, the reverberation of the bells echoed inside my chest. I felt like a bride. I met him on the landing as he climbed the last few steps. His jet eyes, and the strength of his embrace did not disappoint. He was better than I had remembered. We went inside and closed the door. Our clothing was off in less than ten minutes.

After, as we lay together, he tenderly brushed my hair from my face and ran his thumb over my lips, swollen with our kisses and our loving, saying nothing. He just looked at me. Those black eyes were like wells I could happily drown in. We smiled and laughed and he rolled me over, snuggling up to my back as he'd done before. I had to remind myself this was only our third time together. Dozing off, I noted our breathing had synchronized easily and effortlessly. His physical rightness was overpowering. Lying in his arms I thought "husband, husband, husband." The word drummed in my brain with every beat of my pulse. I was too entranced to consider he might be someone else's husband. He had denied he was married when I'd asked.

When we woke from our nap, he asked about my trip, and my work. I stumbled a bit in the language, having never discussed cross-cultural training terms in French before, but he quickly got the gist of it. "I can tell you like your work."

He did not say much about his work or the trip to Tunisia. Too content to probe for more information, I switched the radio on. Before leaving for the US, I had discovered a local Arabic radio station *Id'itti el Shark*, the Star of the East. The announcer was talking about Ramadan, the Muslim holy month of fasting, which would begin on the New Moon tomorrow, June 1st and would run the lunar month, through to June 29th. How good a Muslim was Omar? Would he observe the fast while in Paris? I asked him.

"I usually go home to spend Ramadan in Sfax," he answered.

The room filled with the recorded voice of Um Kalsoum, the most famous of Arabic singers. "*Ya habib albī*" (oh dearest of my heart) the Egyptian woman sang. She had died in 1975, almost a decade ago, the same year the war in Lebanon began. I repeated the chorus, singing the Arabic words softly near Omar's ear, letting myself feel the love I still harbored for the Arab world that had shaped me.

Before leaving, he said, "I'll call you tomorrow around five. Perhaps we can go out for dinner or something."

* * * *

The next day I had lunch with the Romanian partner of the ICM (Intercultural Management) consulting firm I had met at the SIETAR conference in the US. He introduced me to the other two partners, Charles Gancel, the French president and Irene Rogers, an American woman, and longtime resident in France. Their programs and services were similar to those I was familiar with and their Cross-Cultural Communications program sounded intriguing. They invited me to come along and see the next one, scheduled to run soon at IBM's European headquarters.

On my way home that afternoon, my good mood felt positively contagious. Humming as I made the rounds of the shops in my neighborhood, I bought food, flowers, and freshly ground Turkish coffee for Omar. By midnight, however, my high spirits had evaporated. Five o'clock came and went and Omar never called. I tried to keep busy with chores, unpacking from my trip, attacking the stack of unanswered mail, but my mind kept wandering. Why hadn't he called? I began to invent reasons and excuses. He had lost my number. Or he didn't have it on him, and was somewhere inconvenient. Was he with another woman?

Eventually I imagined the worst. He had been in an accident. He was lying on the side of the road somewhere hurt and bleeding. Torturing myself like that was worse than useless. There was nothing to do but wait. I had no number to call him at, except the Hotel George V, where I sent his mail for him to pick up. Omar had explained that once the prince returned to Saudi Arabia for Ramadan, he would be free to spend time with me. Yet he had also said he usually went home to Tunisia for Ramadan. I got undressed and climbed into bed, sitting with the pillows plumped behind me, with the same Star of the East radio station on, remembering how we had lain here so happily, just last night. Would he ever call again?

I scolded myself for being so deluded. I was overreacting and this ought to serve as a lesson. My risk-taking had consequences. I hardly knew this man. How could I be pining for him as if he was a fiancé? My reactions were out of proportion. But how could I forget last night? He meant something to me. Perhaps he was a heartless cad, yet he had made me feel so deeply. Those black eyes, those strong arms, his lips, and kisses, I caressed myself imagining his hands and finally slept, after promising myself if he called tomorrow, with a perfectly logical excuse, I would laugh at myself for having been so upset.

The following evening I wrote in my journal:

Is this the hangover one suffers after being drunk on euphoria? I am feeling quite ill physically. Despite everything with Beirut, I never knew the meaning of the word "distraught" till now, just when I thought normalcy was returning to me emotionally. If I was more cynical, and did things like this all the time, perhaps I would feel nothing, but I feel awful...

A week later this entry:

It's raining in Paris. June rain. The only thing bearable about it is remembering how much worse the weather was last February. Still no word from Omar. I suppose I could let this rain wash him away. Maybe it's time to initiate a cure, to stop building him up, and decide to let him go. But the essential ingredient is missing: the why. What happened to him? Without knowing why he hasn't called, I can't be sure of what I must do. Have I totally misinterpreted the situation between us?

If I have been a fool, I can face that. It doesn't bother me as much as not knowing does. I feel helpless and paralyzed, unable to decide anything until I know what has happened. How can I get angry when I don't know if he's laying in a hospital bed somewhere, needing me? Should I try to get over him? Or think about how to handle him if he ever calls again?

I have no idea where he could be. Apart from the night we met at Calvados I have only ever seen him surrounded by these apartment walls. For me he hardly exists outside in the real world.

This reveals more about me and my condition than him. Omar, Mon Fantôme. Like a thermometer, registering my degrees of fever, my symptoms, of what? Foolhardiness? Greediness? Gullibility? I am certainly being emotionally indulgent.

I'm half off my rocker over this man. It is pitiful.
How far under his spell have I fallen? How to come out of it?

Putting aside my journal I got out the Paris telephone book. I looked under all the possible spellings for his transliterated Arabic name: Chaker, Chakir, Shaker, Shakir. I made a list and began to call each of them. Egyptians, Pakistanis, no Tunisians. On the television that night I heard something about Tunisia. Some Tunisians were holding hostages. So distracted, I caught only a smattering of the news story. Could he be involved in something political? Was he off on a mission of some kind? Or in hiding?

I thought of Georgina's dead husband Ali Hassan Salameh and his work as a mastermind behind terrorist incidents. How much had she known? What would I do if Omar was involved in sinister things and tried to enlist my "help?"

The next day I wrote him a note and took it to the Hotel George V. Before giving it to the officious concierge behind the desk, I asked if he was holding any other letters I had sent from the US for Mr. Chaker. The man rifled through a thick stack of mail and extracted two letters for Omar. Both were mine, sent from the US. One contained the "Mon Fantôme" poem. I had forgotten to ask if he'd received it. I added today's note to the pile.

I could come by periodically to check on his mail here. This was the only link I had. At least I would know, when the letters were gone, that he had returned to the hotel. Perhaps he wasn't in Paris. Paris. This was not the same city without him. He had disappeared without a trace and the City of Light had gone dim. After losing so much it hurt even more to lose what I had let myself want so badly. Wandering back towards Île Saint-Louis dazed and preoccupied, two men tried to follow me, and another asked me for the time while I sat having a coffee. This was annoying. The next few days I took long walks, occasionally noticing when someone's hair or skin or cheeks reminded me of Omar's. Being alone in the apartment was excruciating but I made myself sit there thinking he might call.

* * * *

One afternoon when the phone rang the noise startled me. I'd fallen asleep over a book. It was Fiona, from Waddah's galerie.

"I didn't expect to find you back yet from the US."

I told her I'd only returned the day before, although it was well over a week now. I felt a little sheepish about not calling my friends since returning. I had wanted to be alone with Omar on my first week back. Since his disappearance I had felt too sick at heart to see anyone.

Fiona invited me to another vernissage, at Waddah's galerie tomorrow night. After hesitating for a second, I agreed to go. Might as well start acting like a normal human being again. Ten minutes later the phone rang again. Waddah. This was the first time I had heard his voice since our parting in February, more than three months ago.

"Hello Fetterolf," he said, with an exaggerated use of my family name.

Was this intended to amuse or annoy? As always, knowing what to assume with this man was difficult. Yet something clicked. During the intervening weeks, I had discovered we had mutual friends in Jeddah. Waddah had been the best man at the wedding of a couple I'd known since childhood and stayed with briefly in 1979. Perhaps they'd told him about our family connection with Mazen. This may have led to his sudden coldness and withdrawal, the way Dr. Mousalli's name had such a powerfully negative effect upon Maurice. So why was Waddah inviting me for dinner at his place?

"Tonight," he pressed, "Come. I'll be having some funny friends from Beirut."

I paused, thinking of Omar, and all the nights I had waited for that damn phone to ring. I said yes. Going to this dinner would at least get me out of the house. While getting ready I wondered what Waddah might know about Maurice and me. Had he heard about the pregnancy? I would mention nothing. Before going out of my door, I looked in the mirror and lectured my reflection, "Don't forget how awful this man was to you. Don't forgive him too easily."

The mauves of dusk descended over Paris as I exited the big red door of my Quai de Bourbon home. Strolling along the quays, the sight of the Seine's dark, caressing waters calmed me. After crossing Pont Marie, I threaded through the Marais district, and the lovely Place des Vosges on the way to Waddah's apartment. The beauty of the old square, with its enduring stones and imposed order was also reassuring.

The next day I confessed in my journal:

I woke up at nine o'clock this morning at Waddah's place. Yes I spent the night with him. Why? I'll never know. Until two o'clock he gave no indication that anything would happen. For the entire evening he avoided looking at me and flirted with one of the other women, Sohat, a ticket agent for MEA. She said she remembered my father when he worked with the company.

The women were belly dancing, with scarves tied round their hips, and the food was good. The same Egyptian artist I met on the first night in Paris was there with his wife. At two o'clock when the taxis they had telephoned for arrived, I got ready to leave with the others.

That's when Waddah signaled, "No. Don't go. Stay."

I thought we would talk about why things had gone so badly, but once everyone left he sat down beside me on the couch. Never uttering a single word, he took my hand, like the first time, and drew me to him, and began to kiss me on the mouth. Then he stood up and took me by the hand to his bed. I never spoke a word either, not of protest, question, or anything else. This morning I felt it best to slip away, so I got dressed quietly and left him sleeping. He can be bad tempered in the morning. As for me, there's no remorse. There's not much feeling at all left for him.

It is Omar I want now. Waddah should not be given the impression that I am waiting for him or expecting anything. I doubt this reunion has any sort of lasting meaning except to end our silence. I cannot gauge his interest in me, in public it's non-existent, which can be taken as a convoluted sign of respect. Perhaps he just doesn't want people knowing about his private life. Probably the latter.

If I knew I'd see Omar again, I would not have stayed.

* * * *

Two days later Zvonimir returned to Paris, as he said he would. I had forgotten he wanted to take me to the Adriatic this summer and it was already June. Calling from Zemira's place, he said he had just arrived from the airport, and wanted to see me first thing. Half an hour later I was opening the door for him.

He admired my apartment and congratulated me on finding such a perfect place. As with Waddah, I had no expectations but when he started kissing me, I let go, half hoping this would help me get over Omar. As he plunged into my flesh, I paid attention to my feelings. Deep down I felt detached, more spectator than participant. Omar was still the one I needed.

Zvonimir took me out to dinner that evening. Zemira had gone to Yugoslavia tend some family business so only Freddie joined us. I recommended a gourmet Vietnamese place, knowing how much Zvoni loved Asian food. Maurice had brought me here on one of our many meals out. In a good mood, the three of us polished off three bottles of wine.

I told them about Omar, how we met, and what had happened the first time he came over. I mentioned his comment on the lack of ashtrays, and my reply that I thought kissing a man who smoked was like kissing an ashtray. Freddie started to giggle. Since I had used the word *"baiser"* no wonder. She explained that meant more than kiss in French slang. Its double entendre was the equivalent of sleeping with someone. "Use the word *'embrasser'* next time if that's all you mean."

We had a good laugh, paid the bill and piled into Freddie's Alfa Romeo to head back to Zemira's empty place, where Zvoni was staying, for a nightcap. After getting on the subject of Omar and sex, we continued talking about it. Eventually this gave way to a rather tipsy game of spin the bottle and strip poker. I suspected Zvoni was trying to get the three of us into bed, as it was one of his fantasies. Without any more clothing left to lose, we were soon at a loss about how to continue the game. In the underwater light, coming from the illuminated aquarium in the corner of the room, our flesh glowed strangely. The mood had changed and the fun grew more serious. We decided to continue the game with requests instead of clothing, which lead to all sorts of kisses as the three of us tumbled happily over one another. Moving to the bedroom to be more comfortable, Zvoni promptly fell asleep exhausted, from the transatlantic flight, and the afternoon he had spent with me. Freddie took me in her arms and kissed me slowly and tenderly. The hilarity of the game dissolved into the wonder of these soft sensations, strangely familiar, yet so different.

In my journal the next afternoon I wrote:

The following must be part of what the French call one's "sentimental education." Last night another psychological barrier was crossed. I had my first experience with a woman. There was nothing earth shattering or particularly naughty feeling about it. Everything was so spontaneous. Freddie was sweet and dear and tender. Now this too is no longer some prohibited unknown, relegated to the passive realm of fantasy. It was so completely satisfying that I doubt it will ever need to happen again. It was like making love in a mirror.

But nothing could wipe Omar from my skin — not Freddie, Zvoni, or Waddah. I had certainly tried to get over him, but by the end of my second week back, I was as despondent as ever. Maybe he's dead, I thought. I had to find out. I called Catherine, my French lawyer friend, the one Maurice had introduced me to. "How does one inquire about a missing person?"

Catherine explained, since I was not a family member, the best I could do was to go to the police station in my arrondissement to ask if his name was on the list of accident victims. She also cautioned me about Arab boyfriends, relating the story of a woman badly abused by a vengeful ex-lover. Among other things he had "squeezed a tube of *harissa* (hot sauce) into her vagina."

Nevertheless, I walked to the Rue de Rivoli police station that afternoon. Waiting in the anteroom for about forty minutes, my details were taken by a small overworked man in plain clothes with a red beard. He phoned the central office and gave Omar's name, checking the listings since the May 30th date I'd given, when I last saw him. Relieved to find nothing, I was not quite satisfied however, knowing how many ways his family name could be spelled. Had Omar given me his real name? I had never seen his passport or any official identification.

Perplexed, I inquired if there was anything else he or I could do to help me locate this man. The officer gave me a look of faint disgust, which implied "what do these white women see in these Arabs?" I didn't even thank him and turned heel to leave, shaking with rage at the ignominy of discussing anything so private with such a prejudiced stranger.

On my way back from the Prefecture de Police, I noticed a book in the window of a shop where I often bought my Herald Tribune newspaper. *Beyrouth, Aller-Retour* by Fouad El Khoury, (*Round Trip Beirut*) had just been published this May the clerk explained. The small paperback was full of photographs: shell-pocked walls, empty streets, burned out hulks of automobiles, and a lone child playing among the tombstones in a cemetery, with some text by the young bespectacled architect whose picture was on the back cover. I bought the book and took it home with me, copying into my journal that evening its closing paragraph.

Maintenant, je sais que Beyrouth, c'est-à-dire ce que ce nom signifie pour moi, est morte. Je n'ai pas d'autre choix que d'accepter de le savoir. (Now I know that Beirut, that is to say what that name signifies for me, is dead. I have no other choice but to except to know this).

That is the point I am also approaching.

That night I wrote Omar a last letter in French recounting my visit to the police station and saying I would not write again. If he ever received my letter it would be up to him to contact me. And I wrote to Georgina, explaining that if she had been trying to reach me I had only just returned from the US, and would she please try again now.

Omar, Georgina, and Beirut were now intertwined here in Paris. This was totally unexpected. Was he a detour or an essential part of what needed to be learned about the truth? Surely Georgina had found men distracting too. What goals did she have before the war? And before Ali Hassan Salameh swept her off her feet? What an apt metaphor. To take my mind off these unanswered questions, I picked up a Paris guidebook. Leafing through it before falling asleep I discovered the patron saint of Paris was a woman, Saint Geneviève. Not distracted by men, she'd saved Paris from invasion by the hordes of Attila the Hun. I studied the picture of her statue on the Pont des Tournelles, which connected Île Saint-Louis to the Left Bank. Several times I had passed over that bridge, and seen the tall white stone woman with the child standing at her feet, not knowing who she was. Tomorrow I resolved to make a little pilgrimage to visit her. Hadn't I had tried everything else?

* * * *

As Carla predicted, I returned to the US on another work trip before the month was out. Another whirlwind of travel and training programs during the rest of June kept me too busy to dwell upon Omar or Georgina, neither of whom I had heard from before departing. I focused on work and spent my summer earning money to live on when getting back to Paris.

In July, on my way back to France, I visited Carla again, hoping for some closure. We didn't discuss her prior predictions, which had not panned out. What was the point?

As for Omar, she said, "He's not the one, but he is something you have to go through. It's karma kid. Either his karma owes yours or yours owes his something. He's in hiding now. But he will resurface in Paris. He will give you some story. You will see him for a while yet but it's over for you. He still has his crush on you though. It's chemistry honey."

Three days later Lynda had a message. Omar had called the Greenwich number. He was back in Paris looking for me. I was thrilled to hear this. Despite my desperation over his disappearance my need to know the truth of what had happened to him outweighed all caution. I wanted to run back to Mon Fantôme and Paris now.

Another prediction by Carla had come true a few days after she read the cards for me. "You will return to Paris with a pet and with your luck you won't even have to buy it. Someone will give it to you."

In the back seat of the taxi on my way to the airport, I reached through the grill of a cat carrier to comfort the beautiful pedigreed Persian cat accompanying me to France. Darius Felix was meowing, and I scratched his forehead, above his amber eyes, smoothing his long grey hair. In my bag were all his papers and up-to-date vet records to prevent any problems with immigration and animal control. My Syrian Saudi friends in Greenwich, CT had given him to me, claiming they were allergic. Having his warm body in my Quai de Bourbon home would be welcoming though arrangements would have to be made for him during my travels.

CYNTHIA F. DAVIDSON

Chapter 12

DANS UN HARAM BYZANTIN /
IN A BYZANTINE HAREM

In a Byzantine harem, where, in order to find paradise,

I was disguised as a dog, a slave said to me.

— SERGE LAMA, lyrics to "L'esclave" (The Slave)

July 1984
On my first evening back in Paris again after more than another month away, Omar came up the steps with an extravagant bouquet of roses, orchids, and lilies. He'd never brought flowers before. Kissing me shyly on both cheeks after presenting them, I realized he was not sure I would welcome him back. After inviting him in, I watched him go to sit in the living room as I took the bouquet into the kitchen. Unwrapping the long stemmed flowers, I filled the largest vase with water, arranging the flowers while reminding myself to be tough on him. Where had he been all this time? I needed to know a lot more about him and vowed never to suffer such ignorance again.

Carrying the vase full of flowers into the living room, I set it carefully on the marble mantelpiece before offering him something to drink. He declined politely and motioned for me to sit down near him on the couch. I chose to sit in the chair facing him instead, knowing his touch might weaken my resolve to get to the bottom of this.

"So, tell me, what really happened to you?"

On the phone before I'd left the US, he told me he had gone to Saudi Arabia with the prince. Now he supplied the details.

"The night I left you, I knew the prince was planning to return to the kingdom the next day for Ramadan. I thought I would be free to spend all my time with you. Well, the next morning at Le Bourget (private airport) while boarding his private jet, he asked if I had my passport with me. I did.

193

He told me to get on board with him. 'Come along on a hunting trip.' Not expecting any such invitation, I didn't even have a toothbrush with me. He said not to worry. They could get me anything I needed in Riyadh. I had no idea I would spend the next month and twenty days in the desert."

He did look tanner and trimmer. His story was not preposterous, not to me. As I listened to him, I remembered going in and out of that exclusive airport myself, on Mazen's Learjet, while he was helping to pay my fees at NYU. He had also smoothed the way for my return to work in the Kingdom in 1979. But that was the year I had made up my mind about Arabia, and relinquished all those options. To me Omar's story was plausible because of my previous experience with spontaneous invitations just like it. Omar's prince could bend the strict Saudi visa requirements for foreigners by avoiding commercial airlines. But going into the country on a private plane without a visa was risky. You had to leave the same way and this put you entirely at the mercy of your host. Without a proper Saudi entrance visa, you could not apply for the necessary exit visa. The Kingdom was one of the few countries in the world with that requirement. To depart on a regularly scheduled flight, your visas had to be shown at passport control, or else you would be detained. Unsuspecting Western women, unaware of these rules, had met Saudis at parties in the US and Europe. Impressed by the invitation and the private planes, they were whisked off to Arabia. Once there, they became virtual prisoners in desert villas, unable to leave the Kingdom since they had not entered it legally.

My thoughts returned to Omar and his words. "They tried to get me to stay there on a full-time arrangement. They promised me a Mercedes, a house, and even a nice little Bedouin bride. But I like my independence and I prefer Paris. Besides, I had to come back to you, didn't I?"

A thought darted across my mind. Perhaps this prince was fond of Omar, very fond. Perhaps... Watching his handsome face, hearing his charming voice, and remembering his body nudged my intuition. Trying to ignore this idea only increased my suspicion it might be true.

From everything Omar had told me, his prince sounded like a classic misogynist. Even his constant changing of wives was a clue, for he made a big show of marrying a new woman every few months. As a Muslim man, he was legally allowed four wives at a time, and he took full advantage of this. Yet he liked none of them. Perhaps he preferred sleeping with a man? Now in his sixties, his latest bride was not even twenty years old, according to Omar. While on their Paris honeymoon, at the Hotel George V, this new wife had writhed in pain on the floor for over thirty-six hours. Omar had begged the prince to let him take her to the hospital. But the prince had dismissed her complaints, insisting they couldn't be serious, and it was probably just her time of the month. Eventually Omar had prevailed. An ambulance took the feverish woman to a private clinic, where she underwent a five-hour operation to mop up all the poisons from her burst appendix. The prince divorced her shortly afterwards, saying he did not want a woman with a scar on her abdomen.

Omar once said that he had lasted longer than any of the brides the prince had taken during his five years of employment. Perhaps this prince was as infatuated with Omar as I was.

"You work for Prince Mishari bin Abd ul Aziz, right? Isn't he the one who shot Cyril Ousman, the British diplomat, in Jeddah in 1951?"

Omar said he did not know for sure. If that had happened, it was long before his time, but he had heard some stories.

Crossing the room I pulled a book off the shelf, David Holden's *The House of Saud*. I quickly located the prince's name on the foldout pages detailing all the branches and births of the Al Saud family tree.

I sat next to Omar on the couch to show him the entry describing the incident, translating the gist of it into French for him. The young Prince Mishari had been refused additional alcohol at a British Embassy party in Jeddah in 1951. Already drunk, his unruly behavior had upset the other guests. In the early morning darkness, the nineteen year old, eighteenth son of King Abd-al-Aziz, returned with a gun. Some said he was pursuing Cyril Osman's wife Dorothy. Prince Mishari shot the British vice consul in the stomach and the diplomat died soon afterwards. The prince fled to the home of his half brother, Prince Faisal, who would become king in 1964. He begged Faisal to intercede on his behalf and deal with their father's wrath. By Sharia law, Dorothy Ousman had every right to demand the prince be put to death as punishment for murdering her husband. But the widow agreed to accept the standard "blood money" payment instead, thus sparing the prince's head. She departed for South Africa shortly afterwards and was never heard of again.

While translating these facts from the book for Omar, I added a few snippets about my Arabian days in the 1960s. He leaned over and kissed my neck, caressing my hair.

I paused mid-sentence. "Don't touch me Omar. I swore I would never let you do anything until you told me everything about yourself. After this horrible summer, with your disappearing without a trace, I don't think I could go through anything like that again. You have no idea Omar."

Assured of his power, he smiled and my resolve faltered. Unable to keep a straight face, I added, "I want to know the names of your father and mother and brother and I want your photo and to see your passport, and…"

He took the book from my hands and set it back down on the shelf. Then he put my hands on his shoulders and drew me to him, his hands dipping around my waist.

"My father is dead and my mother too. My older brother lives here. His son is like a brother to me, as we were raised together. I went to live with his family, so I could go to a better school in Sfax. My elder brother is a strict Muslim. He never misses a prayer. Because his wife ran up too many bills calling her relatives in Tunisia, he took out the phone, so I cannot give you any number. What else?"

Then he added, "Here, write down this number in Sfax."

I reached for a pen, and an envelope a bill had come in. Seeing I was ready, he recited the number explaining, "This is my friend's phone. I haven't put one in my place yet since I am not there very often and I don't want the servants using it to call their relatives in France."

His lips brushed mine. "I know it's hard to get to know me. It's how I am. Your fantôme. Remember?"

The cat meowed at our feet. "You haven't met Darius yet," I said by way of introduction. The Persian cat rubbed against him, leaving a large patch of wispy gray hairs on the leg of Omar's navy blue suit. We both looked down and laughed.

"Don't worry. I have a good clothes brush."

Later we went for dinner at Monte Christo's, an intimate Italian place on the island, previously noted for just such a purpose. Over the meal he told me more about his life and work. His nickname was "Monsieur Mille," meaning that he charged a thousand French francs per day. For this fee, he arranged everything for his clients, acting as their majordomo or general factotum. This included driving cars, doing chores at the banks, planning the evening entertainments, making reservations in restaurants. He babysat the other princes and their various offspring when they came through Paris on their way from schools in America, on shopping trips or medical appointments. He supplemented this daily rate with whatever else he could touch, by way of commissions and kickbacks.

I understood just how crucial his sort of assistance was. Saudi royals did not speak French and were used to retinues of staff and servants waiting upon their every whim. But those employees were not useful in a place like Paris, where they did not know the city or the language. Someone like Omar was indispensable, and not just because he knew French and Arabic, but because he could anticipate his clients' particular needs and satisfy them. Omar knew where to go for things like gift sets of jeweled prayer beads, attractive blonde French teachers, and could arrange — on very short notice — to have a meal of roasted lamb on a bed of rice delivered right to the hotel room if his client did not wish to eat out. Competent and discreet, he possessed that je ne sais pas, a touch of class despite his humble origins.

As Omar described his work, I realized how deeply he despised some of them: the pathetic alcoholic son of the prince, the rapacious hangers-on, gouging and cheating everyone involved in any transaction with the prince. "Wolves and foxes," Omar called them, including a male Palestinian secretary who could not keep his accounts straight. Omar admitted he had double billed him on occasion just for spite, adding, "When I worked as his secretary, nobody could get away with that."

His was a strange occupation, with long hours and unpredictable whims that tried his patience. It also required constant vigilance. To keep this post, he had to be available all the time and on his guard. In that jealous scheming milieu, others would always covet his position, and be ready to step right in if Omar did anything to provoke the prince. On the positive side, Omar was making good money. Most Tunisians came to France with only a high school degree, no capital and few connections, except with other North Africans.

After the meal, as we sipped our coffees, I asked how he came to Paris in the first place.

He explained he'd come one summer to visit his elder brother, who was already living and working in Lyon. Before returning from that holiday, Omar managed to secure the promise of a job at a chemical laboratory. Without telling his family, he applied for an immigrant visa on his eighteenth birthday and returned to France to take the lab job.

"During the mandatory physical examination, the doctor asked me to read aloud from the eye chart on the far wall. He told me to read it with one hand held over one eye. Busy filling out the forms at his desk, he told me to switch to the other eye, so I did this." He demonstrated, taking his left hand off his left eye and lifting his right hand to cover the same eye.

"I have an astigmatism in the left eye. I did not want to be refused permission to emigrate because of it. The nurse saw me. She was about to say something but I winked at her and she closed her mouth. That's how I got into France."

"And how did you get this?" I said, my finger running along the scar that crossed through the eyebrow above his good eye.

"Oh, that. A bunch of thugs in Lyon. Some Tunisian had opened the arm of a French kid from the wrist to the elbow with a broken bottle. His pals just wanted to take revenge on the first Tunisian they could find."

He made it sound like a rite of passage in France, just like the Frenchman from Biarritz had, when explaining his scars at Freddie's raclette party months ago. Their nonchalance about racist violence, coming from opposing sides, was oddly matched.

Leaving the restaurant arm in arm, I suggested we walk to the footbridge to see the moon. It would be full tonight. We strolled up the middle of the island with our arms around each other, like teenagers. In the mild September night sky, the moon hung heavily yellow, above the spires of

Notre Dame Cathedral. Omar stood behind me on the bridge, clasping me tightly from behind, breathing into my hair.

Maybe I was a total fool to take him back after what he'd put me through, but I wasn't ready to stop yet. Damn the torpedoes. I'm young, I'm in Paris, and I'm in love. And if I had to get over him, well I have done that before too. It's better than not knowing him. As we turned to walk home, I looked at the tall statue of Saint Geneviève in the distance on the far bridge. Perhaps she could help me. Didn't people pray to saints for assistance?

Back at the apartment, in the living room in front of the mirror above the fireplace, Omar began unbuttoning my blouse. The flowers he had brought were reflected in their vase, multiplied by the mirror glass. I removed my necklace with its gold Saudi sovereign and this prompted another story from him as he continued unbuttoning my blouse.

"Once I had to take some older female relatives of the prince to Geneva to buy jewelry. I had never been there before. So I got up early the next morning and made the rounds at all the fancy jewelry shops, explaining that I would bring them some very good customers, if they would agree to share a percentage with me. By the time they were ready to go out after lunch, I had made agreements with the three stores they made their purchases in, and I got my commission."

What an enterprising man I thought as he finished this tale while finishing to undress me. The sensation of his lips traveling over my breasts and down over my belly made me shiver, as he paused, kneeling in front of me. Naked I wondered does he see me as some kind of client or opportunity? I hope not. I want to be the counterweight to that rich cynical *monde* (world) he works in. My love for him is simple, pure, and good, even redeeming. I hope to be his haven of peace and calm. Perhaps I need someone with his street smarts to protect me from my own romanticism. Soon all thoughts were melting into the fire beneath my skin as I surrendered to his ministrations.

After Omar departed the following morning, I returned to bed with a second cup of tea. Darius also climbed the steps, and jumped onto the bed, to nuzzle beside me. During the night he had walked on our pillows and our heads, waking us. But now I was glad for his furry company. I stroked his back until he started purring. Then I retrieved my pen and notebook from my purse beside the bed. A scrap of paper fell out. On it was the drawing Omar had scribbled in the restaurant last night, explaining some method for winning at roulette. In ten days he planned to go to the Deauville Casino with a Moroccan friend of one of his cousins who claimed to have an unbeatable, computerized way to win. So animated while drawing this, I was surprised he believed such a thing was possible. How often did Omar go to casinos? Was he a gambler? Well, so was I, but my gambling was for truth, love, and ecstasy. I gave the cat a playful squeeze.

* * * *

Two days later, Nabil called from London inviting me for the weekend. "You can come tomorrow if you like. I'll pay for it. I'm only here for a few days from Jeddah and thought you might like to see my new house."

His invitation was a surprise. Although we had kept in touch vaguely since January I'd assumed he heard about Waddah, or the affair with Maurice, and had totally given up. Noncommittal on the phone, I asked him to call back this evening after I met with the company that was offering to employ me in Paris. "I don't want to make any travel plans until after talking with them."

Nabil agreed to call later.

I wondered about Omar after replacing the phone receiver. Should I tell him anything? What would he think? Jumping in the shower, I hurried to get ready for today's nine thirty meeting with the ICM, the Intercultural Management associates partner I had met at the SEITAR conference in the US. Hadn't he mentioned a London office in addition to their Paris one? Going back to London would be fun. Perhaps some old friends still worked at the United Arab Emirates Embassy. I was already talking myself into going.

* * * *

Returning to my apartment after meeting with the ICM associates, I felt like one of the thousands working and living in Paris, a regular. Darius met me at the door, waiting for a cuddle and his dinner. After filling his bowl with cat food, I poured myself a glass of wine, kicked off my shoes, and dropped onto the couch. I replayed the day's discussions in my mind. We had negotiated my daily rate, and ways to get around my current lack of a French work permit. They were ready to apply for one on my behalf. Being in the cadre management category, with a cross-cultural management skill set few had in France, would simplify that process. ICM asked me to design a new cross-cultural mobility program we could offer together at IBM's European headquarters, where I would be their lead trainer. Meanwhile they would bring me up to speed on their existing programs, and certify me to run them solo in the New Year. They invited me to observe the next three-day cross-cultural communication course, to run in early October, so I could co-train the following one, and take over the delivery of the rest of those already scheduled.

Mentioning the possibility of my going to London over the weekend, I asked if there was anything I could take care of there while on my trip. One of the partners was also going and offered to give me a tour of their offices and introduce me to some of the staff.

I decided to tell Omar about my trip, wondering if he'd disappear again during my absence.

When Nabil called back that night, I accepted his invitation. "I can leave on Friday but must be back by Sunday night."

He told me, "Go to an Air France agent and pick up the prepaid ticket." Then he added, "I forgot to tell you the news about Georgina."

"What news?"

"She got married."

"To who? When?"

"Just come over here and I'll tell you all about it," he chuckled.

* * * *

That Friday morning I slipped quietly from bed and left Omar sleeping there. After filling several bowls of food and water for the cat, I finished packing. My fantôme had not arrived until six in the morning after his night out with friends. Before we slept, I gave him my spare key, and asked him to lock the door when he left.

"This is your key now. That way you can come at night when I'm asleep like a real fantôme."

Before leaving I pinned a note to his trousers, "I miss you already."

On the flight to London I chose to interpret the curious ringing sensation in my ear as a sign Omar was thinking of me.

London was surprisingly mild and sunny. I hailed a cab to the city from Heathrow airport. Staring out the window at the passing green commons and rows of semi-detached brick houses, London looked more rundown than I remembered. The capital of another empire that had ceased to exist.

Nabil greeted me at the door of his house, apologizing for the construction mess. As he took my overnight bag to the spare room, workmen were going up and down the steps. Soon he had me helping him choose marble and tile patterns for the bathroom. The place definitely needed a woman's touch but it wasn't going to be me who turned this building into a home.

Over dinner that evening I said enough about Omar to make things clear to Nabil. He did not say much in response. Then I steered the subject back to Georgina and he relayed the story just as he had heard it.

"She married some Lebanese Christian playboy named Elie Salim in July, but they divorced less than one month later."

He added, "We've been invited to lunch tomorrow at the home of Arab journalist friends of mine and they can tell you more about it."

The people Nabil and I had lunch with gave me the name and phone number of another Paris-based Arab journalist, a confidante of Georgina's. They all worked for the same Arab magazine. I was grateful to Nabil and thanked his friends. I had not managed to swing by the ICM offices but on my way back to Heathrow airport that Sunday evening, I considered this trip as a breakthrough in my efforts concerning Georgina.

* * * *

By eleven o'clock that night, I was back home in Paris, wishing Omar would call while making notes in my journal. The phone rang. His voice sounded tired but his banter made me laugh.

"Let's hope I can get away long enough to take you to a Chinese dinner tomorrow night."

"Oh good. I'll be waiting," I chimed back.

"No, I didn't ask you to wait for me," he said, suddenly serious.

"But I will wait for you habibi," I insisted, puzzled about his meaning.

"No. I don't want you waiting and spoiling your evening. You know how these people are. I cannot make promises. I can only say that I hope to take you to dinner." This was *Inshallah*, God willing. Though he hadn't used that word I'd heard the expression so often in the Middle East. One could take it as a sincere acknowledgement of the Almighty or as an excuse for human fallibility.

"Okay, I understand better now. I will be here for you but I won't be waiting," I said, relieved he hadn't meant something else.

"How was London?" he teased.

"Well, I did tell you to come along with me didn't I?" I said this to demonstrate my innocent intentions when explaining my weekend trip.

"You know I cannot leave this job for a moment, not with all the wolves and foxes about," he said wearily.

"I'll tell you all about London and the new developments concerning Georgina too, when I see you." I teased back.

And then I added, "Do you know what I love about you Omary?"

"No, what?"

"You do not snore!"

* * * *

As luck would have it, the following evening we did enjoy that Chinese dinner. Both in high spirits, we laughed, joked, and held hands across the table, our eyes glowing. He teased me about leaving him to go off to London. I told him about the luncheon and showed him the name of the journalist they had told me to contact in Paris, about Georgina.

"If it is the same one I think it is, I can tell you, he likes his whiskey," Omar added. This comment reminded me that Omar knew the "Paris by night" world I so rarely saw, though it had brought him to me.

While eating my spicy meal, I asked Omar what his favorite food was at home in Sfax. When ordering from the menu he had been careful to ask if any of the exotic dishes contained pork. He never ate it and he never drank alcohol either, in deference to Islam. The few times he'd tried, it only gave him headaches.

"My favorite food? You take a piece of our round flat Tunisian bread, and cut it open, and stuff it with grilled chopped meat, onions tomatoes, pignolia nuts and tahini sauce. Then reheat it in the oven, and voila, a Tunisian hamburger."

Then I asked him to describe a typical day in Sfax.

"I get up around seven thirty to walk in the garden for about an hour. The trees are taller each time I go back. But I have to get rid of the gardener. He only really works when I'm there and I want that garden well taken care of."

He said the word garden the way desert dwellers do, for their heaven is not some white mansion in the sky, but an eternally cool green oasis, with streams flowing through it.

"Then I take my shower, and have some fruit, and a coffee around nine. I take the car and go into town, to do the shopping and make my rounds until noon or so. When I get back, I like to take a nap while they prepare the food. We eat our main meal of the day around three. At four thirty I like to take my rifle to go off and hunt pigeons, rabbits, or whatever else is in the hills around the house."

"And do you go hunting for girls?" I joked.

"No, not at all. It is recuperation time in Tunisia, not at all like the life here in Paris."

He continued, "Around eight or nine in the evening, the meal is laid out. I eat, play cards, or receive my friends. Around midnight I go to sleep."

I tried to imagine myself fitting into the rhythm of this life, which sounded romantic to anyone who didn't know it too well. Was I more in love with love than with the reality of this man? I tried to explain this to him.

"Illusions are for poets. I live in the reality. I know I'll survive if you leave me one day, but will you?" As he said this, he grasped my hands even tighter.

* * * *

The following day, I bought him a good razor, a supply of blades, shaving cream in a container I'd seen him use, and a brush to foam it up with. I also got him a pair of slippers and a robe. Later, I dropped off a note at the Paris office of the Arabic magazine where the man who knew Georgina worked. He wasn't in when I stopped by. My note explained how mutual friends in London had told me he knew Georgina and I asked for his help with my biographical project. Then I returned home to await his call.

Unwrapping the things I'd purchased for Omar, and putting them on the bathroom shelf, I reverberated with happiness. I let myself imagine being his wife and making beautiful children together. Then logic kicked in, with a catty, sarcastic voice, berating me for harboring such silly dreams. They could not come true. On the other hand, I refused to pretend I was not having these feelings. They were natural enough. My mother had repeated the old adage, "You'll know he's the one when you want to have his children." After so many years of vowing never to bring children into this rotten world, and ending prior pregnancies, this nudging was new. I decided to regard these as healthy signs. Even if Omar was not to be the father, at least what I wanted was normal. This signaled the changes inside me.

* * * *

Around ten that evening Omar called, sounding sad and dispirited. The work was getting him down. I sympathized, telling him about the little things I had bought for him.

"You shouldn't have gone to all the trouble," he responded.

"Come see me, I'll cheer you up."

"I'll try, but I doubt I'll make it tonight. Perhaps tomorrow night."

I recounted my afternoon visit to the magazine offices, which were near the Hotel George V, and how I had stopped by to look for him in the lobby and the bar area.

"You are so sweet," he said wistfully.

When we hung up, I felt very sad and stared at the phone, willing him to call me back. I wished there was something I could do for him, if only to hold him quietly. Something was bothering him, something he hadn't told me about. Imagining him back in Sfax, out in his garden, or roaming the hills with his rifle, imparted a sense of freedom. It was the exact opposite of his job, catering to the whims of the nouveau riche princes. They were corrupting him, even as he professed to despise their frivolity and lack of responsibility. Constant contact with them could sour him, rendering him too cynical to believe in a peaceful life, like the one inside that garden. Lodged safely within the bones of his rib cage, I envisioned an arbor, with roses blooming inside his chest, a secret garden. Oh to put my hand inside and tend it. I remembered the terrarium I had not purchased for Waddah.

The similarities were stunning.

Both men were risk takers. Their desires to succeed fueled by ambition and competition, to live as well or better than their clients did. To eat the best food, to wear the finest clothes, to drive the fancy cars and frequent beautiful women — they wanted it all. The dream of the garden was too simple to satisfy them now. How many could forget the deluxe life in Paris once they tasted it? Why shouldn't they want the same? Yet my exposure to such fabulous wealth had provided a strange immunization. I did not crave such a life. Lebanon had shown me where the jet set could end up. I wanted the peaceful garden.

Omar had asked why I wasn't married already, a nice girl like me. My answer was, "I could have been but I did not want to give up my freedom for life in a golden cage."

"Oh I don't know. Those cages aren't all bad," he replied, half joking.

What people will do for money, I thought. On this subject, a gulf existed between us. There were many ways to live. Who was I to judge him? If I had been born into his life, would I have done better or worse?

I laid out his new robe on the chair where he always hung his clothes, and placed the slippers alongside on the floor. Although he had said not to expect him tonight, one never knew. Before I climbed the steps to my loggia bed, I looked at the place where he so often sat on the couch, and imagined him there in the future. The image came again of a very young child, with curly black hair, playing at his knee. "Our child" I thought dreamily, although intuition may have intended an entirely different message.

Chapter 13

A PLUSIEURS REPRISE /
THE MANY TRIES

...You're destroying me. You're good for me

You're destroying me. You're good for me...

— MARGUERITE DURAS

August & September 1984

Georgina's journalist friend called the next morning, suggesting we meet at his office at three that afternoon. I was there at the appointed hour but our meeting lasted barely ten minutes. Did that mean the man already had me checked out? Or had he made up his mind as soon as we met? On the phone, his voice had sounded so much like Waddah's and I said this as we shook hands.

"Do you know him?"

"Yes, we went to school together."

He assured me he would speak to Georgina about my book proposal just as soon as she returned from Tunisia. So, thanks to Omar, we now have Tunisia in common too. I assured him she already knew about it directly from me.

"She is seeing Abu Ammar. She only stays two or three days each time she goes. She'll probably be back on Sunday."

I knew Abu Ammar was Yassir Arafat's nom de guerre. Maybe he gave her money when she went there, or she ran "errands" for the PLO.

The man offered me a cigarette. When I declined he asked if it would bother me if he had one. I said no it didn't. It was his office after all. As he lit the French Gitane, I saw how thin his body was and how tired his eyes, remembering how Omar had said, "He likes his whiskey."

I asked if he had ever seen the film *Gone with the Wind*.

"Yes."

"That is the sort of story I have in mind to tell about Georgina." I meant the backdrop of war, the end of a way of life, and people caught up in things beyond their control, with tragic choices and outcomes.

"I have seen that film several times. I agree, Georgina's life could make several films, and a play or two as well." His tone implied that he was quite positive about my chances of getting Georgina to talk to me about her life.

I passed him an envelope with my proposal, an outline, my bio, and some copies of my poems, as samples of my work. He left them sitting on the desk between us. Perhaps he would look at them later.

There seemed to be nothing else left to say. The rest would depend upon Georgina. I rose to leave, not wanting to overstay my welcome, and he did not try to stop me. He said he'd be in touch with me upon Georgina's return.

I thanked him and said goodbye. His cigarette was not even finished as he escorted me to the door but I guessed the process of my being checked out was over. Maybe this would speed up things with Georgina.

* * * *

Back on the pavement, I went towards the metro station, glancing at the Rolls-Royces and late model Mercedes parked outside the Hotel George V. When I'd stayed there with Mazen, during my university days, I had not suspected what I now did in hindsight. Bad enough this old family "friend" had slept with my sister, but he had also dangled me, perhaps as some sort of bait, in front of Kamal Adham and Prince Saud. Why? Since those days I had woken to the fact that a lot more was going on. Mazen had never explained anything. Yet surely he expected some return on his investments, in Georgina too, after she became Miss Universe.

Who had Georgina trusted? Had Salameh told her the truth? Had she trusted him with hers? Without honesty there could be no trust, no true intimacy, even with ourselves. How many lies had I been told? And which types had I preferred to believe? It seemed easier to ferret out lies others told us than the ones we told ourselves. But everything came back to the crises caused by the lies. The betrayals. Being lied to or lied about had caused me the most despair. Wanting the pain of irreconcilable lies to end had prompted me to hold a razor blade to my wrist at age nineteen. How to escape the lies, and stop betraying myself most of all?

When the inner voice sounded, luckily I had trusted it, and the clarity of its message, "You don't have the problem. They have the problem." Did other people hear voices? And trust them?

And what was the problem exactly? Was it the lies or the total lack of trust they caused? Most of us were confused, but it was our job to sort things out: who or what to believe and how to heed our innermost guidance. In the years since I had heard that still small voice, it had made a great difference, although I still sought validation when visiting psychics. All of this made me wonder just how many kinds of truth there were. Intuitive truth. Relative truth. Subjective truth. Objective truth. Factual truth. Emotional truth. Spiritual truth.

* * * *

That Wednesday, the journalist invited me to come see the photographs he had of Georgina's recent wedding. At his office I studied each picture as he handed them to me, one by one. Her young son Ali junior had been there, all dressed up and playing in the London Garden Terrace where the wedding reception had been held. Not wanting to bombard this man with questions, I ascertained as much as possible from the photographs. His standard reply to the questions I asked was, "Georgina can tell you about that."

"You can have some pictures to keep," he offered.

Not wanting to be greedy, I selected a single one, of Georgina and her new groom, Elie Salim. Standing before the priest, their postures and expressions were so serious. He wore a dark suit, with a white shirt and white tie. Though nearly the same age as his bride, he appeared older, his eyes ringed and debauched. Georgina was dressed in a white satin suit, encrusted with sequins around the neckline and shoulders. White gloves covered her hands, which held a small bouquet. Pearl and diamond jewelry flashed at her wrist, ears and neck. On her head sat a fanciful sequined band, decorated with a white netting, descending over her hair. Attached to the band, in the middle of her forehead was large, sequin-covered satin heart, with a spray of white feathers arching back over the top of her head. Unusual and stylish, she was still beautiful to look at, with her high cheeks, fine skin, and sensuous mouth, artfully painted a deep red.

There was no news yet. Georgina had yet to return from Tunis, the capital of Omar's country, but the journalist assured me he had not forgotten my request. He promised to call as soon as he'd spoken with her.

"In the meantime, you might want to get in touch with a Lebanese filmmaker who is currently staying at the Prince de Galles Hotel. He made some films with Georgina in Beirut. Three I think."

After thanking him for the suggestion, I wondered where this Byzantine harem maze was leading me. All I wanted was to hear Georgina's story from her. My questions were not the ones men would ask, like whether she'd had an abortion. Women often leave men in the dark. They don't trust them with the truth. Guys who brag about their kills or how many women they've bedded never hear what women know. If Georgina had stayed with her first boyfriend, Philippe Duke, a swimmer and chemistry student at the Lebanese French University, her life would have been conventional and not worth writing about.

A television interviewer had asked her opinion on premarital sex after she won the Miss Universe contest.

She'd replied, "We must have lots of experience. Marriage is not a simple thing."

Public pressure caused her to qualify her remarks. She said she approved of premarital sex "only with someone you loved or planned to marry." Once again the face shown to the public differed markedly with what went on in private, and that left us all in the lurch, trying to reconcile the two.

* * * *

At midnight, I was still awake hoping to hear from Omar before sleeping. The phone rang. It was him, apologizing for not calling the night before. He had been in Deauville, with the prince's alcoholic son, gambling.

"Not with the man you said had a system for winning at roulette?" I countered.

"Him? He took me for a fool. Imagine, expecting me to hand over the money, for him to go and play with. I understood we would go to the casino together. I asked him what was to prevent him from going straight to the airport with my 60,000 hard-earned francs, god knows."

"So, what happened instead?"

There was a long pause before he admitted the truth. "I played and I lost, badly. What's worse I had to reimburse the prince's son what he had loaned me. His father won't return until the middle of next month. I had to go to all my friends and the banks to get the cash together. He didn't think I could manage it. But I did. I had to keep my word and get the money back to him."

He berated himself on the phone, telling me how stupid and foolish he had been, to squander so much money in a single night. He did not quote the exact amount, and I did not ask. While listening I thought at least he's able to criticize himself and admit to his own mistakes. He said he felt too rotten to come see me tonight, even if he did finish early enough with the son and thanked me for my compassion.

"But what I really need to do is to get out from under these Saudis and start something else — a restaurant, a hotel, anything."

Brightening I said, "We will help each other."

"You are wise you know. And so sweet. You are too good for a man like me. I cannot support you or anything."

"I don't need to be supported now, not until I stop working to have kids, and even then, only for a little while. I am a contributor Omar, not some parasite."

After hanging up the phone, too disturbed to sleep I got out my journal.

Omar called. I'm upset. He's been gambling and lost heavily. I'm ashamed to admit it but I liked things better before. Now I know he needs my help even more but this problem might be too big for me. I need to face reality. I don't need this. He is letting me see him for what he really is, including his weakness and remorse. I suppose I ought to love him more for opening up and revealing this much of himself, but it has changed everything. I am beginning to see and hear again. It's like waking up from a prolonged fantasy. Omar is no pot at the end of any rainbow. I mustn't pretend anymore. The edifice I've constructed of him in my imagination is wobbling. And worst of all, because he is bogged down in this money mess, he is not with me. Thank God he did not ask me for money. What would I have done if he had?

I think I got a good kick in my blind spot tonight. I will wait and see what a difference all this makes when he's here in my arms. My heart hurts. It does not want to give up even one slice of this beautiful fantasy of mine but my cynical and calculating head is finally being heard.

It is wisdom I am after, non? Even though love is lovelier, how else to become wise, except by getting over having been so silly? Maybe there is nothing I can do but love him for as long as it's going to last and hope, love somehow helps him to break out of this vicious circle. He is probably quite the gambler. It sounds like this is not the first time he has suffered such serious regrets.

Putting aside my journal I turned out the light, more certain I could survive being wrong about Omar. Being too afraid to risk loving him, or anyone else, was worse.

* * * *

The next afternoon my go-between, the journalist, called to say he had a long talk with Georgina who'd returned. In principle, everything looked set to go. "Here is her phone number. She asked me to tell you to call between eleven thirty and noon tomorrow." It was the same number Maurice had given me, but getting it this way implied I'd been checked out and deemed acceptable, didn't it?

"Hooray!" I shouted after replacing the receiver. Lifting Darius, I danced around the room with my cat.

At noon the next day the maid answered the phone and said, "Madame has gone out." My heart sank.

"But she was expecting your call. She told me to tell you to call her back in about an hour."

I gritted my teeth, feeling so close and yet so far, made to jump through so many hoops, but we finally spoke on the phone that day.

That evening I wrote to Lynda.

Well, well, well. Almost a year into this, can you believe it? I finally had my first phone conversation with Georgina today. We are supposed to meet next week since she's leaving for somewhere tomorrow. We'll have another talk then. She will be traveling most of October and so will I, as I've got to come back to the US again to earn next month's rent. We will probably not start working on the interviews until November or so.

I asked if she had any scrapbooks. She does but they're in Beirut at the Rue Verdun apartment. She will have to get someone to bring them from there. They might be water damaged since she heard the place had been shelled and the pipes burst in the apartment above.

She didn't remember me from six months ago and thought the book may have been done already. I did not ask why she never responded to my letters...never mind. I think it was the mention of making her life into a movie that really got her interested.

Her voice is very husky. She sounds like one tough broad on the phone. We have yet to talk about percentages or a contract. I have no idea if she'll keep the meeting planned for next week when she returns but at least we are talking. And she answers the phone when I call. Perhaps this is going to happen after all.

How are you doing? My love life, with Omar, is another story. More in next letter.

Much love.

* * * *

For the next three days, there was no word from Omar. I alternated between being sad and getting angry, first at him and then at myself, for boarding this emotional roller coaster. After the third miserable night I decided I had to get over him. He could not even be depended upon to call. It's worse this time because he knows how much it hurts me when he does not keep in touch. Why did I ever take him back?

Perhaps his last phone call had been some kind of test. Had he wanted to see if I would offer help in the form of money? Had he been hinting at this all along and I'd been too dumb to see it? Because I am not proving to be profitable, he's tired of playing along. Maybe he's moved on to someone willing to spend on him. He's a good for nothing rascal. The bitterness rose in my throat. I hissed at the cat, "I have only myself to blame."

Later that morning Omar called as if nothing was wrong. "I can come by around three o'clock today to spend a few hours with you."

Defensively I asked, "Where have you been?"

"Where have you been?" he countered. "I called you yesterday several times, between four and eight."

I was so upset with him I didn't remember I had been at Freddie's getting my hair done and shopping until after hanging up the phone.

All he had said was, *"Ce n'est pas grave"* (It's not serious).

After that call, I burst into tears. Too confused to be happy that we would be together in a few hours, a large part of me resented he still existed. This phantom. Why was I torturing myself?

His secrecy seemed deliberate. Did he fear my interest would wane if I knew the real Omar? How much did I need to know, to maintain my equilibrium and sanity? Surely more than I did. During my morning ablutions I counseled myself. "Don't do it! Don't slip backwards. You know what he is. He's hurt you already, and he'll do it again." I felt like a conflicted wreck, my warring parts drowning my common sense.

At three thirty he was at the door, as handsome as ever, flashing his thousand-watt smile. What a devil. We sat on the couch. He had no idea how worked up I had been, but was it my mistake to be so sensitive? You are a big girl. You ought to know how to play these games, I told myself. But this revealed the problem. It wasn't a game. Not for me. Not with him. Now that he was here in the flesh my body still wanted him. I swallowed my ire and he regaled me with the details of his recent escapades.

The other night at three in the morning, after dropping the prince's son at the hotel, he had been on his way to the garage with the limousine. At a red traffic light he pulled up behind a small Renault 5 car. When the light changed, the two French girls in the little car did not move. Omar flicked his high beams to indicate that the light was green. They stubbornly stayed right where they were, making crude remarks about oily foreigners in their fancy cars.

Omar had whipped the limo around in front of them so they couldn't pull away. Leaping out he stuck his hand through their open window and grabbed the ignition keys. Holding onto a handful of hair, belonging to the girl who was not driving, he instructed her, "Tell your friend to say, 'I beg your pardon Mr. Foreigner' ten times if you want your keys back."

They did as they were told, and he returned their keys.

He said he rarely lost his temper but the attitude toward immigrants in France was sinking to a new low.

"It is different in America," I said. "Immigrants built the country. They are the heroes. We all came from somewhere. I've got Scottish, English, German, and French blood in me. Nobody is better than anybody else. In America only money counts."

"Well it's not like that in France," he went on, giving other examples of the racism he saw far too much of. He'd watched metro officials cursing some poor Senegalese and had gotten involved, paying the man's fine for not having a ticket. He was proud of his recent triumph over the French customs control and regarded it as a kind of revenge.

He explained what he had done to fool them. "You know you are not allowed to take more than five thousand francs out of the country if you are a resident?"

I nodded, familiar with President Mitterrand's infamous financial impositions.

"The last time I returned to Tunisia, they stopped me on the way out at the airport. They asked if I had any cash. I laughed and said, "Of course I do! With these infernal restrictions, my pockets are bulging."

"The guy waved me through laughing. I had one hundred thousand francs on me. They could have confiscated it all."

I could see how he could do things like that and get away with it. Look at what I'd let him get away with.

Later in bed we discussed our relationship. He asked point blank, "What do you want from me?"

"What I have," I answered, hugging him closer. "And I want to find out why you were put on my road and I was put on yours." I also admitted how distressed I had been when he had not called.

"I knew you would be," he said, softening. "And I'm sorry. I often think of you, and know I should call, but I stop myself. I have seen men in love and how women take advantage of them. Men only fall in love two or three times in their lives, and they never forget it. But women? They are always coming with this one and going with that one. They get over things easier. It is better for a man not to show his feelings to the woman. Besides I hate to have to do something, even if it is to call you."

Then he added, "And I hate *arrivistes*. One ordered champagne when I took her out. I left her to pay the bill. I despise phoniness. I like women who have seen life, and know what it is, and are not impressed by it anymore."

Watching him with my chin on his shoulder, I had to wonder what he really thought about me.

"You are so sweet and kind and understanding hayati. And intelligent," he added. "Maybe too intelligent for me!"

He pulled me to him and sank his teeth lightly into my cheek, as he'd done before. My head whirled as he lifted my face to kiss my mouth, rousing me once more. In the midst of our frenzy I opened my eyes to see his eyes, fierce and fiery above me, just before they closed. He gritted his teeth and threw his head back with the final pleasure of possessing me again.

At eleven that night, he left with the note he'd encouraged me to write, after I'd told him about the Lebanese film director who had worked with Georgina. Since he was staying at the Prince de Galles, right next to the Hotel George V, he offered to deliver it for me. Omar had cautioned me to avoid telling this man all my ideas concerning Georgina. "Those two could eat you up you know."

I laughed and agreed with him. "But you'll protect me, non?" Then I added, "You eat me up with worry when you don't call. I cannot work or write when I'm wondering about you."

"I know. I know what you want. Someone here with you, who has things in common with you. To go out with, to talk to, even to live with, until things become more clear."

I felt like blurting out, "It is more serious than that! I want to be the mother of your children," but I held my tongue.

* * * *

The film director, Mohamed Salman called at a quarter to two that morning. Omar had phoned me earlier to say he successfully delivered my note to the man's driver, George, whom he knew and had seen that evening. Mr. Salman suggested we meet at his hotel tomorrow evening at seven. Then he called me back, suggesting I come now, to Calvados and join him for a drink.

I did not think this was a good idea, but since it was for Georgina, I flew around the apartment, swiftly dressing and arriving shortly after two thirty.

He was a caricature of the Hollywood director stereotype: sleazy, nervous, fat, and practically chomping on a cigar. "Could the casting couch be far away?" I mused. The man's flesh spilled out of his chair. He smoked one cigarette after another like a fellow determined to nail his coffin shut, the sooner the better. I shuddered thinking Georgina had ever taken orders from such a man.

I told him a little more about myself than my note had mentioned. There were other people with him so I did not want to say much.

He told me he was a Shia from South Lebanon. Having spent decades in the movie business, he'd started out as a singer and an actor, before moving on to directing. Before long he was asking if I wanted to work with him. Had I, could I write anything about Lebanon?

"Maybe we can talk about that tomorrow," I hedged, seeking a polite way to extricate myself. He got the message. Pressing a five hundred franc note into my hand, he said, "For taxi fare to our next meeting."

This was embarrassing. I tried to refuse it, but he wasn't going to take it back, especially not in front of his friends. I decided this was neither the time nor the place for making a scene. His driver George took me home.

* * * *

The following day I ate dinner with him, and met his daughter and her

213

English husband. When pressed for details about my ideas, I felt it was not fair to talk much about Georgina until after discussing things with her. Having no idea what her feelings were now, concerning this man, I resisted the temptation to go behind her back and talk about her life with other people for over a year already. I feared this would make it impossible for Georgina to trust me.

So this meeting came to naught, although Salman promised to locate the cassettes he had of Georgina's movies when I asked to see his work. The next day he was leaving to meet yet another Saudi prince, who was financing some project. I doubted he would keep his word about getting me the cassettes — and he didn't.

Chapter 14

JE SUIS MALADE /
I AM SICK

I'm sick, that's right I'm sick, you've denied
me all of my songs, you've drained me of all
my words, and my heart is completely sick...

— ALICE DONA, lyrics to "I Am Ill"

October & November 1984

The following week I finally met with Georgina. On my way to her apartment that Saturday evening, I had Darius in the cab with me, for I was also seeing the Burkes for dinner that night. They had kindly offered to cat sit for me since I was leaving on Monday for another month's work in the US. Excited to tell them about the Georgina meeting, I dropped Darius off and assured them I'd return soon for our supper. After so many disappointments, I half expected to be told once again, "Madame just left."

Climbing the single flight of steps to her apartment, I rang the bell. The Filipino maid ushered me inside. Surprisingly Madame was there this time. As I entered I noticed little Ali, munching on something.

"Haven't you finished your dinner?" I asked with gentle friendliness.

"Yes, I'm done," he replied, confidently for six-year-old.

I followed the maid into the black, white, and silver toned salon. Georgina rose from a white leather couch to greet me with a kiss on both cheeks. After all this time, we were off to a decent beginning. Dressed in a long black lounging robe, with a patterned neckline, she introduced me to another Lebanese woman, Najwa. Georgina's hands were full. She had a glass of water in one and a spoon in the other.

"Do you know what this is?" she asked holding out the spoon for me to see its contents.

"It's cigarette ashes!" I answered, astonished. "You are not going to swallow them are you?"

"Yes. I have, how do you call it?" she said pressing her diaphragm.

"Heartburn?" I offered.

Georgina nodded, and drank them down with a swig of water. I was as stunned by the symbolism as the act itself. To eat ashes as a cure...

I had forgotten how tall Georgina was. We sat on the couch together. From the envelope I took my recently reworked outline and gave it to her to look at. While she examined the typewritten pages, I studied Georgina's face. No make up, just a smudge of leftover eye shadow. Her shoulder-length auburn hair fell to her shoulders and curled softly around her face. Although tired, she'd just risen from an afternoon siesta, she was still a great beauty, though she looked more than a year older than me. It was her languor. Her movements were not those of a young woman. She was thoroughly matured in every sense of the word.

Focusing upon her attractive mouth, I realized how such seductive lips could hypnotize men and women too. That mysterious quality of desirable beauty emanated from within, involving far more than the mere surface of her skin. She carried herself with the authority of someone used to being watched and wanted. I could see she wasn't interested in reading anymore of what I'd given her so I began to reminisce.

"My father worked for Middle East Airlines in Beirut. Remember those life-size cardboard cutout figures they had of you?"

"Yes I remember them. I did that when I was about fourteen."

"And remember the white fur hat and coat you wore on the cover of Monday morning magazine? I still have that photo," I added.

"Yes. That was for the opening of the Jet Set boutique."

I mentioned the movie *Gone With the Wind*. She agreed she wanted her life story told like that.

I elaborated, "No need to get too political, just one woman's life, in a country suffering through war. Maybe your story can help where so many newspaper reports have failed. People don't understand what's happening in Lebanon."

"Does anyone?"

I brought up the issue of having seen Mohamed Salman. "I didn't want to tell him anything about this idea without your permission."

"Since my marriage, people have been writing such crazy things about my life and what I am doing. There is even some film being done, called *The End of Death* or something."

She was obviously exasperated by all the rumors and gossip. I hoped this might motivate her to set the record straight by telling her story herself. Maybe for the sake of her little son too.

Georgina invited me to stay and have a drink.

"I'm sorry. I cannot today. I really must go now. My friends downstairs are waiting for me. You know, the Burkes, they live right below you."

Enough had been accomplished for a first sitting. I did not want to say much more with the other woman there. One never knew. They both rose to say goodbye when I stood up to leave. Georgina walked with me to the door.

"We shall meet again here tomorrow night at seven, okay?" she said.

"Okay. But I must go to the US for my work the next day. Thank you."

* * * *

The following evening at seven when I arrived the maid handed me a note.

Dear Cynthia,
I am very sorry I was obliged to leave at six thirty to go to the airport. A very dear friend of mine is transiting through Paris and I have to see him. I tried to call you at home but there was no answer. I will work on your paper and when you come back, we will see each other.
Sorry again. Have a nice trip, Georgina

Later that night we spoke on the phone. Georgina explained she could express herself better in Arabic than English. While I was in the US she would contact a friend in Syria.

"He wrote a book of poems about me. For years he has been asking to do my biography. I could arrange for an Arab writer to come and take down the first draft."

Of course I was not the only person who had the idea to write about her. Competition complicated things. A camel is a horse designed by a committee I thought despondently. Georgina added, "I hope you're not in a hurry. All of this might take a year or more."

"Well it has already taken a whole year to get this far. My clairvoyant in New York said it might take three. I want it to be good, not fast."

"Do you know a good voyante here in Paris?" Georgina queried.

"No, but I can ask around," I offered. So, Georgina must believe in them too.

"Call me when you return from America. I know I'm often traveling, but I am rarely gone for more than four or five days in a row." Georgina said.

"I'll just keep trying until I reach you," I responded, trying to sound cheerful.

* * * *

By noon the next day, I was winging my way across the Atlantic Ocean again. Omar had spent the night and driven me to the airport. Once settled in my seat thirty five thousand feet above the ground, I reviewed our recent conversations, especially the part about children.

On Sunday afternoon Omar had taken me to meet his friends at the Café Les Deux Magots. While drinking coffee and eating pastries, Omar's friends had teased us about what beautiful children we would have together.

In bed later I brought this up again. "So, what's all this about beautiful children? How many do you want?"

He laughed, and answered, "Oh, about a dozen."

"A dozen? Then we better get started right away!"

"Two, two would be enough."

"A girl first. And then the boy. She would help me, the way I helped my mother with the others who came after me."

"No, no, two sons," he said in a markedly sarcastic tone.

"You don't like girls? That's not very evident," I said squeezing his buttock playfully. We fell asleep holding each other.

On the way to the airport, I told him more about the visit with Georgina, remembering to mention the other woman there.

"Najwa?" said Omar incredulously.

"Yes! Do you know her?"

"I helped her arrange a week in Tunisia with that man Elie! She thought he was going to marry her. Then he turned around and married Georgina. What a hypocrite she is! What is she doing in Georgina's house after she told me so recently about that bad woman Elie had run off with and married?"

This was startling news. Without Omar's network I never would have known. I thanked him for the information and silently wondered just what sort of relationship this Najwa had with my Omar. Finally I asked him. He said there was nothing *intime*. They were just friends.

"Well she is dumb for letting you get away," I joked.

* * * *

A month of nonstop work and travel passed before my return to Paris in November 1984. I visited my parents and my sister, and squeezed in time with friends, but with all my moving around, I had heard only once from Omar. Riding the taxi back from Charles De Gaulle airport, I steeled myself for the fact he might not be in Paris. I had no way of knowing if Omar had received the cards I'd mailed to the Hotel George V. I had not phoned to ask if he had picked up his mail after Omar's warning that the concierge was not his friend.

Despite the rare November brightness that afternoon, I went straight to bed, exhausted after unlocking my apartment door.

Omar's call woke me from a deep sleep at seven that evening.

"I thought you would be back two days ago." He sounded worried.

"Did you get my last letter about the delay?"

"No, it didn't arrive yet. I tried calling you but there was never anyone there," he said.

Listening to the concern in his voice, I smiled. For once the shoe was on the other foot. Now he knows what it feels like to worry when the other one doesn't show up.

"What are you doing now?" he asked.

"I'm in bed," I answered, hoping to sound terribly decadent.

"I bet you are only warming your side," he teased back.

"Well, if you were here…I'd give you the warm side," I laughed.

"I wish I was. I do not know the prince's plans for tonight yet. He is due to leave Paris on Wednesday, Inshallah. I'll call you again later, hayati."

After replacing the receiver, I did not move from bed, still feeling incredibly jetlagged. It was worse when flying against the sun instead of traveling westward with it. Turning on the radio to the Star of the East station, the familiar tones of ouds, flutes and drums soothed me while I pondered tomorrow's chores: I had to pick up the cat and deliver a note to let Georgina know I was back in town.

The doorbell rang, and a key turned in the lock, not long afterwards. I flew down the steps from my loggia bed, disheveled but tickled to see Omar coming through my door. What a good surprise. As handsome as ever, in a gray silk suit, with a Bordeaux colored tie, and shoes of the same deep wine hue. He drew me to him and whispered in my ear, "J'ai tellement envie de toi" (I want you so much).

Leading me back up the wooden steps to the bed, still warm from sleep, we celebrated our reunion.

Afterwards as he dressed I asked, "How did you get away from them?"

"The prince was taking a nap. I said I would go check which movies are playing on the Champs-Élysées."

When he got back to the hotel he called to tell me, "Good thing I returned when I did. They were looking for me. But it was worth it hayati."

* * * *

The following afternoon, a man answered the door when I stopped by Georgina's apartment. I had come to collect Darius from the Burkes, who kindly cared for him again, during my most recent work trip. The man's resemblance to Georgina was so strong, I blurted out, "Are you her father?"

"Yes, I am. My name is George. My daughter is still traveling. Won't you come in?"

"I'd like to, maybe next time. Would you please give this note to Georgina when she returns. I'd appreciate it."

He nodded and took it from my hand. We both smiled goodbye. As I went down the steps I wondered if he knew about my project. Perhaps he could help.

Downstairs at the Burkes, Darius was fine, and I thanked them for their help. The family had grown quite attached to him and he meowed in protest when I hugged him too long. Tom had just returned from another trip to Saudi Arabia. As tomorrow was Election Day in the US, we discussed the American presidential campaign. None of us had bothered to vote by absentee ballot because we assumed President Reagan would be reelected, though we had many doubts about his foreign policy. I invited the Burkes to dinner at my place this Friday.

"Maybe Omar will be able to come this time and you can meet this phantom I've told you so much about."

Afterwards as the taxi wove through the traffic towards home, Darius purred contentedly in his carrier on the seat beside me. The sky was a royal shade of blue, such fine weather for November. How long would it stay this nice? I resolved to take some long walks and make the most of these good weather days. We always paid for them, with the wretched winter ones, I reckoned as the cab crossed over Pont Marie to Île Saint Louis and the Quai de Bourbon.

* * * *

Though I'd invited Omar for the Friday night curry dinner I cooked for the Burkes, he had not joined us. Omar had studiously avoided meeting anyone in my circle. This had become an issue. His odd work schedule provided some plausible excuses, but I was determined to have Lynda meet him when she visited on her way to see relatives in Brussels. After all the messages she had taken from him, on the phone this past year, and my numerous mentions in my letters, she ought to put a face to his name. "I need a second opinion. I am far from objective and I know it," I confided.

She was the first of my friends to meet him and even that was by carefully plotted chance. I needed to be able to depend upon her as our go between. "After all, you are the one he wakes up at all hours of the night when he calls the Greenwich place looking for me."

* * * *

The plan was to see Omar at the Hotel Georges V. We would stop by for an aperitif on our way to the theater nearby. I had gotten us tickets to see my favorite singer, Serge Lama. He was starring as Napoleon, in a musical he had helped compose the songs for. On the way there I gave Lynda my mini walking tour of Paris, passing through the Tuileries Gardens, with their round pools, gravel paths, and statuary before continuing on to Place de la Concorde. There we took the Champs-Élysées toward L'Arc de Triomphe. This was my best-loved stroll, done meditatively and alone, most Sundays. When standing at the Tuileries, one could gaze all the way to the L'Arc, several unobstructed kilometers away. This view not only showcased many Paris landmarks, it displayed the pleasing coherency of the city's overall architectural design. If only my life was as well laid out I mused, sighing inwardly. Then I might be able to see my way forward.

As we strode along, the sun set and the sky turned purple behind the Place de l'Étoile. Waiting our turn to cross the boulevard, I told Lynda, "Some say Europe is just a big old museum but Paris is still very special. They built it with beauty and majesty in mind." A fine rain began to fall. Pissing was what the French called this form of precipitation. "Wait till you see Versailles and the palace tomorrow. All that gilt and extravagance. Then you'll know why the French had their revolution."

As luck would have it Omar was at the bar as we walked into the lobby. His friend Hamed was there too, the one who had teased Omar and me about having beautiful children at the Café Deux Magots, before my last US trip.

We sat in the seats nearest them with our drinks. Lynda gave me an "I approve" look. Hamed bent to explain something to Omar, who then leaned over to whisper to me, "The prince is sitting on the red chair there, in the foyer, behind me, with a German businessman, if you want to have a look at him."

I turned my head just as the Saudi prince Mishari stroked his dyed black goatee with a brown hand.

"I'm going to go over there and tell him he's got no right to keep you away from me so much of the time," I threatened, mock seriously.

"Shhhh," cautioned Omar. "It's bad enough I'm sitting here with you while on duty, so to speak. If he sees us with two beautiful women, he'll get jealous."

"I should think he would be pleased to see you happy," I quipped.

"Oh no. You don't know him hayati. He would reduce my *pour boire* (tip) when he leaves, just so I cannot enjoy myself too much when he's not here," explained Omar. He was totally serious. A strange comment, I thought. It sounded like something a jealous lover would do. Perhaps this possessive employer was…I drove the idea out of my mind once again, lacking proof of such a thing.

In the darkness of the theater the suspicion returned however. While trying to concentrate on the musical, this idea wouldn't go away. Was it a piece of the puzzle that was missing from our lovemaking? Despite the fact his flesh intoxicated me, my pleasure with him remained incomplete. All this time I had made excuses for him, thinking Omar was too tired, when arriving so late from his nights out. Contenting myself with the heat of our passion, my focus had been primarily on pleasing him. For quite awhile this had been sufficient as Omar made me feel so warm, so generous, so womanly, and voluptuous but the nagging need for orgasmic release would not go away. Why did I not dare to bring up the subject?

How could he know so much yet not know this? He seemed to care about my pleasure, to a point, but we had never achieved that mystical union, when physical bliss crossed into the realm of the spiritual, at least for me. Surely any man who loves women would have such knowledge. My other lovers had known, almost every one. It was hard to believe a man his age, with his good looks and experience, had yet to discover this secret. This had slowly become my litmus test. Real love doesn't leave us hanging, it completes us. Rather than make this request, I was lying to myself. Why?

I recalled something Maurice had told me before leaving Paris. Maurice had performed this most intimate task with such relish and regularity, I feared my body would dissolve with pleasure. But he had cautioned me, "If you are ever really serious about marrying a man, take my advice. One, make sure he really loves you, by testing him over and over again. And two, don't let him know how much experience you have. It might scare him."

Taking him at his word, I had known he was telling me what other men might believe, though it seemed rather insincere and contradictory.

Instinctively I had not fully revealed my siren side to Omar. In view of his lifestyle and background, I had wanted to be the pure unspoiled person in his tawdry world. Yet this had left me frustrated. Concealing my needs only intensified my desire, which was never sated. I suffered his absences more acutely because my thirst for him was never fully quenched not even when I had him in my arms. Resorting to pleasuring myself alone afterwards, I recalled what we had yet to share.

Several times I had resolved to broach this subject but I had never discussed this exact topic in French. That increased the degree of awkwardness. Thinking to drop the hint in some clever way, I considered telling him my erotic dream in which he bent his head between my legs. But when he was with me, I contented myself with his presence, and became more reluctant to upset our established dynamics.

But without this ecstatic exchange, he would not keep me. Failing to master this was a harbinger of other difficulties. It was a matter of time, and a way out, for he had not yet bound me, and I could still escape. Never telling him what I wanted, I waited for him to intuit it, for him to want to please me more. By my convoluted logic, offering to meet these mutual needs was done freely. Doing it on demand did not feel right.

Unless one was a client. Ugh. I shuddered to think of Omar as a gigolo or the object of another man's pleasure, for money. But that would explain, perhaps, why he had a disdain for certain acts of generosity? If one was accustomed to making others pay…was he my client in a sense because I had not asked him to meet my needs? Had this belittled me in his eyes?

Once he'd remarked that I gave myself so freely without expecting anything in return. He almost couldn't believe it, as if he could not trust someone without discernible needs.

"Don't you want something?"

Truth and ecstasy was what I wanted. After all the blood and lies, ecstasy was wordlessly true. I trusted my body. It was an antenna intuiting what my mind missed, a compass operating inside my chest, pointing me towards other ecstasies, spiritual ones too, though I had yet to grasp that portion of the message. Omar also had intuition, yet he deferred to calculation. Life in Paris had convinced him that everything had its price. The new brides of Omar's prince were generally divorced for approximately $60,000 dollars. And I knew about call girls and escorts, from places like the notorious Madame Claude, whose range of services started at three thousand francs per hour.

Was the corollary true? Do things freely given, without price, have no value? Was it all just commerce? When reducing our lives to numbers, we rarely gained what counted most. A handsome man like Omar, who needed to make money, had certainly found plenty of opportunities to earn it in Paris. Did I want to find out? If I asked him, would he admit such a truth? He must have wondered about me too, but he knew about my job, because my work, and his, kept tearing us apart.

As the musical ended, Lynda and I left the theatre, and I wondered whether Josephine and Napoleon had such problems. The infamous quip, "Not tonight Josephine," was never uttered by Napoleon. I had discovered it was a bit of British propaganda. Rather like the muckraking broadsheets in Paris who invented the phrase, "Let them eat cake" which Marie Antoinette had never said. But unless we dove deeper, we'd never know such things, nor sort out the whys of the lies.

* * * *

Later that week when Lynda went on to Brussels, I had yet to hear back from Georgina. Whenever I called her number, to check if she had returned from her travels, her father often answered. Always polite, he insisted nowadays, "Call me George." But, the response was always the same, "No, she isn't back yet."

One day, after he told me she was "still in Damascus" (where her older half sister lived), my impatience got the best of me, and I tried to enlist him.

"George, could you help me? I have proposed the idea of doing a book about your daughter's life."

"Yes, I know. She told me."

"Then you must also know, she has told me she wants to do it, but I can never seem to get her to work on it. Can you help me with your daughter? I don't want to go behind her back, but if you could find out, the next time you talk with her, if she really intends to do this book, or if she has changed her mind, I would appreciate it. I cannot afford to keep wasting so much time."

"I would like to help you. I agree, you should not go behind her back. I will talk with her and call you back. Perhaps we can arrange to meet for a coffee. What is your number?"

I told him, relieved he sounded interested. "Perhaps you can look at the file I left with her before we meet. Then you will know what I am trying to do."

* * * *

Omar remained preoccupied with his prince whose stay had been extended. He called when he could and our nocturnal couplings remained passionate. Looking back through my agenda book, I realized he visited about once every three days. The next time he called, I joked about this.

"Okay then. Now I won't come back for three days, to make you wait. You'll see!" he bantered back.

"Omar, that's not what I meant," I mock scolded. "You know how much I miss you. I always count the days until I see you again."

Late that night, still unable to sleep, I told myself, if he cannot sleep yet, neither will I. He had promised to ring to say goodnight, from wherever he was. I had just dozed off when the doorbell rang and there he was, his eyes shining with their deep black light, and his arms winding so tightly around me. He kissed me, and licked my lips with a mix of sharp and broad strokes of his tongue. I felt faint, imagining those touches somewhere else, but no, not that night.

After, he held me, with my back to his front, calling me *mon petit lapin* (my little rabbit) softly in my ear. Rejoicing at this new endearment, I decided to be patient. He did love me, in his own way.

* * * *

The following day when George Rizk phoned he had good news. "My daughter will return tomorrow. I have spoken with her about your call. She assured me she does intend to do the book with you. The problem is she just hasn't any time. She will call you, probably tomorrow."

He added, "I found the file you left her. I read your poems. I liked them. I think the book is a good idea, and a movie. If the war had not come, Georgina would have liked to continue her acting career I think. In any case, we will talk about all that. I will try to help you. I will call again soon."

The next day, Georgina called, apologizing, but saying she would have to postpone any meeting for a few days. "I have to meet some people at the airport, and take them to the hospital later today. And tomorrow I must buy things to send to other people. It is all rather urgent. But I will try to call you around five."

I hung up wondering if this was PLO business. Were wounded fighters arriving? What type of items had to be purchased? Medical supplies? Ammunition? The death toll in Lebanon had just surpassed eighty thousand at that point, in a country of three million.

Later that day Omar phoned with the news that the prince had invited him to come along on a trip to America. "But I told him I didn't want to go. I don't know the language or anything."

"I'll teach you habibi. English is not so hard."

"How fast can you teach me?" He added, "I'm leaving for London with him the day after tomorrow. I have no idea how long he will stay there but I would guess it will be about a week. I'll come see you before I leave. And when I return, we will have all the time to ourselves."

The next time Georgina called, my spirits sank to a new low. "Listen," she said in a serious tone. "I know you want to start the book now, but I must postpone things until spring, March or April at the earliest. Now is just not the moment for it. I am so busy. I am trying to get a business started, and I am searching for a new apartment."

"Well, what else can I do? I suppose I just have to be patient. My voyante in New York said it would take three years. I am visiting another one, here tomorrow. I wonder if she will say the same thing," I joked, trying to make light of all this.

"Oh? A voyante? A good one?" Georgina queried, obviously more interested, to hear of one in Paris.

"I do not know. I will tell you after I have seen her, if you like."

"What's her number?" Georgina asked. I read it off for her.

"Well call me tomorrow and tell me how it went with her."

The visit to Rosine the next morning confirmed many things about Omar, things I had hoped to hear. One of Rosine's first comments was, "You have already met the man you will marry, but the wedding is two years away. He wants to get himself established in some business or something before. You come from a higher social class than him. He is afraid to lose you if he cannot take care of you. There will be four children, two boys and two girls. You will be lucky, and have success in an artistic career, as well as a happy family life."

At the end of the reading, she asked if I had any questions. I inquired about Georgina and the book project.

"Hurry up and do it. Even if you have to get her out of Paris and off to someplace calm to help her concentrate. She is all mixed up in her mind. Not very eloquent or coherent. You will have to make it chronological later. And I see she may die soon after," she paused and I winced.

"When the book comes out, she may already be dead. There will be a line in the back of the book, 'on such and such a date…' I see lots of other dead people around her. Her life is definitely in danger."

This gave me the shivers. I did not want to believe it. Perhaps the dead were people who had already perished in Lebanon, like her husband. Returning home, I quickly copied down everything Rosine had said so that I could remember. Before finishing my notes, the phone rang. It was Georgina, wanting to know how the reading had gone.

"I've already made an appointment with her for this Monday evening."

I gulped, not knowing what to say, and babbled about myself instead. "She told me I'd marry my boyfriend and have four kids. And that we should do this book. She was pretty good. Let me know what you think after you see her."

When our call ended, I dialed Rosine, my hand shaking. "Will you be telling Georgina what you told me? She just called and I didn't know what to say."

"Yes, I will tell her, if it is still there when I see her. We should not censor such things. Sometimes these warnings can save people's lives. Or at least get them to put their affairs in order." she added in her deep, calm voice.

After hanging up, I wondered how I'd feel if someone told me I had less than two years to live.

* * * *

During the week Omar was in London, I put my affairs in order. Being in love took up an inordinate amount of time. Thanksgiving was almost here and then it would be Christmas. To accomplish anything before the year's end, I had to get better organized. My next work trip to the US was after the 1985 New Year, which left a decent block of time to devote to the Georgina project, even if she was unavailable. By spring, when she sat down with me, we could flesh out the crucial topics I had already outlined.

Would she tell me the truth? Not if Arafat had to give permission.

Georgina still depended upon him. Burning that bridge would be deadly. Look at what had happened to her husband and so many others. No wonder she was trying to set up her own business. But even if she became financially independent, they would never let her go. Nor her son. For the first time I realized she may have earned money for their cause without even knowing it. If she had been used, photographed with Saudi princes to blackmail them, that would have required an accomplice. Mazen? Salameh? Georgina did not seem the type to mastermind such initiative. And since Salameh's death, the wind had gone out of her sails.

* * * *

As 1984 came to an end, I met again with the ICM people, to finalize prospects for 1985. Things looked hopeful. IBM agreed to purchase the course I had helped to design. Indrei had gently coached me after one meeting, "You don't have to sell so hard, this is not New York. They have already decided to buy the program, otherwise they would not be meeting with us." This was constructive feedback and though it wasn't fun to hear it, I was grateful to be learning what was necessary for adapting to my business role here in France.

Another example of a critical incident, I would later share this mistake of mine with IBM executives, and other clients, as proof of how we were never done learning. Having attended ICM's existing cross-cultural communications program, I would co-train the next one, and then go solo, to fulfill the rest of the dates on the calendar of bookings. It was a great relief to secure this local source of income as it meant less traveling. Completing my business correspondence, I made time to see friends and go to the movies. Freddie did my hair and I met Fiona for dinner.

She told me Waddah's galerie was doing well, though he was traveling endlessly. "He has tried to reach you several times by phone."

One afternoon I went out to post the rest of my letters, drop off dry-cleaning and get groceries in the Le Marais neighborhood across Pont Marie and on my island. Though it was raining, I enjoyed this routine. The "Bonsoir Madames" and the "Merci Madames" in each specialty shop left me feeling like a regular. Eggs and cheese were purchased in one place, meat from another. A pudgy young Moroccan worked the fresh fruit and vegetable shop. His dream was to go to America. He practiced his English with me. "How are you?" After that conversation, I went to the Fournil de Pierre for my favorite six grain bread, and lastly to the crowded Franprix *supermarché* for staples like cat food for Darius.

By then my two-wheeled shopping cart was overflowing and my feet were damp and tired. In the dark drizzle I stopped at my neighborhood cafe, Le Dome St. Paul, for a *grand crème* and a treat of *tarte tartine*, to warm me up before the last leg of my walk home across the windy Pont Marie. Parking my grocery cart just inside the door, near those of the other patrons, I plopped down at the one free table and loosened the scarf around my neck with a sigh.

The waiter came over, inquiring, "*Ça va?*" (How goes it?) They all did these days. Nodding at other faces I recognized made the cafe seem like a public living room. The old fellow with the large red drinkers' nose and the grumpy German Shepard sat at a table beside the wall, sipping his demi. A group of solidly fleshed middle-aged women sat at a window table, complaining about the high prices and poor quality of leeks they had just seen at the market. On my left sat a woman with thick, blonde dyed hair and a large square cut aquamarine ring on her finger. Her pink smock signaled she was a *comerciante* and I knew she was married to the *cordonnaire* (shoemaker), which reminded me more than one pair of shoes in my closet needed re-heeling. These days I walked the leather right off the bottoms in this city I had grown to love.

While awaiting my coffee, I glanced at the irises protruding from my bulging grocery cart. Purchased from the corner flower cart, they glistened with rain droplets, and looked like green flames with tongues of purple and yellow. I had been surprised to find they had no scent when I'd lifted them to my face to sniff. Monet had loved them. Why? Visiting the famous painter's gardens in Giverny was on my list of things to do in France. Van Gogh had also painted them. Every thing in Paris resonated with connotations.

The waiter returned with my café crème and the hot apple tart as requested. He lifted the plate from his tray and set it down on the little round table with a flourish, adding a fork wrapped in a paper napkin. This dessert had personal connotations for me. The first time I had tasted it was last winter after a visit to Georgina's apartment to leave her another letter. At a cafe near her Rue Georges home, I had seen a woman eating one, and inquired which pastry it was.

"Tarte tartine," the waiter had replied. "Je suis désolé mais c'était le denier. (I am very sorry, but that was the last slice).

The French woman sitting near me promptly cut her slice in two, and insisted upon giving me the larger half. People said the French were mean, but they had not been mean to me. Life in Paris had many pleasures great and small. These balanced out the tough times. I said a silent "thank you" for all the enjoyable times and hoped for more of them.

* * * *

The Burkes invited me to celebrate Thanksgiving with them this year too. The traditional feast of stuffed turkey, candied yams, cranberry sauce, mashed potatoes, and giblet gravy, peas, and corn, with pumpkin pie for dessert was my favorite meal of the year. To offset eating such a big dinner, I walked to their apartment from mine, which took about two hours. Taking the route along the Seine, Rue de Rivoli, and Place de la Concorde, it was my favored walk, recently done with Lynda and often with my other tourist visitors. While strolling through the autumnal cool, I thought about the Burkes, who were my only American friends in Paris. This had not been intentional, but most of my friends in France did not speak English. I'd discovered some would, if forced to, when I'd invited mixed groups to my place. The French put such a high priority upon speaking their language properly they assumed others might judge their English as harshly, which inhibited their attempts.

The Burkes had become a second family and alleviated homesickness twinges during holiday times. Since they'd shipped all their furniture from the states, being in their apartment felt like being back in the US, with Tom's all-American vinyl record collection that lined the wall. Always her pert, cheerful self, despite struggling with French language lessons, Janet longed to spend her time with grandchildren in Florida and New Jersey and I wondered how much longer they would stay in France.

Tom would sit in his rocker, sip whiskey, and sometimes puff a cigarillo. I encouraged him to recount his experiences as Senior Vice President of a wholly Arab-owned construction firm, responsible for huge projects in Saudi Arabia. The company was bogged down in bankruptcy. Bad management decisions had been intensified by rapacious partners who did not reinvest in the business. Their invoices were seldom paid on time, if ever, which compounded the problems. The Saudi princes heading government ministries were clients for many of their construction projects and collection issues were rampant. I'd seen Mazen struggle too, to get paid for work completed for princes years ago.

The Burkes had heard every frustrating chapter of my saga with their upstairs neighbor Georgina. Though grateful for their sympathies on that score, what had sealed our friendship was our common history in Arabia. They even knew the road my old home was on in Jeddah and had sweltered through those Red Sea summers and swum in the same Obhor Creek. Their daughter was attending the American University of Paris, but she had gone to my PCS elementary school, although it was in a big new building somewhere else now.

The Thanksgiving dinner was everything I had hoped for. Twelve of us were gathered round the table, including old friends of theirs from the US, visiting Paris for the first time, and English expats, met previously in Arabia. We told jokes and traded stories about our experience with the French, the Saudis, and the Lebanese until two o'clock in the morning, when I phoned a cab. Riding through the dramatically lit streets back to Île

Saint-Louis, I felt sentimental thinking about Christmas time. The Burkes would be back in the US spending the holiday with family and I'd be staying here.

What did Omar know about Christian holidays? Would I have to convert to Islam so we could marry? Civil marriages were not recognized in many Arab countries including Lebanon. You had to be married in a religious ceremony and the husband's religion took precedence. All Lebanese identity cards listed the holders' religion. It was how its citizens were registered. Like Georgina, I had considered converting when engaged to Ayman, but hadn't gone through with it as she had. Did she raise her son to know her Christian culture and holidays too? If Omar and I ever married, and lived in Tunisia instead of Paris, things would be very different.

As lax as Lebanon was, some rules were impossible to circumvent. I remembered my trip to the US Embassy in Beirut to ask if I had to do anything official about converting to Islam. Over eighteen, I believed I was of legal age, with the rights of an adult. The American Deputy Chief of Mission had given me quite a tongue-lashing.

"Your Lebanese boyfriend is in for a surprise. These Arabs marry American women because they expect to get the advantages of US passports, for themselves and their kids. But you can't give your nationality to any offspring. You're an expat. You have not lived long enough in the US. You have to live there until age sixteen, or for ten consecutive years afterwards, before you can legally pass on your nationality. You left at age eight. All you can do now, if you marry a foreigner, is to have a child on US soil, like anybody else in the world."

Yet another set of complications few stay-at-home Americans had to worry about.

* * * *

The next day George Rizk called saying he'd been trying to reach me. Georgina had gone off again but he wanted to assure me that his daughter did intend to work with me, despite these current interruptions. In the meantime, he suggested we get together, as he could tell me a few things before departing on December 1st to spend the winter in Lebanon.

"I will call you back to say exactly when because I am in charge of the boy. I do not like to leave him unless my wife is here. One of the maids has gone back to the Philippines to spend the holidays with her family, and the other one does not know how to cook. Otherwise I would invite you here. It is better if we go somewhere else."

Trying to be helpful, I suggested, "You could bring the boy with you. I don't mind going to McDonalds. He must like hamburgers. All kids do," I was curious to know more about Georgina's son.

"He's too...turbulent," said George with a sigh. "I'll arrange something and call you back."

Turbulent was a rather strange adjective for describing a six-year-old boy but he had been through more than most people several times his age.

Rosine called then, saying she had tried to reach me the other evening, after reading for Georgina and two other women she had brought along. "None of them even forty yet, and all of them widows from Lebanon. I still see death upon her. She did not seem surprised though. I think she has heard this before. You must keep after her about the book or else she will never do it. She is too passively accepting of her fate. I think there might be an accident, something like an airplane crash, around January of 1987. That's why I see the dead all around her. Her son will grow up to be a brilliant politician. She should do this book, for his sake, I told her. She will continue to 'live' if she does this."

Whew. That was a lot to digest. I thought about how soon January 1985 would arrive. It was the birthday month for George and Georgina and the New Year was a good time for making resolutions. Mr. Rizk told me he'd been born on New Year's Day and his daughter on January third. "That's why we called her Georgina, because she was born so close to my birthday." I had since learned that my patron saint of Paris, Geneviève's feast day, was on Georgina's birthday.

If Rosine's prediction was correct, barely two years remained. Should I believe any of this? Had Georgina been told things by other clairvoyants that had come true? Why did she consult them? Carla's accuracy had made me trust her, although the discrepancies still rankled, especially between what each clairvoyant had said about Omar. Rosine said we'd marry. Carla had said this relationship would run its karmic course and pass. Meanwhile I had my own intuitive urgings to sort out.

* * * *

A few days later Omar returned from the London trip with his Saudi prince. We went to the same Chinese place we'd dined at before. He wanted to know what I had been up to while he was gone.

"Alors, raconte-moi!" he ordered (Tell me everything) with a grin while taking my hands from across the table.

Having just finished ordering our meal, I had his undivided attention and began by telling him about George.

"Watch that one," he winked. "I bet he still has an eye for the ladies!"

While recounting my visit to the voyante, and how Georgina had also gone to see her, I included the frightening forecast about her death.

"What did this Rosine have to say about me?"

"Only good things," I answered.

"Like what?" he persisted.

"Oh, the usual stuff, you know," I hedged.

"The usual what?" he pushed. "Listen, I don't really care whether you tell me or not. I don't believe in all that hocus-pocus. Do you? Only God knows the future."

He went on, "I used to work for some phony Arab astrologer here. He charged poor, gullible people tremendous amounts of money. He was a real trickster. He would read verses from the Quran, then tell them he had the power to draw their problems out of them. He said he could take them into his own hands. And then they would see this ball swelling between his palms. It was just a wadded up ball of plastic material sensitive to heat. I used to make them for him. Those people are all charlatans."

When our dessert arrived, he was saying, "Despite what I said, I would still like to know what that woman told you. I think you believed it, didn't you?" he cajoled.

"You said you don't believe, so I am not going to tell you. I do believe that some of them are right, some of the time."

As we climbed into bed later that night, he brought up the subject for a third time, and by now I was laughing. So I told him "marriage in two years, then four children."

"I went to one who also said I'd have four," he told me as he cupped my breasts in his hands. Soon he was drowning me with kisses, so we spoke no more about Rosine and her predictions, though I had noted he had not refuted her statements.

* * * *

The night before my scheduled meeting with Georgina's father, I dreamt I was back in Beirut, staying with her parents in the apartment in the Christian neighborhood. Her mother was sitting on a sofa in the salon, in a housecoat and slippers. As she spoke to me about Georgina's childhood, she occasionally sipped from a small cup full of a sweet dark brew, extending her pinky finger, while balancing the saucer on the open palm of her left hand. I was seated in a chair facing her, with my notebook open and a pen in my hand. On the page I had already written "Catholic Girls School."

"But of course it has been demolished in all the fighting," Georgina's mother was explaining to me. When I woke, for the first few seconds I wasn't sure where I was, in Georgina's bedroom in her parents' house on rue Hopital Orthodoxe in Beirut, or in Paris, in my own place.

* * * *

By four that afternoon, I was already at the Deavois cafe on Place Victor Hugo. George Rizk had suggested this upscale cafe restaurant, with its carpeted floors, dark, upholstered banquettes, hanging lamps, and greater space between the tables. Lovers could rendezvous and whisper here. My neighborhood cafe by contrast had harsh lighting, with hard chairs jammed closer together, and habitués flicking their cigarette ashes onto the bare floor. A café crème here cost twice as much.

While waiting for Mr. Rizk to arrive, I reflected upon my time thus far in France. I'd come here nearly a year ago on a ten day vacation. So much had happened but the project with Georgina had stalled. The affair with Waddah had fizzled but it had been an additional inspiration to relocate. Despite the sad times with Maurice, I was still grateful Paris had become my home. It was no longer some fantasy place. How much longer would it hold me? And Omar, the phantom, how long would I continue to harbor that fantasy? If this Georgina project failed to come to fruition, when would I give up and accept that truth?

The sun came out from behind the clouds. I tipped my cheeks, still chilled from my walk, to its precious yellow warmth. This week I paid too much for a mango at an outdoor stall but I'd needed it badly. My favorite fruit, the heft of its round ripened weight could still be sensed in my palm. Like a concentrated dose of energy straight from the sun it was. I had devoured it the moment I'd returned to my apartment, the sweet juice soaking my fingers. Was I like a mango to the men who'd wanted me? My inner sun still burned, the fire of inspiration had not gone out. I had not succumbed to cynicism. My capacity for ecstasy, for poetry too, kept that fire going. The freedom to pursue or be pursued helped fuel it. Could I continue to feed my fire here when the full force of the dreaded winter was upon us again and I had to face that frozen gray reality? Perhaps I belonged in a place where mangoes grew.

George came through the door a few seconds later. I recognized him instantly though we had only seen each other once briefly when I delivered another note to Georgina's apartment. The father-daughter resemblance was very strong. No one could mistake where Georgina's nose, eyes, and forehead came from. Tall and slim, with his dark eyes set deep into their sockets, he was still attractive. We shook hands. I thought Georgina will look like this in thirty years if she lives that long.

He unbuttoned his camel colored coat, and unwound the white wool scarf from his neck, before settling into the seat across from me. His beige turtleneck sweater complemented the trousers of a similar shade. His leather loafers were expensive and Italian.

"Have you ordered anything yet?" He asked. "I hope I have not kept you waiting."

"No, I just arrived a few moments ago. I thought I would wait for you."

He signaled for the waiter, I asked for a hot chocolate, and he decided on a cup of tea.

"Won't you have a piece of cake or something? I cannot, doctor's orders you know, no salt, sugar, alcohol, or cigarettes." He emphasized this by patting his chest. Had he had a heart attack or some other surgery?

His hand went into the breast pocket of his coat lying across the chair. "Here, I wanted you to have these," he said, opening the envelope as he passed it to me across the table. There were age spots on the back of his hands.

The envelope contained unfranked postage stamps. I took them out. *"Miss Univers,* 1971, Georgina Rizk, *Republique Libanaise."* The same words were repeated in gracefully curving Arabic script above. While studying them, I tried to remember if a stamp had ever been commissioned to honor a Miss America. One large sheet had four stamped designs in the different colors of various denominations: five piaster stamps were green, the twenty purple, the twenty five yellow, and the fifty piaster ones in turquoise. These were the prices from thirteen years ago.

Georgina was dressed in something meant to be a national costume, a red caftan, heavily embroidered with whorls of gold threads. There were two views. One showed her portrait, only head and shoulders, the other full length, smiling, with her hands on her hips, her pelvis tilting forward provocatively. The conical hat made her appear taller. A white scarf draped from its top, and fell down her back in the manner of fairytale princesses. The close-up showed the contours of her perfectly proportioned features. She had a dreamy bedroom look. The curve of her lips seemed in exact harmony with the curve of her eyes. A pair of cheap gaudy earrings dangled at the sides of her head. The whole presentation made me smile. It was another measure of the distance from the truth. Georgina never would have chosen to wear such an outfit. It was all for show in this particular photograph. Her taste was light-years away from this stylized ethnic image. The real Georgina and the real Lebanon were nothing like this.

"Thank you very much," I said, putting the stamps back into the envelope and sliding them into my bag.

"I saved all her pictures and newspaper clippings, from Italy, Austria, America, all over," he said proudly. This surprised me. Despite her marriage to a Palestinian Muslim guerilla fighter, this man obviously loved his daughter. Did he know the whole truth? Most Arab fathers with beautiful daughters zealously protected their honor because the entire family name was at stake. How much had Georgina told him? Were they close? It was exceedingly rare to meet an Arab father whose daughter had become a model, much less one who took pride in it, instead of feeling ashamed and disowning her. Had the Rizk family needed money? I recalled my own father and my fiancé dissuading me, from playing my guitar in public and becoming a singer in Beirut, because that sort of job was frowned upon. It implied the men in my life could not afford to take care of me, and this in turn reflected poorly upon them and their social status, in this part of the world.

George explained he was now retired but had worked in the customs department at the Port of Beirut. This made me wonder if he had capitalized upon that position like my old boss had. Before Mahdi Al Tajir moved up in the world, and became the United Arab Emirates Ambassador to the Court of St. James, he had worked in the Dubai custom office, smuggling gold into India, in the days when that had been illegal. By the early 1970s, he was being featured on the cover of Time magazine as the world's wealthiest man, when I had worked for him in London.

Surely George had managed to salt away several extra thousand a month in such a job. Call them tips, bribes, or expediter fees, undeclared income like that went into Swiss bank accounts. Perhaps George and his wife lived off that nest egg now or the interest it generated.

I told him of my recent dream of being in Beirut with him and his wife.

"Oh, you should come. We would have you as our guest. And you should also go to Damascus, and visit Georgina's sister, Fellucina. You know her mother was married to an Italian. Fellucina is her half-sister. They still speak Italian together sometimes." George had wooed and married Georgina's mother despite her marriage to another man and their child. This echoed what Georgina had done, marrying the already married Salameh.

As he spoke, he drew a small set of *misbaha* — a string of beads akin to a rosary — from the pocket of his trousers and fingered them absentmindedly. The brownish beads were soft and smooth, made of resin or amber. Beirutis of all religions carried these "worry beads."

George admitted he had no control over his daughter. "I would like her to do this book but I cannot make her do anything. You know, every time we come here, her mother and I, we try to take care of the paperwork that has piled up. She doesn't even open her bills. Some are already a year past due. It isn't as if she doesn't have the money. She just lets things ride."

We spoke in French, but we drifted into Arabic, and then English, and back into French. He seemed most comfortable in French, though I suspected he wanted to test my Arabic, and show off his English. Every conversation with Georgina so far had been in English. Which language did she speak with her parents?

George mentioned how good things were on the Christian side of the city now and how I would see this when I came to visit. "We do not lack for anything. People go out at night, to eat, and to the discotheques." He inferred that this was unthinkable in West Beirut, the portion controlled by the Muslims.

"The port of Jounieh is busy twenty-four hours a day. The Lebanese pound is still strong. Business is good. *Al humdu'illah* (Thanks be to God). The only nuisance is having to fly to Cyprus and take the boat over from Larnaca." (Beirut airport was still closed more often than it was open. And from where the planes landed you still had to get across the Muslim controlled parts of town to the Christian side. If making this trip, I would have to go by boat too).

George spoke as if this "minor" inconvenience was the major thing worth mentioning about the war. He probably believed the fighting would be over in another few months. I recalled how my parents had also believed this, for years. Those who'd lived there had the hardest time accepting reality because they clung to the memories of how the country used to be. Was his enthusiasm sincere or just for show? I suspected some of this bravado was for my consumption. Meanwhile he would probably be converting whatever he still had in Lebanese pounds to some less risky currency, like the US dollar. Had he bought a place in Cyprus, just in case?

By the end of the meeting he confided he would like to see me again before leaving Paris but he had a *petite amie* (girlfriend) to see tomorrow. Could I come back the day after that, "Around four o'clock at the apartment to meet Georgina's mother?"

Was he mentioning a girlfriend to impress me? Did he have one? If so my guess was she would be French and about half his age. George had the irreverent boyishness of Arab men whose mothers had spoiled them. Convinced life should revolve around the satisfaction of their needs, they indulged themselves, with scant concern for the consequences others were left to endure. George was certainly past sixty. Part of me wanted to admire his spunk, for he obviously believed in the pursuit of happiness despite the war. But another part of me cringed. He had never grown up. He was a lot like my father. What kind of examples had these men set for Georgina and me?

I replied I could probably come and would phone later to confirm it. This way we would both have an "out" if this invitation was mere *politesse*. You could never be sure if the Lebanese meant what they said. And they would judge you for being too exuberant and thoughtless, about accepting spur of the moment invitations, despite the seeming sincerity. It was like their offerings of food at the dinner table. You should refuse until they insisted for a third time. These customs could be maddening but knowing of them had made me more patient when dealing with people like Georgina.

As he helped me into my coat, George told me, "You are as pretty as my daughter."

What an old flirt I thought. He held me by the shoulders, kissing me warmly on both cheeks as we said goodbye on the sidewalk. Then we each turned to go off in our opposite directions.

* * * *

At noon the next day I phoned George to follow up on his invitation to tea. Georgina answered the phone. What a nice surprise. She was not yet expected back from her last trip. Although it was noontime, I could tell from the gravel in her voice that my call had woken her.

"Sorry to disturb you. Is your father there? He asked me to call him today."

"No, he's gone out. You could try him again this afternoon," she answered wearily. I thought to myself, perhaps the little friend is real after all.

"When we met yesterday to talk about the book, he seemed to think it would be a good idea for me to go to Beirut, and maybe Damascus too this winter. I could do some background work, with your parents and your sister, until springtime when you are ready to talk. I am ready to try anything. I have been here for almost a year already." I said, with just a tinge of exasperation.

I was trying to humor her but could sense it was not a good time to talk. "I just want you to know I am not lazy."

"But I am lazy," she answered, with such unrepentant frankness I smiled on my end of the line. She continued in a different tone, "About your going to Beirut, I don't think it is a good idea. The situation is not good."

She sounded quite serious. Did she know of any upcoming events in particular or was this just a general comment? Was she trying to discourage me from listening to anybody else speaking about her life? How come her father thought it was a good idea? I decided to say nothing more for now. I changed the subject.

"Before I forget to ask, how did it go with Rosine? You never said."

"She was good, very good," replied Georgina. "Listen, I'll be traveling a lot now, through the holidays, but I will call you after the New Year, alright?"

Her impatience was evident.

"Sure. I will be here for Christmas, but away in the US for most of January, working. I guess I'll see you in the spring. Take care of yourself. And please tell your father I called. He can return my call at his convenience. Goodbye."

Later that evening George called apologizing, "There are so many things to do that we have left to the last minute. I am sorry but I think we might have to wait to have our tea in the spring. In any case, I will write to you, and see you when I return."

I doubted it.

Chapter 15

FAITES VOS JEUX /
PLACE YOUR BETS

Pourquoi les gens ont du mal à être heureux.

Why people have trouble being happy.

— MARCEL PAGNOL

December 1984 & January 1985

On a mid-December morning I parked myself on the couch determined to get my Christmas cards finished. A mug of tea steamed up my elbow and the cat curled up beside me as I tackled my list, more than sixty cards to send this year. While addressing each envelope, I considered what to say on the enclosed card. Did they have my change of address? Would I see them again? Though I grumbled about this annual ritual it was how I kept in touch with my far-flung network of friends, and caught up on their news, if our regular letter writing had fallen off. Several cards were going to people met through my training work, fellow expats. I tracked their progress to see how their global careers were panning out and whether our training programs designs needed tweaking. Some were planning to come through Paris to visit. Two girlfriends who worked for my US employer were here this week, hoping I'd accompany them on a visit the palace in Versailles tomorrow. So I had to complete the airmail cards at least so they'd arrive in time for the holiday. The ones for Paris friends, like Fiona and Freddie, could wait a bit.

Addressing one to an American woman, met through my recent ICM work, I recalled her recent remarks. "My husband is French. We have been married for three years and have a ten-month-old daughter. I do not want her to grow up French. I want her to be an American."

How plaintive Ida's tone had been. As if one's identity dissolved as easily as sugar stirred into hot liquid. Yet I also knew from personal

239

experience, just how challenging dual alliances were, even when both parents shared the same passport nationality. During our discussion of the pros and cons of expatriate life, I'd recounted examples of happy couples, like my landlord George Masclet and his American wife, Selma. "They have a little community of friends, mostly in mixed marriages, like their own."

The people in our circles were as important as the place. A third of those on my Christmas card list were friends made here this year. Whenever someone asked me how long I would stay in France, I always answered, "For as long as I like it" because I was here of my own volition. But some of the IBM executives in a recent program had confided their disappointment at living in Paris for two years already without making a single French friend. I invited them to dinner at my place to introduce them to some of mine.

After that dinner, when they departed, my *pied noir* friend Sylvie shared her impressions. "When I asked what brought them here, they said they were on three or five year assignments. It sounded like they were counting the days until they could leave. We Europeans believe it takes time to make a real friend. And with them it's not worth trying. They are in too much of a hurry to get back to America."

I winced and filed away her comments to share at my next cross-cultural communication program. Friendships were crucial. Although I might leave Paris tomorrow, or stay here forever, either way my old and new friends would always be welcome, wherever they or I went next. Relocating was no excuse. After all, my prime reason for moving to Paris was to be with people here. My 1983 agenda book was on my desk and I quickly compared its entries to this year's. In Paris I had gone out more than twice as many times per week than when I had lived in America.

Girlfriends often called, sharing new restaurant finds like Le Fast Fou, good movies, or events worth attending at the Palais de Congres. Staying home alone was rare. People liked to congregate here and my French friends loved to talk. They had opinions about everything and worked to keep up on their pet topics. Equally interested in my thoughts, they had taught me the value of debate and substantiated arguments. In the beginning I had assumed it was more polite to agree and keep the peace, but they expected me to have ideas, and add mine to the mix when issues arose, and to hold up my end of any conversation. This truth was borne out whenever I eavesdropped on the discussions of those sitting nearby in my neighborhood cafe. The average Parisian relished a meaty disagreement and respected those who had good reasons for their difference of opinions. They wanted to hear your facts and supporting logic, and could shred it full of holes, as I'd also discovered to my chagrin. This was evident when issues came up in French politics too, a common subject, although I had yet to grasp sufficient historical background on the candidates or platforms.

France had a wide field of political parties. The US was bland by comparison with only its Democrats and Republicans.

While writing my notes in these cards, there was no ache for eggnog, a Christmas tree of my own, or caroling, since I'd rarely experienced them. Nor was I homesick. Having gone overseas so young, and off to boarding school at fourteen, my relatives in the US hardly knew me, except for my grandmother Hattie Alice LaMotte Trout. In January I would visit my parents in Pennsylvania, if only for twenty-four hours and catch up on their news, and see my sister in New York. My life was here for now.

Zvonimir was due to pass through Paris again before Christmas. The orthodontist still tightened his braces regularly. In his card I thanked him for the good times and hoped there would be more. The last time he had been in town I told him Omar had returned. "I don't think you should come over. It just won't work. He's really gotten under my skin. As long as I love Omar like this, no one else can touch me."

Zvonimir had replied, "I can wait. Let's have dinner at least. I doubt this will last. I knew you before and I'll know you after. Just don't let him hurt you. These Arabs like to be so clever. You are not like that. Be careful."

* * * *

That evening, on the 14th of December 1984 I had a strange dream. It took place in BHV, a Paris department store, where I actually went in real life, and had purchased CDs of my favorite French singer, Serge Lama. In my dream he was there also, looking distraught, in between the aisles.

The next day, when Sylvie called, I mentioned this dream to her.

"Haven't you heard the news?"

"No. Did something happen to him?"

"He's alright but both his parents died last night in a car accident."

The shivers went through me. That night I slid into bed humming one of his sadder songs about a funeral, "Toute Blanche" although it was not as well known as "Je Suis Malade" or my personal pick, "L'Esclave."

Unexplainable connections like these would continue to nudge and direct me for the rest of my life.

* * * *

The doorbell rang the next afternoon just as I sealed another Christmas card envelope. Who it could be? The concierge had already come with the mail. Checking my reflection before opening the door, I saw no makeup, an old sweater, and older corduroys. Omar stood upon the landing, a complete surprise. I had not heard from him all weekend. He hugged me very hard before coming through the door.

"I just wanted to drop in on you and see if you had someone else here," he said.

"How dare you. If you don't trust me, just say so," I flashed back, indignantly.

"Easy! Easy! Of course I trust you," he said laughing as he lifted me off the floor. "I'm only joking."

His mouth searched for mine as if he'd lost me. He broke away long enough to say, "Bring me my robe while I take a shower. And why don't you put on some music?" As I turned to get his things he gave my bottom a slap, as if I was an obedient little wife.

As he showered, I switched on the radio. As usual it was tuned to the same Arabic station unless I had listened to the BBC news. The music of the Middle East filled the rooms, taking me back to less complicated times before the war when the words I could catch were enough, and I was not yet so desperate for the whole truth. The distinct and dreamy pleasure of drifting along returned, reminding me of days before events shook my trust to pieces.

Slipping out of my clothes, I stepped into a caftan that zipped up the front, and turned up the gas fire to warm the rooms. A vase of yellow tulips purchased yesterday sat on the mantel. The additional heat would make them wilt. As I moved the flowers to my desk Omar came up behind me.

"They are beautiful," he said softly, his mouth near my ear. He caressed one of the petals, "like you," he whispered, turning me around to press my full length to his. We swayed to the music not quite dancing. I hoped for this, and ran my hands over his back, feeling the damp ends of his hair at the nape of his neck. I gathered them, pulling with one hand as my other traveled down his muscled back to his buttocks. As he pressed his pelvis into mine I felt his manhood swelling. Slowly he unzipped my caftan and held it open to admire my body in the flickering light of the gas heater.

"How white you are," he said, slipping the gown off my shoulders. It fell in a silky heap at my feet. I stepped from its folds and he bent to spread them over the rug in front of the heater before lowering me to the floor.

"And this?" He said, tugging gently on the scarf around my neck. In my haste to undress I'd forgotten it. Untying it, he whispered with mock menace, "Aren't you afraid I might strangle you?"

"Even though you hurt me a little sometimes, you give me pleasure too. I am not afraid."

"Are you a little masochist?" He teased, pulling the scarf loose, drawing it over my breasts and belly tickling me with it.

"No. But with you, I think I could do anything," I swooned, breathing heavily. He sank his teeth into the skin of my neck. I closed my eyes as his body covered mine with its sweet forceful weight.

Later we were hungry, and I pulled together some lunch for us. Standing at the kitchen door he taunted, "I only came over because I thought something good might be in the casserole."

We sat down over steaming bowls of my Ras el Hanout soup, made with that magical North African mixture of spices that translated roughly as "the head of the grocer."

Before picking up my spoon I pronounced the word *Bismillah* over my bowl (In God's name). This was a Muslim form of saying grace before a meal.

Omar was surprised, "It has been a long time since I've heard that."

"Well, you shouldn't forget your religion. I suspect you will become Hadji Omar someday," I said, referring to the pilgrimage, each faithful Muslim is expected to make to Mecca and Medina before they die.

"Yes I suppose I will," he agreed pensively.

"You know, I always say Ayat al-Kursi before the plane takes off. Sometimes I say it in the car or the train too."

"Yes, I noticed you are wearing it," he waved at the golden amulet on its chain around my neck.

"It is part of what's left over from my upbringing. Since the age of eight I have watched over a million Hadjis coming each year through Jeddah on their way to the Holy Cities. That left a strong impression. Over the years my faiths have melted together. In Lebanon I was ready to convert to Islam to marry my fiancé."

"We do not have Lebanon's problems in Tunisia because we are all Arab and Muslim," he said. What a telling remark.

I got up to open the drawer in the heavy antique sideboard, taking from it a gold chain, with two charms on it, an engraved Ayat al-Kursi, and a blue eye-shaped bead, to ward off the Evil Eye.

"Here," I said opening the clasp to fit it round his neck. "Wear this all the time. Don't take it off, not even to bathe, and it will protect you habibi."

He thanked me with a deep kiss and a long embrace, holding me seated on his lap. He helped clear the dishes from the table before putting on his coat to leave. "Do you need any money?" He asked.

This was the first time he had asked. I was touched that he seemed to care about my welfare. "No, I have only just begun to use what I earned on this last trip but thank you anyway."

He replied, "One can always find money in Paris but when I have it, I should take it right back to Tunisia. If I stay here, I spend it, give it, loan, and gamble. We could always go rob banks, you and I," he chuckled.

"Like Bonnie and Clyde?" I joked back.

"I know a guy who is in prison now. He robbed eighteen banks in the South. They never would have caught him either if it hadn't been for some tourist's film identifying him. He never wore a mask."

Although I thought Omar was only kidding about robbing banks he certainly knew some shady characters. He had seen the underbelly of Paris, the side I had yet to glimpse except like this, through him. I wondered if he had ever been in trouble with the police but didn't ask.

At the door, I questioned, "Will you be coming back tomorrow?"

"Who knows? Tomorrow is a long way off cherie." He blew another kiss as he went down the stairs. I went out on the landing, watching till he was out of sight.

The radio was still on when I came back into the apartment. Shutting the door, I saw the remaining Christmas cards to be written but I was no longer in an industrious mood. Instead I picked up the cat and carried him to the sofa where I sat with his warm gray body in my lap. As Darius purred, I regarded the yellow tulips Omar had touched, and the mirror above the mantle in which we had seen ourselves embracing, and at the space in front of the gas fireplace where we had just made love.

Dwelling on his skin, eyes, and kisses drove everything else out of my mind. All the confusions and contradictions could be reduced to a lovely drowning bath of the senses. I was loath to leave that dreamy world. By closing my eyes I could see his face, feel his arms around me, bend to his body once again. Like a pool his beauty was. I could float in it, reveling in our responses, my questioning brain in suspended animation. Being with Omar sent me flying over the dunes again like listening to this Arabic music. Mon Fantôme was an enchanting mystery but did I want to be lost in a sea of desire that never culminated?

My throbbing body reminded me what was missing. It pulsed, needing climax and release. How paradoxical it was! I could neither possess this man nor be possessed by him without the satisfaction of a proper melding. What bound us was merely a web of pleasure strands, which could break anytime, if the weight of demands or obligations were added. Becoming man and wife was the antithesis of this dreaminess.

This was why I had never confessed, "I want to be the mother of your children." Others could mention it, like his friend Hamed in the cafe, or Rosine in her fanciful predictions but if I said it, the silky threads of our floating world might snap. This afternoon as he licked my breasts and sucked my nipples, I had been on the verge of blurting out, "Make me the mother of your children!"

Thinking of that moment now, I remembered the curly headed child I had intuitively "seen" playing near his knee as he sat on this couch. Was this a sign of normalcy and my improving psychological health or something else? My phantom was not with me because he wanted to be a father. I was sure of that. Desire had beckoned us, pure and simple. When we first laid eyes upon each other, we'd been equals, taking a gamble, obeying a primal law. We had followed beauty in the hope of ecstasy, an end in itself, splendidly worthy.

What had changed since then? I had met his needs but he had not met mine. The unspoken contract had not been honored. We were no longer equal. By not broaching this subject I was further betraying myself as well as the law of primal union. One-sided pleasure lasts only as long as one of the pair agrees to live a lie. But I was loath to request any more, fearing it might break the spell. Was this romantic idealism, my belief that ecstasy had to be inspired, wordlessly? Demands were the death of it.

What other excuse did I have? Perhaps inhibition sealed my lips, for Maurice had advised, "Don't tell the man you want to marry how much experience you have." But I wasn't going to deny my experiences. They had taught me to reject pretense, and live from the truth, of love not lies. And since I had more experience, I expected more, from others and myself. After all their experiences, what had Waddah, Maurice, and Omar expected to give or to get? Reconsidering these men and my expectations made me angry at myself now. The French had a term for what I had done, *faire des châteaux en l'air*, making castles in the air. I had fallen for wounded, unavailable men. They reflected what needed to be healed, inside of me, not just them. And now I had latched onto a phantom. When would I learn?

Rather like my quest for the truth with Georgina, this bid for ecstasy had not panned out and it was time to face the facts. Why had I given Omar more chances instead of listening to the truthfulness of my own body and honoring it? I'd done something similar with Georgina who remained a mirage. Despite being able to charm or seduce others, we cannot force people to love us, or collaborate with us, just because we want them to. In the end, artifice could not take me where I wanted to go. Lies did not bring the truth of lasting love, much less wisdom. I could change myself but I had to accept my limits when it came to changing anyone else.

Omar's beauty had left me in a place of predicament, facing the need to be truthful to myself most of all. I wondered about Georgina's beauty and Beirut's. Had hers brought her ecstasy? Beirut's beauty, like hers, had brought more than a fair share of pain and loss. Had Georgina slaked her deepest thirsts or merely serviced others' needs? The two seemed intertwined. And like all powers, the greater the beauty, the greater the temptation: to exploit it, for gain, money, and more power.

I wanted to reset my direction and return to simple truths. Veering just a few fateful degrees away had already taken me off course. Because it was a true north, ecstasy would always matter, as much as the capacity to relate to it from a healthy place. In the years to come, more skillful lovers would transport me to deeper satisfactions of body and soul, but ultimately what I would discover is how ecstasy evolved, and decoupled us from people altogether.

* * * *

A week later I was in Versailles, enjoying a long Sunday lunch, with Catherine's family. This lawyer Maurice had introduced me to many months ago, had remained a friend. We saw each other periodically, catching a movie, sharing a meal. At those meetings Catherine would fill me in on what Maurice was up to, but this Sunday she wanted to introduce me to another client of hers, a woman in the process of divorcing her Lebanese husband.

Irina was a petite, dark-haired, stylish woman from Kiev, the Ukrainian capital. She had knowing blue eyes and spoke French with a charming Russian accent. Meeting her shattered my preconceived notions about dowdy babushkas waiting in line to buy toilet paper in the USSR. Her soon-to-be divorced husband had gone to Moscow on a university scholarship. The Soviet Union often extended these opportunities to the poor in the Middle East, for reasons of influence, akin to what AUB had done. Irina had been his Russian language instructor, and the two fell in love, married, and prospered. An enterprising middleman, he'd seized whatever opportunities came his way, starting with the Soviet Army's sudden need for umbrellas. Thanks to Irina's help, he managed to procure enough of them, from overseas in short order, and that responsiveness continued. Soon he was procuring all sorts of items, including weapons. Doing third country deals he circumvented the sanctions between Soviet Bloc nations and the rest of the world.

When Irina was expecting their first child, they had gone back to Tripoli, Lebanon, a port city in the North, where his impoverished Muslim family came from. Then the war started, and Irina became yet another refugee, with a small daughter, and another baby on the way. For safety's sake they settled in France, but her husband traveled constantly. Irina had discovered he was keeping a mistress in Moscow, which led her to Catherine, who handled the divorce.

Irina and I took an instant liking to each other. We stayed on, until after five o'clock that first meeting, discussing Lebanon, the war, and even clairvoyants. Irina had just consulted one, over the breakup of her marriage, and swore he was the most accurate she had ever visited. After giving me his name and number, we called him together that day. Gustave said he had a cancellation and could see me tomorrow morning.

"Then you can come have lunch at my house afterwards and tell me what he said," Irina suggested.

* * * *

The following day, I met Gustave at the appointed time. A big bear of a man from Breton, his booming voice and ready laugh impressed me from the moment I stepped into his warm, well-lit apartment in Versailles. Now in his fifties, he had once worked in the corporate marketing world, but he left all that for his Tarot cards, astrology, numerology, and other esoteric interests.

He invited me to sit on the other side of his desk and had me blow on a deck of cards. Then he spread them across the desktop, instructing me to draw a certain number of them for my initial reading. As he studied the cards I'd selected, I studied him, noting how he fiddled with his red scarf, unwinding and rewinding it around his neck. There were no drafts, so I guessed the length of red material was for protection of a spiritual sort rather than a physical one. He seemed quite professional, and I liked him, but was not happy with what he said about Omar. It confirmed all my doubts.

"He is not the one. And you shall soon realize this. You might know it already, despite your tendency to idealize things. He's not evolved enough for you. He is too materialistic. And he has no sense of family life. He loves the night. His work has something to do with going out at night, to restaurants, clubs, and casinos..."

I left his office feeling as though I'd been punched in my solar plexus. Had Irina told him anything? No harm in being suspicious. I reviewed our conversation from the prior day but we'd talked about Lebanon and what was similar about our pasts. The subject of Omar had yet to come up. The supremely logical Catherine never went to clairvoyants, so she had not supplied Gustave any information about me. So somehow he intuited these things without specific, prior knowledge. I sat at a cafe and wrote down everything he had said, having just enough time to fill a few journal pages, before Irina expected me for lunch at her place.

Going to voyantes was risky. Which one to believe? Rosine had told me what I most wanted to hear. Should I put more stock in what Carla had said, now that Gustave had confirmed it? What about my own feelings? Was it possible to mix all three, and approximate the possibilities, if not the truth exactly?

Gustave had been adamant and he'd hit some nerves. Perhaps I ought to heed his words and prepare myself emotionally. It had been awhile since I'd seen or heard from Omar. Not what one expects of someone in love. The two sides of myself were at war within and watching them slug it out was exhausting.

Over lunch in Irina's tastefully luxurious apartment, I repeated what Gustave had said about Omar.

Irina told me more about her life and marriage. "I've always had dreams and premonitions before any major event in my life. Before my husband proposed to me, I dreamt that I was out in a field, a beautiful area, with a blue sky above me, and a crystal clear river flowing nearby. A lovely white dove came and sat on my shoulder and then I had a great desire to enter the river and swim in it. The dove stayed on my shoulder for quite a while, but then it flew away. When this was interpreted for me by an old woman in Kiev, she explained I would marry the prince of a husband, but that he would not stay and we would separate one day. And here it's come true.

"Another time, I was flying over a field, like the one where the river was. Suddenly I just couldn't fly anymore, and I started falling toward a hole where cow manure is put for spreading later upon the fields. I fell right into it, and was covered from head to toe with shit. I woke up, and it must've been four o'clock in the morning, but I had to bathe right away. Shortly after that I learned about my husband's mistress in Moscow."

She reached over to take something from the drawer in the coffee table. "I've recently found these in between the mattresses and above the door. What do you think they are for?"

I took the folded up piece of paper and unwound the thread wrapped around it. The sheet was covered with Arabic inscriptions from the Qur'an.

"I think my mother-in-law wrote them and had my husband put them here. It's some kind of magic isn't it?"

"I will have Omar or someone else take a better look at it, but it starts out with Bismillah. I think it's a blessing, for your protection."

"Yes, I think she does not want us to divorce even though she fought me all the time and wanted a Lebanese girl for her son. She regrets it now. Wait until she meets this mistress of his. She's a bitch."

On the train back to Paris from Versailles, I thought about my new friend Irina, and Gustave the clairvoyant. They were modern, educated people, not superstitious, illiterate villagers living in the Dark Ages. In view of my personal experiences with intuition, and my missteps with interpretation, I certainly had more to learn. Though keeping my mind open, I was wary of charlatans, and people who charged money for things like casting spells. That was the realm of black magic, of money and ego, where the desperate preyed upon each other for power and control. White magic seemed its opposite. Instead of trying to engineer predetermined outcomes, one sought the signs and directions to align themselves with the positive forces in the universe, the "highest good for the greatest number." I'd heard of spells, like the ones Mazen's Syrian wife Fatin had used on him: incantations, putting menstrual blood in his food, and having an egg inscribed with fertility symbols, which had been boiled and eaten. Fatin had managed to conceive a healthy son, Rashad, but she had not managed to keep the marriage going with such a damaged man. His treatment of women was inexcusable yet he also seemed to be punishing himself.

Perhaps turning his back on his German college sweetheart, and other disillusionments, had cost him his self-respect.

Why had she killed herself? In the years since wanting to take my own life I had learned just how common a response it was with men and women. Yet far too many females tended to harm themselves, when betrayed, shamed and mistreated, instead of standing up to the perpetrators. Turning our anger inward, rather than outward, was not going to change things for the better. Likewise, spraying anger and hatred upon others, in the form of words, bullets, or bombs only increased the despair in the world. Surely there were options that lessened grief but how did we discover them? Logic had led us to more lethal killing tools and technologies. Where might intuition take us?

* * * *

That Friday I accompanied Irina to the Hammam Saint Paul, a Turkish style bathhouse, off rue Saint Antoine. Not far from Pont Marie, it was easy walking distance from my Quai de Bourbon home. The establishment was run by two *pied noir* sisters. These French women had been born and raised in Algeria, when it was still a colony of France, but they had to return to Europe after the Algerians won their war of independence (1954-1962). Inside the hammam was another world. Irina said it was like the Russian bathhouses of her childhood but it was new to me. Entering through the arched doorway, I felt the steamy heat wafting up from the lower level. Walking in from the frigid December streets of Paris, I re-entered the sweaty humidity of my childhood, beside the Red Sea.

We were shown to our numbered cabins and given white cotton kimono-like robes, with lavender sashes to change into. The attendant also gave us each a pair of plastic sandals to wear, "So you won't slip on the wet tile floor downstairs," she explained, adding, "If you would like a massage, it is best to reserve it now on your way down."

Leaving our street clothes and handbags locked in the cabins, we proceeded down the curving marble steps, like two lost princesses returning to the seraglio. Downstairs, the room was full of naked women — lying, standing, and sitting around a large central pool of cool water. Two older women waded into it, their bellies creased and loose with age, their pubic hair sparse and gray. A very young French girl brushed past, her supple young skin steaming and red as she made for the pool, diving straight into it.

In all my life I had never seen so much female flesh. An entire world made of women, all ages and races, with flesh of every imaginable hue, from blue veined white to the richest chocolate. A pair of North African Berber women with tattoos on their chins, a blue line of dots running down from their lips, were whispering to each other. An Asian girl bent over her feet, painting her toenails. Behind her a black woman with the slender grace of a model was smearing mud from a plastic bag, onto her face, neck, breasts, and the rest of her body.

Beyond this room, behind the glass partition, I could see another circle of women, sitting on unpainted wooden deck chairs, drawn up around a raised marble platform from which the heat rose, from a boiler underneath the floor. I followed Irina into this steamy room and took off my robe, hanging it on one of the many wall hooks, just as my companion did. Several women were sitting on the lavender sashes that held the robes closed, so I retrieved mine and spread it across the wooden slats of my seat as the others had done, before I sat down. Hardly anyone spoke. The heat made us drowsy.

Some women had their feet up on the round marble dais and the furry places between their legs were visible. For a few moments I was conscious of my own nakedness, having never removed my clothes before in a room full of women, but that feeling was soon replaced by a lovely lassitude and carelessness. With so many breasts, bellies, and buttocks, and all this glistening skin around me, I forgot my own. No one cared. It was like melting into a warm, mothering mass. Everything was already known about the sameness of our bodies and the heat overcame any remaining inhibitions. My arms hung down and my head lolled back. I closed my eyes and surrendered to the probing heat as it drew the moisture from my pores.

My stupor encouraged strange visitations. Like the mirages seen in the Arabian Desert, scenes from my past flickered through my overheated brain. The good-looking face and thick brown hair of an old boyfriend floated towards me. Chuck. My mother had liked him and nicknamed him "Dreamboat." I could distinctly recall the purple cotton fabric of the jersey I had worn on a date with him when I was fourteen. The soreness and bruising of my pubic bone was also remembered. He had ground his erection against me, both of us fully clothed. Sheer physical sensations continued to come. My first kiss with the red haired boy named Stephen during my twelfth birthday party in Jeddah. When he couldn't guess what I had wanted, I took the lead, and pressed my lips to his.

The next recollections were of parties my father had thrown, for sailors from the US Navy destroyer ships when they docked at the port of Jeddah. Reliving his Navy days, dad had invited them to our home on their shore leave in a country devoid of nightclubs, bars, or legal alcohol. They brought the beer and my parents turned up the 1950s and 60s dance music for them. I could see dad doing what we called his "can opener" dance, his arms up and his thumbs raised, to the tune "How Sweet It Is To Be Loved By You." I could smell the beery breath and feel the sailors' clammy bodies as they danced with me in that heat. It was so hot then and it was so hot now. My temples throbbed as the sweat poured from me, beading on my chest and belly. I sluiced off the excess water with my hands. Even this small effort tired me. I sat back in my chair once more.

Then I remembered Yusuf Tawwil,[35] the tubby Saudi who had asked my father for my hand in marriage when I was twelve.

My father had laughed in his face. "Why, she's too young! She's only a child. She hasn't even finished school yet."

His laughter had been a grave mistake. Yusuf was incensed and embarrassed. He considered his proposal an honor to our family. Being a rich merchant, he had only one other wife, and I would want for nothing in his house.

We knew Yusuf because my mother had worked for him, decorating his offices, and a new villa. In return she had been well compensated, but Yusuf had surprised my parents with an additional lavish gift, of a brand-new red Mercedes 190 SL convertible. This present preceded the proposal of marriage. My mother wanted to refuse it but knew this would also offend him.[36]

After my father so rudely rebuffed his proposal to his face, Yusuf returned in the dead of night. Sneaking over the wall of my ground floor balcony, he managed to climb into my bedroom, through the window. I woke up with his roly-poly body already on top of me in bed. The sheet was still between us but he was hoisting up the floor length white jalabiya he wore, and wrestling with the long cotton pantaloons underneath.

Recalling that incident in the sweltering air of the hammam, I realized again what Yusuf's intentions had been that night. By penetrating me, he'd hoped to force my father to acquiesce to his proposal, because I'd be "damaged goods." No longer a virgin, it meant to his way of thinking, nobody else would want me afterwards. Raping me would also redeem his honor, for Yusuf had lost face when my father had laughed at him, and not taken his offer seriously. The escapade had made him an enemy.

None of this was my fault. Screaming, kicking, and punching, my noise

---

[35] Yusuf Tawwil, a Hijazi merchant, was one of the key coup conspirators in 1969. Some 200-300 Saudi military officers were involved in this and it resulted in mass arrests. After this attempted coup, rumor said Yusuf and Daoud had been pushed from a plane several thousand feet above the open desert. Yet after King Faisal's assassination in 1975, both men were released. Their crime was judged as a failed attempt to murder a man, not as treason, against the state. Considered rehabilitated, they resumed their businesses and social roles as far as I'd been able to ascertain.
[36] Despite the ban on women driving in Saudi Arabia, my mother sometimes dared to get behind the wheel when dad was away on flights outside the country and she had to. Covering her red hair with the Saudi men's headdress of *ghutra* and *agal,* she wrapped the cloth strategically and hid her eyes behind a large pair of dark sunglasses

woke my parents. Just as they ran into my bedroom, Yusuf jumped back out the window, having failed in his plan to take me by force. What could we do now? Going to the Saudi police was not an option. A foreigner's word was not worth much against a Saudi citizen. My father expected Yusuf to use his network of powerful friends in the Ministry of Defense and Aviation to have him deported, from his job at Saudi Arabia Airlines. But that never happened.

Rising from my chair, lightheaded, I went towards the cool water to bring myself back from these disconcerting memories. The shock of the cold liquid restored me as I waded into the pool up to my knees. Irina and I spent another half hour in this steamy room before showering. Wrapped in my kimono afterwards, I laid on a chaise lounge until it was my turn for a massage. Irina had insisted on reserving one for each of us.

"You will like Raymond. He's blind but has the hands of an angel. He doesn't chatter like the woman does."

"You go first," I told her. "I want to rest a little longer here." Regarding the golden ringlets of reflection cast upon the ceiling by the water moving in the pool below, I felt a deepening peace. Gone was my hectic conditioning. In this transplanted room, the rushing and chasing fell away. I luxuriated in the deep heat. This was what I needed. Like the women reclining around me, I could slough off preoccupations and just be. Languor. That was the word. I resolved to practice this regularly. Irina was also right about Raymond. His massage was equally transporting. I vowed to return here each Friday evening I was in France. Most of the time I kept that resolution.

That Christmas Eve, Freddie invited me to help decorate her tree. Traditionally the *arbre de noël* is not put up until December 24th. Several friends and neighbors were there already, draping the candle-shaped lights, and teasing about who would place the silvery spike ornament atop the evergreen. Christmas music was playing and we sang the familiar tunes like the Little Drummer Boy. I was surprised to discover how many American carols were popular in French. On my walk home I bought a small paper bag of hot roasted chestnuts from a Pakistani Muslim, also selling inflatable Santa Clauses, along the Champs-Élysées. When I reached my own apartment, I was humming, feeling like this was Christmas. I climbed on a chair to hang the cards people had sent around the mirror above the mantle. I reread the messages as I taped each one up.

My parents' card said, "It sounds as though you are really in love this time. We just hope he doesn't break your heart. And please promise us you won't go to Beirut. It is not safe there and there is little we could do from here if anything happened to you."

George Rizk's letter from Lebanon said he had not forgotten me or the book project. I noticed the stamp at the edge of his envelope. No beautiful girl this time. The current stamp from Lebanon featured a raised fist, wreathed with leaves, and a broken chain beneath.

Lilian, my artist friend in New York, had sent one of her hand-drawn prints, with a message beneath the printed Merry Christmas and Happy New Year. "How lovely to know someone is happy. And thank God you have sense enough to treasure your joy. I hope to visit you in Paris before too long."

After pasting up the final card, I tied on my apron and went to work in my tiny kitchen to finish preparing a meal I had planned for Omar and his friend Hamed. When they arrived they were dressed up and loaded down with goodies from the fancy Lenôtre Traiteur, including a Buche de Noel. The traditional Christmas log cake was large enough for twice the number of dinner guests and they brought along two bottles of good champagne, though neither of them drank alcohol. I took the cake into the kitchen to see if it would fit into the refrigerator, marveling at its miniature marzipan decorations, including candy carrots and mushrooms. Coming back to the living room, I carried a tray with two glasses of juice for the men.

They were on the couch, watching the Christmas festivities on television. Hamed said, "I like that," indicating my emerald green silk blouse. He added, "You look Arab in it."

"Thank you," I replied in French and Arabic.

Omar commented, "Here in France, it is usually considered an insult to be called Arab or Arab looking."

"Yes, I know." But I was also thinking of how many "SOS Racism" buttons I had seen people wearing on their coats and jackets. These featured a small plastic hand with the words, "Ne Touche Pas a Mon Pote." The English equivalent was Keep Your Hands Off My Pal. My new friend Sylvie worked with this organization, combating racism.

"Maybe that's because they never lived in an Arab country or know Arabs in their homes. They only know the extremes: the poor immigrants who come here to do the jobs the French think they're too good for, or the rich Arabs, throwing their money around and carrying on in ways they would never get away with back in their own countries," I said.

"The French are particularly envious of other people's money," said Hamed. "It drives them crazy to see these oil-rich sheikhs speeding around town in their Mercedes. But they won't get off their asses and work to earn more money themselves. They'd rather just bitch about it and live on *chomage* (unemployment compensation). Foreigners are the only ones who really work here. The rest expect the government to take care of them."

Omar took my hand and made a place for me on the couch. "You don't know how lucky you are that I didn't have to work tonight," he said smiling.

We watched the television in silence for a while, seeing Christmas pageants from all over Paris and a few from the provinces. After observing the singing at Notre Dame cathedral, Omar said he preferred the Protestants to the Catholics. "At least they are not extorting money from the poor to build more cathedrals and keep the priests fat."

Hamed nodded in agreement.

During our dinner, Omar mentioned having heard one of Georgina's friends mention the book project. "She told her she wants to do it but just hasn't got the time."

He added, "Too bad you are not offering her money. The Lebanese are always interested once they've seen the color of the cash."

"I know. If I told you how much it's already cost me just to be here and wait for her, with nothing to show for it, you would say I belong in the crazy house."

"You are wasting your time with her," Omar said. "I bet she has no trouble finding time for shopping and going to parties."

"Well, it's her life," I said in Georgina's defense. "You can't force someone to sit down and tell you the story of their life unless they're ready. I can't even get you to keep your promises to call me," I said pointedly regarding Omar.

"That's because I am a man who detests having to tell anybody where I am going or when I am coming back or who I am with. You know me hayati, I can't stand it when I call you and you ask, 'Are you coming over?' I'd rather not call when I cannot come. It's easier that way."

Hamed interjected, "Believe me, you see a lot more of him than his friends do. He's always working and has no time for us."

"Don't listen to him. He's just a bum. He's a nice bum, but if it wasn't for me, he wouldn't even have money for his cigarettes." We all laughed.

After finishing the meal and dessert, we moved back to the living room for coffee. The talk turned to families. Omar complimented me on the many cards he saw above the mantel place.

"You know, my mother had eleven children. I don't think I ever told you this, but only four of us survived. She lost seven. Every boy she named Muhammad died. The longest any of them lived was six months. A few months before I was conceived, a visiting dervish passed through the village and my mother went to him for help. He told her she must not name the next son Muhammad no matter what, but that Allah would give her another boy. When I was born she named me Omar, after the second Caliph, and here I am today. God rest her soul."

Hamed said, "In our village there are a lot of irregularities with identity papers. I have my dead brother's. It's a long trek to the registrar's office into town. If the baby dies after receiving a birth certificate, the mothers keep that one and use it for the next child that comes. Why go all the way into town for a new one? The authorities never know exactly how many children there are."

While watching the midnight mass, Omar leaned over and said near my ear. "I know what you want for Christmas. A nice house, with a big salon, and a library room for all your books and papers, and two kids, any good man for a husband."

I leaned to place my hand on his chest and kissed his cheek, expecting to feel the chain I had given him through his shirt, but it wasn't there. I patted him again before asking, "Where is it?"

"Oh I sold it. And the proceeds fed me for four days. Have you forgotten what a gambler I am?" I wasn't sure if he was joking or not. Clearly my puzzlement was evident.

He added, "No, I didn't sell it. I just left it at my brother's when I took it off to have a shower."

"You don't need to take it off. It is real gold. It won't turn you green you know,"

"I know hayati. Don't worry, I'll be wearing it the next time you see me."

But this incident upset me. After they departed I climbed the steps to my loggia bed thinking it was a harbinger of bad news to come.

* * * *

On Christmas Day, Omar was busy and could not come help eat the cake as promised, but he called twice, sounding almost like a husband.

"I am so fed up with this work of mine. I have to change my life and get into some other line of business, so the money comes in regularly, every day, every month. I've always taken everything I've made back to Tunisia, to make the house and furnish it, but now I need to get some money together here.

"Maybe we could buy a little hotel somewhere, and knock down some of the walls on the top floor to make a little apartment for us to live in. And you would have a place to write while I took care of the hotel."

"I could help out with the hotel too," I said, quite pleased to hear him say these things. Perhaps he was really planning our life together.

"No wife of mine is going to be ironing sheets and working."

"So, you want to spoil your wife then?" I teased back.

"You are very intelligent you know, but I've always said that, haven't I?"

"Yes you have." I didn't ask him when he would be coming now. I held back those words remembering what he had said last night.

255

"I'll be there tomorrow night. And since the prince has come back today, I am sure I will be with him for New Year's Eve, in case you want to make other plans."

The following night I waited until five thirty in the morning but Omar never appeared. As the sun rose, I tried to sleep and cursed myself for the lonely night of waiting, when I could have gone to the party Irina was having. In a little more than a week, I would leave for a month or more to the US for work. I wanted to spend every possible moment with Omar. Lately he seemed like a different man, full of loving words and plans for our future each time he called. But when he did not show up, my doubts rushed back. I chastised myself for believing there was any change.

* * * *

At eleven that morning Omar finally called. His voice was weary and haggard. He explained that the thirty-seven-year-old son of the prince had died of a heart attack in Riyadh. Omar had spent all night calling to find a private plane to take the prince and his other son back to the kingdom for the funeral. "He was the only good son he had. We've done business together. He'd invited me to his wedding next month. He was planning to marry again."

Though his news had melted my anger, I mentioned having waited up for him.

"You know how I live hayati, like a cloud in the sky. When they are here sometimes I don't even have a moment to take a shower. I am ashamed of all this, this life and them. You know I never meant to hurt you when you do not hear from me. I know you wait for my calls. That makes it worse. It is terrible I know, but you must not count on me during these times. I don't ever want to hear you say I knew a Tunisian once, what a bastard he was. You know I adore you. You have all the qualities I want in a woman. I never want to cause you any pain. That's why I must get out of this life if we want to be together."

Holding back my tears I declared, "Omary, I love you. I would never say you were a bastard. I know it wasn't really your fault you could not call. It's true I was upset last night, but I get over it quickly, once I know what happened. You know how I always imagine the worst since you disappeared."

"Yes, but you took me back," he reminded.

"Yes and I forgave you."

"And I will always call you, you know that, even if it's not on time. But we cannot go on like this. I have to get out of this life once and for all," he declared with finality. Then he added, "I'll come see you just as soon as I can, but I have not slept for two nights now. I've just got to get some sleep first. In the meantime, can you do me a big favor?"

"Of course I can. What is it?"

"Please go to the post office today, and send telegrams to Riyadh for me, in the name of the prince and his surviving son Muhammad. They need to be in English. You're the writer, compose something, condolences, etc."

"Go to sleep now. Consider it done."

* * * *

On New Year's Eve, Omar had to work. Upon returning from his son's funeral, the prince went out to the Raspoutine nightclub with his guests for the year-end celebrations. This disgusted Omar.

"He's practically dancing on the grave of his son. His body is hardly cold. I think I care more about the memory of that poor man than his own father seems to."

He promised to call me from the club to see how my evening was going and to wish me a happy new year just after midnight.

I hadn't committed to any invitations because Omar had not known if the prince would return to Paris so soon after burying his son. If he'd been free, Omar and I would have planned to stay in for a quiet night. My only friends who didn't already have other plans were Freddie, her new Yugoslavian boyfriend, and Zemira so I invited them over.

Everyone brought something along and the four of us enjoyed a real feast together. Beginning with champagne, and going on to several different wines, and back to champagne after the meal, we toasted the arrival of 1985. Freddie's foie gras had been specially packed in the province by her uncle. So smooth and buttery going down my throat, I tried to forget it came from enlarging the livers of force-fed geese. Then we ate smoked salmon, followed by my spicy lamb curry, the dish they'd requested: full of okra, zucchini, onion, tomatoes, peas, and bits of sweet potato. Then came the Boursault cheese, figs, and *marron glacés* (sweet, conserved chestnuts).

Good for his word, Omar called just after midnight, to wish me, and Darius the cat, "Love, health, happiness, and a long life."

"And I hope it is all with you!" I said, blowing him a kiss through the phone.

"I'll come as soon as I'm done with them. God only knows when that will be."

Omar did not arrive until seven thirty that morning. Our joint slumbers were interrupted around noon by Darius the cat, jiggling the telephone receiver near our heads, to request his breakfast. Downstairs in the kitchen I was glad all the party dishes were done before I slept. I hate waking to a messy kitchen. Standing at the sink, after the guests depart, I enjoy savoring what has happened. That night, while showering I consciously washed the

257

old year off me, imagining it swirling down the drain in the bottom of the floor. This New Year had to be better. Toweling myself off, I had an overwhelming sensation of being loved, of love coming toward me, and of love flowing out of me. I felt so light, as though some warmth shone out, from within me.

After feeding the cat, I did not write in my journal first thing as is my habit upon waking. Instead, I climbed back up the steps to slide back into bed beside Omar. His body was so warm and solid and real. He stirred and drew me to him.

"Is your new year off to a good start, mon petit lapin?"

I nodded and nestled closer to him.

* * * *

On the third day of January 1985, I stood at my window watching the snowfall onto the courtyard cobblestones below, dusting the rooftops, streets, and bridges of Paris. The statues in the parks, with their eyes ever open, would be cloaked in fresh whiteness, muffling the eternity that surrounded them. I touched my Ayat al-Kursi amulet around my neck, which spoke of this everlastingness, and remembered today was Georgina's thirty-second birthday. I phoned to wish her well but no one answered.

The following day it snowed again. I walked to the Place des Vosges wanting to see it covered in white. That square had become a Paris reference point, now seen in all seasons: winter, spring, summer, fall, and back to winter again. Observing its alterations firsthand had intertwined them with my changes. In another month or so the bereft branches of these blackened trees would put forth tiny green buds and the children would return to play although the frozen ground was covered with snow today. I felt reassured. By allowing nature to flow, my life would also bud and bloom in unison. At the cafe I sat at the same table where I'd eaten a string of solitary breakfasts a year ago after things had not worked out with Waddah. I ordered the boeuf bourguignon. When my steaming serving came, I devoured it like a hungry peasant, wiping my plate with the good crusty bread. On my way back home I detoured past the tall white statue of Sainte Geneviève standing as always upon her bridge. Facing upriver, with a young child standing in front of her, they faced the world together. For a long time, I gazed at the pair, the falling snow cloaking my shoulders with the same mantel being drawn over theirs.

Late that night, just as I finished packing, Omar arrived. This was to be our last night together before my departure for a month or more of non-stop work and travel elsewhere. His mood was quiet and serious. He sat me down on the couch beside him to speak of his hopes and plans for this New Year.

"Hayati, I know you are counting on me and I'm counting on you. As marvelous as love is, it does not fill one's pockets. Before we can marry and have a family we have to have the future laid out. We must pose a solid base. I know the horror of orphans and families broken up because of money problems. I don't know how long it will take me to get established but —"

I interrupted him, "Why do you think you have to be rich first? Any woman would marry a rich man just for his money. I love you now. I can help you. We can build our lives together. My parents had only twenty-two dollars between them when they married."

He smiled, shaking his head as he took my hands in his. "I'm afraid you are not being realistic. I don't want to lead you on and tell you everything's fine when it's not. I want you to go on this trip and work hard and make lots of money and then come back to me. In the meantime I'll be hard at work on my various projects trying to get set up. You don't really know anything but my good side. Did you know that my own brother cannot even read or write? Sometimes he sits for hours doodling with a pencil. He tells me if he could write like I can, he would do it all the time. You know I am a man without a real trade or a degree of any kind. You, you have a bank in your head. You can always make money, anytime. Me, if I haven't got cash in my pocket, I feel rotten and depressed. And I can't face you. You know how I stay away from here when I feel down."

He paused before continuing. "I don't want any wife of mine to have to work outside the home once we're married. And I could never live on your back. I have to have everything arranged beforehand. I never want to hurt you or make you suffer because of me."

We sat quietly then, holding hands, with me imagining future possibilities if everything worked out. My head dropped to his shoulder. The scent of him was just detectable through his shirt and sweater. I had heard mothers could pick their child's shirt out from a pile of clothing, just by its smell. Chemistry. I shut my eyes and breathed him in deeply not knowing how long it would be until I could do this again.

He put his hand under my chin and tilted my face to his. The heat rose in us as his mouth found mine, our passions matching in response. I wanted us to be wholly connected once and for all, to place everything except us outside the circle of our embrace, to banish all obstacles. It was not that I wanted to escape from the real world but I wanted to complete something in it. To tie a knot at the end of this bright thread of pleasure and hold on to something solid after so many months. That day, as he dove into my skin, I plunged deeper into his, hoping to go all the way through him and through myself, to reach some third thing, neither his pleasure nor mine, but ours. To fuse all our forces into one great transcendental ecstasy, the security of our love made absolute. But once again, it did not happen.

The next morning we hurried to leave for the airport and my flight. Omar drove me, recounting on the way, a dream he had overnight. "I'd been given someone to guard, perhaps a Palestinian. The prince and the other royals were involved with their cause, though it was not clear to me if it was 'for' or 'against' — although I guess it would have to be 'for,' non? Anyway, I became convinced somehow that I should kill this man. Then I woke up for a few seconds, but I went back to sleep, and finished the dream. In it, I killed the man, I strangled him I think."

"Do you think you did the right thing in the dream?" I asked, wondering how to interpret all of this.

"Yes, I did. I had to kill him. He was a bad man. But then, I had all the royal family after me, and I was on the run."

We drove on in silence for a while. I recalled something Lynda had written in her Christmas letter. "Carla asked me how you were. I just went back to her for another reading. She said she did not think your Omar would stay in France. She said he has secrets and that he'll have to leave the country." I said nothing of this to him but I held him for as long as I could, my eyes welling with tears, before turning to go through the doors of Charles de Gaulle airport.

Omar had said, "If you don't stop crying, I'll send you home to your mother for good."

The rich red and yellow scents of curry powder accompanied our take off on Pakistan International Airways as I headed back to the US. This was my first time on PIA. The tickets were well priced for this flight, which had originated in Karachi, the city dad had called "the armpit of the universe," after flying through it many times. Gone was the cool navy blue and white efficiency of Air France. This plane was packed with crying babies, flashing dark eyes, and golden bangles clinking on brown wrists. Anklet bracelet bells tinkled as sandaled women walked the aisles, their footwear slapping their bare soles.

The riot of their colorful costumes cheered me. Most passengers wore the modestly cut Punjabi pantaloons and tunics, with long trailing scarves, accentuating their femininity. My mother had worn such an outfit to Jeddah parties, with tiny mirror pieces sewn into green and white silk fabric, the handiwork common in the province of Balochistan. The stewardesses uniforms were of the same emerald shade of the blouse I had worn on Christmas Eve when Hamed told me I looked Arab. This Islamic green, from a dune brown country, was also the color of the Saudi flag.

Pushing my seat back, I thought about Omar and where he had come from. On this airplane I was closer to his original environment than I would be in the world I was flying towards. When Omar had admitted his older brother could not read or write, and his mother had born eleven children and seen only four live to maturity, my heart had gone out to him. For him, there was nothing romantic about the desert. Born in a Tunisian village, into the poverty of a rigid colonial social system, his opportunities were limited to say the least. North Africans often left their farms and villages as soon as they could scrape together enough money to get to the nearest big city or across the sea. Some Americans did the same. In search of their fortunes, these Tunisians and other North Africans ended up in France, the former empire their lands had been a part of, when they'd been forced to learn its language. The French had been in Tunisia since 1881, longer than they'd been in Lebanon. And the Tunisians had not gained their independence until 1956. Some returned periodically to their villages, like Omar did, to build a house for his neighbors to envy. Seen as a prodigal son, his advice, favors, and money would be sought; and with it the responsibility to help feed an extended family. Few would be able to fully comprehend how Omar had earned the bread, which went into their mouths.

Hamed had said he could never go back to live in Tunisia. "Nobody would really understand me. I've been away too long and gotten too used to another way of life." His other reasons were that he had made no money and had nothing to show for all his years abroad. This meant he would have no standing in his society nor receive any respect. He'd become one of those who could not afford to return, literally or figuratively. And Omar? Could he bring a foreign wife back to the close-knit world of his village relatives? I hadn't given this sufficient consideration. What the two of us knew about each other's lives in Paris was less than half the story.

Sfax, Tunisia would be nothing like France. Having never met his brother or extended family, I knew how bad the odds were. Making it past our differences was a long shot at best. It was far more likely we'd fall out of this precarious love orbit and be sucked into the impenetrable maze of our societies' cross-cultural conundrums. And what about Omar's latest dream? Was it a warning about an upcoming break with this Saudi prince? To leave his service would require "killing" the subservient Omar. He said he wanted change, to no longer be the man I knew currently. Could he manage such a transformation? Committing a murder in the dream had shown him someone's life must end, but was it his own inner "bad man" or an external one? Meanwhile, I was living in a fantasy too, with a man who was as much of a phantom as Georgina and Lebanon were. When and how would my self-deceptions cease?

* * * *

My first month of 1985 was spent in the familiar work routine of flights, hotel check-ins, unpacking, meeting people, running programs, re-packing, and flying on to the next destination. Some nights while falling asleep, I imagined having Omar along. What would he think of New York, Dallas-Fort Worth, and Denver, Colorado? While in Boulder, at the Midwest offices of my MS&B I ate lunch with a Lebanese couple brought in as resource people for our pre-departure training program. We discovered the husband had once been a pilot for Middle East Airlines and knew my father. The wife Nadia invited me to dinner at their home. That evening we reminisced about Beirut in the good old days. They felt lucky to have immigrated before the war had worsened. They had family in the US already and said they were done with Lebanon. This gave me a perverse kind of hope. If a Lebanese family can get over the place, surely an expatriate like me ought to be able to manage it.

I told them about my Georgina book project and they thought it was a good idea.

As we parted that night Nadia told me, "When you get back to Paris, I want you to call Mona, an old girlfriend of mine. We've known each other for many years and she knows Georgina very well. They used to model together. She lives in the South of France on the Cote d'Azur now. Maybe she can help you."

Gratefully I took Mona's name and number, remembering how the original information about Georgina's Paris whereabouts had come through the friend of a friend.

My final two days of the trip were spent visiting my parents in Pennsylvania. My mother had left the Christmas tree up with my presents beneath.

Dad was happily working for a small cargo airline with a big United Parcel Service contract. He called it "the night boxes business, with no passengers to worry about."

I was relieved to see them settled in and doing well. I didn't want to talk about Omar and they avoided bringing up the subject of my love life. In my parents' garage, I went through a file cabinet to dispose of superfluous things, like six-year-old Christmas cards. Coming upon a sheaf of magazine articles and newspaper clippings about the fighting in Beirut ten years ago, I broke into tears. Had those horrors been so easily forgotten? The faces of terrified children and crying mothers running between the ruins of their homes seemed to reproach me. The armed men, and abandoned buildings, burnt out and shell-pocked, those corpses in the streets; that reality had certainly dimmed for me in Paris since Omar had entered the picture. Was this good or bad?

I also found the partial draft of a poem I'd scribbled two years ago in 1982.

My rifle eyes you in the street
Scurrying to some animal's task
As my cheek lays against the smooth
Wood of the stock, I cock
The metal curve of the trigger
And with one cool click
My streaking fire blows
The last breath out of you.

[Excerpt from *Measuring Distances* poetry collection]

In that moment I too had felt the murderous urge described in my poem. Raised with a greater likelihood of becoming a sniper than a poet, I had picked up a paltry pen instead. And yet, even the great French conqueror Napoleon had admitted, "Il n'y a que deux puissances au monde, le sabre et l'esprit : à la longue, le sabre est toujours vaincu par l'esprit." which translates, "There are only two powers in the world, saber and spirit; at the end, the saber is always defeated by the spirit." Napoleon Bonaparte also had the dubious distinction of getting the most men killed in a single battle, over sixty thousand at Borodino in Russia in 1812. His life had started on an island, Corsica, and ended on another one, in exile on Saint Helena, though he had thought the English were sending him to North America after trouncing his troops at Waterloo.

That night I tried calling Omar via the Hotel George V not knowing if he was back in France yet. I missed him badly and wondered if he'd received my letter with my return date. Why rush back to Paris if he wasn't there? That thought depressed me. Meanwhile there were chores to take care of in the US, like selling my car, and some of my furniture, to get us extra money. Over the past year on each trip to the US, I had put off these chores but now felt certain I would never live in Greenwich, CT again. If Omar and I were going to try making a future together, my BMW would add to our little stake.

While returning my remaining papers to the filing cabinet several index cards fell out. The quotes upon them had been copied out years ago:

"The violence done to Lebanon will overwhelm you." Hebrew prophet Habakkuk in 600 B.C.

"The formation and deformation of Lebanon are rooted in the same forces." Lebanese sociologist Samir Kalaf.

"I am not afraid for the Lebanese, but I am afraid for Lebanon." Ex-Prime Minister of Lebanon Selim El Hoss, in 1980.

"Lebanon continues to survive as a state, despite so many foreign occupiers and wars, because it is no longer enough to wreck the government to destroy the country. You have to knock down each individual. But precisely because every Lebanese is shortsightedly focusing on his own individual domain, it is easy for outsiders to come in and play havoc with their country" Thomas Friedman, New York Times bureau chief.

* * * *

The last night before flying back to France, I stayed with Lynda in my old place. With no word from Omar, I gave her the keys to my car and asked her to help me sell it. Overnight I had a strange dream that seemed a warning from my subconscious.

I was driving a car, and someone was with me, but I was not sure if it was a man or woman. We were coming off a mountain road onto a highway and the traffic was backed up for miles. I saw a possible shortcut and turned to take it. Then I saw all the other drivers who had the same initial idea were turning back.

The next thing I knew I was standing on the ground and so was the other person but the car had plunged down the mountainside into a crevice. No one was hurt. I had no recollection of getting out of the car yet remembered something precious was in it. I could not say what it was exactly or whether the car could be recovered.

As Lynda drove me to JFK airport the following day I recounted this dream. We attempted to interpret it.

"Maybe it relates to the Georgina project, becoming impossible, and going off a cliff, figuratively speaking," I posited.

Lynda suggested, "Maybe it relates to Omar. Then again it could just be anxiety about selling the car. Don't worry, I won't let anything happen to it."

* * * *

Back in Paris there was still no word from Omar for several days and I fretted about it but Freddie called saying she had good news. She had taken care of Darius for me and when she brought him back to my apartment, I made her dinner. She confessed things had gotten serious with the Yugoslavian boyfriend Zvonimir had introduced her to.

"He'll be coming to Paris to live with me and learn French. Then he can look for a job. I think we'll be getting married."

"The best of luck to you both Freddie," I said hugging her tightly.

Relieved to not be the only one with marriage on my mind, I was hoping her good fortune might be contagious.

Resuming my Paris routine, I met Irina at the hammam that Friday and had dinner and saw a movie with the Burkes over the weekend. At my neighborhood cafe, the regulars were complaining about their weight gains over the holidays. And in the mail was an invitation to a reception being held by the mayor of Paris, Jacques Chirac at the Hôtel de Ville (City Hall). The occasion was the French translation of a book of poetry written by Prince Abdullah al Faisal Al Saud. How my name had gotten onto the invitation list was a mystery. Perhaps Waddah? Or my old Mobil Oil boss? They were among the many who knew I wrote poetry. Responding to the RSVP I decided to attend and find out more.

The overly ornate interior of the Hôtel de Ville was full of elegantly dressed people when I arrived on the appointed evening. The honor guard was going up the steps, and we paused to allow the soldiers to go through the flourishes, drawing their sabers. Their uniforms were crisply pressed, their boots and buttons gleaming. The trappings of empire, I thought while following them up the carpeted steps. Inside the large reception room, huge chandeliers hung from the ceiling where frescoes of naked women and cupids frolicked in eighteenth century style. These would never be seen in the City Halls of Riyadh or Jeddah, I noted dryly while passing beneath them.

Jacques Chirac,[37] a former Communist party member, and previous prime minister of France was now the mayor of Paris. He seemed harried and sweaty when I shook his hand in the receiving line. His speech that evening droned on about the long special friendship between France and Saudi Arabia. I thought of details he was leaving out and ruefully recalled the real story. Years ago Mazen had told me about how his father, Dr. Rashad Pharaon, became the first Saudi plenipotentiary and ambassador to France. Although Syrian born and without a drop of Saudi blood, Rashad Pharaon was sent to represent Saudi Arabia after the Second World War because King Abdul Aziz Al Saud trusted him. Having become the king's personal physician, Mazen's father had treated extended members of the royal family, curing them of syphilis too, if those rumors were correct.

At first the French government rejected Dr. Pharaon's diplomatic credentials. His name was still on their most wanted list. During the French

---

[37] Jaques Chirac would become the President of France from 1995 to 2007. Later disgraced, and sentenced for corruption in 2011, he was the first head of state to be prosecuted in France since Marshal Petain, the infamous Nazi collaborator president. His Middle Eastern connections were his downfall.

occupation of the Levant (Syria and Lebanon) he had joined the resistance movement. Having been part of a group that ambushed a patrol and killed a French officer, he'd become a wanted man. Rather than risk arrest and torture, Dr. Pharaon fled south into the desert and had ended up in Riyadh. There his medical talents were much appreciated. Since his medical degree had been earned in France, he spoke the language, and understood the colonialists' thinking. The Saudi king held fast and forced the French government to accept the former resistance fighter as Ambassador Pharaon. During the years of his father's posting, Mazen was born in Paris. Already in labor on the way to the hospital, his mother gave birth to him in the car on a bridge over the River Seine. He never said which of the city's thirty-seven bridges it had been.

Now the featured poet took the podium, graciously thanking the mayor for his remarks. This Saudi Prince Abdullah was a brother of the current Saudi Minister of Foreign Affairs, Prince Saud. Both were sons of the assassinated King Faisal, whose reign I'd lived under in Arabia. Prince Abdullah spoke exclusively in Arabic but I relished the fact we were all listening to poetry, the universal mystic language no matter which tongue delivered it. As he made his remarks and recited his poems, Abdullah often stroked his nearly white goatee. Such a familiar gesture, I'd seen so many Muslim men touch their beards just like that, often vowing *Wahayat Allah*, by the beard of the Prophet, when doing it.

Later, while the guests partook of the drinks and canapés, I spotted an old friend from my New York United Nations days, the Ambassador of Bahrain, Dr. Salman Al Saffar. In the six years since I'd last seen him, his hair had gone more white than gray. Now he was the Bahraini Ambassador to France. I congratulated him. We caught up on each other's news and that of our mutual acquaintances. He had not heard about the suicide of Mahmoud's nephew.

As the guests began departing, Salman offered me a lift home. His chauffeur had driven the dark blue Mercedes to a convenient spot, and opened the back door for me to get in. Looking at him, I thought it could just as well be Omar.

Salman sat up front beside the driver as the car glided through the traffic. At a roundabout another car approached the right-hand side, coming a bit too close. Quick as a flash Salman's hand was in the glove compartment pulling out a loaded revolver.

"You never know these days. Too many diplomats have been murdered in Paris. The Arabs are more afraid than anybody of kidnappings for ransom. It is not the same city I knew when I studied here as a boy. You remember the UAE ambassador? He was killed near the embassy residence on Avenue Foch. I'm not taking any chances. This car has bulletproof windows."

Another reason to be relieved that I am not part of that world, I thought. As we pulled up to my big red door on Île Saint-Louis, I thanked Salman, and invited him to a dinner party I was planning for next weekend.

"I'd like to come, but I think I'll be in the countryside. Would you like to go there with me instead?" He gave me a sly smile.

I knew Salman already had a French wife and perhaps I read more than he meant by his invitation, but I demurred.

"No thank you. As a matter of fact I'm engaged to a very nice man, and will probably be getting married soon," I said, stretching the truth in my attempt to be diplomatic.

"Well, you can tell him I said he's lucky. Please keep in touch. I'll call you about the dinner party."

That night while trying to fall asleep I worried about how much longer it might be before any word came from Omar.

The following day he called having just arrived from Tunisia. "I found your letters waiting at the hotel. I'll come see you tonight, unless you've already found yourself another man," he teased.

Hanging up the phone I reflected upon last night. Why did I want the driver Omar when I could have had an ambassador? And why had Georgina wanted Salameh, the refugee freedom-fighter terrorist, when she could have had a prince, or some member of the elite establishment. Because we loved who we loved. And we had seen through the corruption of the system and were willing to buck it. Idealistic, foolish or strong willed enough, we somehow realized our rights as women, even to love freely, were entwined with all those whose rights were threatened. I could do without ambassadors who no longer impressed or intimidated me. Could Omar do without princes?

When Omar arrived late that evening, he seemed subdued. For a long time he held me to him. "You are prettier than I remember."

We sat on the couch and he asked what I'd been up to. Among other things, I recounted the Hotel de Ville reception.

"I was wishing you had been there beside me. We have never been seen in public together really."

He curtly replied, "I have no place at such a function."

I looked down at my hands. What a mistake to bring that up. He saw his place in society as predetermined, whereas my sense of social mobility must seem ridiculously romantic, and unrealistic to him.

I changed the subject, "What is your news then?"

"Nothing really. I got fed up with Paris and went back to Tunisia for a rest. I brought my nephew back with me. I need to find him a job in a bakery."

"And your projects? You seem depressed Omary."

"Things aren't so good, they're just not working out the way I had hoped. This time I got caught, taking 50,000 francs in cash, out of the country. You know we are not allowed to take money out. They confiscated it all. The man who is my friend in customs wasn't there. So that's the end of it I suppose. It was meant to be a little stake to get us started."

"Oh habibi! I'm so sorry," I said reaching over for his hand. "What is the down payment on a little hotel? How much do we need?"

He gave me a look of surprise but I persisted.

"Have you ever saved any money or bought any property before?"

"No. I did not want to be tied down anywhere by something like property. I've only bought my car, to make me more mobile. I've earned money and saved just to be free in between time, to write and think."

He asked me how much I had made on this trip and I told him. He regarded me practically with pity as though earning less than $50,000 per trip made me a child or something. It made me angry. After all, I was not the one who had lost my money.

Then his tone turned soothing. "Hayati, let's not talk about this anymore. I don't know how much you have or don't have, but it's enough to know that you seem ready to share it."

"I was going to stay in the US longer to sell the car and bring back the money in case we needed it, but I never heard from you. I didn't want to stay extra days, so I hurried back here to be with you as soon as my work was finished."

He smiled weakly. "Why don't we watch a little television now? And you can take off your boots and change into something more comfortable to come sit with me."

I started with my boots but when I was down to my slip, his eyes rolled over my bared shoulders hungrily. He unbuttoned his shirt and slipped off his shoes before leaning towards me. I noticed that the chain with the charms I had given him was still missing when his shirt came off. We never went out for dinner that night.

The prince returned the next day and Omar resumed his hectic schedule.

"At least I'll recover my losses," he joked on the phone.

Two days later he called me at two thirty in the morning to say, "I'd love to see you cherie but I don't even have time to wash my hair these days!"

"I miss you. We have only managed to see each other once in a month and a half," I reminded him.

"Yes I know. This is how I lost my past girlfriends. No woman can stand this life of mine. You have lasted the longest you know. You're the most understanding."

"I just keep reminding myself it may be hard to wait for you but at least I'm comfortable at home in my own bed while you are out there somewhere in the night."

* * * *

The rest of February included a string of days with temperatures below freezing. Keeping busy with friends, visitors from out of town, and my work with the French consulting company, I only heard from Omar when he could call. He sounded tired and more harassed. One night he turned up at three after calling at midnight to see if I was home. He hadn't told me he'd be coming over.

"So my phantom returns," I said sleepily as he slid into bed.

"I am not a phantom anymore in your life," he said, seizing my flesh and bruising it with the force of his hunger.

* * * *

On Valentine's Day Omar called to say he would come late but be there. Upon arrival he was buoyant and full of plans.

"I've decided to buy a good, used, new model Mercedes, and drive it myself when the prince is not here. Instead of driving for agencies, I will have my own car, and make twice as much. And when I'm busy with the prince, I can put Hamed to work driving it. It will cost 200,000 francs, but it will bring in 2,000 francs a day."

He was rattling off numbers and how many workdays were required to pay off the amount before starting to make a profit. He spoke so fast my head spun though I clearly heard that 100,000 francs was needed for a down payment.

"Best of all, I can be with you every night until your next trip," he added.

That night he made love to me with such slow deep kisses and with such deliberation that I cried out, "What are you doing to me? I'll die of pleasure!"

"I haven't done anything yet," he said through clenched teeth.

As we lay together afterwards, our breathing returning to normal, I said, "I bet none of your princes have ever been loved like this. How I love you Omary."

The following morning I told him about my upcoming trip and additional work expected now with the French company.

"Good! You will soon have to open an office."

"I'd much rather have kids first," I replied, knowing this was risky.

"One never knows in this life. One day it's this, another day it's that. We cannot see into the future. Children come when they come."

"Well, we do have choices you know," I said a little impatiently. "If I didn't take precautions, I could just let them come."

"And you would be the loser," he swiftly answered.

"I'd never do that," I retorted. "I have too much respect for you and myself. We will have kids when we're good and ready."

He changed the subject, "You know you were laughing and chuckling in your sleep last night. I wondered what you were dreaming of."

"Why didn't you wake me and ask? Then we would both know!"

"I didn't want to wake you," he said, tenderly taking my hand from across the breakfast table.

Then he told me more about his plans to invest in the car. "I had to turn away business in the past, from Bahrain, and other places, because I didn't have my own car. But now, if I do, I'll be my own boss, and free to work three or four days with this one or that one. And when I get set up, there will be other clients."

At the mention of Bahrain, my mind went back to the night of the reception, and Salman. We all have to start somewhere, I thought. The man who'd become the first UAE Foreign Minister had been a taxi driver once upon a time. I mentioned none of this to Omar however. All I said was, "If you have the car, you'll be able to have a more regular life, and be here with me every night."

Standing, I went to his side of the table and sat on his knee to hug him. I touched his chest and asked, "Where is the Ayat al-Kursi I gave you? You said I would see you wearing it again but I never have. If you really sold it because you needed money, I could give you other jewelry that would bring in more. I meant for it to protect you."

"Keep your jewelry hayati. Gold things cost two to three hundred francs a gram to buy but only bring in fifty or sixty francs a gram when you sell them. Be glad you have fallen into my hands. I know plenty of men in this city who would be glad to sell your jewelry." He bit my cheek.

"And you will see me wearing that chain again, I promise!" And he kissed my forehead, pulled on his jacket, and went out the door.

I made a second mug of tea and sat down on the couch with the cat on my lap, thinking about Georgina. Spring would soon be here. Maybe we would start working together when she returned to Paris after my next work trip. Sitting at my desk I wrote three letters: one to Georgina, one to my parents, and one to Mona, the friend of my friend who lived on the Cote d'Azur in the South of France.

* * * *

The next time Omar visited we discussed the car project again.

"Another fellow has promised to loan me part of the sum, since the banks will not."

"Too bad you cannot use my car," I said. "But it's only a two door BMW, and too expensive to ship, and it's not new. On this next trip I can sell it and we can invest the proceeds." So far Lynda had not found a buyer.

For the first time he replied as if he thought this was a good idea. "You will get your money back at the end of the season after we recoup the investment. Eventually we will sell the car and invest all the proceeds in the hotel business. Then we'll see," he said, tweaking my cheek.

I reminded him that he had said he'd be with me every night when the prince departed but it had not worked out that way.

"I know, I've got such a crazy hours now, but I need all the work I can find. I don't want to be any bother to you. You need your rest before this trip. Besides, you would soon tire of me if you saw me every night."

"I would not!" I replied heatedly. "I never get enough of you, and now I'm leaving in two days, for another month away."

"But this time, it's once and for all," he said gently, before kissing me.

* * * *

Two days later, on the flight to New York, I wrote down everything Omar had said about the plans to invest in the car. I concluded it sounded too good to be true. He hadn't mentioned things like the cost of insurance or garage, etcetera. With my businesswoman hat on, it was easier to see this get-rich-quick scheme would probably backfire. Was it just a ruse to get money from me? If I handed Omar seven or eight thousand dollars I suspected he'd go straight to a casino and that would be the end of it. What then? My cynical side warned me not to be a total dummy. If I gave him the money and he lost it, or did not give him the money, the outcome would be the same. Either way he could disappear, yet I would be poorer, and feel even dumber, if I tried to buy his affections. Perhaps my offer of financial help is why he had been so lovey-dovey lately. Ouch. Was this the sort of truth I had come to Paris to learn?

* * * *

As things turned out a corporate client in Michigan postponed a program on that trip. And the French consulting company ICM asked me to come back to Paris early to help them with booking conflicts. Suddenly they had more business than expected for March. I cut short my US stay, leaving me no time to sell the BMW. I tried to reach Omar to discuss this change of plans, but like last time, I had no luck reaching him by phone. Miffed he had not tried to contact me since my departure, I decided to postpone the car sale until my next business trip. On my return flight to Paris I had a strong premonition the failure to sell my car would become an issue between Omar and me. We were headed for some kind of crash, for sure.

* * * *

Less than an hour after I got home, Omar was at my door, with an armful of flowers. Obviously he received the message I'd left at the hotel with my new arrival date. He wasted no time getting to the subject of his plans.

After a sweet welcome back kiss he said, "I hope you have a good news for me hayati because all my other plans for help have fallen through."

I hesitated but decided to tell him straight. "Actually I was hoping you would call while I was in the US to discuss the car and everything. Did you get the message to call me?"

"No, I only got the one saying when you'd return."

"I left it with the concierge and told him it was urgent."

"Oh, him. He and I have quarreled. I won't get anything out of him until the prince returns and he has to cooperate with me."

"As you can see I came back early to do more work with the French company. I wanted to ask you how urgent your need was. I could have said no to this offer of extra work, so I could stay to sell the car, but I need the business too. If I improve my relationship with this company in Paris, I won't have to fly back to the US every other month and spend so much time away from you. Since I did not hear from you I decided to come back now and sell the car on the next trip."

He went rigid with disappointment and said, "I thought I made it clear before you left that this time it was 'once and for all' and for you to do the necessary. Remember, I did not ask you for help, you offered it."

His words stung. For a few moments I said nothing and did not look at him. I thought, this is what it all boils down to, money.

"Listen Omar, I'm sorry." I paused before adding, "If we were married, everything I have would be yours too, you know."

"Don't mix up the subjects," he said with frost in his voice.

"I could do a lot if things were clear between us. I have friends I have known for years who might loan us money and — "

He cut me off in mid sentence, "No. And I don't want you discussing any of this with anyone else you understand? It's between us only."

This irked me. Maybe what he really means is that anyone else could see right through the scheme. They would tell me just how blind I've been. Casting about for something else to say I offered, "Perhaps I could borrow the money from the bank, and buy the car in my own name."

"Me work for you?" He retorted. "You are not even a resident. You have no papers. It would probably be illegal. Besides, I can take risks that you cannot. I have my ways and my connections. I can get out of any trouble. You could be deported."

Was he trying to scare me? He had certainly sized me up. The vehemence in his tone and "me working for you?" hung in the air.

"My lawyer friend could help. She could take care of the necessary paperwork. Don't tell me a nonresident cannot buy a car in France." The paperwork was already underway for my residence permit and work permit with ICM though I didn't mention this.

"No. I thought I made it clear to you from the beginning. All I need from you is the cash. You don't need to get involved. I was going to add your money to mine, and then pay you back once I'd made the money and sold the car."

"I gave my girlfriend instructions to sell my car in my absence. She has all the paperwork," I offered.

"Forget it. Let's just drop the whole subject. It's too late now anyway." He sounded thoroughly dejected.

"I'll be honest with you Omar," I said after a deep breath. "I'm afraid to give you money. It's not that I don't trust you, it's just that if the plans did not work out as you hope or you lost the money, you'd be too ashamed to face me, and I'd lose you."

"No you wouldn't lose me. Money comes, money goes," he said.

Upping the stakes I added, "You've been careful to never make any promises to me. On the one hand, I respect you for it. You have always said we have to be reasonable, and build the base first, before we could talk about marriage and all that. On the other hand, I worry that there isn't any future for us. It always seems to be more my idea than yours. Maybe all of this is just a way of stringing me along."

He looked at me. His eyes were very hard. The soft shining black light I had seen in them so many times had gone out. He answered, "We will just have to see what this summer season brings. I have to work very hard now until autumn, and then we'll see how things look."

This was not what I wanted to hear him say.

A short while later he took a handkerchief full of rings from his pocket and showed them to me. At first I thought he was giving me the choice of a present, but he said, "A friend gave me these to sell. We're going to split the profits, and I'll pay him back the rest when I can."

I examined two of the rings. Did he expect me to buy one? The workmanship was poor and the style so démodé. He would be lucky to get what their weight was worth. The stones were just chips. "I doubt they will bring very much."

Then he took "a gift from someone else" from the breast pocket of his jacket. This gold three-piece set had a watch, a ring, and a matching lighter in what we called "gaudy Saudi" style. "I should think these are worth more than the rings," he said somewhat triumphantly.

I thought it strange that anyone who knew Omar would give him a lighter. He never smoked. Were these a gift or had they been stolen?

"Remember Najwa?" he asked. "The woman you met at Georgina's? She once offered me 20,000 francs to invest for her. Recently she tried to get in touch with me, leaving a lot of messages at the hotel. I never returned any of her calls."

Even if this was true, it was low of him to throw this in my face. Seeing this as a tactic, it bothered me less. It revealed how far he would go and how badly he wanted money. I was tempted to say, "then go to her," but I held my tongue. Now I was one hundred percent sure, I would never give him any money, not after this conversation.

Our discussions did not dampen his ardor. We made love on the living room floor in front of the gas fire, but it no longer felt as special.

After he had gone, the phone rang. It was Georgina's father, welcoming me back to Paris and inviting me over for tea at five thirty tomorrow. What a nice surprise.

* * * *

The following afternoon I arrived at the appointed time. The Filipino maid and little Ali Junior opened the door and led me into the apartment. After removing my coat, George gave me a hug and planted two hearty kisses on my cheeks. I followed him into the salon and had the most powerful sense of déjà vu. Georgina's mother was sitting in her house robe after her siesta, just as I had seen her do in my dream. She was even sipping Turkish coffee from a small white cup, balancing the saucer in her other hand. It gave me the chills.

After greeting the tiny woman, I took a seat on the sofa between the chairs Georgina's mother and father were sitting on. The maid went off to make me a coffee and little Ali lifted a big box of fancy chocolates opening it to offer me some.

"After you," I said, trying to be polite.

"Oh no, he mustn't have any. He eats far too many sweets. The doctor says sugar is bad for him," explained George. He pointed at a bowl of carrot sticks on the coffee table. "Ali, you may have some of those instead."

The boy took one and then sat on the floor near us, resuming his game with playing cards. I asked him what the game was about.

"I am making the kings fight," he said, slamming one card into another with such a violence and force, it completely crumpled.

This saddened me. It was an apt re-creation of what went on in our world, especially in the Mid East. I recalled an article about Lebanese children not knowing what normal life was. Their games were full of killing, their drawings full of guns, bombs, and dead people. At least my childhood had not been that chaotic.

George asked me about my holidays and so I chatted about them before asking him and Madame about their holidays.

They had spent them quietly, he explained, going to Larnaca, Cyprus for quite a while, "Where it was calmer," stressed Georgina's mother. So Georgina had been right to warn me things had not been safe for me to go to Lebanon this winter.

George said to his wife, "Didn't I tell you she was pretty?"

Mrs. Rizk nodded. George added, "Madame was more beautiful than either of her daughters."

"I'm sure she was," I countered. "The two of you did produce a Miss Universe after all." They seemed pleased, almost like children, and it irked me.

Meanwhile Ali's game grew louder and rougher. His grandfather asked him to quiet down, "Or else you'll have to go play in your room."

I said, "Ali, would you like to play another game? With your papa and me?"

"My papa's dead," he stated, simply.

I winced, deeply regretting my slip of the tongue. "I'm sorry. I meant to say your grandpa."

"We're rich you know," he said then, as if it was somehow related to the subject of our conversation. I thought the riches you most need cannot be purchased: your father, your country, peace, and the natural things of family life.

Next George said, "We've had some more bad news. Georgina's sister Felicina has lost her husband in a car accident in Damascus. Georgina is there now, helping her sort everything out."

"She wants to come to Paris and remake her life," added the mother.

"It will probably be good for the book," added George. "If her sister comes here. She always has a good influence on Georgina. She calms her down."

"Someone offered Georgina $2 million to be in some film project about the war in Lebanon, but she refused," added Madame.

I wanted to ask who, when, and what it was about, but this was only our first meeting, and that would seem too aggressive. Then it dawned on me Madame was dropping a big hint about money. What would be in it for her daughter if she did this work with me? It was a classic negotiating ploy and I had almost missed the point entirely. I had been away from the region too long. Naively I'd believed Georgina would welcome another woman's help to write about her life. In return I had planned to offer her an even share of the profits, if there were any. But how could we hammer out an agreement when she did not keep her commitments to come to meetings we had set up? What difference would money make if she'd refused $2 million dollars? I was self-financing all my efforts instead of expecting anyone to offer me anything.

George went on, "She made three films: one with Lulu, one called *Aida* and *Guitar d'Amour*, which I thought was the best."

"I'd like to see them. Do you have copies on videocassette?"

"Everything is still in Beirut. But we could ask someone to bring them and the scrapbooks. People are always going back-and-forth," said George, optimistically.

The discussion shifted to the war and events in Lebanon. George said, "It's terrible the way Solange, Bashir's widow, is fighting against her own brother-in-law Amine, now that he's president. She heads her own faction, against the government. It's really not what the country needs now. We don't need fighting amongst ourselves."

He meant the infighting amongst the Christian factions. I thought of all the blood Bashir had spilled and how he had taught Solange. In his ruthless efforts to wipe out his fellow Christian rivals, he had ordered his henchmen to slaughter the entire families of two previous Lebanese Christian presidents. Live by violence, die by violence. These atrocities could not be blamed upon Muslims, Israelis, French, Americans, or anybody else. The Christian Lebanese could not even get along with each other, much less anyone else. What would Georgina say about all of this?

As the visit came to a close, Georgina's mother seemed to have warmed up to me. As we said our goodbyes, she told me, "My daughter is very stubborn. I warn you now, you will need to have lots of patience with her."

"I am trying my best. I have already been working on this for more than a year but I do not have forever."

George helped me back into my coat and kissed me goodbye assuring me we would be in touch. Despite the bitter March wind that hit me when I left their building, I decided to walk home. The meeting had left me depressed. Reviewing how they had divulged the few things they'd told me, I doubted they could do much more. Did they really believe their older daughter had more influence over Georgina then they did? It was foolish to expect them to be much help going forward.

* * * *

The following morning it was snowing one minute and sunny the next, and the changeable weather continued for several days, an accurate reflection of my emotions and state of mind. In addition to the interminable wait for Georgina, Omar was also being unpredictable. For several days I would not hear from him. Returning home to hear the phone ringing, he would be on the other end of the line asking, "Where have you been?"

"What do you mean 'where have I been?' Where have you been? I've been here for two days waiting to hear from you."

"Well, I've been calling you since six. I want to take you out to dinner."

"I was at the hammam with Irina. I can't sit at home all the time."

"Get dressed. I'll be by to pick you up in fifteen minutes."

He was all bright and cheery over the meal. My hopes rose again. When departing the following morning, he suggested that I prepare a little pot-au-feu for Sunday night. Dreams of domestic bliss flared up.

But Sunday evening came and went. I heard nothing from Omar until ten that night when he finally called to say, "I'm feeling rotten cherie. I'm sorry, but I'm just not very good company tonight. Things are not going well at all. The people I expected help from have all let me down. And now the Prince won't return until July. I think I'll go back to Tunisia at the end of the month."

A quick little calculation made me realize April, May, and June would go by. Was this his way of telling me he'd be away for the next three months? The pot-au-feu was still simmering on the kitchen stove. It's aroma filled the room. Damn him I thought.

"When you go through these depressions Omar I don't know how to handle you. When you're working, you're too busy to see me. And when you're not working, you're too depressed to see me."

"I know. It's not your fault," he paused, before adding, "Save me some pot-au-feu. It will taste even better tomorrow. I'll come over and we'll have it for lunch, together."

* * * *

The next day I was drying my hair when the phone rang.

"Cherie, I've got a client. I've got to go out to the airport now." He was nearly breathless.

"What about our lunch?" I asked, already knowing the answer.

"I'm sorry. I guess it will have to wait again. I've got to run now. I'll call you from the airport."

I was so angry I slammed the phone down. My night had been miserable. I had tossed and turned, with one nightmare after another, trying to kill the same witch, over and over. Each time I thought I had crushed her for good she reappeared in another form. I felt for sure these bad dreams were indicators of futility regarding Omar though I had not wanted to listen.

An hour later he phoned from the airport.

"How can this ever work?" I said. "Your clients are always more important. How come they can always reach you and I cannot? This is too crazy. When I put that pot-au-feu back into the refrigerator for the second time you canceled on me, what I really wanted was to just throw it out the window."

"Calm down hayati. We can eat it some other time. I called the big hotels, like I do all the time when I am not busy with the prince. And today the Ritz said they needed somebody who spoke Arabic to go pick up the director of something or other at Charles de Gaulle. This job should last about a week. You know I could use the money. But I hope to be free in the evenings."

Sniffling into the phone, with equal parts anger and sadness clashing within me, I could not speak.

All sweetness and light Omar reassured me, "Take heart mon petit lapin. Don't lose your courage. This will pass. It's not much longer now."

After hanging up, I had to get out of the house. I went for a long walk and took myself to see a movie.

* * * *

At two thirty in the morning Omar called from Deauville. "He just won 300,000 francs at roulette. I think we're going to be here for another day or so."

I knew his Arab clients always shared a percentage of their winnings with him and the other drivers, bodyguards, and interpreters.

My spirits sank even lower. I knew what Omar would do with any money he earned and if he had any of mine, he'd also be wagering and losing it. I consoled myself. At least I had not been a complete fool. While trying to get back to sleep I comforted myself with the fact that I knew him well enough now to be certain of the truth. He would gamble everything away.

Chapter 16

ÇA FAIT MON AFFAIRE /
IT'S OVER MY AFFAIR

The most mediocre libertine has dreamed
of oriental princesses; every rotary carries
about inside him the debris of a poet.

— GUSTAVE FLAUBERT

March - May 1985

Needing a change of scene, I accepted Irina's invitation to visit her in Versailles the following day. She was fast becoming my best friend. We spent a lovely sunny weekend with her two young daughters and the Pomeranian dog Kiki. Long walks in the nearby forest were therapeutic, as was her genuine homemade *borscht* soup and *pelmeni*, Russian pasta.

Upon my return to Paris I felt much better. Walking by my neighborhood cafe, I saw the waiters putting the tables back out on the sidewalk, another sign that spring was surely on the way.

But the news from Lebanon was particularly upsetting. In the wake of the Israeli withdrawal, the chaos in Lebanon was worse than ever. The retreating Israelis had fired on a press car, killing two CBS employees, a cameraman, and a soundman. Feeling badly about their deaths, I also reflected it could have been me in that car, dying with them, if I hadn't left the network news business. I had left it because I wanted more than one minute and sixteen seconds to tell Lebanon's story, I reminded myself bitterly. And here I was in Paris, going into my second year, and no closer to my goal.

I went to the phone and called Georgina. Her father answered, "She is still in Damascus but might return next week."

Dammit I thought but what could I do about it?

279

* * * *

For the next ten days I did not see Omar and rarely heard from him. As far as I knew he was still in Deauville. As another birthday approached I grew more melancholy remembering my thirtieth one in Paris last year, and Maurice, and the baby I had not kept. What had been learned since then?

* * * *

It had been four days since Omar's last call when I finally heard from him. He phoned late at night and from the tone of his voice I could tell he'd been gambling.

Somewhat coolly I reminded him tomorrow was my birthday. "The Burkes are having a little party for me, and they've included you in the invitation."

"I'll come, and I'll pick you up, and drive you over."

This was a surprise. He had strictly avoided meeting any of my friends in the past.

When he arrived at eight thirty the following evening, we had a talk, or rather, he talked and I listened.

"You want to know the truth? I'll be frank with you. I always have been, haven't I? I've spent the money. I played and I lost. When I saw that nothing was working out, I just didn't care anymore, so I blew the money. All my plans finished in the water. I don't know how I'm going to get out of all these problems now and there are no jobs in sight either, so I'll have to go back to Tunisia." Resignation rang in his voice.

"I don't want you waiting and being unhappy because of me. I hate to feel guilty. I've never had to account to anyone. I don't want you, or me, to become a victim of love. I know life without love isn't life, but I've lived free as a bird for thirty-four years. It takes time to change.

"You know, I never used to stay more than five or six days with the same woman? I've never lived with a girl. And I've never told any woman that I loved her. Do you realize that?"

I shook my head.

He continued, "I love you a lot hayati. You have all the qualities I want in a woman, tenderness and goodness. But I cannot come and live on your back. So I don't like to hear you talking about a family and all that. First I have to pose the base [lay the groundwork], and change my lifestyle, and then we'll see. I want you to always be strong, like you were when I first met you. I cannot stand weak women. Don't lose your personality because you're in love. It will only make you unhappy. If it was over between us, I'd be sad for a week, but I'd get over it. My character is stronger than yours.

"Don't forget, I'm an Arab, a Tunisian, from the milieu of the immigrants. I don't even know the actual date of my birth. You have only ever seen my good side. You really don't know how I am when I'm there with my family. We are very proud you know. There may be poverty on every street in my country but we have pride. Arabs are the worst racists. If any friend of mine were to say anything against my aunts or my sisters, I'd cut her off, especially a foreign wife. My sisters don't even speak French. We all live together in the houses nearby. People are coming and going all times of the day and night and you have to serve them. Did you really expect that kind of life? Mixed marriages have a forty percent divorce rate."

"Marriages between people of the same country aren't doing much better these days," I said defensively.

"I know cherie. And if anybody could make one work, it's you, but you're missing my point. In my neighborhood there are people who live on five hundred francs a month and somehow manage to feed ten kids. I don't want to live like that. I have to be sure I can take care of you. I want my children to go to school, not live like I did. What if something were to happen to me? If I got sick or died? What would you do? You'd want to take the children and go away, non?"

"No, I would not. They would be my family too at that point."

"And would you accept it if I just went off for a month or two at a time?"

"You do now and I take you back. Just as long as it wasn't a story about another woman, I could probably accept it." I was trying to lighten the tone of our conversation. I pulled playfully on his tie while speaking the last phrase.

"You know Arab men are allowed to do things their women cannot do, but even an Arab woman would not accept my disappearing like that. You are too good." He tweaked my cheek.

"Don't let any man ever blame you for something not working. You've just had the bad luck to fall on me." He paused again, then said, "Don't you think it's odd that a man my age is alone, and still the way I am?"

"Not really, in our day and age. Do you think it's odd that I'm turning thirty-one today and I'm still single?"

"Cherie, you are too sentimental."

The discussion finished in the car as we arrived in front of the apartment building where the Burkes and Georgina lived. For a few moments I sat in the parked car not moving to open the door. Over a year ago, on this very spot I had sat with Waddah in his Range Rover when we kissed for the first time, and he invited me to spend the night. Look how that turned out. And now this, everything was dissolving: most of all my ideals of love and truth. Those great illusions I was trying so hard to believe in. Why? I swung the door handle and climbed out of the car. After all, there was a birthday party to attend, friends to see, and a cake with candles to blow out.

* * * *

I enjoyed the party more than I expected to. Omar did not say much as he could not speak English. On the way home he said he wanted to show me something. We drove a little out of the way to the infamous Rue Saint Denis just after midnight. It was busy at this hour. Girls loitered in every doorway, in various states of dress and undress. Tight neon colored sweaters, with white belts and no skirts underneath, just fishnet stockings, and very high heels. Some wore garter belts, with black stockings, and blew their cigarette smoke out provocatively. A black woman, with huge jiggling breasts, in a bright red satin push-up bra was laughing with another girl bending to re-tie her boot laces, which reached halfway up her bare thighs. Some wore coats, to keep off the early spring night chill, opening them to passersby, revealing nothing except g-strings or tiny panties with swaying fringes.

The car rolled very slowly as I stared at the streetwalkers in their working clothes. As horrible as it was fascinating, I couldn't take my eyes off the spectacle they made, parading their wares. The gawkers and customers jammed both sides of the street, overflowing the sidewalk. Silently I wondered what are they looking for? They all want something. What is it like to pay for sex? To be paid for it?

Omar spoke, "Most of them come from the provinces. They run away from home and come to Paris looking for a better life. They meet a man who buys them dinner and gives them a place to stay. They fall in love, or think it's love, and one day he says he's having money troubles. 'Would you mind working a little to help me out?' Of course she has no real trade, so he brings her here, telling her how much she can make in a single night. Some use drugs with the girls, to get them addicted, so they'll do anything for money."

Why was he was telling me this tonight? Had the equivalent happened to him? I knew about pimps and prostitutes. I had seen these "ladies of the evening" on the streets of New York but never such a mass of them at once, or the male variety.

Then Omar said, "You are lucky you fell on me. Some other man might have brought you here. I think it's dangerous the way women are blinded by love. I think I could get you to do anything for me."

No you couldn't I thought, but out loud I said, "I don't need to use my body to make money. I have my education and career." As soon as the words left my mouth, I saw how they could offend. And were they true, exactly? Men had given me things, after I'd slept with them. Although I had never asked for money before or after sex, I believed marriage was also based upon sexual exclusivity. Education made Omar and me more different from each other than culture, religion, or ethnicity. Perhaps Omar had used his body to make money. Did I want to know the truth if he had? Months ago my intuition had flickered with a blurry image of him sliding out from between the sheets, after being with someone else, probably his prince.

He let my comment pass and did not reply.

Later at home in bed I asked him, "Omar, after what you've told me, would it help relieve the pressure on you if I stop taking you so seriously? I could try to love you less."

"It's impossible to control such a thing. Either you love someone or you don't. There's no middle ground and not too much you can do about it," he replied.

"Well then, do you want me to wait for you or not?" I said, my frustration evident.

"What kind of question is that? Indeed, after all we've talked about tonight? You should know better than to ask it."

His reply did not satisfy me. I thought it could be read either way. Lying in the darkness beside him, I tried to sleep but could not stop thinking. What an inconclusive birthday. And the anniversary of our first meeting was less than a month away. Would we last that long?

* * * *

That Sunday, on my long, solitary, walk I reveled in the arrival of another spring. Leafy little green flags had unfurled on the branches overhead. Some of the city's half a million trees were releasing their powdery pollen balls, and these had filled the gutters, and blown to float on the River Seine. Oh Paris, what a taskmaster you are, despite your many gifts. Later at home, I watched a television documentary about the city. It explained how Paris had been laid out in a deliberate series of compass points, which began from Ground Zero, marked by a stone in the pavement facing Notre Dame Cathedral. All twenty arrondissements unfolded in a great circle from that center, with the lowest address numbers closest to the river.

The French had thought themselves the center of the universe from the 1600s to the 1900s. Even the mundane tasks of their Sun King, Louis XIV, getting out of bed in the morning and going to bed at night, were ceremoniously observed, in the daily lever and coucher ceremonies. Each empire had taken its turn thinking it was the be all and end all, like the Chinese, who had called themselves the Middle Kingdom, and the Egyptian Pharaohs believing everything revolved around them. Today Americans put the US in the center of world maps. But just as surely as the pollen balls I had seen today, the abuses and excesses of each empire had seeded their downfalls. Did any one possess the wisdom necessary to break these cycles of war and destruction and bequeath the world a model of peaceful coexistence instead of shortsighted self-interest?

The program mentioned the many protectors Paris had over its seven thousand year history. Saint Geneviève remained the best-known Patron Saint of the City. Among other things, her prayer marathon was credited with keeping Attila's Huns from besieging the city in the year 451. For hundreds of years afterwards, every new King of France had sought her blessing, visiting her tomb immediately after being crowned. No wonder I felt drawn to her, this preventer of war, violence, and death. Her example was missing in Beirut and the US. Saint Geneviève was the antithesis of the dead woman strung up by her neck in an empty apartment. I thought of this upright French mystic, whose acquaintance I had made via her statue on the Pont de la Tournelle. Though she had died in 512, almost 1,500 years ago, the example of how she used her energy lived on. Her eyes never closed, she never ceased in her watch. This was a female equivalent, of what the Ayat al-Kursi described in the Muslim protection prayer, I'd recited so many times.

Here in Paris all around me tonight, people were eating, reading, watching television, or preparing to go to bed. Some were lonely, some sick or sad, others happy. Despite the troubles in the world, and my troubles with Omar and Georgina, peace and continuity were palatable here on this little island. In the middle of it all, with the River Seine flowing round us and Saint Geneviève standing guard, these were solid spiritual reminders of alternative ways of doing and being.

On my way up to bed, I carried my birthday gift to myself, the big, beautifully illustrated book, Paris by John Russell. I wanted to read more about my fourth arrondissement and Île Saint-Louis as well as Saint Geneviève. Before sleeping I copied two of its quotes into my journal:

"It is a city in which to act on impulse is one of the secrets of happiness, and Occasio, the bold goddess of opportunity, should at all times, be propitiated."
"Paris exists in order that we should become more, not less, like ourselves."

* * * *

The Burkes came to dinner at my place the next night. Cooking for them was my thank you for the birthday party. They were eager to tell me they had liked Omar, the mysterious phantom, after hearing about him these many months.

"We were a little afraid to meet him, in case we didn't like him. Since we care a lot about you, we would've had to tell you the truth, if we didn't think he was good enough for you. We thought he was great."

I smiled, thinking of how charming he'd been, and what he said about how we show our good sides first. It takes longer to get to know someone.

* * * *

The next time Omar came to visit he told me he'd narrowly escaped being rounded up by the police.

"They came to the Hotel George V. I don't know what I'm doing in this life sometimes, or what's coming next, but Allah always protects me. I was in the bar the night before last and heard some fellow speaking Tunisian Arabic. We struck up a conversation. He had some other people with him, and invited me for a drink, and to join them later if I was free. They were younger. I guessed none of them were even thirty. I thought it strange they were claiming to be Saudis, when their Arabic wasn't Saudi. I even asked the guy. He claimed he was half-and-half, that his mother was from Tunis.

"But other things didn't fit, like him saying his watch had been stolen. A real Saudi wouldn't mention that. Once it's gone it's gone. No more comment. I thanked them for inviting me, but said I was busy, and 'maybe later.' What luck, because when I did return to the hotel, I found the police had arrested them all and were cleaning out their suite, a real bordello. They must have had twenty-three whores upstairs and took everyone to the police station. I'm so glad I wasn't with them. I've never had any trouble with the police."

I was particularly glad to hear him say that.

He continued, "They know me at the hotel and would have vouched for me but still. I was just discussing this with the bartender. He'd heard the hotel called to check on the gold American Express card they'd presented. The bank told them it was good. I said they had probably met the owner and he had not reported it stolen yet, or perhaps he was unable to. He told me they had all the man's papers: his traveler's checks, his passport, the works. Nothing had been reported to the police or the Saudi Embassy. I think they must've killed him. If I had made off with around 3 million francs, like they did, I would go off somewhere, and surely not stay at the George V, and throw all that money around so stupidly."

In bed later that night he also told me, "Remember I said that the prince had married again, about two months ago? Well he's already divorced her. At least she had her eyes open and her plans ready. She will use the settlement money to open a daycare center in Riyadh."

The next night I had another dream about Georgina. It seemed to be nudging me back on track. I was listening to her talk while she showed me pages of notes already written up. The word château was on one of the pages. There was a discussion about money. The figure, $17,000. I wasn't sure who was paying whom. Or if this was some profit we were going to split.

Georgina mentioned some man, "an Israeli spy I went to school with."

In the dream I asked if she knew where he was now, and if she kept tabs on him, or if he kept tabs on her. Upon waking I felt more motivated than ever about my self appointed task.

But when I called her apartment the next day, the answer was the same. "No she is not back yet," her father George said, sounding old and tired.

* * * *

On the day before the April anniversary of my fateful first meeting with Omar, I noticed signs announcing a traditional sciences forum inside the Paris Grand Hotel while walking past. Inside the dimly lit room, various readers, palmists, astrologers, and clairvoyants sat at their tables receiving customers. After touring the room, my intuition directed me to sit at the table of a thirtyish, blond haired woman named Marjory.

She instructed me to put my hands on the table palms down. After stroking the tops a few times she said, "Very evolved. You have creative hands, artistic, and very capable. But you're not daring enough yet. Put your ideas into practice. They are good ones and will be successful. You'll be quite well known in the future for your talents. You are lucky and fortunate, and you make a pretty good living now, but there will be changes for the better."

I thought she could have said that to just about anyone walking in off the street.

But then she added, "You are sublimating yourself sexually."

How had she known? It was my deepest regret with my phantom, a reminder of all that was not real.

"You are not married yet are you? But you will be, to someone who has money and social position. You will inherit money and property. You like children and will have them."

"Will I marry the man I'm with now?"

"Does he have money and a social position?"

"Well, not yet," I hedged.

"Do you have a photo of him that shows his face?"

I took one from my wallet. Marjory studied it before saying, "He likes money and luxury this one, all the finer things in life, but he does not want to work very hard to get them. He's not on your intellectual level. He's a bird of the night. He loves you, in his own way, but you shouldn't live with him. You don't need him. You are going to succeed with or without him. Amuse yourself with him, until Mr. Right comes along. Keep your autonomy no matter what."

Walking home I realized how right Marjory was and I was finally ready to listen. This was the third time I had been told the same thing: by Carla, Gustave, and now this woman. How would it end? In some angry scene? Or would Omar just fade away? Would I meet someone else?

As I passed a kiosk, the cover of *Le Point* magazine caught my eye. The feature story was about the clairvoyants of Paris. After buying the magazine, I flipped through the article at home. How astonishing. Paris had fifteen thousand credentialed taxi drivers compared to twenty-five thousand working clairvoyants. The French with all their Cartesian logic obviously needed to consult intuition, its balancing opposite, concluded the article. I cut it out and put it in my journal before writing my entry.

Tomorrow it will be a year since Omar and I met. It has taken all this time for me to understand things between us. A year to know better and that is a gift in itself. I mustn't forget the good times even as I recognize all that has been missing. Becoming bitter would be wrong. He is what he is. Why blame him for it? I did adore him so. The sheer beauty of him, those shining dark eyes, and his dear sweet flesh. I've learned what it is like to be infatuated. But it's coming to an end now. I can feel it, slipping and shrinking, and it's for the best.

How curious that Marjory has been the catalyst to free me from my passive melancholy. I wasn't ready until now but it is time for something better. Loving Omar has made me feel more worthy of being loved. Omar does not love me as I love him but he never could. It's not what he's looking for. I have yet to communicate any of this to him but my change of heart is final. It feels as though the pool I've been floating in is being emptied of its contents. A huge drain is swirling beneath me, dissolving what used to hold me up. There is no other way but to let go.

I came to Paris for the truth, to learn about Lebanon, love, and illusions. This era is drawing to a close. Suddenly I am on the other side of this strange territory, having crossed it with Omar. And Georgina? What's the connection between these two disillusionments of mine?

The following afternoon I phoned Georgina expecting her father to pick up. When she answered the phone there was genuine pleasure in her voice. She asked me how I was. I broached the subject of going to Nice, to visit Mona, an old friend of hers we now had a friend in common.

Georgina responded very positively to the idea, saying, "If you can stay over that weekend, I might be able to come down and join you."

By then end of our conversation, Georgina was calling me "darling." We had come a long way. Just as I prepared to give all this up, I thought, replacing the receiver in its black plastic cradle.

* * * *

Two weeks went by with no word from Omar. The day before my departure to Nice, he phoned from Sfax. Hearing his voice made me seethe this time.

He dared to ask why I had not phoned him, saying, "I asked my friend at the hotel everyday if there were any messages for me."

Withholding the full force of my anger I replied, "What do you mean you did not hear from me? I didn't even know you had left for Tunisia. Don't try to put the blame on me Omar."

"Well, I am coming back now. The prince has changed his plans. He's returning to France, so I'll be coming back to work," he said.

"Good for you. I'm leaving for Nice tomorrow, to stay with one of Georgina's girlfriends. I am trying to get some work done on this project." I gave him the number at Mona's house. We said nothing more on the phone. I decided it was best to have it out, face to face, if we ever saw each other again.

* * * *

For a change, I took the train instead of flying to the south of France. As the French countryside rolled by my window, I thought of all the blood that had soaked this ground: religious wars, Catholics against Protestants, and French kings against English kings and queens, battling century after century, right up through both World Wars. The Lebanese certainly had no monopoly on violence.

The news from Lebanon had been bad that week. The Christians had left the south, fleeing north, as their Israeli protectors pulled out. The Druze forces moved in to fill the vacuum. Many Christians were in Jezzine, cut off from their fellow Christians in the north by the pincher tactics of the Druze leader, Walid Jumblatt. How many more times would those lands change hands?

The rain began to fall once we arrived in the port city of Marseilles. I scurried down the platform to change trains, scolding myself for believing an umbrella would not be necessary in the sunny south of France. On the move once again, I fell asleep, waking to the sight of the spreading blue acres below the rocky, craggy shoreline. This was the same Mediterranean Sea whose waves washed up upon Beirut's beaches.

Mona had kindly arranged for me to stay in her third floor guest room although she would not return from Geneva until the following day. Her American husband was off on a business trip somewhere, so the housekeeper let me in.

After unpacking, I looked out over the grey waters and equally grey sky from her villa windows. The rain had followed me here and seemed a bad omen. This Côte d'Azur was devoid of the azure hue its name implied. The horizon could not be made out. Rather like my life at the moment I mused, trying to discern where the water ended and sky began, where emotional fantasies cease to meet the hard edge of reality.

The television news that night was all about the 1985 Cannes Film Festival starting tomorrow. The lack of "sun and fun" was a concern if this dreary weather continued. One reporter observed the Americans were conspicuous in their absence this year. Even tough guy Sylvester Stallone was staying home. He feared being kidnapped or hijacked.

* * * *

My weekend visit turned into a ten-day stay with Mona. Georgina never made it down, but Mona, the tall, flamboyant ex-model vividly reminded me of what I'd forgotten about the Lebanosh mentality. With her long purple fingernails, dramatic clothing, and makeup, Mona still turned heads. Despite her genuine hospitality, the glitz and superficiality were defenses, nearly impossible to penetrate. How to investigate deeper issues or get any real work done on this visit when all we did was party?

Mona's Lebanese friends had come to town and wanted to have a good time. "Let's forget about the war for a while." They swept me into their whirlwind of lunch and dinner invitations. Mona and I often danced with them until dawn, in Monte Carlo, a short drive away. Resistance was futile. Adapting to the situation, it reminded me of Beirut in the old days. Having acquiesced, I turned on the charm; singing, dancing, telling jokes, and pouring wine, doing my part to maintain the vacation ambiance though my heart wasn't in it.

These five Christian Lebanese men were too desperate to enjoy themselves. Their money, time, and energies were expended with neurotic frenzy. The food had to be the best, in the best restaurants, with champagne all around.

As one explained on the drive back to Mona's at dawn from a disco, "I could catch it in a car bomb tomorrow upon my return to Beirut. There's no sense in saving money when there is no tomorrow. We have learned to live for the moment, as each good time might be our last."

I realized anew where I'd gotten that idea although I'd begun to outgrow it.

Crawling into bed in my third floor guest room each morning, I listened for the sea sounds, needing to hear the waves slapping the rocks below. They anchored me to reality after these nights spent with ghosts. These guys believed in nothing solid. No tomorrows, only now, and the past.

* * * *

One afternoon, Mona was suddenly ready to talk about Georgina. She invited me to sit down across from her in the black and gold toned living room with its low couch, lamé pillows, and metallic wallpaper. I had yet to meet her constantly traveling American husband. There were no children and not a single book on the knick-knack lined shelves. Taking notes in my journal as she spoke, I did not interrupt.

Mona prefaced our conversation by saying she didn't think Georgina could or would do the book. "You cannot tell the truth you know. It is dangerous ground. She knows that. In Beirut I told a visiting German reporter that the Israelis had not killed Abu Hassan (code name for Georgina's dead husband) though they had taken all the credit for it. I told him who was really responsible for the murder. That reporter was killed the next day."

This sounded melodramatic, yet I knew how easy it was to get killed in the Middle East. Trigger fingers itched over the smallest slights. Wrong assumptions had led to horrific slaughters. Nevertheless, Mona was still at large after sharing this information. Maybe "they" considered her harmless. Who were "they," as in those responsible for killing Salameh? Perhaps she conveniently spread disinformation for them, whether she realized it or not. This Muslim woman had so many Christian friends. I guessed that Salameh's killers could even have been rival Palestinians. Trouble was always brewing between their rival factions. I didn't ask Mona outright and let her speak.

"You have probably guessed that Georgina and I totally disagree about politics and it's not just because I am Muslim either. The Palestinians have brainwashed her. All the problems in Lebanon were brought on by them. They can't get their own country back, so now they've wrecked ours."

From her tone, I surmised Mona would like them to all rot in hell. But blaming all her country's ills on the Palestinians was a bit excessive. What about the killings in 1860? Long before former Palestinian territory had morphed into present day Israel, there had been a lot of bad blood between religious sects in the Levant. Palestinian refugees had certainly exacerbated the situation but a "situation" had already existed. No use contradicting my hostess, a modern Muslim woman. Besides I was curious to hear her out.

She was most comfortable talking about the past, and the many shows and modeling jobs she had done, with Georgina and her half sister Felicina Rossi, in the good old days. Unfolding a brochure, she handed it across the coffee table. "Here, you can keep it," she said.

The color photos were mostly covers from Arabic language magazines and the fashions were all the rage during the 1960s and 70s. Mona appeared in everything from knee-length suede boots and hot pants, to haute couture gowns, and far-out metallic outfits a la Paco Rabanne. Her tawny features, chiseled cheekbones and strikingly dark eyes stared coolly back in every pose, with her false eyelashes and thick black eyeliner on the lids.

"We were trying to promote Lebanon as a fashion capital. We even traveled on tours to other countries. I have three suitcases full of press cuttings back home in Beirut with my mother."

"Why didn't Georgina leave Lebanon for the US or somewhere else to continue her modeling and acting career?" I inquired. She had come to France after the fact, after the disastrous war and her husband's assassination.

"She's not the type," Mona replied. "If I had her looks, I'd have done differently. It became unpleasant for her. I remember being in the Gulf together, after she won the contest. It was so bad she couldn't even go downstairs to eat in the dining room. We had to hide her in a closet. Men were ready to break the doors down to get at her."

I shuddered at the idea of Georgina being pawed and worse.

"Did you ever go to Abla when you were still in Beirut?" she asked, shifting the subject.

"No. Who's Abla?"

"She was the fortuneteller who told Georgina she would be 'seated on a throne, with a crown upon her head, and all the world at her feet.' That was less than a year before she became Miss Universe. I don't need to tell you, Abla's business boomed after that."

I remembered Josephine had been told something similar and became the Empress of France after marrying Napoleon Bonaparte. All of that had ended in tragedy too.

Mona rose to fix us some Turkish coffee. I heard her giving instructions to the housekeeper about the laundry. When she returned, she asked if I believed in the Evil Eye.

"Yes, I do actually." Thinking of the incontrovertible negativity of jealousy and envy.

"Then do you know what it is like when someone puts one on you?"

"Not really. I don't think anyone ever put one on me, but one was put on my mother. Two different readers saw it in her cup. She had a woman come to the house, and burn things in certain corners, and carry something out with lit candles. After that, the readers didn't see it anymore. I think my father's mistress had it put on her."

"There's one on me," Mona volunteered. "I've been to see a witch in Geneva to try to get it taken off me, but her power is not strong enough. I'm telling you all this because the man who put on me is coming here tomorrow and I would like you to help me."

"Sure," I answered, wondering what I was getting into, but also feeling obligated by her generous hospitality.

"He's a Saudi. He even knows my husband. I have told him I am happily married, and given him every other excuse in the book, but he just won't leave me alone. When he found out my husband is away on business, he decided to come here. Last time he got a photo of me and, on the pretext of having it repaired for me, he got a hold of my Qur'an necklace. They need to have something you have worn against your skin, plus a photo to work a spell. He took these to Egypt, and had a very strong magic man put a hex on me."

"How do you know?" I said.

"I can feel the bad vibrations coming towards me. I am very sensitive to these sorts of things. I'm quite psychic myself, and have lots of dreams and premonitions. Recently I dreamt that my mother cut herself, and she called the next day. I told her I already knew she had cut herself, and she hardly needed to call to tell me.

"Anyway, this man half-admitted it the last time I refused him. He swore if he couldn't have me, he would ruin me, and I would regret it for the rest of my life unless I went to bed with him. And since he had this spell cast on me, I've had two car accidents. Everything I try to do or plan won't work out. I'm half afraid to leave my house. It's driving me crazy.

"When he comes tomorrow, I don't want to be alone with him. No matter what, when we come back here after lunch, I'd really appreciate it if you would stay right here, and not leave the room for a single minute. He'll try to pounce on me. I know his type. He's an animal," she said with such a grimace I thoroughly believed her.

I agreed to remain in the room, although I did not believe in black magic. This hex was obviously real to Mona, in part because of her belief in such spells.

The man came the next day in his Rolls Royce with his silk shirt unbuttoned nearly to the waist. Its melon shade was most unbecoming against his complexion. The sight of him made me feel sick to my stomach. He was ugly, with a thin, caved in chest, and an awful pallor. Sparse black and grey hairs dotted his chin in a weak beard and formed a scraggly mustache on his upper lip. He was the most repulsive person I had ever seen. All of that was as real as the nose on my own face.

As soon as Mona introduced us, he guessed why I was there. He bristled with fury. Barely ten minutes later he left the house enraged. After he'd gone, his anger still radiated through the room. I shuddered and glanced at Mona with genuine concern. That had been the most vivid display of evil I could remember witnessing in a while. The incident upset us both.

* * * *

Not all of Mona's male friends were like him thankfully. One of her Lebanese bachelor pals Joe, had taken a liking to me. In his late thirties, he had yet to marry and was quite persistent, joining us for meals regularly and asking me out, though I was never alone with him and did not want to be.

According to Mona, "He's had every available woman in Lebanon."

A real skirt chaser I concluded. I know the type.

At one point, this Joe had been the king of the black market *mazot* (diesel, heating oil, and gasoline supply) on the Christian side. He had recently switched to "pharmaceuticals" as he called his drug dealing business. Had the money for our partying come from the misery of addicts? Ugh. Yet another "truth." It hurt to know.

During lunch at a seaside restaurant in Beaulieu, Joe had confided in me things looked "doubtful" in Lebanon. "I am looking into doing more business abroad, and researching the possibilities. But Europe is full. The US looks like the best bet now."

Did he see me as some sort of ticket to America?

Between courses, he expounded on "the oriental mentality" saying, "We really aren't civilized you know. We have no civic education in the Western sense. We don't know our limits. For example, if two French families move into the same apartment building they say, 'Bonjour' in passing each day, but things rarely go any further. With the Lebanese, it's 'Bonjour' on the first day, 'Comment ça va?' on the second, and by the third day they are knocking on your door, inviting you to dinner, with all kinds of ulterior motives. Believe me, I know, because I do it myself.

"The only way to handle us is to make us fearful," he added, after a moment's contemplation as the waiter served the main dish.

"When I ran the market, I made sure to threaten the people bigger than me, so they'd pacify me, and do what I wanted, out of fear."

He reached across the table to take hold of my hands. His were beautiful and I told him so. But what had he done with them?

"I know," he replied, squeezing mine tighter in his grip.

So confident of his charms. What a playboy.

When we returned to the apartment, he tried to kiss me.

I pushed him away, saying, "I'm engaged for heaven's sake." This was not technically true, but it was the best defense of my honor I could come up with. I even told him a little about Omar believing this would cool his ardor.

All Joe said was, "How long have you known him?"

"About a year."

"Then I'll bet he never marries you," he predicted with brash confidence.

"He can't, not until things are better financially, and he's gotten away from working with these Saudis." I had said too much and sounded too defensive.

Joe countered, "Those are just excuses. Let me give you a tip. Arab men take women for granted. You have to be mean with them. It's the only way to handle us. Otherwise, the more you give, the more we take. Look at all the famous women in history. They weren't very nice, were they? You are too sweet and good. He'll never marry you, unless he's afraid he's going to lose you."

My cheeks reddened. Despite having already decided to leave Omar, Joe's words hit a nerve. Yes, I may have been foolish, but it was not fun to have this be so obvious to someone I'd just met. As far as I knew, Omar had not called me either, as he'd left no messages for me on Mona's answering machine, despite my being in Nice for over a week already.

* * * *

Joe left for Paris on business the next day saying he would be in touch. As I waved goodbye I thought, what good is a man who can only love a bitch? He had told me what I needed to hear even though I didn't like it. Coming to Paris, I had wanted the truth more than anything else. Well, here was some more of it. Men knew other men in ways women could only guess at. It did not pay to be too nice. People walked all over you. I had been good to the point of boring, and far too naïve about Omar, but I needed the lesson obviously. And perhaps he'd needed one too, of the opposite type.

I stared at the ring on my finger. Ayman and I had co-designed this engagement ring, with two diamonds, our Aries birthstones, flanking a fire opal, the stone of mystery, passion, and ecstasy. When leaving Lebanon for London, Ayman insisted I keep it for good luck. When Omar admired it, I'd said it was from my ex-fiancé adding, "He loved me."

Omar had quipped back, "Because you didn't love him?"

"Oooh, I'll make you pay for that!" I had countered.

Too near to the truth perhaps. I had loved Ayman less, and he had loved me more for it. And with Omar, the shoe was on the other foot. I'd done the loving work for us both. Women usually did, didn't they? I did not want love to be like this. If pretense was the only way to keep a man, we had to spend our lives pretending. I was tired of these games. Either you loved or you didn't. Otherwise, you were merely using each other. But didn't we want to be useful in our lives? Was dignity and fairness possible between the sexes? Or was it all ruthlessness? The last thing I wanted to believe was love was just like war.

The weather had grown even uglier on the Southern coast of France. A dense wall of clouds rolled in and sheets of rain were falling as I stretched out for an afternoon siesta. Mona was also napping to prepare for another night of merry making. But these rounds had become a chore over the last week. When I woke, the sun was a pale wet blur, drowning in a sea without a horizon. Where is the solid ground, the land I can stand on so as not to drown in these watery emotions? "Cry me a river...I cried a river over you," the lyrics of that song, not heard for over a decade, drifted into my consciousness. The message was clearly delivered. It was someone else's turn to cry now.

I dressed quickly, wishing again I'd packed warmer clothing. Downstairs in Mona's bedroom, I waited while she finished getting ready. This had become our routine. While peering into her vanity mirror, she carefully applied her false eyelashes with glue. The spidery things were poked into place on her lids with a toothpick.

How many times had I watched my mother do the exact same thing while my father taunted, "Put your face on..."

I had never worn false eyelashes. Artifice was not my domain.

When done, Mona sprinkled herself with gold powder, the finishing touch, before stepping into a tight, black suede dress with a cut out back.

In a conspiratorial tone, as we left her bedroom, she shared, "Don't laugh, but guess what Joe told me before he left?"

I lifted an eyebrow quizzically.

"That you're the girl he ought to marry. He said you'd make a good mother too."

Shaking my head I started to laugh, "Just because I would not let him kiss me!"

I could never love Joe. He was far too cynical although Omar was too. My phantom scarcely deserved to be loved so much, yet "being deserving" had little to do with the inspiration to love like I had — if that's what it was. Despite what Joe had told Mona, I would never get involved with him. These games were so predictable. I wanted less and less to do with them. Perhaps Omar had taught me the lesson I most needed to learn.

* * * *

At one thirty that night, I was alone in another room in Nice, making an impromptu journal entry on a sheet of the Hotel Beach Regency's stationary.

By the most improbable series of coincidences, as I entered the lobby of this hotel tonight with Mona, Omar was just getting out of an elevator with the prince. He walked straight toward me. You would have thought we had an appointment. I couldn't believe it.

"I thought you were in Paris!" I said, astonished at the sight of him.

He made some snide comment about "what was I doing in such a hotel" as though the only single women in such a place were prostitutes.

I pointedly ignored his question, the way he had ignored mine, and asked, "Why haven't you called me at Mona's?"

He said, "I lost the number."

"How can I believe that?"

Then he slipped his room key into my hand, saying he could not talk now, as he was on duty. I could go up later, when I finished with my friends, and wait for him. He had no idea when he would be done with the prince. They were probably going to the Monte Carlo casinos tonight.

So here I am, writing to pass the time, and to collect my wits. I have a confession to make. I shouldn't have, but since this is the first time I have been in a room he's slept in, except for mine, I have taken the liberty of going through his pockets. In a way, I wish I hadn't, but now that it is done, I can see how much of an ostrich I have been, with my head in the sand for far too long.

I found a note that sounds awfully domestic. It starts with "Mon Amour" and ends with "Je t'aime," and it is signed Mami, Sfax. It's a list of items, for things like creams she wants him to bring her from Paris. The script is crude without any commas or periods. He cannot tell me it is from one of his sisters because he has already said that they do not speak French. So, it must be from his little wife.

I thought about leaving the note on his pillow, with a sheet of this hotel stationary beside it, and one large question mark drawn upon it. Although that sounded gallant, it would not have given me the answer to the question, "Who is Mami in Sfax?" Plus, I would forfeit the element of surprise, as he would have time to invent some story before calling me again. No, I am not going to run away. I am staying right here to confront him. It is as good a way as any to do what must be done.

I paused, feeling sad seeing those words in print, but carried on writing.

Luckily, I also found my spare apartment key in another one of his pockets, along with a chip from one of the casinos. This saves me the humiliation of asking for it back. It's in my purse now. How shall I bring up the subject when he finally returns to his room?

A little over an hour later, Omar returned. When he entered the room, I said nothing, waiting to see what he would do.

He commented on how lucky we had been to run into each other.

I nodded. He kissed me.

I let him make love to me, knowing this would be the very last time. I forced myself to keep my eyes open so as not to sink below the surface of consciousness. I was determined to remember every detail: the way his hair moved when he looked down at me from above, the way his body arched, the suppleness of his skin, and the veins upon his neck. I enjoyed it more, knowing he had no idea what was going to happen next.

And afterwards, a single tear crept down my cheek. For him, it was the first sign something was wrong.

"What is it hayati?"

I let him coax me a while longer. Then I dropped the crumpled note onto his chest. The whole time I had held it tightly in my hand reminding myself he had lied. He had a wife.

"Who is Mami in Sfax? You are married, aren't you?"

When I had "seen" the curly headed child, thinking it might be ours in the future, it had actually been intuition showing me his real daughter. But I hadn't wanted to admit the truth of that possibility to myself. I had been too hungry, like a starving person at a banquet.

He kept his calm. I had to give him that.

He waited quite some time before quietly answering, "I'm yours, if I am anyone's."

What a liar. A pretty liar but a liar all the same. He expected me to believe him. He still thought I was dumb enough to swallow his words. At least he said this in an effort to keep me. He probably assumed things would continue as they had.

"You know, any other woman finding that note in my pocket would have been gone when I got back here."

"But I am not any other woman. I wanted to hear you make excuses."

I stopped short of telling him it was over. Not yet. Let him stew in his own juices, and wonder, like I have for so long. We fell asleep in each other's arms.

In the morning, a room service breakfast left me feeling pampered and victorious. Outside, the sun was finally shining, for the first time since I'd arrived on the Cote d'Azur. Standing on the Corniche Boulevard later, I stared at the Mediterranean Sea so calm and brilliant now. These waters also lapped at the Corniche alongside Beirut. Some subterranean circle felt completed. I felt warm and radiant, and sure I had done the right thing.

In the taxi back to Mona's, lovely classical music was playing on the radio as we followed the curving coastline. I remembered the other voice heard in my head last night demonstrating what it was like to be cynical, to think one thing and say something else. I wanted no more of that, despite the phantom pleasures. They were no substitute for the truth of real ecstasy.

That night, I rode the Train Bleu back to Paris.

Chapter 17

LE COÛT DE LA VIE /
THE COST OF LIVING

The city, built by human beings, is indifferent to
their desires...it educates even the most successful
megalomaniacs in the smallness of their dreams.

— GRAHAM ROBB

June 1985

Back home in my Île Saint-Louis apartment, I began the process of getting over Omar. Though my mind was firmly made up, my body suffered the physical loneliness of withdrawal. Mon Fantôme had been an addictive drug. Some afternoons those first few days, I curled up on the couch in the fetal position, wallowing in the process of letting go rather than pretending I was fine. The improving weather and the season of rebirth were additional healers. I talked to Darius, confessing my idiocy, while stroking his warm purring body. Though I judged myself pathetic, the practice was therapeutic. My stubborn faith was another comfort. I had chosen this man, and by the same powers that had brought him, I could banish him. Although I had to keep reminding myself, I did believe in my ability to recover from situations, especially the ones I'd put myself in. That truth had certainly been tested often enough.

I took the photos of Omar out of my wallet and put them in a drawer. I threw away the slippers, brush, and shaving soap purchased for him but found the most difficult task was breaking my habit of listening for him when I went to bed at night. The distinctive click of the big red door latch opening would trigger my recollections of the times he'd crossed that cobblestoned courtyard. Now those footfalls belonged to others who were unknown to me. I consciously resisted dwelling on memories of his voice, his humor, and his arms encircling me, and how our bodies had fit together with our breath matching as we fell asleep.

Oscillating between the need to be alone, and my determination to put myself back in circulation, I methodically called my friends. It was time to be with other people. Answering my correspondence, I realized how much I had neglected while being preoccupied by Omar. I wrote him one last letter explaining it was truly over and never to call me again. On a day of sun and clouds, I walked to the Hotel George V to deliver it personally to the concierge. Once the letter had been handed over, I returned to my island still in mourning yet certain my healing process was working.

* * * *

In May, on little Ali Hassan Salameh's birthday, I called to wish him well. Georgina answered the phone. "We celebrated it on Saturday, so he could have his friends over for a party."

"I had a very good time with Mona" I added. "We wished you could have been with us."

"I couldn't get away. I was too busy here," she said. "I saw Joe last night. He told me he met you."

"Did he?" I responded. What else had he said?

"He thinks he's in love according to Mona," Georgina confided. Her tone of familiarity was too new to be used to.

"Let's have lunch, tomorrow or the next day," she suggested.

"Sure," I replied, surprised by her increasing warmth. I could hardly believe what my own ears heard. What had caused this change? Something Mona had said? Or Joe?

"Just say when and I'll be there," I added before hanging up.

Waddah called that afternoon. "I've been trying to reach you for days. Are you free tonight? I've invited some people over. I think you'll enjoy meeting them," he said in his cryptic way. "Oh, and you haven't seen the new place yet. I've also moved to the island." He gave me his address, on the other side of Île Saint-Louis, a short walk from my door.

Curiosity got the best of me. I dressed for the evening in a new outfit of richly patterned cloth and cinched my waist with a wide brass belt. Leaving my hair loose, I dabbed on some recently purchased Coco, Chanel's latest scent. My nails were painted orange. Since returning from the Riviera, I'd developed a passion for that color. I suspected Waddah would try to take me to bed. It would be a test, and perhaps a cure, to chase out from under my skin whatever remained of Omar. Could I close my eyes and feel pleasure without thinking of him?

Just before nine o'clock, I left Quai de Bourbon to walk to Waddah's new place. Almost June, but the night temperatures still required a jacket or sweater. The address was on a quiet street corner and the stone building was as ancient as Quai de Bourbon. After pushing the buzzer with his initials, a small wooden door swung open automatically. Inside the central courtyard was a tiny garden with a single willow tree. A poignant reminder of the terrarium I'd almost purchased for him as a present so many months ago. Walking past it another memory surfaced, of the tree I'd seen from the clinic window, with the emptied nest, after deferring the birth of my child. These were oases in the deserts of our lives. Waddah and I would never share more than these watering stops with each other.

Passing through the mirrored entranceway, I climbed the steps to his apartment on the second and third floors. Waddah met me at the door. His eyes were bright. Having shaved off his mustache he looked younger. In rare form, he kissed my cheeks and I noticed how very good he smelled.

Sniffing the air I asked, "What's that wonderful scent?"

"It's called Aleppo earth. The women use it when they go to the hammam. They rinse their hair with it. Wait I'll bring you some."

He darted up the curving wooden staircase where I assumed the bedrooms were. In his absence I glanced around the living room. The long French windows gave onto a splendid view of the Left Bank across the river. The shimmering lights from the Seine filled the elegant room with glittering fluid reflections. A *bateau mouche* went by, its refracted spotlights playing against the walls and exposed beams of the high ceilings. The wood had been decorated long ago with the blue and gold *fleur de lys*, symbol of French royalty. The paint had faded, like the powers of the old rulers, and the lighting further softened their delicate hue. From the tour boats recorded voices in four languages could be heard faintly, explaining the history and significance of the monuments being passed as the tourists glided down the river. Once he shut the window, those sounds muffled away.

Waddah had preserved the essential oriental ambience, which had made me feel so at home in at his former apartment. I recognized the striped red sofa, paintings, and carpets, pleased at how skillfully he blended eras and cultures, reflecting what was best in both our lives. Arabic music played softly in the background and further layered the atmosphere. Here I was in Paris and yet not exactly. We were on this island in between. I spied the small dark bird, lying on the mantle above the fireplace, the sculpted one, with folded wings. When Waddah came back down the stairs it was warming in my hands.

"Here," he said, removing the stone bird to set a brownish lump in my palm. I bent my head to sniff it.

"No, like this," he said, pinching several grains and rubbing them between his palms. The friction reduced the grains to powder, releasing the fragrance. I repeated his movements and the ancient dust of the desert and the night wind rose from between my hands. Breathing it deeply in, I detected rose petals, their perfume carried from some hidden garden near Aleppo, beyond the Syrian wilderness.

"The women dissolve this in the last bowl of water they rinse their hair and bodies with. I can remember my mother and sisters smelling of it when they came home from the hammam."

He regarded me closely. He knew something had changed.

I returned his level gaze and said nothing.

He took my hands in his as we stood in the middle of the room. "What can I get you to drink?" he asked.

"Some wine. You are the expert in that department," I answered smiling.

He returned the smile and went off again, towards the back of the apartment where the kitchen was. A few moments later he reappeared with a bottle in his hands. A woman followed with a silver tray and several crystal goblets, edged in silver. Dressed in a navy blue maid's uniform with a white apron she was not the woman I had seen before. This one was looked Moroccan, in her fifties I guessed.

"This is Mina," he said by way of introduction. We exchanged smiles. "She's a superb cook. I was very lucky to get her. She used to work for the Americans who had this apartment. But they went back to California, and she did not like it there. The concierge told me about her."

Mina set down the tray and returned to the kitchen from which more enticing aromas wafted. And what a super chef she was, as we discovered when she served the dinner: whole poached salmon, in a very delicate sauce, baby lamb chops broiled to perfection with wild herbs, tiny fresh snow peas, sweet onions, baby carrots, frisée salad with walnuts and small round balls of aged cheese from the mountains of Lebanon, all topped off with a flaming platter of Crepe Suzette.

As exceptional as this dinner and the setting was, what added to the memorability of the evening was the guest who arrived, just after I'd tasted the wine Waddah had opened. He introduced me to Maurice's brother Jean.

"So you're the poet my brother told me about," he said warmly, as we shook hands. Jean took in every detail, appraising me. I did the same to him. He possessed Maurice's voice and mannerisms. Their physical resemblance sent me into the eerie territory of simultaneity where memory and present overlap. Freshly done with Omar, he was a vivid reminder of my life with Maurice, just before Mon Fantôme entered the picture. Would this reconnect me to my emotional independence?

Besides the poetry, what else had Maurice mentioned? I racked my brain for details Maurice had shared with me about his brother. Hadn't he been the Chief Executive Officer of the same Arab construction company Mr.

Burke had worked for? Yes, and more facts resurfaced. Jean had once enjoyed the dubious distinction of being the highest paid Arab executive in the world. But I knew, from Tom Burke, that Jean's efforts to introduce Western management techniques and proper accounting procedures had not succeeded. He had left the company in disgust.[38]

After the meal everyone returned to the living room where a fire had been laid to take off the evening chill. Jean sat on a floor cushion near me. Staring into the fire, he said, "I would have been a Zoroastrian if I had been born at a different time."

Hadn't they been a sect of fire worshipers? I nodded and asked, "What are you doing these days?"

"I have gone back to school, imagine that, at my age. I am doing a PhD at London University on war studies. I'm planning to return to Lebanon next month to spend some time studying resistance movements. I think the most interesting events of the war are happening now."

"Interesting" was hardly a word to use with wars I thought as Waddah handed Jean a glass of brandy. Jean contemplated the amber liquid, rolling the glass between his palms to warm it. I thought of the bird on the shelf I'd warmed between my palms earlier. Its wings were eternally folded but mine weren't. I had taken flight. Freedom could be chosen any time.

After a sip of the brandy, Jean continued. "I already know I'm a good manager and executive. I know that definition of success and I don't want to spend the rest of my life doing what I've already done." Ah, another person who wanted to be free.

Waddah was passing a box of cigars around to his guests now. Jean put down the brandy snifter and took a cigar. The ritual of preparation began. Clipping one end carefully with the proffered silver tool, he moistened the tobacco between his lips, before striking the long match to light it. As he drew several breaths through its brown length, I remembered Moudi with a pang, having immortalized his identical motions in my poem "His Havana Cigars." What had happened to him? I'd relinquished so many. Life steers us onward and elsewhere. Some friends would forget me too.

After several puffs, the orange tip glowed brightly and Jean spoke again. "I want to be a better person, a better Arab. I am a Christian in my brain, and in the way I relate to God, but in my skin and in every other way, I feel like an Arab, and a Muslim. My culture, my food, my lifestyle."

I understood that duality, for I also felt it, albeit it in different degrees, along with the added ambiguity of an American passport. Jean indicated the

---

[38] The firm was in receivership and total disarray, robbed by its own partners. Akin to the mess Mazen's brother Ghaith was in, with the REDEC scandal, having earned a spot on the FBI's most wanted list. Ghaith Pharaon could no longer travel to the US and Mazen no longer spoke to him.

artist, Adam Henein,[39] sitting across the room with his wife.

"I'd like to ask him to create a work of art for me, something to convey this Christian depth and Muslim surface I have."

Would Henein accept this commission? Jean needed expert help. To visually convey what Jean meant would require more skill than was evident in the hodgepodge art collection I'd seen on the walls of the Paris apartment he shared with Maurice. Refinement. To satisfy not only the eye but a deeper need for order. That took more than money. It demanded loyalty, to a higher set of principles, ones which transcended manmade differences of culture and religion. It was quite a feat, to originate a novel overarching pattern. But we would recognize it, those of us who resisted being forced into either/or camps, with their outdated enmities.

Jean was asking for the magic of alchemy. I too had sought the melding means, via poetry and ecstasy, needing some process for redeeming our fragmenting multiculturalism. Could splintering people be regrouped? Could one plus one make eleven, not merely the same old two?

Staring into Waddah's fireplace, I pondered the qualities which made people and things, satisfying. Only symbiotic relationships had any chance of sustaining this. The pairing of equals might combine what inspired evolution instead of devolution. But how many possessed the aptitude or background required to accomplish such unusual endeavors? No wonder Jean needed the artistic genius of a person like Henein. And this hinted at why Maurice and others had gravitated towards a synthesizing poet like me.

Then it struck me, every sentence Jean had uttered, began with "I." The unexamined egotism. It blinded even executives who were taught to say "we" as I discovered in my corporate work. Who dares to correct or contradict the powerful? Surrounded by "yes" men and women, who are paid to agree and acquiesce, the truth becomes dangerous. Even when we request it, from our intimates, those with little practice rarely admit it, as I'd just learned once more, with Omar.

Was Jean a genuine seeker of truth? My guess was his interest in a poet like me was for novelty's sake, some escapist adventure, not an in depth discovery. I remembered the tearful scene over a year ago, when I had begged Waddah to tell me what was wrong, after we'd started out so well. He'd gone silent and stormed out of the apartment at three in the morning. And I'd responded by getting angry and ending things, incapable of doing anything else at the time.

Since then I had inferred my former connections with Mazen were the most likely reason, yet we had never discussed them. And Maurice, the last time we had spoken, had spit out Doctor Mousalli's name, by way of

---

[39] After living in Paris for a quarter of a century Henein returned to Egypt. In 2014 the Adam Henein Museum opened in Cairo, a gift from the artist to his country

explanation. Yet Maurice had been just as guilty. Both men were married. Would others say they had taken advantage of me? Or would they blame the "loose woman" rather than the loose men with their double standards. I had not seen myself as their victim. When the fairy tales of male rescuers and protectors had proven untrue, I had not gone under, I had learned. Born into "a man's world," I'd been taken advantage of since childhood, as most girls were. There was little I could do about the Biblical and Shakespearean sins of the fathers, including my own dad's, but they had not cost me my personhood.

And I would not carry their shame, or my needs, in silence. I would use my hard-won education to speak up and write down the truth of my personal experiences. Some might howl and damn me for doing it but others might find comfort in my discoveries, and make use of them. I still wanted to be useful, if only to remind them, we did not have to imitate those who consumed our love, time, and energy with no intention of being fair or truthful.

The conversation in Waddah's living room had turned to the many disasters the Arabs had suffered. An elderly guest mentioned the dashed dreams of pan-Arabism, the thorn of Israel, the displaced Palestinians, and Lebanon. I was weary of it all. Rather than rehash recent history, I wanted to know what could be done about these problems. Instead of engaging in their debate, I resumed my musings about Jean's Christian inside and Arab Muslim outside. Who had managed to transcend those labels? Only the mystics.

Indeed, the most moving, unforgettable elements in religion, art, and writing had come via transformative experiences. And the mystics had done the unusual work: Saint Geneviève here in Paris, Moses with his burning bush, the forty days Jesus endured in the wilderness, and the visions of the Prophet Muhammad. The fruits of their quests for oneness had fed the hungers of meeker souls for centuries.

Mystics strove for first hand connection to Source, according to what I had read. They refused to content themselves with human intermediaries and second hand stories. Their quests were born of personal needs for healing, to cure the unbearable separation from the divine, no matter which name they gave it. In pursuit of this connection, they risked everything. Some of these seekers had gone insane. Others had endured baptisms of fire, figuratively, but some were successful, merging ultimately with that pure, unifying energy. In their ecstatic visions they transcended physical, mental, emotional, and spiritual boundaries, proving it was possible to overcome the separations of opposing forces. Mine-versus-yours transmuted into one great ours.

Achieving the human equivalent of nuclear fusion had transformed them. But it also set them apart. Feared and envied more often than revered while alive, the small-minded and the powerful felt threatened, by what the mystics knew firsthand. Once they were dead, the religious establishment had capitalized upon their stories, canonizing the mystics, collecting money in their names and building edifices. Much to the dismay of the mystics themselves, surely, for they had bravely let go of worldly needs for approval, or political power, in their search for absolute unity.

Perhaps my quest for truth was heading in another direction entirely. I needed to question my relationship to ecstasy. It had been far too much to expect Mon Fantôme, or anyone else, to be my absolute be-all and end-all.

I got up to stretch my legs and put more wood on the fire. Watching the many colored flames lick the burning wood, I wondered whether it was genius or insanity to believe ecstasy held the answer. Physical passion was a great conductor of this power, because it gave a fusing glimpse of emotional and spiritual ecstasies. My mistake had been to limit this to Omar or any one human being. My expectations needed readjustment. Despite our lovely frictions, people were not designed to do what this fire was doing to the logs.

Why had I fallen for a phantom? Because it was the best way to see through my illusions, even where ecstasy was concerned. I had jumped into the well of Omar, like a woman dying of thirst, and nearly drowned. But my foolish enthusiasm had been instructive. Having emerged on the far side of my temporary insanity, I could see it for what it was. I didn't blame him anymore than myself.

My needs had been enormous: to have my fill, to stop feeling empty, and endlessly on the road. Driven to overcome the violence and separation of the war, I remembered the damage it had done. My wounds were nowhere near the magnitude of those I had found squatting in my old room, when I went by my Beirut boarding school dormitory. The last time I had been to Lebanon in 1979, I had stopped for a few days to visit my father, while on my way to work in Arabia. There I'd discovered that Palestinian refugee family. With no idea where they'd come from, or where they would be going, we had just stared at each other. None of us uttered a single word. My tears didn't come until I turned away. The black hole of space between us was the same one I had witnessed inside the eyes of the Holocaust victims in my father's German history books.

I reached for another piece of firewood to drop upon the grate, and the sparks flared, behind the protective screen. They reminded me of our angry, embittered ancestors, and how their unreconciled contests had set us up for centuries of conflict. Sitting back down on the couch, I silently vowed to do things differently. Having seen the whole Earth, inviting us to enlarge our experiences, I could not go backwards. Our essential oneness was real to me even if it was not to others. They could use labels like foreigners and refugees but I would embrace my fellow Earthlings. The whole was more important. Did this orientation make me a burgeoning mystic?

The guests were beginning to leave. I shook off my reveries and stood up. Jean took my hand to say good night. "Can I reach you through the lawyer Catherine Genis?" he asked. He lived in London and did not come to Paris very often.

"Yes, anytime. I've enjoyed meeting you. Good luck on the trip to Lebanon. I would like to read your thesis and your findings. Give my regards to your brother Maurice when you see him." Did I mean any of it? Mere politesse, a habit perfected in the Middle East.

After bidding farewell to the artist, his wife, and the other guests, I reached for my purse but Waddah leaned to refill my champagne glass. I knew what that meant. As he saw the last guest to the door, I added yet another log to the fire. He returned and we were alone in that lovely elegant room, full of the black river's trembling reflections. He put on a record he wanted me to hear. Soon the high notes of a single wooden flute filled the room, rasping slightly, like the desert night wind. As timeless and haunting as the wandering Bedouin with their foldable tents, and their flocks, on the move, like Waddah and me.

My eyes filled with tears. They streamed down my cheeks unchecked. Waddah wiped them with his fingers before gathering me in his arms. He held me very close and stroked my hair while I sobbed. "I know it's not my country Waddah, but it is my past, it's the only past I have."

He nodded, and continued to hold me, rocking me gently.

And when my sobs were spent, he led me wordlessly up the curving steps to the high bedroom. The night came in through its many windows and I thought it was the most beautiful bedroom in Paris. As he laid me down, I glimpsed my protectress, Saint Geneviève, her familiar tall stone form standing guard on the bridge beyond. And then everything dissolved into skin and its rhythms.

At three thirty in the morning the golden tones of a saxophone woke me. The music was coming from across the river. Waddah's regular breathing assured me he was still asleep as I slid out of his arms to go to the window. The musician's solitary figure was hunched over his curving brass instrument, as he played his lonely solo in the shadows of the embankment where the Pont de la Tournelle crossed the River Seine and Saint Geneviève stood guard. Naked and shivering I lingered by the window, not wanting to miss this. Looking at Waddah on the far side of the room, I thought of how he represented my past, finally put to sleep, and to rest. As the last notes of the music faded, I slipped back between the covers thinking, some things will just always be.

* * * *

In the morning Mina made us a delicious breakfast. After leaving Waddah's, I walked toward my apartment. Such a gloriously sunny day could not be spent working alone in my studio. I turned toward the Pont de la Tournelle instead, wanting to visit Saint Geneviève. Upon reaching the bridge and her solid stone body, I felt deeply comforted. Near her towering form I rested. A strong sensation came, as if my island home was shifting shape, being transformed into a boat ready to move through the water. Ready or not, it was carrying me forward, heading out to sea. Standing on the deck of this spirit ship, the ancient motto of Paris came to mind, *Fluctuat nec mergitur.* Latin for "She is tossed by the waves but does not sink."

It was time to honor the death of my loves. What had animated our connections had to be released before the rot set in. To surrender any remaining attachments to Mon Fantôme and the others, I summoned what was left, knowing this watery burial must complete the process of letting go. As reluctance gave way, the remaining tentacles of regret loosened. Leaning upon the bridge railing I shoved everything overboard with a final great heave. Down into the frothy waters went this strange emotional package to sink in the wake of moving on. Rather than being dragged under, I let it all go. The River Seine was flowing on, showing me how to live.

Freeing them freed me. There was nothing more to learn. The soul of my love could take flight now and roam. I would follow wherever it leads. Another love would reanimate me for I still had my capacity for ecstasy. Loving like I had would make the next time better and perhaps a tad wiser.

The following week I threw a big dinner party and invited friends who had never met each other. Waddah came. The Burkes met Irina, and Freddie met the lawyer Catherine. Newer friends, Sylvie and Cherifa came, and an old friend of Zvonimir's, named Elizabeth and her husband. My grandmother would also visit, my brother and my parents in the coming year.

Joe called and took me out to dinner before returning to Lebanon. He said he'd come back to see me but we never reconnected.

* * * *

Lilian arrived next, pausing in Paris on her way to the south of France. She would be staying and painting in the homes of friends during the summer months. Calling to invite me to her hotel for drinks and dinner she explained, "I'm too exhausted to do anything else after that transatlantic flight. I'm over eighty my pet, don't forget."

Seeing her and listening to her talk about the Paris she'd known in the old days was wonderful. Full circle for her and for me. Coming here since before both World Wars, she had witnessed the city's descents and resurrections. I'd come here wondering if Beirut would ever return to life in my lifetime. I realized with a start it didn't matter as much to me anymore. I had turned some invisible corner and recovered somehow. The French word *blessé* came to mind. Although it meant wounded, and described the condition I had been in when moving to Paris, and some of what had transpired here, in English the word sounded like blessing. Ruminating on this odd insight, the image of Saint Geneviève came in a flash.

Lilian asked for my news, interrupting this train of thought. I told her about Omar and how it had ended on the Cote d'Azur.

"I always thought you were too classy a dame to be wasting your time on the likes of him, especially after you told me how he'd disappeared. But I guess it was something you had to go through. You've been mothering him you know. Let me tell you, if you want to be a mother, get yourself a real baby. Don't baby a man. You don't really want that kind of man. I could see it in his face when you showed me his picture the last time you were in New York. I also knew it would do no good to tell you that then. You were so in love. But it's been good for you. Just don't go backwards now. Promise me, you'll never go back to him, even if he crawls across Paris on his knees to you."

"Cross my heart," I promised, drawing my finger across my chest.

"May I propose a toast?" she said, raising her glass. "To a lesson learned that does not need repeating."

"If he ever calls again, I'll say 'Omar who?' and hang up." And we clinked our glasses together.

* * * *

More than two weeks passed and Georgina never called so I finally did, only to be told, "Madame is traveling." When would she be back? I really didn't care anymore.

Nabil came to Paris, saying our mutual friend Mazen would arrive the following day. "Let's surprise him," I suggested. "Don't tell him I'm coming but when you're with him, call if he's in a good mood, and I'll come over."

Nabil agreed to this plan.

CYNTHIA F. DAVIDSON

Chapter 18

MÉTRO-BOULOT-DODO /
SUBWAY-JOB-SLEEP

Paris isn't made for mystic confessions, is it?

— EVA DE VITRAY MEYEROVITCH

The following afternoon, I went to Mazen's posh Avenue Foch address. Closed circuit cameras bristled above the gates and an armed security guard sat just inside the door. On my way there I had passed the residence where the young United Arab Emirates ambassador had recently been gunned down. Who might be next?

Riding to the third floor inside a creaky cage-like elevator, I thought of the ensuing six years since I'd last seen Mazen in Jeddah in 1979. Whatever use he had of me had passed. My hand trembled slightly when ringing the bell. Nabil answered and escorted me into the study. From behind a large desk Mazen rose, dressed in a long white cotton jalabiya, his beard streaked with gray and white, lizard skin boots on his feet. He crossed the floor to greet me with his customary warmth. Obviously Nabil had not kept my visit a secret.

Tea was served and we reminisced. His green eyes still sparkled mischievously and he laughed as often as ever. Life appeared to be treating him well. He showed me a large portrait photo of his son, who had grown so much. There was no picture of the boy's mother Fatin, the Syrian wife his mother had found for him. After getting the male heir demanded by his family, Mazen had divorced her.

Beside his son's picture sat one of his little half sister, as blonde and fair as Mazen was. He had managed to get a daughter to spoil after all. Her mother's portrait photo was on display. A blue-eyed American with long curling locks and large diamond earrings, she had once been a stewardess. Had she agreed to have the child on Mazen's terms? How much had he paid her to do this without the benefit of marriage? I didn't ask though I wondered what would become of that mother and her daughter in the coming years.

Mazen took me on a tour of the huge apartment, full of absurdly expensive museum quality furniture, including a genuine Louis XV writing desk, once owned by Cardinal Richelieu. A gigantic eighteenth century clock, on a marble base, he explained, had once been a present from the king of Prussia to the king of France. That piece alone had cost him a million francs. The tour depressed me. Why did Mazen need or want all this? I was not impressed. On the contrary, I thought of all the conniving and cheating it took to obtain this kind of money. In 1979, I knew he'd been selling weapons in Sudan. My sadness turned to disgust when he took me down the hallway and opened one of the bedroom doors to show me "the girls." Inside were three young women, in various stages of dress and undress, although it was past noon. Only their first names were used in the introductions, two Americans and one German, and not a single one over twenty-years-old.

"There are more upstairs. You can meet them later at dinner," he said as he closed the door. I could hear the women carrying on inside, yelping like puppies in a kennel. The randy old satyr, I thought while following him back through the salons to the study. I was profoundly disturbed. This man had never grown up. He'll probably be cavorting with teens in his sixties and pimping them out. Had his behavior ever been excusable?

* * * *

Returning home, I changed quickly and went straight to the hammam, striding across Pont Marie and through Le Marais neighborhood in a great hurry. I had an enormous need to sit, steam, and get clean. To be calmed and massaged. While watching the pool waters reflect upon the ceiling, I sweated out as much as I could, going into deeper layers of experiences not faced in ages, determined to bring everything up for a final contemplation.

I had been one of them — a young and vulnerable giggly girl — and my sister too. Her relationship with Mazen had started when she was even younger and more vulnerable. Their affair had lasted longer and done more damage. After finishing high school in Beirut a year behind me, she had gone off to college in Maryland, with Mazen paying her tuition and buying her a Datsun. I had left for England. Living in different countries by then, she and I had never discussed any of this.

When deciding to go to university at age twenty-two, I had accepted Mazen's offer of money, for NYU's fees. By my reckoning, he had already forced me to pay for the most intimate education, let him pay for the institutional, publicly sanctioned one. Education has enabled me to support myself, to never be abused or beholden again. Whatever other ways Mazen had considered me useful were never fully disclosed, beyond his mention of our collaborating on a tell-all book someday. He was often angry at Saudi royals and what he put up with, to secure projects, and get paid for work already completed by his companies. But that was no excuse for his treatment of women. The irony was in how dependent he'd become upon females, yet he seemed to have no remorse for how he had used us.

During my 1979 year of work in Arabia, an introduction, to a certain Saudi government official, was "engineered." But he and I could see what was going on. We jointly agreed to refuse the bait. Another story that must wait for it is not yet safe to tell it.

As a kid I'd been grateful for this entrée, to an otherwise inaccessible level of society, but I had no experience with the quid pro quo part of its functioning. Of course Mazen had wanted something in return. And he had been connected to a circle of master puppeteers with all kinds of agents and informants. Perhaps he'd expected me to make more financial demands than I did, seeing as how women were kept as dependent as possible upon men in the Middle East. From what I had witnessed, I had wanted out, not in. My diploma was a bargain, my ticket to independence.

Mazen had not been strong enough to choose independence. His failure to stand up to his parents was the seminal moment to me. I recognized it because of what I had faced when my parents responded so angrily to Ayman. But Mazen had caved under pressure, unable to resist his cultural conditioning, his family's status, name, money, and reputation. Yes, this was only a single incident, yet that experience was formative, because he had treated women as expendable ever since, even the wife his parents had forced him to marry.

Had his first love been pregnant when he turned his back on her? What else made a woman lay her head in an oven? A German woman no less, in a country with its history of Holocaust ovens. How convenient for Mazen she was gone. Yet her death must have remained on his conscience. When I first learned this story I had been too young to comprehend its impact on subsequent decisions. It was relevant to the story of my own conception, the choices my parents had made, and even my unplanned pregnancies. I had no more questions for Mazen. My life had gone in another direction and was about to fill with very different answers.

* * * *

With this latest shift in perception in the hammam, I attended the dinner Mazen had invited me to that evening. Twelve of us were seated around the table at the swank Olivia Valere nightclub. Only three were men: Mazen, Nabil, and a German he did business with. Everything was laid on including the grey caviar in cut crystal bowls atop mounds of shaved ice. We never saw a menu or price list. After the meal, we moved to the lounge area beside the dance floor, accompanied by bottles of chilled rose champagne in sweating silver buckets. The young women were bored and danced with each other. I danced with Nabil a bit but he soon tired and sat down. I continued on my own. The champagne had loosened my limbs and inhibitions. The music pounded and my body swayed, my loosen hair twirling as I reveled in my newly reclaimed freedom.

A handsome man, in a blue and white striped shirt and white trousers, was watching me. Standing atop a short flight of steps near the bar, he held a glass of beer. Good white teeth, a tanned, well proportioned face, dark hair, and dark eyes, a tasteful gold neck chain, and open collar. He stared for quite a while before I acknowledged him with a smile. He smiled back. I danced on and he moved closer, watching me intently. Under his gaze I felt hot and moist, animated by the flashing lights and thumping music. Round and round I swirled, growing dizzier and feeling sexier.

With one hand I motioned for him to come join me on the dance floor. Immediately he understood, and got rid of his glass, coming down the steps, grinning all the while. We danced for each other and then the DJ slowed the music. The man stepped closer, matching my movements easily. A good dancer he was, healthy and happy inside his skin. I was so hot I raised my arms to lift my long hair off my neck. My skin glistened. To cool me, he blew gently on my neck and face. This tickled and I laughed, dancing over to retrieve my champagne glass to offer him some. We passed the cool fluted glass back-and-forth. He laid it against my flaming cheek and I closed my eyes.

"My name is Mimo," he whispered, close to my ear. The music was so loud I asked him to repeat it, and he did, adding, "I'm Italian. I can see you are with those people, and I don't want to make any problems for you. I would like to give you my number. Will you give me yours? I will call you tomorrow."

Pulling my head back I regarded his face for a long time before nodding yes. We danced a bit more and then I excused myself. Leaving the dance floor, I retrieved my evening purse and headed for the ladies room. Once inside, I looked at myself in the mirror.

"What are you doing?" I silently inquired of my reflection. Shaking my head, I repaired my lipstick, and brushed my hair. Taking out one of my business cards, I changed my mind, and put it back in my bag. Tearing off a scrap of paper I wrote only my first name and number. I left the bathroom with this piece of paper folded in my hand, thinking of the night I'd passed such a note to Omar at the Calvados, and what was different this time.

The man was standing near the bar. Discreetly I pressed my slip of paper into his hand as he pressed his note into mine.

"Ciao," we both said as I turned to rejoin Mazen, the German, Nabil, and "the girls."

* * * *

The following afternoon Mimo phoned to invite me for drinks that evening.

"I cannot come until late. I'll be having dinner with the people you saw last night at their place on Avenue Foch."

"I'm not like that," he said. "I have only a simple studio on the Champs de Mars. I want to see you. If you want to see Mimo, you come tonight. Meet me at the Bar Alexandre when you finish with them."

His confidence was admirable. I knew where that bar was, across from Fouquets, at the top of the Avenue George V.

"Okay, I will try to be there by midnight."

The dinner at Mazen's was ridiculously excessive for the size of the group. The meal was catered by a Lebanese restaurant. Several of them had opened in Paris since 1975 when war in Lebanon sent so many Lebanese fleeing here. Though the *mezze* dishes featured my previously favorite foods, I had no appetite. Most were barely touched. After dinner as everyone settled in front of a large screen television to watch a movie, I bid my goodbyes, for a final time.

Outside I hailed a cab to my rendezvous, wondering what to say to this total stranger. I needn't have worried because Mimo did all the talking. Sitting at an outside table with another beer in front of him, he greeted me profusely. He wanted to order champagne but I insisted on my regular Campari and soda.

As I settled into my chair, his regard made me realize he had not been sure I would come. I smiled, "Where did you get the nice tan? Summer's only just started."

"In Tunis," he replied. "I only just returned from there. I am not 100% Italian. My mother's father was from Sicily. My father is Tunisian, but here in Paris, it is better not to say you're an Arab. My real name is Mohamed."

A lump coagulated in my stomach. "And what do you do here in Paris Mimo, I mean Mohamed?" Why had he decided to tell me the truth? Perhaps he had noticed I was with some Arab people last night.

"Call me Mimo, everybody does. I lived in Italy for quite a while and speak Italian. I work with the Saudi princes when they come to town. I do a bit of everything: public relations, driver, bodyguard, accompanying them to the casinos. They pay a percentage you know, even if they lose."

I could hardly believe the coincidences and had to ask. "Do you know another Tunisian, named Omar? He's in your line of work."

"Of course I know Omar. We have worked together, with Prince

Mishari."

This was too much for me. Of all the available men in Paris, fate served up the one who knew Omar. What if he came along now and saw me here? This was his neighborhood.

I told Mimo, "I know Omar too. We were together for about a year."

"So you're the one? He said something to me about six months ago, how he had this American girlfriend, who loved him and kept coming back from America, just to see him. When I asked him if he loved her, or planned to do anything about it, he never answered. He has a wife and daughter in Sfax you know."

And so he did. There it was again, the truth, as plain as could be. If only I had realized it when my intuition had shown me a curly headed child playing at his knee. It wasn't some future child of ours. It was the daughter he already had. Would she grow up to realize her father was a lot like mine? That stomach wrenching cycle, I wanted no part of.

Mimo went on, "I'm not really close with him. For me he has not been a friend I could count on and I noticed his relations with women always end badly. We shared a woman once. The trouble is he wants to be rich one day. I want to be rich too, but I know it doesn't happen in one day. He is always trying to get women to give him money for one thing or another."

I took a big swig of the red Campari and swallowed hard. All these confirmations were additional forms of closure.

"And I don't like the way he licks the prince's hand. Some people say he sells his ass. I don't know. I would not believe it if I didn't see it with my own eyes, but I hear it and I wonder."

The lump in my stomach was turning into a ball of knots. A wave of nausea rose. I had to leave.

"Listen Mimo, it is getting late. I don't feel very well. Perhaps it's something I ate. I really ought to go home." I stood up.

He put out his hand trying to make me sit back down. "Don't go yet. You only just got here," he protested.

I gave him a look that was nearly green and he went quiet.

"I'll get you a cab. Can I call you tomorrow?"

I nodded and gave him a tight little smile.

The ride home to the safety of my little island seemed long that night. When the taxi pulled up in front of my big red door, I was so grateful. Halfway up the steps, the tears started, making it difficult to get my key in to unlock the door. Darius was meowing inside. I scooped him up and sobbed into his fur.

* * * *

That Friday two of my newer friends, Sylvie and Cherifa, came over for dinner. On the spur of the moment, I invited Mimo to join us. Each time he called, I had put him off but decided it was silly not to face him. Besides, I was curious to see what else he might reveal about Omar. He arrived a bit late and the women had already finished their aperitif. This had given me enough time to fill them in about Mimo, "Of all the people in this city, I met the one who knows Omar."

When he came through the door, he quickly sized up the apartment and the other women. He was making calculations, and considering my status, with approval. Amused by his utter transparency, I thought Omar must have done the same, but I'd been oblivious. Mimo ate as if he had not had a good meal in weeks, stabbing his fork into the serving platter, and shoveling in his dinner.

My girlfriends looked at each other, and then at me. I smiled and shrugged. Mimo did not contribute much to the conversation and picked his teeth with a toothpick after the food. We moved into the salon for our dessert and coffees. I watched him pat his stomach and strut into the next room like some cocky little rooster.

I stifled the urge to laugh. Sylvie and Cherifa did not stay much longer and Mimo seemed to be waiting for them to leave. He made no move to go with them when I escorted them to the door.

Sylvie winked at me, and whispered, "C'est un homme gadget. Amuse-toi bien." (He's a gadget man, amuse yourself well).

I winked back at her and smiled broadly, before kissing them both good-bye.

Returning to the living room I found Mimo sitting on the floor with one of the sofa cushions propped behind his back. For the next hour in a great incessant outpouring, he told me the story of his life.

Born in a Saharan village, in Southern Tunisia, he never had much schooling. He'd worked at various jobs in hotels and restaurants and had gotten a taste for the good life from his encounters with visiting tourists. His affairs included German, French, and Scandinavian women. He claimed one man had paid him to make love to his wife while he watched.

Eventually he went to Italy with an older woman named Dolores and lived with her there for two years, which was how he had learned Italian. She took care of him, but got "too jealous" according to Mimo, and the affair broke off. I remembered Freddie's friend, the woman from Nice, with her handsome young live-in boyfriend at the raclette party. There were so many ways to live, I thought while listening to Mimo recount his experiences with Europeans.

He was earnestly trying to entertain me, impress me, and please me. His striving revealed his insecurity about my reactions. Omar had probably thought the same about me. All my explanations and efforts, to please him, to adapt to him, to be nice to him, had ironically produced the opposite effect.

The topic of Omar, our mutual acquaintance, came up. Mimo insisted Omar wasn't even handsome, "though he fancies himself to be a real Casanova."

Pure competitiveness and jealousy, I thought while fetching Omar's photos from the drawer where they'd been put away. I had to be certain we were talking about the same Omar. Mimo confirmed it was him flipping through my handful of Polaroid snapshots. He repeated what he had said about Omar at the Bar Alexandre, touching again on the two most upsetting issues: his habit of asking women for money, and his relationship with the prince, which seemed to involve more than the duties of a majordomo. So my other intuitive image of his slipping out from between the sheets where a man's body lay had also been true.

"I would prefer if we dropped the whole subject now," Mimo said. "And I would also like it if you made these photos disappear. I am a man after all."

He handed the pictures back to me. As I reached to take them and the space between us closed, he laid his hand upon my cheek. "You are too sweet, you know? He isn't good enough for you. I should teach you how to be more *mechant*."

This was the French term for "mean," which applied to ferocious dogs as well as catty women.

He did not try to kiss me then. Instead he said, "My shoulders are aching," and asked if I would rub his back a little.

I complied, expecting only a friendly back rub. He stretched out on the rug and I bent to massage his back, remembering Raymond, the blind masseuse, and his ministrations at the hammam.

Before long, Mimo asked if he could take off his shirt.

"Yes," I answered, leaning back to give him room to sit up and undo the buttons.

The sight of his smooth brown hairless torso pleased me. Lying back down, I resumed my kneading work, but touching his warm bare flesh made it different.

He sighed, "I could take weeks of this."

As my hands tired my strokes became caresses. I loosened my hair and drew it across his back, seeing the goose bumps rise on his skin. He sighed again. Pressing my lips to his shoulder blades, I kissed his backbone, slowly tracing its entire length. The heat rose in me like a fire under a cauldron. I felt like a witch putting him under a spell, wanting to enchant him, as I tried out my powers after gathering my energies back into myself.

Wordlessly he rolled over and removed his trousers. His eyes searched my face as I put my hand upon his stiff desire. He unsnapped my blouse, and finished undressing me, his fingers shaking slightly. When I was naked, he laid me down on my back and began kissing me and reciprocated all my touches, beginning with my forehead. Brushing his lips gently across my skin, he touched my eyelids, cheeks, ears, and neck, my shoulders and on down to the insides of my elbows.

As he progressed toward my breasts, he began to bite and suck, his teeth and tongue on my belly, over and around my hip bones and down the inside of my thighs to my knees. He took my toes in his mouth, his tongue sliding between each one, before he traveled back up the inside length of my leg, his pace quickening and his breath coming faster.

My body tensed beneath his mouth and I held my breath waiting to see if he would nuzzle me where Omar's lips had never touched. Mimo slid his hands beneath my buttocks, and he raised my pelvis before bending to devour me with the same gusto he'd shown at the dinner table.

All the tightness in my body melted away as he continued. He had certainly done this before and he knew how to please. Everything else fell away as the room dissolved, until there was nothing left of me, except that hot bright point of light between my legs which intensified until it burst into a wave of stars of every color. I wept from the sheer joy of it, released as I was, from a year of pent up fury.

From above, Mimo moved, his wet face finding mine as he plunged into me. His lips and tongue tasted of the sea, of me, as he took my body again in great forceful strokes. I blessed every other woman he had ever been with, who had taught him so well, before pressing my ankles together behind him as the pleasure echoed from my body with every thrust.

And when he had spent himself, he held me gently, shyly, stroking my sides, telling me how much he loved the curve of my waist and hips. Profound calm settled over me as I closed my eyes beside his warmth.

* * * *

The following evening I was at the Burkes for dinner. More than a month had passed since we'd seen each other and we had news to catch up on. They'd attended the funeral of Tom's father while in the US but there had been a happier reason. Janet beamed when showing me the pictures of the brand new baby, their first grandchild.

Would I ever have a family of my own?

I told them about my trip to the South of France and the ten days spent with Georgina's friend Mona. "It gave me the willies going out with those Lebanese friends of hers, like spending time with ghosts. They were so desperate to have fun, knowing they could die tomorrow. The country is in hopeless shape, so they want to live every moment they've got left, intensely."

Janet said, "Georgina has been having lots of noisy parties too lately.

The IBM family in the apartment above hers told us it has been bad while we've been gone. Parties practically every night. Sounds like a herd of elephants jumping on the ceiling."

"The least she could do when she keeps you up all night is to invite you to join the party," I chuckled, wishing I had been invited. Since the day she so warmly suggested we have lunch sometime, I had not heard from Georgina. She always had plenty of time to party but had none for working on the book. I resolved to call her tomorrow.

I could picture Georgina and her friends enjoying themselves and didn't begrudge them their fun. The elephant herd noise had probably been the Lebanese dabke dance. Everyone lined up in a row, facing the same direction, with their arms over each other's shoulders. The two dancers on either end held handkerchiefs or scarves, which fluttered from their fingers. Everyone raised their knees and stepped sideways, in unison, stamping down. I had done this dance in Beirut though I doubted I'd ever dance it again.

The biggest news from the Burkes was their recent decision to move back to the US, for good.

"The plan is to return to Florida by the end of the summer," explained Janet. "We've been house hunting on this trip. I found one I really like. You'll see it when you come and visit us."

Tom piped in, "I'm going to start my own consulting firm."

I knew he'd been thinking of this while watching the disintegration of the Arab firm he had worked for. His Middle Eastern experience would certainly be valuable to American clients. Perhaps my old company would be interested in some of his contacts.

"I wish you both well, but must confess I don't like the idea of you folks leaving me alone here in Paris. It just won't be the same without my adopted family." I remembered fondly how often we had socialized together, going to places like Calvados, and Conways when we were hungry for real American food, coleslaw and spare ribs.

I decided then to tell them my other news.

"You remember Omar don't you?" I began. "There are several reasons why I decided to call it quits with him, but the main one is his gambling. It's a disease as bad as alcoholism. I don't want to be barefoot and pregnant with him in debt by a million French francs in a few years. It hasn't been easy to get over him. I've had a real 'case' as your daughter would say, but my feet are firmly back on the ground now." I paused to let this information sink in before continuing.

"Tonight around eleven a man named Mimo will stop by to pick me up. I met him at a disco recently while out with some other friends. He knows Omar. They are both Tunisian and both work with the Saudis. Mimo told me Omar is already married and has a daughter back in Tunisia. I am glad I decided to give him up even before I knew that."

The three of them had a mixture of surprise and concern on their faces. Tom raised his after-dinner goblet of Cointreau, "To a good decision," he pronounced, toasting me.

Janet and her daughter nodded in agreement.

"Thanks," I said as the two women came to hug me.

The daughter reminded me what I had told her earlier that year, when she broke up with her college boyfriend. "You said something like, 'Men are like buses, there's another one every five minutes.'"

I laughed, "Yes, that's what my father always says, though he says it about women. The same can definitely be said of men."

Fifteen minutes later, Mimo arrived, dressed in black leather pants and a white sweater. When offered a drink, he asked for whiskey with ice and no water. Perched on the edge of the couch, with his glass in his hand, he was nervous, but charming. At least he spoke a little English, I thought, listening to his responses to Tom's questions.

At a quarter to midnight we said our goodbyes and departed. Mimo put his arm around me and pecked me on the cheek as we walked toward Avenue Victor Hugo to catch a cab.

"I liked your friends. They are very good people."

"They only saw Omar once at my birthday party. He never wanted to meet any of my friends."

"Let's not talk about him. Let's go dancing. Or would you rather come to my place?"

I hesitated but I knew I really wanted more of the same, more of what last night had been like.

"Let's go to your place, I'm too tired to go dancing," I said snuggling closer.

His place was a second floor walk up, on a side street off the Avenue Bosquet in the seventh arrondissement. A modest studio, with a tiny kitchen alcove and a bathroom, it was messy in the way of single men, who concern themselves only with comfort and practicality. A fur covered mattress on the floor behind a gauze curtain, a low brown couch, a poster of two lion cubs in a basket, and an open Qur'an, in a glass and wooden box, nailed to the wall, with a set of prayer beads hanging from it. On the coffee table, a full ashtray, a pair of brass knuckles, a radio cassette player with a stack of tapes beside it, and a wine bottle with a candlestick in the neck, its sides covered with wax drippings in various colors.

"This is Caroline," Mimo said, patting the Sony Trinitron television set. I smiled and asked to use the bathroom.

He came around to open the door for me. Inside it was spotlessly clean, not a single hair in the tub. The porcelain surfaces gleamed as if they'd just been scrubbed. This reassured me. I sat down on the toilet seat and took out my compact, checking my face and hair. My eyes were bright and my cheeks flushed as if with fever

I told myself, "I'm here because I'm taking a cure. I'm with this man for one reason. This affair will not last long but it's the best way to rebound from Omar." I flushed the toilet and rearranged my clothing before going back out to Mimo.

He was already naked, his erection jutting out in the candlelight. A Farid el Attrash cassette was in the recorder and the familiar music played as he said hoarsely, "Come here, come over here."

Taking his outstretched hand, I obeyed. We made love until the morning. It had never been so good or so intense. Mimo knew more about sex than anyone I had ever been with. At times he was rough, slapping my buttocks, calling me *salope* (bitch), and grasping a handful of my hair at the neck to pull my head back. He told me in vividly descriptive French, just what he was going to do to me next.

By the time I went home, my entire body felt bruised and sore. I wasn't used to this. I wasn't sure I wanted to get used to this. But it was a useful lesson in surfeit. This man thoroughly quenched my thirst.

Darius mewed loudly as I opened my door that afternoon, fumbling with the stack of mail left in front of it. One letter was from Lynda. Before reading it, I opened the cat a can of food and refilled his water bowl. Lynda had written, "I had a confusing dream about you recently, but it ended well. What is going on over there? Are you all right? It's been too long since I heard from you."

She was right. My letter writing had fallen off again after the post Cote d'Azur burst when I'd told friends it was over with Omar. But what to say now? Mention Mimo or not? That he turned out to be an acquaintance of Omar's? Or that he had made love to me until I thought I would die from the pleasure? No one had ever written to tell me such a thing. But the truth was, I was grateful for a good…fuck. That word came reluctantly but it was the truth of it. Why call it anything else? It wasn't love. I promised myself I would never call things by other names again. Mimo had satisfied me, utterly, on the physical level. But nothing else fit. I wanted a larger form of ecstasy and transcendence, though how to achieve this was yet to be determined.

And though I never wanted to be called a snob, I could recognize Mimo was not my social or intellectual equal. I doubted he read anything except the crime pages in the newspaper, like Omar. Had either of them wanted a formal education? They were at the level of stud and chauffeur. Would they stay there all their lives? Why had I seen Omar differently? Both men had used what they could to escape into a larger world. Hadn't I done the same?

A child who'd started life in a Tulsa, Oklahoma trailer with two parents who'd never gone to college, what level was I at? I did not think myself so high and mighty. Obviously I needed what Omar and Mimo provided or they wouldn't have attracted me. I would not denigrate that need. It was real enough and so were our struggles to survive in this warring world. What we had in common was more important than what separated us. At least I wasn't as ignorant anymore. Seeing how we'd all been set up, by those who'd used us, left me more determined than ever. This truth had inspired me to find a way out. Surely there were other choices besides killer or victim, exploiter or exploited. Aware of my aching muscles, I leant back in the chair, and suddenly remembered Irina. We had an appointment at the hammam this afternoon and had planned to eat dinner together. In a rush, I gathered my things, and left the house, craving the cleansing steam.

Irina was already downstairs when I arrived. We greeted each other warmly and took our customary seats on the wooden chaise lounges. The heat was wonderful. I surrendered to it completely feeling it penetrate to the marrow of my tired bones, massaging mind and body from within. As the sweat beaded upon my abdomen, I reached to sluice it off.

A flashback came, of Mazen ejaculating upon my belly when I was fourteen. He'd been thirty-two at the time, more than twice my age. The events returned in Technicolor replete with sounds and smells. We'd been in Obhor, a Red Sea inlet north of town, which most expats called The Creek. We often snorkeled, fished, and picnicked at our rented cabin nearby on the weekends but this time we were at Mazen's beach house, the same A-frame where my mother said she'd met Georgina.

What had formed me then had since informed and healed me.

Mazen had invited us for the weekend. My mother, sister, and brother were along but dad was off somewhere on a work flight. I was home for the winter holidays from my first year at boarding school in Switzerland. After dinner that night, Mazen had asked me to sing and I'd taken out my guitar. Since kindergarten, my parents had found it amusing to wake me to sing for their guests so I was used to performing. They'd given me a guitar on my birthday years before. When everyone one else went to bed, Mazen had urged me to continue.

The desert night sky was full of stars, the Milky Way fully visible, so far from the city lights. As our world turned upon its axis, I remembered its beauty while singing "*Ne Me Quitte Pas*," the Jacques Brel song. As I finished Mazen reached to lift my guitar from my hands. Moving closer on the couch he started kissing me. My body responded but my brain knew this was wrong.

My "uncle Mazen" was not supposed to be doing this. The clashing emotions were difficult to sort. I was not ready, had not learned yet to wield my own power. His was being thrust upon me, literally.

The following day I felt constantly nauseous but never told a soul what Mazen had done. Upon my return to boarding school after that vacation, Mazen took up with my younger sister and no one protected her either. That year was 1969 turning into 1970. That summer Georgina won the Miss Lebanon contest and by the following year, Mazen was boasting about paying Georgina's expenses for the trip to Miami to compete in the Miss Universe pageant, which she'd won. Surely he had done more with her.

None of this was ever discussed in our family. My sister had joined me in Switzerland at Collège du Léman during my sophomore year. A troubled teenager, she went through a kleptomania phase, filling her dorm room with items pilfered from Geneva stores. Her behavior had been a misinterpreted cry for help. Craving love and affection, she lacked the money to buy such gifts. Knowing nothing yet about the psychological trauma accompanying childhood sexual assault, I had not connected her behaviors to her experiences — nor mine.

My parents had poured the blame on her when the school reported what she'd done. When did they finally suspect Mazen? Dad needed the booze Mazen provided in Arabia where alcohol was illegal and scarce. And the glamour, parties, and high life of the jet set had blinded my mother. But we young daughters had paid dearly.

We finished high school in Beirut at ACS where Mazen had greater access to my sister. While I went off on my own to England after graduation, he paid her college tuition in Maryland. Had their affair ended before he'd started up again with me? In the years since the tables had turned. Now I saw how someone like Mimo or Omar might be considered my male equivalent. Would I turn into a female version of Mazen? No, but I was done wanting the right thing from the wrong men. This time I expected nothing except the most basic satisfactions. That limited the confusion while I discerned what was next.

As I surrendered further to the hammam's steam and heat, snatches of recent conversations surfaced, like Mimo crooning to me, "I could never get enough of you even if we stayed together for years." It was bed talk but I liked hearing it just the same. "You are a real woman," he had said, whatever that meant.

"Would you like to have a baby? We'd have beautiful kids. You're beautiful. You'd make a good wife and mother."

How ironic to hear those words now, from a man I had no intention of being serious with, I concluded wiping the beads of sweat off my chest.

But then he had spoiled it, saying he could bring me clients, people who would want to watch us make love together, or pay for my favors. Was he teasing about this to make me feel more desirable? I did not fantasize about rich men or diamond bracelets. Having seen enough of that I believed those baubles were bribes. Something inside me passionately resisted reducing life to mere financial transactions. Some things were not for sale. Besides, I knew all of that could disappear in a moment. Beirut had schooled me.

I realized a newer truth — that I would rather be the client. Mimo made me feel like one, already asking for money. "Just a little loan, to tide me over until the next client. I'll pay you back, I promise. The girls I usually borrow from are out of town."

He told me how he sometimes arranged for them to meet his clients and shared some details. The strange requests: being tied up, women in pairs, champagne bottle necks inserted in various places…and worse. Though I was curious about the darker side of life in Paris, I wanted no part in it. Buying or selling sex was not a business I wanted to be in after being this close to it. Like crossing the border into another country, I knew my limits of adaptability did not extend that far. Things would only get unhealthy.

I thought of the girls at Mazen's fancy place and the night Omar had driven me down Rue St. Denis implying I could have ended up there. But I hadn't. I never would. Oddly, I expected more of others and myself. The ecstatic truth remained. Although I had yet to learn what else the power of pure energy exchanges could be put to, I had never faked ecstasy or sold it. I held on to that capacity and what was uncorrupted within me. More years would pass before this would redirect me towards the mystic shamanic path. For now it was enough to discern which direction not to take.

Omar had told me, "Paris isn't really your place you know. It's not where you belong."

What had he meant? That I wasn't sufficiently ruthless? I should've asked him, "where do you think I belong?" but I hadn't thought of it until later. Where did he belong? That question also needed asking.

I'd replied, "Yes I know. But Paris is in between where I was and where I want to be." America and the *"Moyen Orient"* as the French referred to the Middle East.

He had countered, "But you would not like it there anymore. Even I cannot stand it for long. I don't like all the questions. Everybody is always on top of each other: my sisters, my aunts, everybody's nose in everyone else's business. You don't know what it's like to be part of an Arab family. I can't buy a kilo of meat for myself without buying a kilo for each of them."

True. Though I knew the psychic dislocations of expat life, I had never been a member of an Arab family, especially a poor one. I did not know what that was like. Yet I had been close enough, long enough, to have some idea of how difficult it was.

Did I want to go back anymore? Not really. While sluicing the sweat from my sides I finally accepted another truth. Lebanon was broken beyond repair in my lifetime and Arabia was no longer what it had been.

Everything had changed and so must I. Those places could not be reconstructed. How best to relate to their phantom natures now? Everything that enriched me could be secreted inside the safe deposit box of my memory bank. I would never deny my history with people and places in dire straits now, but I had to go forward or I could never help anyone, not even myself.

I was so tired of war. I resented its existence. I wanted to defy death and destruction. Here in this steamy hammam, I was joyously voluptuously alive. There were so many ways to live. Omar was probably right. I did not belong in Paris anymore. What had brought me here was concluding. The old mystery of Waddah was settled. It would never be more than it was, the same with Maurice and Zvonimir. Omar was over and done with. Of all my reasons for coming to Paris, only Georgina remained, the first and the final piece of the puzzle. Did she have similar difficulties?

Georgina. Beirut. Omar. Each had evoked the same hunger for resolution and release. Like a starving person at a banquet, my needs had been too great. Like Mimo gorging himself at my table and on my flesh, I saw how my cravings had made me desperate. Since losing Jeddah and Beirut, I'd clung to any potential for happiness, the lack of joy, and the fear of loss, warping my relationships. Sated now it was easier to grasp this.

Omar had once accused me of smothering him. "You're too afraid of losing me," he retorted, when I rebuked him for not calling me, and making me worry he had disappeared again.

He was right. After losing so many homes, friends, and familiar environments, I thought I'd accustomed myself to loss, but I had not. My emotions had not caught up with that logic. Likewise a task as supremely rational as writing a book would not bring me the emotional and spiritual peace I sought.

Why had I been so attached to him, and Georgina, of all people?

Because they'd reflected my blind spots. I'd failed to see how others perceived me. Taken in by my own needs and miseries, I'd missed so much. The lesson was in the ending lines of Mon Fantôme: des cadeaux, aussi profound, aussi beaux.

They'd given me what I thought I wanted, my desire to offer gifts as profound and as beautiful, but this had yet to be accomplished. I had gotten what I needed, in ways I did not want or expect.

Coming to Paris to find the truth, I'd been forced to face its opposite, the liars and their lies. The serendipity of the right catastrophes, like meeting Omar, this had achieved the success my original project never could have. I'd been using Georgina, as a substitute, when the story I had to confront was my own.

"Don't think your truth can be found by anyone else," Andre Gide had written.

Fate had conspired to arrange outer realities to mirror my inner turmoil so I could recognize it. Hadn't I warned my program participants to be ready for this moment of rupture and change? Their reasons for accepting a foreign assignment would never suffice to keep them overseas when the going got rough, as it inevitably did. Other reasons would have to be discovered when things failed to meet expectations and they were shaken to their cores. The same had happened to Georgina, and Omar, me and all the others.

"Would you mind scrubbing my back?" Irina asked. Her request returned me to reality.

Nodding I took the bright orange glove from her hand. We turned in our chairs so I could reach her back. Waves of heat rolled over us from the boiler beneath the marble surface of the central dais. It radiated like a hidden invincible sun, like the underlying energies powering us from within.

Sloughing off the dead skin cells I thought of the Turkish word for this: *kasa*. The bath attendant at the hammam I'd visited in Istanbul on my last business trip had taught me that word. I had a lot to slough off psychologically too. Tonight I was Irina's attendant. While I rubbed her pink back with the rough glove in long downward strokes, from her shoulders to her hips, I reconsidered what I knew about this petite Ukrainian whose life was as charged with change as mine.

After her father died, contracting an infection from contaminated, reused needle in a Soviet hospital, she had left Kiev for Moscow. There she'd become a Russian teacher and met a foreigner in one of her classes. They'd married and moved to Lebanon. But not every Soviet citizen was granted a passport. Because Irina was a loyal member of the Communist Party she was allowed to travel out of the USSR. Before they agreed to let her leave however, she had to sign another document. It promised her "full cooperation" if the KGB ever required her assistance overseas.

My strokes softened while recalling the births of her two daughters and how those births had differed. In the USSR the Russian midwife had massaged her perineum with warm oil to prevent her skin from tearing during the delivery of her firstborn. In France they'd cut her open. The stitches of the excessive episiotomy incision had gotten infected. She'd been practically incontinent until it healed. The tremendous suffering of that second birth had turned her off sexually and contributed to her husband's infidelity. So many disappointments and adaptations, and just when we decide what we want, life shifts and transforms everything into fresh challenges.

Irina signaled for me to stop. Enough. She would shower now. I handed the glove back to her, motioning I would stay, so she could have the first massage appointment. We floated along like this with no strain and hardly any planning. Scrubbing each other's backs and sharing this companionable silence left me feeling closer to this woman and the truth of life, than frantic activities or conversations. Paris had shown me the allure of languor, and the odalisque, in sharp contrast to my compulsive doing. All my striving, organizing people and activities, taking charge and being in control needed to be reexamined. These behaviors were linked to my upbringing. As the eldest child of an alcoholic, it would be a few more years before I made that connection. My father had mocked my "mother Cynthia" tendencies, unable to realize I'd been trying to parent myself.

Peace was like this, floating in the hammam pool.

* * * *

Just after ten that evening, returning home from the hammam, my phone rang. Picking up the receiver I heard him ask, "Hayati? Is that you?"

Omar. I said nothing. Reaching for the arm of the chair to steady myself, my knees went soft as I lowered my body onto the cushion seat.

"How are you?" he asked with the old familiarity. Perhaps he believed he could take up where things left off over a month ago.

"Did you get my last letter?" I kept my tone level.

"There is never any last letter between us. You shouldn't write down such things you know. It is easier to take them back when you only speak them."

"But I don't want to take them back Omar. I meant everything I said in that last letter. It is over between us." Despite my resolve, tears were coming.

"Oh come on now. You don't mean that. I'll come by for you. We'll go have a coffee together and talk."

"There is nothing to talk about. You should know that. You never loved me, never."

After a long pause, he said softly, "I wish I could love the way you do, but I cannot. Maybe I should see a psychiatrist or something. I'm incapable of feeling strongly for anyone. I read your letter but had no reaction really. Maybe I could change, maybe someday I'll reach that level."

No you never will I thought. "You don't deserve me Omar. You know it, you said so yourself. After that night in Nice, you knew how sensitive I would be, but you never called, not once."

"I stayed in Monte Carlo with the prince."

Ah, yes. What had the two of them been up to? Surely he'd been gambling too. Now he expected to crawl back into my bed. No wonder he thought he could. He'd done it before. Yes I had been a fool, but I really didn't regret it, not now.

When I said nothing else, he added, "I went back to Sfax for a while."

"To see your wife and daughter," I replied.

Now it was his turn to say nothing. I held my tongue, tempted to mention Mimo, but why? Let him wonder how I found out about the daughter. Blurting out that I found another man, a friend of his, who had satisfied me more on the first night than Omar had in a year, would lower me in his eyes. I wanted him to regret losing me.

He changed the subject. "I saw your friend Georgina, and Najwa too, in Nice after you left. How is the book coming? I bet nothing has happened. Why do you wait for her? You should know, you cannot count on the Lebanese."

Nor could I count on you I thought. I was moving on, leaving all that. Saying nothing, I let the silence sit on the line between us.

"Too bad you fell on me, the most savage man in Paris. I always thought I if didn't make you I'd break you," he said.

"You never believed in love or even your own value to me. You could have changed your life, become a better man. Love has the power to do that, it changes people," I insisted.

"Human beings never change and love is for poets," he quipped. "I've seen too many unhappy victims of love."

"Don't tell me you've never seen any happy lovers? That is also possible you know."

"But love doesn't last, the years pass."

"But something else replaces it, the love of family, a sense of peace." I wondered why I was bothering and stopped. The threat of tears had ceased.

"Come on now, let's go have a coffee, for old times, for friendship sake."

"No Omar," I said sternly. "It's better to leave things as they are. I'd rather not see you again. I've buried you." In my mind's eye, I saw Saint Geneviè, the Pont de la Tournelle, and the River Seine rushing beneath as I let go, consigning him to the dark green waters. Instead of my going down, I'd emptied myself out. My love, my soul, had truly taken flight. That surrender had cleared me, leaving a new space within for the next truth to come and dwell.

"Can I call you again sometime?" He asked, evidently comprehending my seriousness.

"No. I really prefer you don't. Do me that favor." With great finality, I added, "Goodbye Omar, and good luck."

"Goodbye hayati," he said.

Dropping the heavy black receiver into its cradle, I looked at the phone, feeling my tears drying on my cheeks. Their saltiness prickled and I went to wash them off. They were the last I would ever cry over him.

In bed later, before sleeping, I tuned to the old Arabic radio station. A deep voiced male reader was chanting Quranic verses. The rich vibrating syllables transported me back to the desert before other peoples' interpretations confused me. *Jahaliyyah* I thought, the Arabic term for the ignorance of pre-Islamic days, before an illiterate camel caravan driver named Mohamed married his boss, a richer, older woman named Khadijah. She had been the first to believe in him and his visions. Would the religion founded by the Prophet Mohamed, the world's first Muslim, exist without Khadijah's generosity?

What about my persona jahaliyyah? Everyone had a before state of ignorance, but what came after? Disillusionment was more common than enlightenment. I thought of Omar, the modern driver of fancy cars rather than caravans. He worked for a debauched prince rather than a woman who believed in him and his evolution, though perhaps his wife did. Who believed in me and supported mine? That was a revelation. We were all ignorant. Men's ignorance about women and our ignorance about them was as challenging as our ignorance about each other's cultures, beliefs, and experiences. And that ignorance was our enemy, not each other. These musings soon released me into a dreamless sleep.

* * * *

A few weeks later, I got home too exhausted to join Irina at the hammam that Friday evening. After feeding Darius, I checked my brand new answering machine for messages. None from Mimo. That was odd. Desperate for business, he was usually waiting by his phone, praying for clients. At bedtime I took the airmail version of the New York Times book review up the loggia steps with me to see what Americans were reading. Were the chances improving for another version of this book project or not? Darius curled up on the other pillow and purred us both to sleep.

At two o'clock in the morning my phone rang. It was Mimo.

"Can I come to see you?" he pleaded. The edge of desperation in his voice was frightening.

"Where are you? Why haven't you called?" I queried defensively.

"It's a long story. I prefer to tell you in person. I just got out of prison."

Half afraid to refuse him, for fear he'd come anyway, smash on the door, yell, and make a scene, I said, "Yes, you can come." What was I getting myself into?

"Have you got anything to drink in the house?"

"There might be some wine or some whiskey."

"Good. I'll be right over."

In less than twenty minutes he appeared, looking haggard and older, as if he had not slept. At the sight of him my fear dissolved. He embraced me, kissing both my cheeks.

"Can you smell it?" He asked, raising the arm of his jogging suit jacket up to my nose.

"Smell what?" I asked sniffing the fabric.

"The prison, at Bois d'Arcy. I don't know if I'll ever get that smell out of me. It's horrible."

"Go take a hot shower," I suggested. He nodded, stripped off his clothes, and disappeared into the bathroom without another word. While he showered, I got out the bottle of whiskey I kept for guests, some ice cubes, and a glass, setting everything on a tray.

When he reemerged, wrapped in my terrycloth robe, I asked, "Where would you like to sit? Here at the table or in the salon?"

"In the salon," he replied, walking in and taking a cushion off the couch to sit on the floor as he'd done before. I set the tray down in front of him on the rug and got a cushion for myself.

"You are a super girl, really super," he said after taking a long swig of the whiskey.

"What happened Mimo?" I asked impatient to hear his story.

"I opened up the face of some Lebanese wimp outside the Prince de Galles Hotel the other night. He was asking me for coke but I don't deal drugs anymore. Everybody knows that. Anyway, I didn't like his attitude. He would not take no for an answer, so I hit him with my fist. I guess my ring opened up the skin on the side of his face," Mimo admitted, running his hands down over his own cheek to simulate the gash.

"Then I just went home. About an hour later the gendarmes came. They turned my studio upside down, looking for drugs or a weapon, but they didn't find anything. They dragged me off anyway. The guy had pressed charges." He paused to drink some more of the J&B.

"It's terrible. I can't tell you how bad it is. They even take away your name. You get a number and you have to answer by it. And the people inside…they even have their own language. They say things like 'ta mmefe' instead of 'ta femme'." (Inverting the first letters sounded like school kids using pig Latin).

"They have a special vocabulary. It really is another world. They put me in a cell with a young French drug addict, Francois. He's spent more time in prison than out of it. Last time he got out, he beat up his girlfriend pretty bad, so they put him back in. He can't live on the outside anymore, he's too used to being in there. He asked me to write to him and find out what happened to his girl."

He went quiet then, taking his time to light a cigarette. After several long puffs he looked at me, and began again. "My Saudi friend at the Embassy got me out. He heard about the incident even before I called him. Just like the American movies, they let you make one call. They came to my cell at midnight and woke me up. I didn't know what was happening. They took me through all the gates and doors, and gave me back my clothes. Until then I had not understood I was being released. They just shoved me out the door. I had to hitchhike back into town. Luckily a truck driver stopped for me.

"The food was awful. No salt or anything in it. That costs extra. You have to buy it from the guards." He stared off into space remembering.

"Are you hungry? I think there's some cold chicken left in the fridge. Shall I warm it up?"

"Don't bother. I'll eat it cold."

In the kitchen as I got out the food and a plate, I heard him pouring another drink. He raised his voice so I could hear him, "Bring some more ice too."

Ravenously he gnawed the meat off the chicken bones with his bare hands. The grease made his brown fingers shine. I remembered learning the art of eating that way. Only your right hand went into the communal dish and your mouth. In the desert the left is your potty hand. With practice, rice can be rolled into little balls you pop into your mouth with your thumb. Camels don't haul silverware around. In the desert without water there is only sand to wash with. In a flash, the memory of a Bedouin campout resurfaced.

Mazen had taken a group of us expats in a caravan of dusty Land Rovers, out to a *wadi* (valley) for an overnight stay. I'd been twelve or thirteen. After leaving Jeddah, it took the better part of a day's drive to reach the campsite. A long black tent had been set up there, complete with beautiful rugs and pillows to sit and lean upon. The Bedouin women wove these tents and carpets with the hair of their goat and sheep. We were served a sumptuous feast, a whole roasted lamb upon a steaming platter of rice. For dessert the retinue of locals brought us piles of fresh fruit and tiny cups of green, cardamom spiced coffee. With a flourish they poured it from their curving metal pots. The spouts were stuffed with palm tree webbing to strain out the grains of coffee beans.

My little brother had pitied the lamb too much to eat its meat. Mom had not wanted him to witness the ritual slaughter but he'd seen the men slice its neck while intoning the prayers. The carcass had been suspended afterwards to drain out all the blood. Those procedures made the meat *halal*, acceptable to Muslims, whose dietary restrictions resembled those of observant Jews whose food had to be kosher.

I sang for my supper that night, playing my guitar under the stars. My thoughts cycled back to Paris, and Mimo eating at my table, using his hands exactly as I'd used mine so long ago. He glanced at me occasionally, as if needing confirmation that he wasn't dreaming. Was I real? Or would he wake up back inside the walls of Bois d'Arcy prison? Was he real to me? Which scenes were dreams? Which were memories?

When Mimo finished, I carried the plate back to the kitchen while he went to wash his hands. Would he be able to sleep now, or was he too keyed up? As I came back out of the kitchen, he wrapped me in his arms. Soon he opened his robe, lifted my nightgown, and caressed me, motioning for me to bend over, and hold onto the table. It was quick, simple, and poignant, as if he feared his parts may not function. Later I wondered what parts of me were functioning, or not. After washing, we climbed the loggia steps to bed, and slept until late the next afternoon.

Once Mimo left I sat on the couch wondering how to end this. A police record tipped the balance. How to tell him it was over without provoking him? Mimo had quite a temper obviously. If he could haul off and hit a man hard enough to open his face, what might he do if he was angry at me? As far as this relationship was concerned, I had learned my lesson. Another long work trip was coming up, a perfect opportunity to slide out of the picture, like others had done with me.

* * * *

The following day I sorted the latest batch of mail and found a letter from Georgina's father. Short and sweet, he asked about my news, saying he did not know when they'd return to Paris. Should I bother to reply? The whole project felt hopeless. He'd enclosed two photos: one of him with Georgina's mother and the other of a marina they'd been standing near.

Georgina's parents looked like any middle-aged couple. Studying them, I noticed George's legs were as thin and vulnerable as my father's. "Bandy legs" he'd called them. His wife was dressed like the matron she was, in pink and white cotton. My father would've called hers "Lebanese piano legs."

"Lima Echo Bravos." He'd used those aviation call letters for the Lebanese. I'd heard him tell the worst, racist jokes about the Arabs, yet he'd given them his best working years. So which was it, love or hate or something else? He'd almost left my mother for his Lebanese mistress Amal Mousalli, Dr. Amin Mousalli's sister, and never explained or apologized for his behavior.

Still holding George's letter, I thought of other names, the ones Saudis and Lebanese had called us. Because we were not Muslims, American expats were "infidels" first and foremost. Popular terms for us were *ajanib* (foreigner) or *q'wajah* (Westerner). Disaffected expats used derogatory epithets for the locals, like "rag heads" and "sand niggers." Since my father and I had the same dark hair and eyes as most Arabs, we fit in better and caused less of a stir in public. By contrast my tall, redheaded mother and blonde sister attracted attention. In the souk, women had stroked my sister's golden locks and touched my mother's freckled skin.

My attention returned to the other photo Georgina's father had sent of a marina in Larnaca, Cyprus. That island country was a known haven for smugglers, money launderers, and spies in the region. Three Mossad (Israeli intelligence) agents were killed there a few months later, Avraham Avnery, Reuben Palzur, and his wife Ester Paltzur (various spellings depending upon which transliteration is used). If one believed the public record, this female operative Ester Paltzur, had been instrumental in the assassination of Georgina's husband six years ago. "Erika Mary Chambers" was one of several aliases used by the agent Ester, whose forged British "Erika Mary Chambers" passport had been found. The British government was publicly furious after revelations of how many Israeli operatives favor stolen British passports.

According to journalistic accounts this "Erika Chambers" (aka Ester Paltzur) lived in Beirut in 1979. Her visa had been granted for "charity work" in the Palestinian refugee camps. This ruse provided Ester access and information crucial to planning Salameh's assassination, not just to avenge the 1972 deaths of the Israeli Olympic athletes in Munich, but for all the operations Georgina's husband had orchestrated as head of Palestinian intelligence. Ester was credited with timing the detonation of the car bomb that killed Salameh and eight others on January 22, 1979. Pretending to be an artist on the balcony of a rented apartment in Ras Beirut in 1979, Ester posed as an artist so she could observe the comings and goings by Georgina and her husband, from their Rue Verdun apartment. Verdun. Not a good omen to live on a street named after the largest, longest battle of the First World War.

I had wanted to ask George Rizk about the man who'd married his daughter and sired his grandson. Had George called him Ali or Abu Hassan? The latter was Salameh's PLO nom de guerre, because his first son by his first wife was named Hassan, after Ali's own father. How much did George know about Salameh's activities? In their shoes, surrounded by such duplicitous people and so much carnage, he and Georgina would not risk telling me anything controversial although the photo of the Larnaca marina might have been meant as a message that had meaning a few weeks later. Did I believe George would do that? No.

I did remember what another Lebanese friend had told me years ago, "Americans are like open books. You listen to them for five minutes, you know what they're going to say for the rest of their lives." Ironically this was why some of them had trusted me with their truth.

Worn down by these endless intrigues, and the lies within lies, I realized anew just I wanted nothing to do with this rotten world anymore. What good could come of confirming more awful lies and betrayals? Determining the truth required a more definitive process. And all I had managed to really prove was the importance of doubting everything.

The most stunning thing Mona had told me was, "The Israelis did not kill Ali Hassan Salameh."

Then who had? Why would the Israelis take the credit if publicizing that story had gotten their operatives killed later in Larnaca? Had they been outed because their handlers wanted them killed? Or because the Palestinians wanted revenge on the Israelis in general and the Mossad agents who had killed their Force 17 intelligence leader Ali Hassan Salameh? All the double-crossing in the region was further obscured by planted rumors and the fostering of conspiracy theories.

I had looked into Mona's assertion that the Israelis had not killed Salameh, and the man she'd told the truth to — about his real killers — had himself been murdered shortly afterwards. My research turned up a German journalist named Robert Pfeffer who had been killed in Beirut on May 24, 1979. Was he the one Mona had told the truth to, about who killed Salameh in January of that year? In 1981 I'd seen a German film about the war in Lebanon, *Die Fälschung* (*Circle of Deceit*). The title reminded me of Omar's question: had I ever been deceived?

Lebanon had certainly deceived me and so had Omar. But something else was also true. I had survived those deceptions. Unlike that time in Beirut when I was nineteen and wanted to die because of my family's circle of deceit, today I wanted to live. And believed I could do it without becoming like them, without having to accept that this is the way the world worked with those I would choose to live with after this.

The deceits Georgina had dealt with were far worse than what I'd imagined. Among them was the how the CIA had used her husband, in exchange for the promise the US would further the Palestinian cause. Salameh would help protect American lives in Beirut in return. After his assassination, it had been open season on Americans in Lebanon, especially those in the intelligence community. Salameh's CIA contact Richard Ames, and most other US intelligence operatives, local and American, had been wiped out in the spring 1983 bombing of the US Embassy in Beirut. And that autumn, when 241 US Marines had died in a truck bombing of their barracks, who had been behind all those casualties? Which group had gained the most since? The Palestinians had certainly lost the most.

Laying aside the letter and photos from Georgina's father, I thought about my most recent encounters with the Beirut micro world recreated by the Lebanese partiers, in the South of France. During my stay with Mona, I had adapted right back to it, but there was no substance in their hall of mirrors.

Joe had asked me, "What do you want?"

More than a year ago Omar had asked me the same thing. If I'd said to either of them "I want the truth" they would have laughed in my face. But such bald questions did reveal the truth of how they operated. I had to give them credit for mastering the art of exploiting needs and greed. And they excelled at manipulating naiveté, like mine. But what did they want? I had never asked because I'd assumed they'd never give me a straight answer. A simple life with people who told the truth was inconceivable to them.

Joe had cautioned me about love, insinuating I was a fool to believe in it, or Omar.

"Only the bitches get ahead," he had said with great certainty.

Was this an accurate reflection of the Lebanese mentality? If so, its costs were terribly high. Having little or no faith in the most intimate of our relationships did not augur well for the public ideals of civic life or governance. It was a bit of a stretch, but for me this refusal to believe in love or fidelity, was a contributing factor in the destruction of Lebanon. Any country has reached a dangerous tipping point when a majority believes cheating is smart. Once lying is elevated above truth telling, the rot of corruption has set in. The same could happen anywhere including the US.

Beirut and Paris had not turned me into a bitch. Instead that kind of thinking had made me look harder at where those beliefs eventually led. The ruins of Beirut were warning enough for me. As my patience waned with Georgina, so too did my belief in this quest. I did not want to follow her example or Omar's.

* * * *

The following night I went to dinner at Sylvie's. Our friendship had blossomed over the past several months. My word for Sylvie was *drôle* (droll) because of her wry sense of humor. Mohamed, Sylvie's Algerian boyfriend of several years, had promised to cook the North African specialty dish, couscous. Semolina grains accompanied this intricately spiced meat and vegetable stew instead of rice. The French loved couscous the way the British loved their Indian curry. Sylvie had started joining Irina and me at the hammam Saint Paul on our regular Friday nights. Sitting in the heat together, sweating profusely, we amused ourselves telling jokes and inventing outrageous kidnapping plots.

Climbing to the fifth floor of her pre-war building that evening, the rich aroma reached me before I got to their door. The pot of lamb, beef, and chicken was simmering on the stove, with marrows, carrots, tomatoes, onions, chickpeas, potatoes, cumin and other spices. This was a couscous royale, to be served with fried Merquez lamb sausages, long, thin, and red with peppery spices.

I gave Sylvie the bottle of Algerian Sidi Bou Said red wine, and bizoux greetings, before washing my hands to help Mohamed. In the kitchen at the stove, with an apron wrapped around his middle, he was rubbing the softening grains between his palms. I wanted to learn to prepare this dish, which was fast becoming my favorite. The semolina grains had to be steamed, three times, and rubbed by hand with oil or butter to separate them. These steps were rarely done in restaurants where the specialty never tasted as rich as the homemade version. In early 1980s couscous was still being served more often than any other dish in Paris restaurants.

We had a gregarious evening. I met several new people, including a French woman who had lived in France's former colonies of Senegal, Malawi, and the Ivory Coast. She'd regaled us with tales of life there and gave me a ride home, a little after eleven o'clock.

When I got home my phone was ringing.

"We're having a party!" Mona said, her tone a mixture of overly bright and peevish. "Where have you been? We've been trying to reach you all evening."

"Sorry Mona," I began, annoyed at having to explain myself. This was the first time I'd heard from her since returning from my ten-day stay at her place in Nice.

"I was out, having dinner with friends. Are you in Paris?"

"Yes, I got here last night. Georgina's here too. She's asking about you," she replied. "Listen, we're sending the driver over to get you. Give him your address."

"I —" started to ask, whose party, where, but the receiver was already being passed to the chauffeur. Music playing in the background sounded like "*Habbaytak Bissayf*" ("I Loved You In Summer"), my favorite tune by Fayrouz the famed Lebanese singer. A lump formed in my throat.

"Your address please," a man asked, his Lebanese accent similar to Mona's.

"#15 Quai de Bourbon, in the fourth arrondissement on Île Saint-Louis," I replied, feeling both resigned and intrigued.

"I will be there in fifteen minutes," the man assured me. "I will call you from downstairs on the car phone when I arrive."

In the next twenty minutes, I threw some clothes back on. Sure enough the phone rang as promised. Soon we were gliding along the black waters of the River Seine in a shiny gold Rolls Royce. The brother-in-law of Adnan Khashoggi, a wealthy Saudi businessman I'd met in New York years ago, was also in the back seat. We exchanged pleasantries. Small world. Small talk. We were heading towards the luxury apartments in Neuilly, Paris's expensive suburb.

Mona met us at the door with effusive air kisses. Taking my hand, she led me into the living room to meet the others. Hanging prominently in the entryway was a large, framed portrait of the assassinated Lebanese Christian president-elect, Bashir Gemayel.[40] This clue helped orient me to the politics of whomever this place belonged to. Bashir had been dead for almost four years now. His older brother Amine Gemayel had assumed his place and was Lebanon's current president.

The Palestinians had been wrongly accused of killing president-elect Bashir. When the truth finally came out, we learned it had been one of his fellow Maronite Christians. Habib Shartoni had planted the TNT inside the Beirut headquarters of the Phalange Party. The explosion collapsed the three-story building, killing 26 instantly and wounding another 100. Shartoni, since convicted and imprisoned, had said Bashir "deserved to die because of his cooperation with the Israelis."

Elie Hobeika,[41] Bashir's bodyguard, had assumed the Palestinians were responsible. On September 16th, 1982 he led 150 Christian Phalangist fighters into the Sabra and Shatila refugee camps to wreak revenge. They proceeded to slaughter 2,463 men, women and children.[42]

The invading Israeli troops in Lebanon, under the command of General Ariel Sharon that September, had kept the camps surrounded to allow no escape while the butchery continued for the next three days and nights. The Israeli government had the massacre investigated by Kahan Commission, while found General Sharon "bears personal responsibility." Yet he became Israel's prime minister nineteen years later. A stroke soon afterwards rendered him mute and motionless for the remainder of his days.

The 1982 Israeli invasion of Lebanon and the Shabra and Shatila camp massacres had led to the creation of Hezbollah, the Party of God, a lethal political and military force. They may have been responsible for the assassination of AUB president Malcolm Kerr and many others.

As I greeted Georgina, repeating the air kisses, I thought of the note

---

[40] Bashir Gemayel had vowed to rid Lebanon of both the Syrian Army and the Palestinians. He'd conspired with the Israelis to accomplish this. When they invaded Lebanon, in June of 1982, the Israelis had a deal with Bashir Gemayel. He would sign a peace accord with them and together they would wipe out the Palestinian "problem." But Bashir had been killed before taking office.
[41] Elie Hobeika, the sadistic head of security for the Christian Phalangists, also met a violent end. Nicknamed Cobra, he deceived many colleagues and turned against the Israelis too, becoming a Syrian political puppet. A car bomb killed him in 2002.
[42] PLO leader Arafat "was shown a videotape of the massacre. He angrily told reporters Phil Habib [the American President's envoy] had personally signed a paper pledging [the Americans] to protect the Palestinians living in the refugee camps." (From Kai Bird's book *The Good Spy*).

found in the bloody breast pocket of her Palestinian husband, Ali Hassan Salameh in January 1979. Bashir Gemeyal had personally penned him a warning, despite the supposed enmity between the two. Both men had died in violent explosions, four years apart.

Georgina gave me a top to toe regard, and remarked, "You look wonderful. You've changed — a lot. For the better." Her compliment was genuine and so was my "Thank you."

I couldn't say the same of Georgina. I did my best to conceal my shock at her appearance. The former Miss Universe looked awful. Her pupils were dilated, her face was pallid and puffy, her skin sagged beneath her chin. Her voice had shifted downward, settling in a deeper, smokier register. No make up. Only an oversized white cotton shirt and a pair of washed out blue jeans.

Just as Beirut has destroyed itself, Georgina seemed to be disintegrating.

Mona escorted me round the room. I shook hands with the others, fewer than ten in all.

Taking my seat on the sofa, between Mona and Georgina, I watched the beauty queen drain her scotch and rise to pour herself another glass.

"What can I bring you from the bar?" she asked on her way to the other side of the room.

"A Campari and soda, thanks."

Over the next two and a half hours, Georgina refilled her scotch glass at least four times. I waited for her to bring up the subject of our book. Eventually she did: "I still mean to do it. I just haven't got the time now."

The same excuses, a year and a half into this project. How much longer would I wait? As much as I had wanted to tell her story, I had to accept it was never going to happen. My inner conflicts were resolved. As the ice cubes in my glass melted and swirled in their red liquid, I made up my mind. It was time to tell her I was done with it all.

"That's too bad Georgina, because I haven't got any more time left to wait for you." The words were out. No way to take them back.

She glanced over at Mona, and her friend registered surprise too, but said nothing as Georgina sank back down into the couch cushions.

"I'm going to go ahead and use what I've got. You will still be in it, of course, but not as the main character. It will not be the book I originally intended to write, but you...may never have the time. I just hope my book won't cause you any trouble when it comes out."

After being at the whim of this woman's frequent trips, sudden delays, postponed meetings, and relayed excuses from her Filipino maids, I had finally broken free. I would figure out something else.

While my words registered no one said anything for a few moments.

Our host removed a photograph from the red leather briefcase laid across his knees. "Remember this?" he asked Georgina as she took the black and white picture from his hand.

"It was my wedding in Beirut," she replied, so the rest of us could hear.

"We didn't know each other then," he added, his pronunciation of the word "know" implied Biblical connotations.

Georgina pointed at a handsome man standing behind her in the crowd of well-dressed guests in the photograph. "He was a dabke dancer. He killed himself. He jumped from a balcony at the Cairo Sheraton Hotel in 1976." Her tone was matter-of-fact.

So many people she'd known were dead, yet Georgina seemed curiously detached, untouched, at a remove from all the tragedies in her life, her family, her country. I had thought that much death and dying affected people, could even ennoble them, but Georgina's eyes had not deepened. What sort of affect had I expected? If such suffering does not endow us with greater knowledge and wisdom, what chance was there for any redemption?

Only a bleary fatigue registered upon Georgina's face. A drinker's face, rather like my father's.

I looked at the other profoundly dis-spirited guests. The socializing was forced and joyless. The liveliest things in the room were the whiskey glasses, going up and down, hand to mouth, constantly replenished. Hadn't Georgina herself said, "No one is optimistic anymore."

I did not want to be like this group of ghosts. I wanted real joy. I wanted to live. At three thirty in the morning I said my goodbyes, shaking each hand and kissing each cheek because I knew this was my final farewell, to them and the Beirut of our past. This evening had proven there was nothing left, nothing to understand, except more pain. My decades of emotional dependence had come to this realization, that ghosts and phantoms had no substance. All that Rizk (sustenance in Arabic) had been squandered, stolen or strangled. I felt a pang of sorrow then, for having been one more needy person, seeking to wrest something from Georgina. Her needs dwarfed mine. What a bitter truth. I felt powerless now, to respond in kind or with kindness anymore. It was over.

Georgina rode down in the elevator with me, insisting I call her tomorrow, "We must get together soon," she repeated, the words mingling with her whiskey breath. Had she heard what I said? My decision was final, not some feint or manipulation.

I would call again, just to confirm Georgina could not keep a promise. For her there might always be excuses but for me, real work was waiting. Since I doubted we would ever meet again, I took one last look before walking out the door.

The low-slung moon in the late night sky shone through the window as I settled into the deep leather seat in the back of the speeding Rolls alone. Perhaps my attachments were like lunar phases, waxing and waning. Arabia,

Lebanon, my men, even Georgina, each with their darkness and light, generated and reflected, like my own. I had tried my best but I had aimed at the wrong target. Relinquishing my attempt to tell Georgina's story was like letting go of Mon Fantôme. It was time to face a deeper truth. Neither phantom had been an antidote to Beirut's betrayals, they were more of the same.

CYNTHIA F. DAVIDSON

Chapter 19

CE LE MOMENT OU JAMAIS /
IT'S NOW OR NEVER

Self-knowledge is no guarantee of happiness, but it is on the
side of happiness and can supply the courage to fight for it.

— SIMONE DE BEAUVOIR

June 1985

In the middle of June 1985 I was in my little studio, catching up on
correspondence, and planning to meet Irina later at the hammam as my
reward. Turning on the television to the familiar Antenne 2 channel, I heard
the first announcement in French after the introductory music, "Details are
still coming in, but a TWA plane on a regularly scheduled flight from
Athens to Rome was hijacked today, shortly after takeoff. The aircraft and
its passengers are on the runway in Beirut." The hijackers were members of
Hezbollah and the Islamic Jihad. They were demanding the release of seven
hundred fellow Shia Muslims from Israeli jails.

"The hijackers have released all passengers on Flight 847 except for the
thirty-nine Americans. Their Shia brethren are being held without trial. To
dramatize the seriousness of their demands, they have shot one of the
passengers, a young American Navy diver. His body has been dumped on
the tarmac. They say they will blow up the plane and the rest of the
passengers if their demands are not met. We will bring you more details as
the story develops."

I snapped right back into panic mode. Obviously I was not yet done
with Lebanon and its torments. Having flown TWA through Beirut so
often, I could have easily been on that plane, likewise my family or friends.
Perhaps I knew someone on board. Would the remaining passengers be
executed like the Navy diver, Robert Stethem? The chances for a peaceful

343

resolution seemed doubtful. So many hostages[43] were being held in Lebanon now: Arabs, Americans, French, West Germans, and others.

Those hostages in Israeli prisons were also being held without trial. Despite the millions in aid money the US gave to Israel annually, the Israelis did whatever they wanted, and they preferred Entebbe-style rescue missions. This time Americans had been singled out, not the Jews or Israelis. Could the US government force these hijackers to negotiate? Was Iran or Syria behind this group? Among those thirty-nine American passengers, how many even knew the names of Iran or Syria's presidents? Their lives depended upon one of them and the whims of their followers.

Every two-bit, gun-toting bandit in Beirut knew how lucrative hostage taking could be, and how spectacularly it could be used to focus attention on one's cause. After the Iranian student revolutionaries seized sixty US Embassy staffers inside the US Embassy in Tehran in 1979, the whole world was forced to pay attention to Ayatollah Khomeini's new Islamic Republic, at least for those 444 days. I had been on the foreign desk at the CBS Nightly News during those days and saw how that crisis was handled. All three networks blew their news budgets covering the story.

Because the plight of those American captives led the news broadcasts every night, the Iranians had us over a proverbial barrel. They forced us to pay $5,000 a minute for whatever video footage they chose to send and they sent the same video to all three networks. We could not shut off their satellite feed after what we'd seen. Grimly we joked about how we were subsidizing the revolution via the ridiculous fees we were paying to the Ministry of Information.

In the spring of 1980, President Carter authorized a rescue mission but nothing went according to plan. A sandstorm in Iran reduced visibility to near zero at the staging point and wreaked havoc on US equipment not designed to cope with such conditions. An American helicopter crashed into a transport plane, triggering an explosion and a fire that killed eight US service members. It was a terrible day in the newsroom too. As we took in the satellite feed from the crash site, we saw the Iranian troops celebrating. They were dancing with the charred skulls of the dead Americans raised on their swagger sticks in front of the camera. Both my boss the Foreign Editor, Brian Ellis and our Managing Editor, Walter Cronkite decided not to show this footage to the American public. And the other networks also withheld those images, fearing ordinary Americans might take things into their own hands and charter planes to Iran, if they saw such desecration.

But Americans had not felt desperate enough to do things, like hijack

---

[43] Many hostages were taken in the decade between 1982 and 1992 when the Lebanese Civil War was at its height. A total of 104 foreign hostages were seized then and eight died in captivity.

Syrian or Iranian airliners, to force the release of their fellow citizens being held captive in Teheran or Beirut. Such an idea seemed outside our realm of contemplation. Likewise few Americans could comprehend the thinking of those who did such things, although the behavior of radicalized Muslims closely resembles that of Christian fundamentalists and the early Christian martyrs, unafraid to die for their cause and glorifying martyrdom.

The handling of that particular incident, that self-censorship at CBS, finalized my decision to leave the news business. The truth is the truth. It needs to be told. Americans bragged about our freedom of the press. Yet when it came right down to it, I'd seen other examples of voluntary censorship and exclusion. What else had been withheld over the years and why? The more I learned about the rationale of television news executives, the less I wanted to be like them, or risk my life and limbs in pursuit of stories the establishment did not want told.

The man who had sent us that gut-wrenching video was Sadegh Ghotbzadeh, who soon became head of the Iranian Ministry of Information. Cronkite's nickname for him was "Goats breath" which he said once on air by accident. The Georgetown University educated Ghotbzadeh had been Khomeini's press attaché during the Ayatollah's exile in France. When the 1979 Islamic revolution drove out the US backed Shah, Khomeini returned triumphantly to take over Iran. Ghotbzadeh's star rose too. Eventually, after heading up the Ministry of Information he became Iran's Foreign Minister and even ran for the Iranian presidency, unsuccessfully.

But three scant years after that revolution, Sadegh Ghotbzadeh was shot by a firing squad, executed against the wall of Tehran's notorious Evin prison. Accused by his competitors, of plotting against the Supreme Leader, his death was also a warning to all Iranians who spoke English, harbored non-Islamic ideas, and had too many friends in the West. This type of risk is taken by all multilinguists and those bridging gaps between warring worldviews.

Before he died, Ghotbzadeh alleged that the presidential candidate Ronald Reagan and the Republicans had colluded with him to delay the release of the American hostages. This strategy was a way to disgrace incumbent Democratic President Carter and prevent his reelection in 1980. It worked. Carter lost by a landslide. The Iranians released the American hostages the day of Reagan's swearing in. The Republicans had pulled one over on the God-fearing former peanut farmer from Georgia. Previous Republican President Nixon had engineered something similar, sabotaging peace talks between North and South Vietnam, to win re-election. His other nefarious activities had forced him to resign in disgrace in the summer of 1974, the first US president to do so.

This ruthlessness rippled outward from politicians, palaces, and parliamentary buildings the world over. When first learning about such things in the Middle East, I had not suspected they were equally true in the US, but over time the universality of corruption became obvious.

* * * *

At the hammam later that evening, Irina and I discussed the latest hijacking in Beirut and speculated upon the fate of the thirty-nine American hostages. She reminded me how few Russians had ever been taken.[44] As we laid in silence afterwards, on the wooden slatted chairs and took the heat into our bodies, fewer negative flashbacks surfaced to me to deal with. That was a relief. The shadows of repressed memories were no longer holding me hostage.

Late that night as I fell asleep in my loggia bed, I recalled my father's torments with powerlessness and grief, and the times he'd been held hostage in Beirut. Both had happened in 1975, the opening year of the war, when I'd been living in Caracas. The first kidnapping was short and brutal. The Mourabituon (Sentinels) had taken over our Rue May Ziade neighborhood in that summer of 1975. A socialist, pro-Nasser, pan-Arabist militia, they were primarily Sunni Muslims. They had grabbed dad off the street, roughed him up in their car, and dumped him back on the sidewalk in less than an hour. None spoke much English but he'd understood their message. "Buy your black market cigarettes, gas and alcohol from us, or else. We run this section of the city now."

The second time, in December of 1975, was more serious. By then the police had disappeared and the Lebanese Army had disintegrated into Muslim and Christian factions after failing to quell the Palestinian uprising in the city's refugee camps. In the absence of law and order, roving gangs of various militiamen set up roadblocks, and extorted cash "taxes" from those leaving or entering the territories they controlled.

For weeks dad had not been able to go to work. Beirut airport was closed. Its runways were too near the Palestinian camps and the aircraft made tempting targets during takeoffs and landings. A deal had to be struck with some Palestinian strong enough to prevent the other groups from shooting down the planes. Navigating on the ground was equally

---

[44] Three months later, four Soviet diplomats became the only Russians ever kidnapped in Beirut. When the Soviet group sent to rescue them learned the Islamic Liberation Organization kidnappers had killed the Soviet consular attaché, the Alpha commandos grabbed one of the kidnappers relatives, castrated him, killed him, and cut him to pieces. They sent the grisly proof to the kidnappers and threatened to do the same to other relatives. The remaining hostages were hastily dropped off nearby the Soviet Embassy soon afterwards and no one dared to seize another Soviet citizen.

dangerous. Airline employees had to drive through too many factions' roadblocks to reach the airport. Neighborhoods had changed hands several times already, and they were likely to do so again. In the uneasy winter of 1975, snipers lurked on rooftops, monitoring every move made by other fighters hiding behind the blackened window frames of burnt, looted buildings on the contested streets of most city blocks.

Mundane errands became matters of life and death. Getting water, food, electricity, or medicine required heroic efforts. The banks had not been open in six weeks. In the days before ATMs, one stood in line to see a bank teller to make a withdrawal or deposit. Hearing a rumor that the banks would open during a ceasefire that day, my father got up early. He joined those forming a line outside the local bank that morning. The men waiting with him were jittery, glancing around in fear since any parked car might contain a remote controlled bomb. Everyone knew there would be a run on the banks and all the cash would be gone by noon. No one had come to deposit anything, only to make withdraws. Inflation had arrived so no one accepted credit anymore. The prices rose constantly, especially for staples like rice, sugar, coffee, and bread. In the latest wave of robberies, even the British Bank of the Middle East had been cleaned out. I'd seen pictures in the newspapers of its plundered safe deposit boxes, littering the floor like toys, twisted by oversized monsters.

The airport was supposed to open that day too, so Dad had dressed in his MEA uniform. After visiting the bank, he planned to drive on to the airport. The airline had decided to relocate the flight crews and ferry the aircraft to safer places like Saudi Arabia. By offering limited service, from outside Lebanon, they hoped to keep the airline afloat financially. Dad waited at the bank until its metal doors were finally pushed opened by the heavily armed guards.

When his turn came, he pushed his withdrawal slip through the old fashioned grillwork at the window and watched the harried, middle-aged clerk. He counted out $5,000 US dollars worth of Lebanese lira using his excessively long pinky fingernail to count the bills. All Lebanese moneychangers grew these nails, expressly for this purpose.

After stuffing the bulging envelope into his inner suit pocket, dad left the bank, and got into his dusty Volkswagen to drive back to the underground garage beneath the Rue May Ziade apartment building he still called home. In the privacy of the subterranean darkness, he unzipped his ankle high black boots and removed his socks. Dividing the money into equal piles, he laid the cash against his bare soles and slipped each sock back on. This held the bills in place as he pulled on his boots. He'd learned this trick during his Navy days, when he also began to stash his pack of cigarettes against his ankle inside his sock.

Now he had to get to the airport. Because the neighborhoods between

Ras Beirut and the airport were a series of battle zones, the airline employees had decided to form a convoy for safety's sake. After converging at the meeting point, they fell in behind one another, their cars moving like a funeral procession. Winding through the rubble-strewn streets, they saw the piles of uncollected trash and the splintered glass glinting everywhere on the pockmarked sidewalks. It was not safe for garbage trucks to do pickups, nor was mail delivered anymore. Water and electricity worked only a few hours per day if at all. A telephone line with a signal was a luxury.

The negotiated ceasefire seemed to be holding, at least for today. Their little caravan of cars was waved through the series of roadblocks without being stopped and forced to show their identity cards or passports. When passing the dividing lines between the factions, they saw evidence of the worst fighting. Burnt furniture had fallen through the concussed walls and shattered windows of residential and commercial buildings. Many structures were beyond repair, their walls were riddled with holes after the continuous machine gunfire and rocket propelled grenades. Overkill. Emotions completely out of control.

Nearing the airport, at a traffic roundabout near the Sabra and Shatila Palestinian refugee camps, a mud spattered car suddenly entered from a side road. It prevented my father's Volkswagen from exiting the ring road to remain with the convoy. As the other cars stayed in line and left the traffic circle to turn onto airport road, the gun-waving men in the dark car gesticulated and shouted at him. My father braked and put his hands up.

What could his colleagues do? In their rearview mirrors they watched what was happening but instinct kept them moving. He hoped they would send word and do something to get him rescued if they reached the airport. No one had wanted to discuss their options if something like this occurred but the thoughts kept them awake. Most of the airline employees still in Beirut drank themselves to sleep each night. Fatalism also helped them cope with their situation, along with macabre jokes. Sharing war stories was one thing but each of them knew no amount of tough talk could ever stop a bullet with your name on it.

A second car joined the keffiyeh draped driver and his cohorts in the first one. My father realized he was being escorted elsewhere and suspected the destination was the notorious "Sabra Hilton" where kidnap victims were routinely taken by the Palestinians. Like most other groups, they were in the ransom business. Its profits paid for additional weapons and ammunition. Some captives were targeted for their information, or to intimidate relatives with resources. Sometimes unintended hostages were scooped up and kept until decisions were made, about how best to take advantage of them. Hostages were traded when competing militias had seized the men. As with all social breakdowns, there were "professionals" who thrived in the chaos like the psychopaths and torturers whose "creativity" knew no bounds in this lawless place. The gruesome condition of the body, of my dead journalist friend Salim El Lawzi, and others was sufficient evidence of this.

The cars flanking my dad's ignored all the stop signs and sped on. The traffic signal lights no longer worked. The bulbs had all been shot out earlier that year in a perverse kind of target practice, which was also responsible for the absence of all birds, and their songs, in the smoldering hell of Beirut. Metal gates suddenly opened to admit the cars into an enclosed area and the guards swung them shut just as swiftly. Hustled out of his Volkswagen, dad purposely left his uniform hat with its black patent visor and shiny brass MEA logo pin, on the passenger side front seat as a clue. He hoped someone would see it as confirmation he was being held there. His black leather flight kit, with its tools, flashlight, and flight log would be rummaged through, as would his suitcase. He doubted he'd ever see those items again even if he was lucky enough to be released.

Brought to a main office area, a man in green military fatigues addressed him by name. "Mr. Fetterolf, you've worked for MEA how many years now?" He was holding dad's American passport.

Before entering this room, two other men had patted my father down and had passed the confiscated passport to the interrogator boss who spoke excellent English. The fact that he worked for MEA might offer a bit of leverage as these men were professionals. Dad could tell they'd been doing this a lot longer than his Mourabitoun kidnappers. After a few more questions dad realized the man in charge already knew all the answers. My father was taken downstairs and locked in a cell. He had no idea what might happen next. Not knowing was the worst part.

"They made me strip that night," he later recounted. "After the day shift, the men on overnight duty wanted some amusement. I think they let me keep my socks on because it was December and very cold that night. They never found the cash. They waved an electrified cattle prod at me, mainly to intimidate and humiliate, and show me who was boss," he explained to us after his ordeal.

"Thirty-six hours later a man from MEA arrived with a briefcase and I was released. I even got my car, flight kit, and suitcase back," he marveled. My father was never told what was inside that case and he never asked. Cash? Ticket vouchers? He felt indebted to the company after being rescued. His loyalty kept him with MEA for another seven punishing years, some of it spent living on a Greek freighter in Jeddah harbor, when the airline could not afford hotel accommodations for its employees.

He'd told his story when all of us congregated in York, PA to celebrate the Christmas holidays with my maternal grandparents that December of 1975. Such a family reunion had not happened in years. Prior to the kidnapping, my mother and brother had fled the fighting in Beirut. After spending a harrowing night in the parking garage, while their apartment building was looted, and the Hagazian Armenian College burned nearby, they took an extended hiatus. For awhile they stayed with other expat friends in Paris hoping the war would end. But as the fighting dragged on, it became apparent that the schools would not reopen. It was too dangerous. My mother moved back to Pennsylvania temporarily so my brother could finish high school. He was never sent to a boarding school. My parents would also pay his college tuition, and advance him the down payment to buy a house. Patriarchy is designed to provide its sons more advantages, while handicapping the daughters, and this truth was borne out in our family too.

* * * *

A decade after the tragic events in Beirut, I was still trying to shake them off in Paris. And despite the continuous manmade mayhem in our world, it was the mild, golden weather I appreciated in June of 1985. Taking my customary Sunday stroll from Île Saint-Louis towards the Champs-Élysées, I noted the light and fluffy dresses worn by the passing women. They rivaled the frilly finery of the trees summer leaves. After winter's trials and privations, nature was trying to woo us back. That April when it had snowed in Paris, I'd sworn never to spend another winter in Europe. Did I want to be won over again, against my better judgment?

Reaching Fouguet's cafe, I had just enough time for *un grand creme* before seeing the new film, *Le Thé Au Harem d'Archimedes*. Mehdi Chareef, a young Arab immigrant had written the script. The title was a play on words. Instead of *Le Theorem de'Archimedes* (The Theory of Archimedes), it translated as "tea in the harem of Archimedes." Twenty-three centuries ago, the Greek philosopher Archimedes had attempted to describe the workings of the universe through its basic principles. Since then many others had tried to do the same. (And so would I, a decade later, with my Wisdom Wheel.) I glanced around the cafe while waiting for my coffee. Something uncomfortable hung in the atmosphere of its plush, red interior. Two old women sat at a far table. Their dyed black hair was teased high above their foreheads, plastered with ghostly makeup. Were they former call girls? Fouquets was a place they frequented. You could spot them, applying their lipstick in public, signaling their readiness to entertain the next customer. A few months ago I had been mistaken for one. Standing on the sidewalk in the predawn darkness outside the ICM offices, I'd awaited my colleague coming with the office key. The drivers of passing vehicles had slowed down to take a better look at me. A few had called out, "Ça fait combien l'heure?" (How much per hour?)

Embarrassed and flustered I had made a big show of switching my briefcase from one hand to another, and looking at my watch, trying to pantomime a different message. Despite being dressed in a regular raincoat, with a briefcase in hand and a scarf on my head, they'd persisted. Spotting an unaccompanied female had been enough to trigger them.

This afternoon, I studied these harridans. What had their lives been like? Darkly malevolent, staring out of kohl-ringed eyes, they wordlessly surveyed this battleground. Death heads I thought with a shudder as the haunting image resurfaced of the used up old whore hanging from the electric light cord, in a deserted Beirut apartment.

Having lost my appetite, I took two sips when my coffee arrived and put down exact change and left for the cinema.

Emerging two hours later, after seeing the film, I was more depressed. Mehdi Chareef's movie was a dismally accurate portrayal of immigrant life in the subsidized housing projects on the outskirts of Paris. The French government had encouraged the first generation of North Africans to come to France. At the time their globalizing conglomerates had needed cheap labor, to build Renault cars, and work in other factories. Economic prospects in Algeria, Morocco, and Tunisia were bleak. Families much like Omar's and Mimo's had exchanged their farms and village homes, in the former French colonies, for this desolate industrial landscape outside Paris. There they tried to raise their bicultural kids while risking the mire of hopelessness when those jobs moved back offshore.

Scruffy bars and grimy cafes squatted between the graffiti covered concrete apartment blocks. Petty thieves and hustlers reigned in the alleys while the rats rattled the *poubelles* (trashcans). By dint of ambition, chance and the willingness to do anything, Omar and Mimo had managed to escape this, to some degree. But where would they, or any of their kids end up, if they remained in France and did not make it? As other moviegoers streamed past me, I paused to get my bearings. Remembering the nearest metro station was Franklin, I walked towards it thinking of the four term US president it was named after.

While FDR was in the White House, the country had endured a Great Depression. "The only thing we have to fear is fear itself," he had said, but it was corruption, recklessness and the unequal distribution of wealth that spawned the era's poverty. When the Second World War started it created a great demand for weapons, planes, tanks and ships. The US had geared up to manufacture these, profiting financially, before sending our boys over to die, in that European war. After US troops helped defeat the Nazis, and their Fascist allies, we helped ourselves to the spoils, remaining overseas to fill the power vacuum left by the war-depleted empires. In the process we became one, lording it over the world. Which war would bring on the US coup de grâce? It was all too predictable unless we did something different to break the sorry chain of consequences. Unpopular foreign wars, bleeding the treasury dry, and fomenting unrest at home as taxes were raised to pay for them. Even the Romans had learned that lesson the hard way.

Continuing towards the metro station, I passed a kiosk where a headline caught my eye. "Former Lebanese President Sarkis Dead." Only sixty, he'd just died of cancer here in Paris on the 28th of June 1985. His predecessor, Suleiman Frangieh, had been responsible for inviting the Syrian Army into Lebanon, "for the sake of peace and order," he promised at the time. The Syrians would overstay their welcome by thirty years. Militaries do not excel at exit strategies. Invasions are their specialty.

I fumbled in my purse for my Carte Orange pass while going down the steps with the crowd of metro passengers. Once through the station doors, I inserted my reusable cardboard ticket into the machine slot that releases the turnstile. As I went through, two young men vaulted over it. Decidedly Arab in appearance, they risked being fined if caught without tickets. If they could not pay the fine in cash on the spot, the police would arrest and jail them.

On the platform another young man was waiting for the train. Regarding his reflection in the glass protecting an advertisement poster, he fluffed his black curls with his fingers. Vanity sometimes thy name is man, I thought wryly. Noticing me watching, he turned in my direction. I lowered my gaze and stared at the tracks below littered with candy wrappers and cigarette butts. I guessed he might be Iranian, with that complexion and abundant hair. The train arrived quietly on its rubber wheels. I opened the door that stopped in front of me. He followed, boarding the same almost empty compartment, waiting to see where I'd sit. When he took the seat facing mine I didn't feel threatened. He smiled shyly. The corners of my mouth curved though I turned to peer out the window. The buzzer sounded and the doors closed as the train pulled out of the station.

"Where are you from?" he inquired, in English, with a hard to place accent.

"America," I answered. "Sort of. And you?" I did not want to get involved with a stranger on a train but the habit of being polite was so ingrained.

"Greece," he replied.

Was my relief audible?

* * * *

Autumn 1985

For the next several months I threw myself into my work, welcoming its distractions, enjoying the people I met and the training sessions I conducted. Busy with Intercultural Management programs at IBM's European headquarters on the outskirts of Paris, I also traveled a lot, to places like Turkey and Egypt on contract work for my old New York employer. The president of that American company, Brian Moran, asked me to set up a meeting with the president of the French company I worked with in Paris. So I arranged their get together while back in Paris briefly.

Performing the introductions on the appointed morning I explained, "Brian Moran, this is Charles Gancel, president of ICM." The two men shook hands and we took our seats around the conference table. The small talk went to a leading question often used by the French when sizing someone up.

"How was your last vacation?" Charles inquired. Europeans regularly pegged your status by where you spent your holidays.

"Oh, I haven't had time for a vacation in the last five years," Brian boasted. "I'm far too busy developing our company."

Charles glanced at me, raising an eyebrow. That answer landed badly. It immediately ruined any chances for a partnership. Oblivious to any of this, Brian further exacerbated this negative impression by declaring shortly afterwards that he was in a hurry.

"I don't want to waste your time so I'll get right to the point. My company is interested in buying yours."

Charles demurred, trying to be charming. "We know you are interested, but this is a bit like a courtship. Even when both parties want to marry they still have to get to know each other."

Later, after the meeting concluded and we left the conference room, Charles confided to me, "That man doesn't know how to live. We could never do business with him. He's a checkbook cowboy."

Their exchange left me the task of interpreting why negotiations had stalled. Brian had never taken any of the cross-cultural training courses sold by his firm, and it cost him dearly. He laid his failure upon the French, "who didn't recognize a good deal when it was staring them in the face." Charles had also reacted with French bravado, attributing faults elsewhere, as we all tend to do.

Without directly quoting Charles, I explained to Brian it often took years to bridge cultural differences and build good working relationships. I asked him point blank, "How much time can you afford to spend wooing this opportunity?"

Already in a hurry and onto the next deal, as the post mortem debrief revealed, he was like a man being chased. This incident demonstrated how crucial small talk can be. Long before the mention of any price or selling points, the attitudes being revealed can torpedo any chance for partnership. Likewise, being curious and open-minded can pay handsomely.

* * * *

353

That autumn, while working on a program for General Dynamics and Pratt & Whitney in Beni Suef, Egypt, I discovered one of my former trainees had been among the thirty-nine American hostages hijacked that summer on TWA flight 847. Now employed on the Peace Vector Two[45] project, he agreed to come speak to the managers and wives as a resource person at my cross-cultural training sessions.

Most were surprised to hear his seventeen-day ordeal as a captive had left him more sympathetic to the Shia cause in Lebanon. He counseled these new expats to keep a low profile and not panic if such a thing happened to them. "Always be polite and show respect. That's what they want. It helps a lot if you know some of the language. Keep some of whatever they give you to eat too. You don't know when they will feed you again."

He explained why he'd chewed up his PX card. "After seeing the Navy diver singled out, I destroyed any proof of my service in the US military."
The US Navy diver Robert Stethem had been chosen because he was on active duty. After being beaten and shot, his body was thrown onto the runway from the parked plane to send a message. The remaining Americans had been released unharmed in the Syrian capital of Damascus. Reverend Jesse Jackson was credited for their safe return at the time. The Syrian dictator, Hafez el Assad was willing to negotiate with the black American civil rights activist, pastor, and politician. The Israelis released over 700 Shia prisoners over the next several weeks while denying it was related to the hijacking.

---

[45] Six separate Peace Vector programs have been implemented since US President Carter's historic Camp David accords, which specified that Egypt would re-equip its military with western weapons. Egypt is one of the world's top customers for the F-16 Fighting Falcon. The Egyptian Air Force has over 220 F-16s. Following the 2013 Egyptian coup d'état, the Pentagon said the jets would continue to be supplied, although this was in direct violation of US human rights legislation known as the Leahy amendments, which are supposed to prevent any American military assistance or weapons sales to leaders who violate human rights.

Chapter 20

VOYAGE AUX ÎLES CANARIES /
CANARY ISLANDS VOYAGE

What we believe to be the motives for our
conduct are usually but the pretexts for it.

— MIGUEL DE UNAMUNO

Spring 1986: Six Months Later

By the spring of 1986 the violence in the Middle East was spilling onto the streets of Europe. Bombings occurred almost weekly in Paris, thirteen in total that year. Avoiding the word terrorism, the French government labeled these attacks *les attentats*. Just after my thirty-second birthday that March, I bought a pair of earrings on sale at a Champs-Élysées boutique whose windows had been shattered by a bomb. Mes bouces d'orrielle d'attendat (my incident earrings). They prodded my conscience. I had come to Paris to accomplish a goal. But what power did a book have against so many bombs?

That April Simone de Beauvoir passed away. Reading her detailed obituary renewed my appreciation for women of intellect and tenacity. This French author had survived two world wars, economic upheavals, and great personal betrayals, yet de Beauvoir got her work done — and her lessons inspired me despite how poorly my initial introduction to her had gone. While working in Saudi Arabia in 1979, I had read her post Second World War landmark book *The Second Sex*. By then her 1949 classic was twice as old as I was. Its truths had threatened what little air remained in my romantic balloon. Practicing what she preached, de Beauvoir never married and had no children. A quick search through my journals turned up her quotations copied years ago:

"...her wings are cut and then she is blamed for not knowing how to fly."

355

"Man is defined as a human being and a woman as a female — whenever she behaves as a human being she is said to imitate the male."
"The body is not a thing, it is a situation: it is our grasp on the world and our sketch of our project."
"All oppression creates a state of war. And this is no exception."

After the mayhem of two world wars, de Beauvoir and her pal Jean Paul Sartre had not become mystics. They had rejected anything divine about the human situation and chose to describe life as an existential crisis. Because you existed, you were forced to choose, even in the absence of any good options. Her existence, and her passing, made me vow to pay greater attention to other women who had also been educated by life, especially in Paris. What had they learned and shared? To become a wiser woman, I needed wiser teachers.

That year I accepted every program offered to me by my old and new employers. By the end of that summer I had managed to save enough money to sit and write for four to six months. The constant work and extensive travels to Turkey and Egypt and elsewhere had taken their toll but it was time to decide two things. What to write about, now that collaborating with Georgina was no longer an option. And where I could afford to live while I did it. Paris was too distracting and expensive. With the changing exchange rate, the French franc had risen in value against the US dollar, almost doubling my rent.

Autumn 1986
On my first Friday back in France that September 1986, the weather was wonderfully warm as I strolled across Pont Marie to meet Irina at the hammam Saint Paul. We had a lot to catch up on. Irina was very worried about her mother. Bitterly she recounted how her mother's throat had almost swollen shut after she'd marched in the May Day parade in Kiev, Ukraine right after the Chernobyl nuclear plant explosion. On communism's most important annual holiday, the Soviet government had wanted the world to see their citizens celebrating, not cowering at home as they should have been. Fearing mass chaos, they had withheld the truth, denying the dangers of Chernobyl's radiation. But nearby European nations were monitoring the Chernobyl's radiation release and reported it accurately. Soon the morgues in Irina's hometown of Kiev were overflowing. By the first anniversary of the Chernobyl disaster, her mother had become much sicker and before the end of 1986, she died from thyroid

cancer.[46]

* * * *

After our bizoux and exchange of news, Irina told me, "Gustave asked how you're doing. He wanted me to pass along his greetings."

"You can tell him I'm alright, but I need to consult him again. He promised to pump some sunlight into me whenever my confidence waned. Now that everything is over with Georgina I don't know how to push on to the end of this writing project. Shall I turn my notes into a novel? I've never written fiction. My training was in journalism."

"Well, you have to tell these stories somehow and you know Gustave can help. He certainly pointed me in the right direction. I saw him while you were gone on your work trips. He told me a new man would be coming into my life...and he has."

Despite their steam-heated pinkness, a blush rose in her cheeks, accompanied by a telling oh lala look.

"Good for you!" I chortled. "You do seem more *bien dans ta peau* (well in your skin)." Irina knew less than two-dozen words in English so we always spoke French.

"He's quite the lover," she admitted bashfully. "We're doing things I've never done before. He works in a bank. He's French. Divorced. One child, a daughter. His name is François."

Smiling, I thought of all the times Irina had patiently listened to my woes over Omar. My heart went out to her.

"Amuse toi bien," I said. She deserved some satisfaction at this stage of her life. I suspected this man might keep her too busy to spend as much time with me but didn't mention that.

"Ah, life!" I joked. "It's too easy to have fun in France and avoid the hard work!"

"I'm enjoying this time," she said, "though who knows where this affair will go. I made an appointment with a plastic surgeon to have my eyes

---

[46] The explosion and fire at the Chernobyl nuclear plant in the Ukraine on April 26, 1985 caused the largest release of radiation in civil nuclear history. The copious amounts of radioactive iodine and cesium blowing across the Ukraine, Belarus, other parts of the USSR also reached the rest of Europe. In Sweden that summer of 1985, the strawberries were gigantic, full of the radionuclides carried by the borderless winds. Forty-seven Chernobyl workers died soon after the accident. Nine children perished from acute thyroid cancer shortly after. The entire town near the damaged nuclear reactor was permanently evacuated and tons of ground soil hauled away. Estimates of worldwide premature deaths attributable to Chernobyl's radioactive contamination varied widely, but the Russian publication Chernobyl, concluded the approximate total would be 985,000.

done." She pinched the upper skin of her eyelids. "He can tighten up this droopiness. And do a small incision to take up some lines here too," she explained, moving her fingers to a spot in front of her ears and pulling back the flesh of her cheeks.

Plastic surgery worried me. What about mistakes? Infections? After all, her father had died from a dirty needle. And she'd been badly infected after her episiotomy. At least she was already happy seeing someone and not taking this step in the hope of attracting a man and some romance.

Concerned I offered, "I'll take care of you after the operation."

"Oh, that shouldn't be necessary," she replied, "but I'd surely call you if it was." She patted my hand and we sat a while in companionable silence.

"I got the money for the plastic surgery operation from selling my first load of paintings," she confided.

"Oh! I forgot to ask what happened when you went back to the USSR." Miffed at myself, I remembered she'd not only gone to see her mother after the Chernobyl accident but to visit the widows of artists she'd known of. The initial idea to deal in art had come from Gustave several months ago. During a reading with him she'd inquired about the kind of work she might do to support herself.

"I see you in auction halls," he'd told her. Following up on his suggestion, she'd settled upon the idea of using her contacts to try auctioning Russian artwork.

"My ex-husband reduced my alimony by an additional 3,000 francs per month," she added. "I bet he's found out about François. And he told me he was taking our daughters to Cyprus during their summer vacation but he really took them to Lebanon. His mother wants to move back to Tripoli now. I doubt his new Russian whore wants to follow him there. Surely she sees him as her ticket to Paris."

Previously she had told me about the woman he was currently seeing in Moscow. I'd commiserated and warned her about losing her children. "You know Muslim men have the right to take their sons back at age seven and their daughters at age nine after a divorce. That's Sharia law. Don't let him take them there again. You would have a very hard time getting them back if he decided to keep them."

"I didn't know that," she said. "I will have someone care for them here when I do the next trip."

"You're going back to the USSR?"

"Yes. I need to buy more artwork. All the paintings I purchased last time sold quickly at the auction hall. I more than tripled my investment."

"That's wonderful! Let's celebrate," I responded, genuinely pleased for her.

"I've done more research. I have a better idea now, which widows to see next time. It was not as difficult as I thought. Most of the women were ready to meet with me. They're desperate for money. I had to tell them I had never done anything with art before and didn't have much capital. And no one knows if there is any market for the work of their dead husbands so I could not afford to pay much. I bought the canvases that looked salable to me but I am no artist. At the Moscow airport I had to pay the *pour boire* (bribe) and the excess baggage weight fees but they never examined my luggage and didn't see the paintings."

"How soon will you leave?"

"As soon as I can arrange for my girls to be taken care of. This has to be done quickly before people catch on and the government puts on tariffs and restrictions. I'll buy as much as I can next time. Maybe take a big truck load out, via Turkey if I can make a friend or contact at the borders, to be sure they'd pass through."

Seeing my friend in this light made me raise an eyebrow. I lifted an imaginary champagne glass to toast her, "Bravo! And I will definitely contact Gustave to get his advice on my future after seeing how accurate he's been about your success!" I promised.

Later that evening at home on TV, I saw Sade for the first time. In rich alto tones, the gorgeous half Nigerian half English woman sang "Smooth Operator." The perfect anthem for Omar I surmised, ruefully.

* * * *

The following week I met Gustave at a Rive Gauche apartment. Jovial on the phone when I'd called to make the appointment, he reminded me it had been almost a year since my first reading at his place in Versailles.

After my compliment on his Paris digs, he laughed. "I read for several ministers and government employees and that has its perks. One of them gave me this apartment to use whenever I want." Ah, the super rational French. They still needed help to balance their analytics with their romantic superstitions, and so did I.

He showed me into the salon. The airy attic room was filled with sunlight. Bare wooden beams supported its sloping roof, and the recessed skylights set between them framed the changeable art of the Parisian sky above the rooftops. Gustave indicated a chair on one side of the table and I settled into it. He took the opposite seat asking how things were going in my life.

After briefing him, I zeroed in on my main reason for this consultation. "I'm worried about getting this project done and not exactly sure how to proceed. Paris is too...distracting. I need to go someplace where no one knows me so I can hide away and do nothing but write!"

Smiling and nodding his shaggy head, he reached into the battered leather satchel lying beside his booted feet. Extracting a burgundy velveteen bag, he laid it on the table. Then he went to the low built-in bookcase and drew a large atlas from its shelves, putting it beside the bag on the table.

"We shall find where you can go to make this effort," he sighed. "From the windows or the doors, you must do it, or you will never write anything else." His tone was ominous. "Your creative pipes will remain clogged unless you get this done."

Opening the atlas he stopped at the map of the world, which covered two glossy pages. Satisfied, he shook the contents of the drawstring bag into his palm. A clear, pointed crystal, with a fine link chain attached to one end fell out. "This is a pendulum. Have you ever used one before?"

I shook my head.

"It's very simple and very accurate. Give me your hands."

Reaching both my palms out, turned upwards and open, he dropped the pointed crystal into my right hand. The chain curled beside it tickling slightly.

"Breathe upon it. You're right handed, n'est-ce pas?"

I nodded.

"Let your energy infuse the crystal and we'll see what it indicates. Forming the right question now is as important as clearly interpreting the response," he insisted.

After a pause for composure, I stated, "Please, by whatever powers there are in this universe, direct me to the proper place for this work, where I will be both safe and productive," I intoned.

"Good. Now we hold it over the map. If the crystal turns to your right, that is a 'yes.' If it twists to the left, it means 'no.'"

My curiosity was certainly piqued. Having never heard of such a thing, I wanted to see if the stone moved at all.

"How will I know you're not turning it?" I inquired.

"Oh, you're going to hold it. And we'll confirm the message, to read the results properly."

Taking another look at the map, I held up the crystal with my right hand, suspending it by the chain over the middle of the opened atlas. Nothing happened. No detectable movement.

"Relax," Gustave encouraged.

Resting my elbow on the table made the crystal relocate over the Pacific Ocean region. Almost imperceptibly, the point turned to the left. My eyes caught Gustave's and he smiled.

"Go on, slowly, keep searching."

After a while, my arm was tired. I changed hands, dropping the crystal into my left palm, and resting briefly before another try.

"Perhaps you'll have more luck with your non-dominant side. The left is the spirit side of your body. Less blocked up with the stuffing of preconceptions," he joked.

This time, before lifting the crystal over the atlas, I closed my eyes, determined to focus upon the feel of the movements instead of the locale on the map. After the initial stillness, the crystal started swaying clockwise for the first time. Controlling my urge to peek, I went with the movement, as certain that it had come to a different place, as I was that the crystal was turning on its own.

When the circling motions were regular and rhythmic, I had to see where this was happening. My inner skeptic was still looking for reasons to scoff but when my eyes opened, I saw a place I'd never heard of. It was out in the Atlantic Ocean off the coast of Spain. "The Canary Islands?"

"Haven't been there yet, have you?" commented Gustave. "Go ahead and confirm it now. Use your other hand."

Switching the pendulum to my right, I held it over the same spot. After a few seconds, it was definitely twirling to the right. Impressed, I nevertheless wanted to be totally convinced, as this was such a big decision.

"You do it!" I insisted, handing him the divinizing instrument.

"D'accord," he agreed. The same right circling results occurred. It was undeniable.

I studied the map more intently now. "There are seven islands." I noted. "How to know which is the right one?"

"That's not too difficult," he winked, flipping through the atlas to the page with the Spanish section of the flattened globe.

"We'll ask again now," he instructed, pointing to the page with the enlarged map of the area. I read off the names of the seven islands: Gran Canaria, Tenerife, Fuerteventura, Lanzarote, La Palma, La Gomera, and El Hierro.

Suspending the crystal for a final time, the movements were unmistakable as soon as I'd reached the town of Santa Cruz on Tenerife.

"Well, for the first time in my life, I'll be following rock solid guidance," I chuckled, intrigued by this divination process. Now with some direction, how would such a plan materialize? Leaving Gustave, I was committed to the idea that Tenerife was worth a try. If I got my affairs in order and trusted this guidance I would also figure out an alternative to my original Georgina writing project.

* * * *

Before the end of that September 1986 I was on a plane flying to Tenerife amazed once again at the efficiency of the universe. Once the decision was taken even my housing situation in Spain had fallen into place. One of Zvonimir's friends directed me to Teresa Pino, a Canarias friend, since their childhood pen pal days. Teresa and her husband Leoncio lived in Santa Cruz and had two teenage children. With their son in the US this year as an exchange student, they had a room available to rent in their apartment. The family would meet my flight tonight.

Leaving Paris had been equally smooth. Monsieur Masclet, my Quai de Bourbon landlord, agreed to keep my deposit for the final month's rent. This further supplemented my nest egg. Maria from the ICM office adopted Darius. They had already bonded while she'd cared for him during my extended work trips this year. Taking him along was not an option as the Spanish family had a dog. Irina agreed to store some of my things in her basement until the book was finished and my next move was determined.

My plan was to sit tight and write until after New Year 1987. Living with the Pino family meant no need for food shopping, preparing meals, or cleaning up afterwards. This cleared the decks for full time writing. Our arrangement also provided me an instant social circle, which beat sitting alone on a Spanish island. Both my French and American employers had agreed to revisit our arrangements after this hiatus when my project was done.

My journals were in the overhead compartment of the plane. Too precious to risk losing in the luggage hold, they'd made my carry-on bag excessively heavy. Could a novel be excavated from my Paris notes? Still hazy on the process, I could not bear to imagine all my efforts going to waste. The war had left far too much of that in its wake. In Beirut the bodies may have been buried but the psychic wreckage remained strewn everywhere.

Had my time in Paris been wasted? People were dying while I'd behaved like a spoiled libertine. Should I feel ashamed? No. Ecstasy had restored my will to live although my personal healing was hardly the end of the process. What could be done on behalf of others? Become an activist? Work in the refugee camps? Take a job with the United Nations Reliefs Work Agency or some other non-governmental organization? Those choices might assuage my survivor's guilt but they would do nothing to change minds. What I really wanted was to prevent these conflicts. To accomplish that we needed to address their root causes. The ignorance of the many enabled wars as much their profitability benefited the few. My deepest purpose had been to discover the truth, and educate myself, and share what I had learned in the hope of enlightening readers.

Since relinquishing the Georgina biography concept, the best alternative I'd come up with was a semi-autobiographical novel. Fiction was hardly my forté but other journalists had managed this crossover. Attempting another genre without any training, beyond the close reading of my favorite books, was daunting. The only thing so far decided was to name my protagonist Sandra. This was a nod to my desert childhood and the great hourglass of time where each individual fell through like another grain of sand.

Seeing myself as Sandra, some separate character who'd lived in Paris, was a revelation. Reviewing my major decisions I saw how incomprehensible my choices would seem to others. Love and war were common themes in literature but not my preoccupation with truth finding and ecstatic experiences as ways to inner peace. Who would want to imagine themselves in Sandra's shoes? Having substituted Georgina's story for so long, as a foil for facing my own, I was reluctant to trade places and become the focal point.

Gustave's prediction echoed in my mind. "You must complete this work...or you will never be able to write anything else. But I tell you, it will go into a drawer and stay there for more than twenty years afterwards. Something else must be invented before it resurfaces. And it will not be published in the original form." His precise instructions were completely baffling.

Wrestling with my demons in Tenerife I wrote for four months straight until the end of January 1987.

By then my American employer asked me to return full time to the New York office. Needing the money, I agreed. On my way back to the US I spent a few days in Paris. Bidding farewell to Irina and the others was bittersweet. My return flight to New York fell on the fourth February since my move to Paris.

In my wallet was the forty dollars remaining from my nest egg. In my carry-on bag was a three hundred and seventy-seven page manuscript.

CYNTHIA F. DAVIDSON

EPILOGUE

There are books which one should not
attempt before having passed the age of forty.

— MARGUERITE YOURCENAR

May 2013: Twenty-Seven Years Later

"Fasten your seatbelts," insists the uniformed steward in his crisply
accented English. He strides down the aisle checking our seat backs are in
the upright position as we ready for takeoff. On this Air France flight from
New York's JFK to Paris, my feelings flutter like restless city pigeons
refusing to be strapped down. When leaving France more than a quarter of
a century ago, I never imagined returning, much less for the motive behind
this trip.

In 1987, I had missed my Quai de Bourbon home and friends so much I
often sent my spirit back. Laying abed in an apartment on the Upper West
Side of Manhattan, that part of me had risen from my center to pass
through the window. In seconds I'd cross star speckled sky to land on the
Pont de la Tournelle, right beside Saint Geneviève. Her statue remains a
spiritual lightning rod. Who could have guessed her mystical example would
replace Georgina as my guide towards an entirely different life after Paris?

Has the city changed as much as I have? Although the particulars still
baffle me, my Paris sojourn sealed the wounds. I am at peace, yet the world
is not. Things are worse than ever in the Middle East. More of the region is
engulfed in "perpetual war," now the official ideology of the US
government, since our invasions of Iraq and Afghanistan in 2003. Sixty-five
million people are straining the resources of the world's refugee camps,
more than we had at the end of the Second World War. When guns are
easier to get than educations, they guarantee a steady supply of misery and
violence. The search for peaceful coexistence is beyond the reach of those
struggling to stay fed, clothed, and sheltered. Only those who feel safe can
afford such ideals.

The desperate try to flee. Some sell a kidney for cash to pay the smugglers as illicit trips to Europe are expensive. Packed on rotting fishing boats, or flimsy rubber dinghies, the overloaded vessels are often abandoned after being pushed out to sea. Thousands of men, women, and children have drowned in the Mediterranean or died in detention camps. (34,361 at last count for World Refugee Day by Dutch NGO United for Intercultural Action). Those who manage to reach the shores of Italy, Greece, or Spain face ferocious dogs, border guards, modern day slavers, and sex traffickers. Some good-hearted residents try to help, but other citizens become more protective and nationalistic, as the woes of war boomerang around the globe.

Our jet turns onto the runway and into the wind. The sun setting over JFK is briefly framed in the oval of my Plexiglas window. Half a century has passed since this airport first launched me overseas as an eight-year-old child. The world seems a lot smaller now than it did then. What if I'd stayed in one place and let life come to me? But I didn't. Each move built on the next one: leaving America, loving Arabia, being enchanted by Beirut, until the worst happened. To set my mind and heart at rest, I went to Paris, where my release was granted by methods unimaginable at the outset.

What happened to everyone else? My family and friends, the movers, the shakers and the stay-at-homers? My brother seems happily married, but he avoided repeating my parents' mistakes by never becoming one. My sister had one daughter but rarely saw her, after her ex-husband won full custody, and moved away. My mother chugs on, but my father passed away in 2004, at age seventy-one of lung cancer. He was grateful to die in his own bed, though he wished he'd quit the cigarettes sooner. I still remember his little rituals. Each time he returned home he'd step inside the house, shut the door, and ceremoniously drop his black leather flight kit on the hallway floor. "Another trip without a fatal accident," he'd say. On the night of 9/11 he told me by phone, "There is no way the Arabs could've pulled this off on their own." After giving the best years of his working life to training Arab flight crewmembers, he earned the right to that opinion. I continue to question the official explanation of events on September 11, 2001 along with other incidents.

While awaiting our turn to takeoff I think back to 1984, the year I went to France. That boss who tried to convince me to stay, "and become our first female vice president," left the company soon after saying that. MS&B was sold off in 1988 to become part of Prudential Intercultural. Not deferring my dreams for their promises was a good decision. After my return to the US in 1987, I remained self-directed, establishing my own consulting firm to specialize in the human side of globalization. I was the first to fuse cross-cultural training with management development. For the next decade I pioneered the field of global management development, designing and delivering programs for executive clients. The best of these were six weeks long, and covered all core competencies, and major world regions. And I had fun branching into other things, like my Global Paradigm newsletter, and producing and hosting a live two-hour PBS special "Gaining The Global Advantage."

The money was great but I spent a hundred days a year on airplanes and my housekeeper was raising my children. Yes, those who knew me in Paris, when I swore "never to bring children into this rotten world," would be shocked to see me return as the twice-married mother of three biological children. Their father Nissim was born on the North African coast, in Casablanca, Morocco, about nine hundred miles from Omar's home in Sfax, Tunisia. We met at an ethnic folk dance in New York's Greenwich Village, in April 1987. Things moved quickly: he proposed two weeks later, I moved in with him in May, we got married in June, and I got pregnant on the night of the fourth of July, the same holiday I'd been conceived. Our daughter was born on April third, a year to the day when her father and I first met, and a week after my thirty-fourth birthday.

My eldest daughter Mira is my reason for flying to France tonight. Without any scheming on my part, she has spent the last four years at the American University of Paris, with a junior year in Buenos Aires, Argentina. After high school she traveled and worked, doing a couple of years in Zanzibar, Tanzania, where she learned Swahili and made films about emerging local artists. Her considerable competence on these self-directed projects earned her a scholarship to the sixth most expensive university in the world. For her sake alone, I am happy to cross the Atlantic Ocean to be at her commencement ceremony.

During the ecstatic moment of her conception white light surrounded me. I knew she'd be a girl and to name her Mira, which means "look/see" in Spanish, "princess" in Arabic, "light" in Hebrew and "peace" in Croatian/Russian: look, see, princess light of peace. Her dear sister Naomi was born sixteen months later and their brother Michael five years afterwards, just before my fortieth birthday. Their stories each deserve memoirs if I live long enough to write them.

Having the "foreign" at "home" enabled me to stay in the US. Despite other differences, Nissim and I laughed at the same jokes, employed the same Arabic curse words, and served our shared favorite couscous meal at our wedding. An Arab Jew, Nissim's mother tongue is Arabic. His Bar Hanin ancestors once lived in Spain, during the Golden Age, before King Ferdinand and Queen Isabella's Spanish Inquisition forced them to emigrate. Five hundred years ago they ended up in Morocco until war uprooted them again, the Arab-Israeli one in 1956. They went to France, where his elder brother died of a childhood fever, before they settled in Israel. But because his background was Sephardic, and not Ashkenazi, he felt treated like a "nigger of Israel" (his words) by European Jews. So he

367

immigrated to the US. Yet another discrimination casualty.

Though we remain on good terms, I left the marriage after a dozen years, because of his addiction. Like Omar, he's a gambler. I should've known better but did not realize at the outset how compulsive his habit was. Yes, our marriage was a gamble too, but three great kids came out of it. After vowing to never marry again, an Englishman named Malcolm became "my king of hearts" in the summer of 2000. Our partnership has outlasted my first one, and his previous two, as we near the two-decade mark.

By 1999 my heart had gone out of corporate work. Like many others, I faced the dilemma of corruption. Once we realize the systems and the people we report to, are purposely designed to take unfair, criminal advantage of others, we have two options. Either we agree to adapt and become like them or we move on. Fourteen years after my final corporate assignment, for the globalization initiative at McKinsey & Company, our former CEO appeared on the cover of the New York Times. Arrested for the largest insider trading scandal in the history of the US Securities and Exchange Commission, the Indian-American finance wiz, Rajat Gupta, publicly proved the corruption I had privately witnessed.

I remember another newspaper headline, the one about Malcolm Kerr's assassination, for it galvanized my move to Paris. And my two-year pursuit of Georgina Rizk, the woman who could not tell me the truth. The manuscript I toiled on after that comeuppance is in the overhead luggage rack. "It will not be published until something else is invented. And it will come out in a different form." Gustave's predictions have come true, though he died of HIV long ago. Since penning that first draft in Tenerife, I've done plenty of writing for business and pleasure but the original effort "sat in a drawer for over two decades" just as he said it would. On this trip I plan to reread it. High time to put what the French call a *pointe finale* on everything and transform it from middling novel to a truthful memoir.

The last time I saw Gustave and his partner Pierre they had come with Irina, to lunch at my Quai de Bourbon place, before my departure to Tenerife. That day Irina gave me the hand knit sweater, of multi colored yarn interspersed with leather cording I'm wearing tonight. Caressing its woven strands I wonder what has happened to her. Unable to locate her, via her former married name, I realize anyone looking for me is also challenged by the last name changes when we women marry. Pierre died during my time in Tenerife, my first friend to succumb to HIV. Gustave lived a while longer. In my single days we worried about getting pregnant or needing antibiotics but the stakes are much higher now. You have to worry about dying when sharing a bed. Hardly conducive to the kind of adventures I had before settling down. Since saying my wedding vows, I have never strayed.

During my first year back in the US, Lilian MacKendrick passed away. Not long afterwards I became a mother suckling my babe. The exact pose of the woman in her portrait, the one I'd been standing next to, at her Wally Findlay retrospective, when Zvonimir told me it was his favorite, and opened my doorway to Paris. Lilian had painted the existence I had yet to believe in. What a great gift. It had the power to steer me subconsciously nonetheless.

Time for take off and here we go. Our bodies sink into our seat cushions as the engines roar. Their thrust propels us down the runway. This is my favorite part of flying. My mantra is "Plus three, minus eight." Most air traffic accidents occur in those first three minutes before and during takeoff, and the last eight minutes when landing. Not much to worry about inflight. Thanks to a father who flew planes for a living, my brain is crowded with such facts.

Knowing the truth, about crashes and so much else, prepared me to survive and prevents me from feeling frightened. Automatically, I've counted the number of seats to the nearest exits, behind and in front of me, in case we have to crawl out in the smoky darkness. Doing these things relaxes me on these buses with wings. Dad showed me how to inflate those rafts, stored in their overhead compartments, when he let me tag along to the recurrent training programs for crewmembers. He taught me the most dangerous part of flying, statistically, is the drive to the airport.

We race along the tarmac gaining speed to over one hundred and fifty miles an hour when the wheels lift off the ground. This is what freedom feels like to me, this moment of exhilaration, when gravity loosens its grip. Dying will be like this when my day comes and my spirit leaves my body for its last flight in this lifetime.

Once airborne we bank and turn, our ears popping. The waterways of Jamaica Bay gleam below. The buildings, roads, and cars shrink to toy-sized proportions. As we climb to cruising altitude another one of dad's sayings comes to mind, "If it ain't Boeing, I ain't going." Inside this slope-walled fuselage, as we head over the darkening ocean, I marvel once more at the winged magic of these silver jets. These mechanical birds have woven our world ever tighter. And none of us can fly backwards.

* * * *

Reclining my seat to a more comfortable angle, I watch my fellow passengers settle down for our seven-hour flight. Ready or not, all of us are in this together. If anything happens to our flight, like it has to others, who cares enough about us to pursue the truth, long enough to find it? There are so many unknowns I have had to accept. I will never know who shot my sister or which men kidnapped my father. But what produced their murderous desperation is as much to blame as their behavior. We are all embedded in a dysfunctional system. And each of us has to decide what we can do about it.

I went to Paris believing the truth would set me free and it has. But I started with wrong assumptions: thinking someone else possessed the truth and they would tell it to me. In France, as my days took me up and down, more flaws were revealed in my reasoning. How rare truth tellers are. We are so reluctant to reject the romance of our favorite lies. It was Omar after all, the charming liar, who inspired me to admit the most intimate truths to myself. Our relationship changed my trajectory. Along with Georgina, whose refusals did the trick. Whatever she could have told me about her story, it never would have accomplished as much as her withholding did. By not cooperating, she forced me to face the truth of my own story, for which there are no substitutes.

While waiting for the seat belt light to go off, I am itching to get up and move around. This old restlessness brings another revelation. I am in the classic flight or fight mode. These responses are predictable when reacting to danger — real or imagined. Eons of experience have conditioned us to run or fight like other species. Flight includes an entire spectrum of avoidance behaviors, from constant travel to the escapism of addictions — to drugs, games, alcohol, sex, work, or money. We fight when we don't feel safe, in the world or our own skins. This makes firearms and firepower so popular.

I relax with these realizations, remembering the third option, to freeze, like animals who "play dead." This psychological paralysis I first noticed in Moudi corresponds with a myriad of other symptoms of post-traumatic stress and self-harming behaviors. Since leaving Paris I've learned more about them and discovered how common promiscuity is among us. I saw it in my father before recognizing it in others and myself. Hurt people hurt people. Those around me had their own traumas to overcome, which stymied their chances of finding peace and settling down. I chose painful ways yet they did more than alienation and isolation would have. My relationships in France restored my willingness to love, and to act, however unadvisedly. To feel desire and joy again, even to want a family of my own.

So much has been laid to rest. But my long ago vow, to bury my finished book — like a sacrificial offering — in the blood-soaked land of Lebanon has yet to happen. The country has been without a president for two years. After the assassinations of so many, who wants the job of leader? With the Syrian civil war raging next door since the spring of 2011, Lebanon shelters more refugees now than citizens. How many will find their bridges to peace, like I did in Paris?

The beverage cart makes its way down the aisle. The stewardess uses the same practiced perkiness with each passenger. Eventually she reaches me, "What would you like to drink?"

"I'll have some of that spicy Bloody Mary mix please. No ice. And just the bloody please, not the Mary." We both smile. After pouring as much as the clear plastic cup can hold, she hands me the can with the rest. I offer a silent toast to all memories who'll visit me, before taking the first sip.

I want to remember my Paris friends tonight. After a few years of exchanging Christmas cards with some, we lost touch. Maintaining far-flung friendships was harder before social media came along. I recall them in roughly the order of our first meetings. Dear Hugette, she was working the counter at Charles De Gaulle airport the day I departed from Paris, and kindly waived my excess baggage fees on that Air France flight back to the US. We once spent four hours eating an outdoor Sunday lunch at her Normandy home, and walked the beach afterwards, to revisit the spot where her brother was killed during the Second World War. So many men gone. So many women left behind with untold stories.

Zemira. Her plans to build a little house were ruined by yet another war. That one erupted after the Yugoslavian dictator Tito died. The Serbs, Croatians, and Bosnians tore the place, and each other, to pieces from 1991 to 2001. Yugoslavia had been cobbled together from former Ottoman Empire territories. It's ancient enmities generated atrocities that rivaled Lebanon's and broke up the Yugoslav nation.

Freddie's Croatian Yugoslavian husband had been lucky to leave the country before the war began. Did they have any children? Does she run her *salon de coiffure* anymore?

Zvonimir is still painting. He weathered the Yugoslavian war and his part became the newly independent country of Croatia. His two grown kids are doing well. He spends most of his time in his Adriatic hometown. Mira met him there while on a holiday trip with fellow AUP students and he treated all her girlfriends to dinner. Another full circle.

Waddah moved to Barcelona after Paris, then to Thailand, before ending up back in Beirut, where he'd vowed never to return. Thanks to Facebook we are in touch again, and also with his nephew Omar Sabbagh, who writes poetry and teaches at AUB. The whereabouts of Maurice,

Doctor Amin Mousalli, and his sister Amal remain a mystery. My old fiancé Ayman became a member of the Lebanese parliament.

Mazen is also in Lebanon now. Social media put me in touch with his son, who lives in Asia, and claims to be writing a book about the fall of kings. This reminds me of Georgina's little son Ali, and his violent card game, "making the kings fight." Georgina has soldiered on. In 1990 she married Walid Toufic, a Muslim actor and singer, born in Tripoli, Lebanon in 1954. They have two children, Walid junior and daughter Nourhan. Her son by Salameh, Ali junior married in 2004. His wedding to a Jordanian woman Dina Ghalayini was held in Cairo. After both attended college in Canada, they live in Egypt. Georgina continues in the beauty pageant business as a judge nowadays. Will she ever tell her story? Since the death of her first husband, Palestine has lost more land, and spawned more suicide bombers. Instead of bridges, Israel has built more walls. The US continues to support its militancy with billions of tax dollars. Peace talks are not even mentioned as a condition for receiving our largess anymore. Why?

I never heard another word about Omar or Mimo. Their old employer Saudi Prince Mishari died in 2000. The Arab Spring erupted in their country of Tunisia in 2010. A despairing street vendor nicknamed "Basboosa" sparked a movement that toppled kings and dictators across the Middle East. Basboosa's real name was Tarek el-Tayeb Mohamed Bouazizi. His food cart was confiscated by a city official who said he lacked a vendor's permit. Basboosa did not have the money for the bribe to retrieve his fruits and vegetables. Most say single cart operators do not need a permit. After declaring he could no longer bear the harassment and humiliation of corrupt officials, Basboosa set himself on fire. His self-immolation received posthumous recognition, as Person of the Year in The Times of England as well as the Sakharov Prize, but it also ousted Tunisia's president Ben Ali.[47]

Despite their transition to democracy, poverty and joblessness cause continuing unrest in Tunisia. One unemployed graduate lamented, "We have freedom but you cannot eat freedom." After terrorist attacks on tourists in Tunisia, the jobs of 400,000 Tunisians working in the tourism industry are in jeopardy.

What if I'd gone there to run a small hotel with Mon Fantôme?

---

[47] After 23 years in power, Ben Ali fled his country in a private plane. France denied him landing rights so he flew on to Saudi Arabia where he still lives. Tried in absentia, the Tunisian court found both the former president and his wife, guilty of money laundering and other crimes. Sentenced to life imprisonment, he remains hiding in exile in my old hometown of Jeddah. The Swiss government has frozen their ill-gotten gains and Interpol has a warrant out for Ben Ali's arrest.

The airline cart returns with our dinners, covered in foil, on white plastic trays. While eating the chicken and rice I remember the Sunday luncheon at the parental home of Maître Catherine Genis where I first met Irina. What has happened to my Ukrainian friend and our lawyer? And the Pino family in Tenerife whose home provided a safe writing haven?

A recent Google search brought up the website of my Paris employers, Intercultural Management associates. Their work continues. After the meal I doze off.

* * * *

The sun is shining the following morning as my Paris retour begins in earnest. A vibrant energy rises from the cobblestoned streets and puts a spring in my step. I take my grown daughter to see my old haunts before her graduation tomorrow. We come to Pont Marie and begin to cross over to Île Saint-Louis. The urban rush fades. The quiet swells. Our steps slow to a stop midway across the seventeenth century bridge. Peering down at the eternal flow of the River Seine, I pay homage to her, the Grande Dame of us all. Mother Nature plopped herself down upon the banks of this River of Life to soak her misshapen island feet in these cooling green depths long before humans named it the Seine, after an encircling fishnet. For centuries she has shaken out her skirts here, and twenty arrondissements have unfurled around her bustling petticoats, giving rise to every kind of relationship.

How amused she must be by our antics. She has been wooed, bullied, and worshiped here. Some went so far as to construct great cathedrals in her honor, like the towering Notre Dame (Our Lady) on the nearby Île de la Cité. That project took two centuries to complete in 1345. Others plotted her demise, having failed to control her in human form. All these attempts to corral and harness her have their echoes in our flesh, and the fate of our female bodies, here in Paris and elsewhere.

To her I owe my health, wealth, and happiness. After three years under her tutelage, 1984-1987, I was cured of hopelessness, helplessness, and naiveté. Now a crone, I am old enough to tell the truth about the importance of Paris. When asked about my time in France I say, "Every woman ought to live a year of her life in Paris." Our Grande Dame has more in common with Occasio, the chortling, goddess of opportunity, than the modestly robed Madonnas or the cool Mariannes, who've personified the French Republic since the 1700s.

Paris will make or break you. From me, Paris took my wounded girl self, and put her through her paces, transforming me into a woman who wanted wisdom more than anything else. Thankfully I survived the process. France has one of the highest suicide rates in Europe. Twenty-seven people take their lives here each day. Over a hundred jump into these murky waters annually. The Brigade Fluviale personnel save as many as they can, but each year they recover fifty bodies too late. For centuries, women have flung themselves off the city's thirty-seven bridges, some with the unborn curled inside their abdomens. Their hearts too battered to take anymore, the Seine carries them away. My old premonition of the lone woman strung up in a Beirut apartment is almost forgotten. Having considered the solace of these dark green waters long ago, today I grasp the hand of the daughter whose birth I once deferred. Though I say nothing, I am certain I have done the right thing.

As we walk onto Île Saint-Louis I think of my current home, Chippaquasett, the six by two mile islet in Narragansett Bay. I have lived there since 1999. By age forty-five I'd had my fill of manmade insanity and formally apprenticed myself to Mother Nature. This island can only be reached by ferry and I have lived there longer than any other place in my life. After all my wanderings, I was finally able to set down roots, creating a modest spiritual retreat center to offer others a place to rest, reconnect and heal. We all need time and space in Nature's embrace, for doing the inner work that can balance our outer journeys. And I developed my version of Archimedes' theory of everything, the Wisdom Wheel, with its natural, universal, spiritual laws to live by. Teaching it quietly for the past two decades, I have watched others use it, and teach it in their study circles. Watching the benefits it has brought them has convinced me, anyone can use it to find their way.

Though we may start with physical ecstasy, we can learn to balance this with emotional, mental, and spiritual ecstasies. The ancients understood this and left us rituals and ceremonies for the work of incorporating all this. From my indigenous First Nations friends I first heard the concept *omsetnogama*, which means, "we are all related" in their language. This globally inclusive ethos is one I can resonate with. For over a dozen years, I have been a grateful student of my Mi'kmaq elders in New Brunswick, Canada and earned the right to share some ceremonies in my community.

Our walk on Île Saint-Louis today has brought my daughter and me to the curved stone archway of my old home at #15 Quai de Bourbon. The large wooden doors are still painted a deep shade of burgundy. After we snap a photo, someone inside buzzes the door open. They leave and before the door can swing shut again, we slip inside. Everything is the same inside the courtyard. Undamaged, unmolested — unlike my former homes in the Middle East. Up the curving stone staircase we go. I tell my daughter, "Almost thirty years have gone by in a flash. Did I dwell here once upon a time? It seems like another life."

The entry door to my second floor studio apartment has a shiny varnish of forest green paint. Who lives here now, I wonder as my daughter takes another picture. Holding the polished brass doorknob briefly I think of the people I welcomed into this home and my life during my years here.

Hungry after our walk, we eat nearby on Rue Saint Louis, at the Auberge de la Reine Blanche (the Inn of the White Queen). New to us both, this will make memories that are ours alone. *Terrine de canard*, with artichoke salad to start, followed by lamb stew for me, served piping hot in black cast iron pot, and fish kebab for my daughter, which arrives on skewer suspended from a hook over her plate. There was more than one White Queen, although this inn was named in honor of Blanche of Castile. At age twelve, in 1200, this Spanish born princess was married to French King Louis VIII. Their son became the next King, Louis IX, the only ruler of France canonized as a saint. Île Saint-Louis was named after him.

Wandering back towards the Avenue Saint Michel apartment, where Mira lived with her French host family the Malherbe's, we stop beside the statue of Saint Geneviève on the Pont de la Tournelle. While paying my silent homage, the warm yellow tones of a saxophone waft up from the quay below. Just like the golden notes that accompanied my ultimate understanding regarding Waddah and so much more, "Some things will just always be." We can do something about the rest.

* * * *

The following morning we make our way to the Théâtre du Châtelet for the commencement ceremony. I carry my daughter's freshly pressed graduation gown to the building near the River Seine. Before entering, I gaze across the water at the smooth, pale, stone walls of the Conciergerie on the west side of Île de la Cité. Once a medieval palace, it became a prison during the Revolution. Queen Marie Antoinette and others were held here before their final trips to the guillotine. Today it houses the courts of law. Such a turbulent swirl of history has carried us to where we are today. Turning to enter the theatre, I give thanks for women's education and pray we never go backwards. Our world needs wise women more than ever.

Inside the auditorium my daughter goes off with the other students to get ready as I take my seat. This commencement marks the fiftieth anniversary of the American University of Paris. Compared to the American University of Beirut, AUP is new. It was founded the same year I moved to Arabia in 1962. My alma mater NYU was going to purchase AUP but the financial crash of 2008 ended those plans. The president of AUP is a woman and the student body is truly global. Behind me the Kuwaiti parents of two students are speaking Arabic, and a stunning Nigerian mother of another wears a regal head wrap, sitting beside a blonde

California mom, dressed in a lavender shift and spiky heels. All of this co-mingling greatly pleases me.

Last night, I met some of my daughter's friends. One has Yemeni Jewish parents, now long time Londoners, another is Canadian, and her family owns a goldmine. Her boyfriend is half Paraguayan and half Austrian. Ah, the mixed tribe. Our numbers are growing.

As my daughter crosses the stage in her robe and sash this morning, I watch her receive her diploma, magna cum laude. My heart swells and my eyes fill with happy tears. I recover in time to snap a few photos of her, in cap and gown, diploma in hand.

Later that day my daughter casually asks how my writing is going. "Will you tell the truth about Paris?"

Oh yes my child. I certainly will.

AUTHOR'S NOTE & ACKNOWLEDGEMENTS

> I may not agree with what you have to say but
> I will defend to the death your right to speak.

> — FRANÇOIS-MARIE AROUET (VOLTAIRE),
> as quoted by his biographer, Evelyn Beatrice Hall

Rather than rolling a grenade into the room, I have written this book. Because I abhor violence, my aim is to inspire others to share their truths and resolve their conflicts, by peaceful means. Be more curious. Make new friends. Share a meal and a meaningful conversation. Learn another language. This book was inspired by those who struggle to understand people we do not agree with. Growing up, I often heard my father Andrew Norman Fetterolf repeat Voltaire's comment, albeit in English, "I may not agree with what you have to say but I will defend to the death your right to speak." I took those words to heart in my life, and when writing this book.

Voltaire was exiled more than once for what he wrote because the establishment felt threatened by his truth telling and I realize publishing these stories comes with risks. In October 2018 I almost shelved this project when another modern truth teller, Jamal Khashoggi, was butchered in the Saudi Embassy in Istanbul, Turkey. He was killed for exposing the corruption between our countries. What I find even more chilling is the fact no one has been prosecuted for his gruesome murder, nor the murders of nearly fifty other reporters killed in 2018, for writing about corruption. Jamal Khashoggi last words, in a posthumously published article were, "What the Arab world needs most is free expression."

If we won't tell the truth ourselves, we can hardly demand it from others.

I am not putting my memoir in the category of Khashoggi's revelations. Nor do I imply it has the quality of Voltaire's work, but I resonate strongly with the belief that people have the right, even the duty to speak up, especially when there is disagreement. And when we have lived truths to contribute to the understanding of a subject, so much the better.

If you found this book hard to read, imagine how difficult writing it was. Although many of my life decisions were made quickly, this project took decades, from 1984 to 2019. I kept telling myself, I lived it, I ought to be able to write it down. But facing myself on the page was much harder than writing about other peoples' lives as a journalist. I had to trust my take on my own life and because I was inviting readers inside my head, I had to accept my thoughts and behaviors would be judged, not just my writing style. What I share came from fallible personal experience.

Knowing how many controversial subjects are mentioned in my story, it would be naive to expect every reader to agree with everything. All I ask is that you consider each instance, when my words challenged your assumptions or world view, as a "critical incident," like those I wrote about using in my cross cultural training programs to illustrate differences in values and beliefs.

The rewards of self-acceptance are enormous when writing and sharing our stories. This became more apparent when attending my first memoir writers' conference in Oakland, CA. I was stunned by the positive, life-affirming attitudes of my fellow memoirists. Here we were, howling with laughter about things we had cried our eyes out over years before. What a wonderfully healing return upon our investment of efforts.

I must acknowledge every other author whose work encouraged my soul and spirit. As for those who deserve to be personally thanked, my dear family is at the top of the list. My husband Malcolm F. Davidson and my children Mira, Naomi, and Michael deserve more than I can ever repay them. Working on this book took a lot of time away from you. I hope the finished product explains some things and that we can catch up on the fun going forward.

I must also thank my parents, sister, and brother, and all those mentioned in this memoir. It is my homage to our shared experiences. All those mentioned in these pages were integral to my life lessons and transformational years in Paris. Each contributed to the inspiration for writing these stories down and for that I am grateful.

Gigie Hall also deserves a huge high five. My graphic designer and editor extraordinaire, we know how much the final product owes to your talents, competence and unflagging energies. Not only did you handle my blind spots admirably, you also asked key questions that unlocked emotional spaces I had yet to explore. I look forward to our collaboration on the other projects we have planned for the Wisdom Wheel and my next memoir, *Every Day Is Sun Day*, about my spiritual life and community.

Sheila Cardente-Capece helped me deal with the emotions that surfaced while writing. She kept me on schedule, listening to this book ten pages at a time every other week and shepherding it to completion. Traumas can prevent us from facing or telling our truths. Her professionalism, as a behavioral therapist, was much appreciated, as was her generous warmth. Getting help is a sign of strength. Ask for it, especially if you don't think you need it. Equal appreciation is due to Gail Straub and our prior Red Thread writing retreats at the monastery in New York's Hudson Valley.

My weekly writing group at Westerly Library deserves a virtual hug here. What a great group of human beings. Allow me to cheer you on in print. Several of you have projects every bit as worthy of attention as anything I have written. I look forward to many more years of meetings and productivity. The same for my fellow poets who meet regularly at the Savoy book store.

Another Rhode Island library, in Narragansett, must also be thanked. Much of this memoir was rewritten in their Elaine Loffredo Memorial Reading Room. Elaine was on her way from New York to Paris, in July 1996 when she died in the crash of TWA flight 800, one of 230 killed. A nod goes to her husband Robert for donating this quiet room. We writers need our rooms but finding one in a library has special benefits. Those librarians have taken good care of me, even finding a lost earring and my mislaid car keys!

One more RI library deserves my gratitude, the Langworthy in Hope Valley. It is also the meeting place of a cherished book club, for there is nothing as satisfying to an author as a group of dedicated readers. My other favorite book club, on Prudence Island, must be mentioned, and Connie and Jane who started it in 2000. I salute all the members and the countless good reads we shared over many years.

Thanks goes to Lynne Bryan Phipps and her book club. They were the first group to read an earlier version of this manuscript. Including me in their discussion gave me some practice at answering readers questions and whet my appetite for more visits to book clubs in the future.

The Story Circle Network and its founder Susan Wittig Albert also need my heartfelt thanks. Those SCN conferences in Austin, Texas over the last decade were the first places I read aloud sections from this memoir and found the support and courage to be heard on these topics.

She Writes Press and its founder Brooke Warner, have also been integral to the process. Much gratitude for the feedback. Also Linda Joy Meyers, the feisty founder of the National Association of Memoir Writers. Their joint course "Write Your Memoir in Six Months" was instrumental, although it has taken me a lot longer.

My many beta readers included patrons and staff at Starbucks and Panera in Wakefield, RI. Never underestimate those who care and have more to contribute than coffee, food, and workspace.

Last but not least, my formal, legal disclaimer. Any mistakes made herein are my own. I assume no responsibility or liability for any errors or omissions in the content of this memoir. Although I have verified as much as possible, the information it contains is provided on an "as is" basis with no guarantee of completeness, accuracy, usefulness, or timeliness.

Addendum

Malcolm Kerr's son Steve, coach of the Golden State Warriors basketball team, strongly criticized Donald Trump's ban on travellers and refugees from seven Muslim-majority countries. He said it had personal resonance: "…as someone whose family member was a victim of terrorism, after having lost my father, trying to combat terrorism by banishing people from coming to this country, is really going against the principles of what our country is about. It's the wrong way. If anything, it could breed more anger and terror. So I'm completely against what's happening." (Associated Press January 2017) His father, Malcolm Kerr, was killed by two gunmen in 1984 while he was president of the American University of Beirut. Islamic Jihad, a precursor of Hezbollah, later claimed responsibility for the murder.

Malcolm Kerr's only daughter, Susan Kerr van de Ven, wrote an account of her family's search for truth and justice, *One Family's Response to Terrorism*. "My father had so much background on what had happened in the Middle East. He knew about good American values and bad American policies. He knew that the US government doesn't always understand the places where it throws its weight around. And there he was, suddenly on the world stage. He didn't necessarily want all that attention, but he wanted very much to be at AUB."

She said her "family struggled with doing the right thing for the right reasons. Revenge versus understanding. In the world of politics I now inhabit — you see different styles. Some love to attack; some search for common ground." Now a politician, Susan serves as an elected Liberal Democrat councillor, on South Cambridgeshire District Council and lives in Cambridge, England, where her husband Johan "Hans" van de Ven is a professor of Modern Chinese History at the University of Cambridge.

Andrew Kerr, Malcolm's youngest son, worked at the US National Security Council. His access to intelligence reports allowed him to become better educated about Middle Eastern politics. He eventually discovered a crucial piece of information suggesting his father's assassination had been commissioned by senior Hezbollah authorities. Officials of the Iranian government were also implicated.

In 2001, the Kerr family filed a lawsuit, agreeing not to file for punitive damages. During the ensuing months of the investigation the family learned the US government had withheld crucial information. Malcolm Kerr's activities in Beirut had been tracked by the CIA as they had him under surveillance. Within three weeks of his assassination the US government knew the identities of Malcolm Kerr's killers but never told his family. In their search for closure, the Kerr family's lawyers finally managed to get the US intelligence reports by agents in Beirut.

CYNTHIA F. DAVIDSON

A READER'S GUIDE FOR

THE IMPORTANCE OF PARIS

1. Why do you think the book was titled *The Importance of Paris?*

2. What was important about the place and the people Cynthia met in France? Each chapter had at least one item of importance. Did you have a favorite scene or interaction you remember?

3. In your view, which of Cynthia's decisions was most important in retrospect? Her original goal morphed into something else. Has this happened in your life?

4. Can there be more than one "Paris?" Discuss what you learned about the "Paris of the Middle East" and the history and politics of that region.

5. How many taboos were mentioned in this story? Which incidents did you feel uncomfortable reading about? What were you most surprised to learn?

6. Discuss the issue of truth telling. What prevents people from finding out the truth or sharing what they know to be true? Why does telling the truth upset some people?

7. You met a lot of characters in this story. Who did you like the most? Who did you detest? Why?

8. Do you know anyone suffering from PTSD? Should survivors share their stories? What happens when they do?

9. Do you believe in revenge? How best to overcome feelings of powerlessness and victimization?

10. Could this story have happened anywhere else?

Suggested Reading

PARIS

Etel Adnan, *Paris, When It's Naked*
Sylvia Beach, *Shakespeare and Company*
Hélène Cixous, *The Laugh of the Medusa*
Malcolm Cowley, *Exile's Return*
Ernest Hemingway, *A Moveable Feast*
Alice Prin, *Kiki's Memoirs*
Penelope Rowlands, *Paris Was Ours: Thirty-two Writers Reflect on the City of Light*
Thirza Vallois, *Around and About Paris*
Edward White, *The Flâneur*

LEBANON

Etel Adnan, *Sitt Marie Rose*
Kai Bird, *The Good Spy: The Life and Death of Robert Ames*
Robert Fisk, *Pity the Nation: The Abduction of Lebanon*
Ann Kerr-Adams, *Come With Me From Lebanon: An American Family Odyssey*
Susan Kerr van de Ven, *One Family's Response to Terrorism: A Daughter's Memoir*
Salim el Lozi, *The Emigres* (also spelt Salim El Lawzi)
Omar Sabbagh, *The Square Root of Beirut*
Kamal Salibi, *A House of Many Mansions: The History of Lebanon Reconsidered*
Zeina Abirached, Mohamed Abi Samra, Abbas Beydoun, Elias Khoury, Alawiya Sobh, Yasmina Traboulsi, Hassan Daoud, Tamirace Fakhoury , Imane Humaydane-Younes, Charif Majdalani, Rachid El-Daï, *Les Belles Étrangères: Douze écrivains libanais*

POETRY

Etel Adnan, *The Arab Apocalypse*
Davidson, Cynthia F., *Measuring Distances*
Lynn Fetterolf, *Through Sand and Sorrow*
    Some Days Honey, Some Days Onions
    I Speak for Those Who Have No Voice
    Guided by Grief
Carolyn Forché, *The Country Between Us,*
    Against Forgetting: Twentieth-Century Poetry of Witness, editor
Deena Metzger, *The Woman Who Slept With Men To Take The War Out Of Them*

MIDDLE EAST

Robert Baer, *See No Evil: The True Story of a Ground Soldier in the CIA's War Against Terrorism*
  Sleeping with the Devil: How Washington Sold Our Soul for Saudi Crude
James Barr, *A Line in the Sand: Britain, France and the Struggle for the Mastery of the Middle East*
William Blum, *Killing Hope: US Military and CIA Interventions Since World War II*
Kimberly Dozier, *Breathing the Fire: Fighting to Survive, and Get Back to the Fight*
Karen Elliott House, *On Saudi Arabia: Its People, Past, Religion, Fault Lines - and Future*
Joseph A. Kechichian, *Iffat Al Thunayan: An Arabian Queen*
Malcolm H. Kerr, *The Elusive Peace in the Middle East*
  Islamic Reform: The Political and Legal Theories of Muhammad Abduh and Rashid Rida
Kameel B. Nasr, *Arab and Israeli Terrorism The Causes and Effects of Political Violence, 1936-1993*
Michael B. Oren, *Power, Faith, and Fantasy: America in the Middle East, 1776 to the Present*
Ilan Pappé, *The Ethnic Cleansing of Palestine*
Nawal El Saadawi, *The Hidden Face of Eve: Women in the Arab World*
Edward W. Said, *Orientalism*
Penelope Tuson, *Playing the Game: Western Women in Arabia*
Robin Wright, *Sacred Rage: The Wrath of Militant Islam*
  Dreams and Shadows: The Future of the Middle East
  Rock the Casbah: Rage and Rebellion Across the Islamic World

Suggested Authors

Georgii Adamovich
Mirra Alfassa
Simone de Beauvoir
Marguerite Duras
Mona Eltahawy
Gustave Flaubert
Omar Khayyam
Eva de Vitray Meyerovitch
Marcel Pagnol
Graham Robb
Gertrude Stein
Miguel de Unamuno
Simone Weil
Marguerite Yourcenar

ABOUT THE AUTHOR

American-born Cynthia F. Davidson (née Fetterolf) spent the first thirty years of her life living and working in Saudi Arabia, Switzerland, Lebanon, Venezuela, England, Spain, and France. Her expatriate decades led to careers in journalism at CBS News and global management development. Cynthia later returned to the perennial teachings and created The Wisdom Wheel, which she has taught for the past twenty years from her Rhode Island home. Married, with three grown children, Cynthia is available for speaking engagements, writes a bi-monthly newsletter, and offers regularly scheduled workshops on memoir writing.

www.cynthiafdavidson.com

CPSIA information can be obtained
at www.ICGtesting.com
Printed in the USA
LVHW032206240420
654379LV00001B/126